Statistical Methods for Recommender Systems

Designing algorithms to recommend items such as news articles and movies to users is a challenging task in numerous web applications. The crux of the problem is to rank items based on past user responses to optimize for multiple objectives. Major technical challenges are high-dimensional prediction with sparse data and constructing high-dimensional sequential designs to collect data for user modeling and system design.

This comprehensive treatment of the statistical issues that arise in recommender systems includes detailed, in-depth discussions of current state-of-the-art methods such as adaptive sequential designs (multiarmed bandit methods), bilinear random-effects models (matrix factorization), and scalable model fitting using modern computing paradigms such as MapReduce. The authors draw on their vast experience working with such large-scale systems at Yahoo! and LinkedIn and bridge the gap between theory and practice by illustrating complex concepts with examples from applications with which they are directly involved.

DR. DEEPAK K. AGARWAL is a big data analyst with several years of experience developing and deploying state-of-the-art machine learning and statistical methods for improving the relevance of web applications. He is also experienced in conducting new scientific research to solve difficult big data problems, especially in the areas of recommender systems and computational advertising. He is a Fellow of the American Statistical Association and associate editor of top-tier journals in statistics.

DR. BEE-CHUNG CHEN is a leading technologist with extensive industrial and research experience in developing state-of-the-art recommender systems. He has been a key designer of the recommendation algorithms that power the LinkedIn home page and mobile feeds, the Yahoo! home page, Yahoo! News, and other sites. His research areas include recommender systems, data mining, machine learning, and big data analytics.

For Bharati Agarwal and Shiao-Ching Chung

Statistical Methods for Recommender Systems

DEEPAK K. AGARWAL
LinkedIn Corporation

BEE-CHUNG CHEN
LinkedIn Corporation

CAMBRIDGE
UNIVERSITY PRESS

CAMBRIDGE
UNIVERSITY PRESS

University Printing House, Cambridge CB2 8BS, United Kingdom

One Liberty Plaza, 20th Floor, New York, NY 10006, USA

477 Williamstown Road, Port Melbourne, VIC 3207, Australia

314-321, 3rd Floor, Plot 3, Splendor Forum, Jasola District Centre, New Delhi-110025, India

79 Anson Road, #06-04/06, Singapore 079906

Cambridge University Press is part of the University of Cambridge.

It furthers the University's mission by disseminating knowledge in the pursuit of education, learning and research at the highest international levels of excellence.

www.cambridge.org
Information on this title: www.cambridge.org/9781107036079

First published 2016

A catalogue record for this publication is available from the British Library

Library of Congress Cataloging in Publication data
Agarwal, Deepak K., 1973– author.
Statistical methods for recommender systems / Deepak K. Agarwal, Yahoo! Research, Bee Chung-Chen, Yahoo! Research.
pages cm
ISBN 978-1-107-03607-9
1. Recommender systems (Information filtering) – Statistical methods. 2. Expert systems (Computer science) – Statistical methods. I. Chung-Chen, Bee, author. II. Title.
QA76.76.E95A395 2016
006.3′3–dc23 2015026092

ISBN 978-1-107-03607-9 Hardback

Additional resources for this publication at https://github.com/beechung/Latent-Factor-Models

Contents

PART III ADVANCED TOPICS

Preface

What This Book Is About

Recommender systems are automated computer programs that match items to users in different contexts. Such systems are ubiquitous and have become an integral part of our daily lives. Examples include recommending products to users on a site like Amazon, recommending content to users visiting a website like Yahoo!, recommending movies to users on a site like Netflix, recommending jobs to users on a site like LinkedIn, and so on. The matching algorithms are constructed using large amounts of high-frequency data obtained from past user interactions with items. The algorithms are statistical in nature and involve challenges in areas like sequential decision processes, modeling interactions with very high-dimensional categorical data, and developing scalable statistical methods. New methodologies in this area require close collaboration among computer scientists, machine learners, statisticians, optimization experts, system experts, and, of course, domain experts. It is one of the most exciting applications of big data.

Why We Wrote This Book

Although much has been written about recommender systems in various fields, such as computer science, machine learning, and statistics, focusing on specific aspects of the problem, a comprehensive treatment of all statistical issues and how they are interrelated is lacking. We came to this realization while deploying such systems at Yahoo! and LinkedIn. For instance, much of the focus in statistics and machine learning is on building models that minimize out-of-sample predictive error. However, this does not address all aspects of practical importance. Statistically, a recommender system is a high-dimensional sequential process, and it is equally important to study issues like design of experiments as it is to develop sophisticated statistical models. In fact, the two are closely related – efficient design needs models to tame the curse of dimensionality. Also, most existing work in the literature tends to build models for univariate response, such as movie ratings, purchases, and click rates. With the advent of social media outlets like Facebook, LinkedIn, and Twitter, multiple responses are available. For instance, one may want to model click rates, share rates, and tweet rates simultaneously for a news recommender application. Such multivariate response models are challenging to build. Finally, given the machinery to obtain such multivariate predictions, how does one construct utility functions to make recommendations? Is it more important to optimize share rates relative to click rates? Answers to these types of questions can be obtained through multiobjective optimization working in close collaboration with domain experts to elicit some utility parameters.

The goal of this book is to provide a comprehensive discussion of all such issues that arise in the context of recommender systems. This is in addition to a detailed and in-depth discussion of current state-of-the-art statistical methods that include techniques like adaptive sequential designs (multiarmed bandit methods), bilinear random-effects models (matrix factorization), and scalable model fitting using modern-distributed computing infrastructure. Our goal in writing this book is to draw on our vast experience working with such large-scale systems in industrial settings and to bring these issues to the attention of the statistical, machine learning, and computer science communities. We believe this will be beneficial in a number of ways. It may help in advancing methodological research in high-dimensional and big data statistics, especially for web applications. We understand that conducting such research in an academic setting requires access to software that can run on massive data. To facilitate this, we supplement the book with open source software: https://github.com/beechung/Latent-Factor-Models. We also believe the book will help in bridging the gap between theory and applications. It will provide problem owners with a good understanding of the statistical issues involved and modelers with an in-depth understanding of statistical issues that arise in practical applications that are rather complex.

Organization

We divide the content of the book into three parts.

In Part I, we introduce the recommender system problem, challenges in the problem, main ideas used to tackle the challenges, and the required background knowledge. In Chapter 2, we give an overview of classical methods that have been used to develop recommender systems. Such methods involve characterizing users and items as feature vectors and then scoring user-item pairs based on some similarity function, standard supervised learning, or collaborative filtering. These classical methods usually ignore the explore-exploit trade-off in recommender problems. Hence, in Chapter 3, we discuss the importance of this issue and introduce the main ideas that will be used to solve the issue in later chapters. Before we delve into technical solutions, in Chapter 4, we review a variety of methods for evaluating the performance of different recommendation algorithms.

In Part II, we provide detailed solutions to common problem settings. We start with an introduction to various problem settings and an example system architecture in Chapter 5, and then we devote the next three chapters to three common problem settings. Chapter 6 provides solutions to the most-popular recommendation problem, with a special focus on the explore-exploit aspect. Chapter 7 deals with personalized recommendation through feature-based regression, with an emphasis on how to continuously update the model(s) to leverage the most recent user-item interaction data and quickly converge to a good solution. Chapter 8 extends the methods developed in Chapter 7 from feature-based regression to factor models (matrix factorization) and, at the same time, provides a natural solution to the cold-start problem in factor models.

In Part III, we present three advanced topics. In Chapter 9, we present a factorization model that simultaneously identifies topics in items and users' affinities with different topics through a modified matrix factorization model that uses the latent Dirichlet allocation (LDA) topic model. In Chapter 10, we investigate context-dependent recommender problems, in which the recommended items not only need to have high affinity with the user but also have to be relevant to the context (e.g., recommending items related to a news article that the user is currently reading). In Chapter 11, we discuss a principled framework for optimizing multiple objectives based on a constrained optimization approach, where we seek to maximize one objective (e.g., revenue) subject to bounded loss in other objectives (e.g., no more than 5 percent loss in clicks).

Limitations

Like all books, ours has limitations. We do not provide an in-depth coverage of modern computational paradigms, such as Spark, that can be used to fit some of the models presented at scale. Online evaluation of models when users form a social graph cannot be done properly with traditional experimental design methods. New techniques that can adjust for interference because of social graphs need to be developed. We do not cover such advanced topics in this book. Throughout, we address the problem of recommendations through a response prediction approach using regression as our main tool. This is primarily because we believe that output from these models is easy to combine with downstream utilities. We do not provide a comprehensive coverage of methods that are based on direct optimization of ranking loss functions. A comparison of the two approaches would also be a worthwhile topic for discussion.

Acknowledgement

Our special thanks to Raghu Ramakrishnan, Liang Zhang, Xuanhui Wang, Pradheep Elango, Bo Long, Bo Pang, Rajiv Khanna, Nitin Motgi, Seung-Taek Park, Scott Roy, Joe Zachariah for many insightful discussions and collaboration. We would also like to thank our colleagues both at Yahoo! and LinkedIn for all the encouragement and support without which many of the ideas we had would not see the light of the day.

PART I

Introduction

1
Introduction

Recommender systems (or recommendation systems) are computer programs that recommend the "best" items to users in different contexts. The notion of a best match is typically obtained by optimizing for objectives like total clicks, total revenue, and total sales. Such systems are ubiquitous on the web and form an integral part of our daily lives. Examples include product recommendations to users on an e-commerce site to maximize sales; content recommendations to users visiting a news site to maximize total clicks; movie recommendations to maximize user engagement and increase subscriptions; or job recommendations on a professional network site to maximize job applications. Input to these algorithms typically consists of information about users, items, contexts, and feedback that is obtained when users interact with items.

Figure 1.1 shows an example of a typical web application that is powered by a recommender system. A user uses a web browser to visit a web page. The browser then submits an HTTP request to the web server that hosts the page. To serve recommendations on the page (e.g., popular news stories on a news portal page), the web server makes a call to a recommendation service that retrieves a set of items and renders them on the web page. Such a service typically performs a large number of different types of computations to select the best items. These computations are often a hybrid of both offline and real-time computations, but they must adhere to strict efficiency requirements to ensure quick page load time (typically hundreds of milliseconds). Once the page loads, the user may interact with items through actions like clicks, likes, or shares. Data obtained through such interactions provide a feedback loop to update the parameters of the underlying recommendation algorithm and to improve the performance of the algorithm for future user visits. The frequency of such parameter updates depends on the application. For instance, if items are time sensitive or ephemeral, as in the case of news recommendations, parameter updates must be done frequently (e.g., every few minutes). For

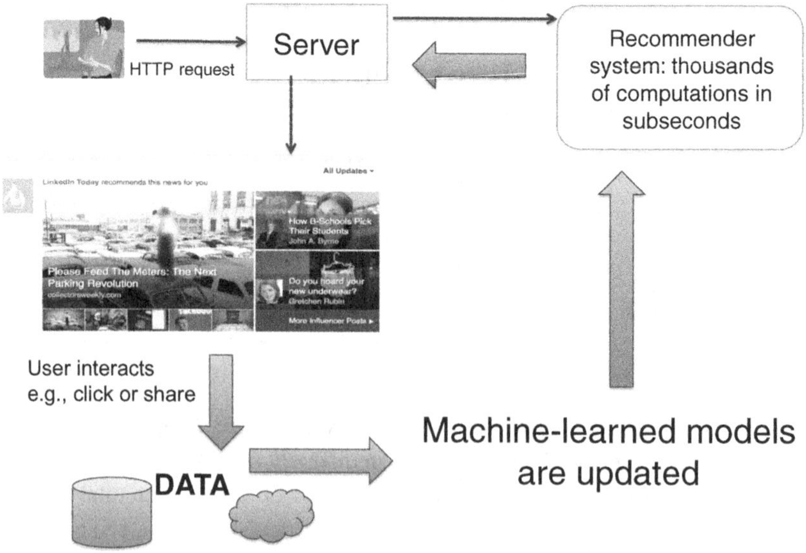

Figure 1.1. A typical recommender system.

other applications where items have a relatively longer lifetime (e.g., movie recommendations), parameter updates can happen less frequently (e.g., daily) without significant degradation in overall performance.

Algorithms that facilitate selection of best items are crucial to the success of recommender systems. This book provides a comprehensive description of statistical and machine learning methods on which we believe such algorithms should be based. For the sake of simplicity, we loosely refer to these algorithms as recommender systems throughout this book, but note that they only represent one component (albeit a crucial one) of the end-to-end process required to serve items to users in a scalable fashion.

1.1 Overview of Recommender Systems for Web Applications

Before developing a recommender system, it is important to consider the following questions.

- *What input signals are available?* When building machine-learned models of what items a user is likely to interact with in a given context, we can draw on many signals, including the content and source of each item; a

user's interest profile (reflecting both long-term interests based on prior visits and short-term interests as reflected in the current session); a user's declared information, such as demographics; and "popularity" indicators such as observed *click-through rates* or CTRs (the fraction of time in which the item is clicked on when a link to it is presented to users) and extent of social sharing (e.g., the number of times the item is tweeted, shared, or liked).
- *What objective(s) to optimize for?* There are many objectives a website could choose to optimize for, including near-term objectives, such as clicks, revenue, or positive explicit ratings by users, and long-term metrics, such as increased time spent on the site, higher return and user retention rates, increase in social actions, or increase in subscriptions.

Different recommendation algorithms need to be developed based on the answers to these questions.

1.1.1 Algorithmic Techniques

In general, a recommender system needs algorithmic techniques to address the following four tasks:

- *Content filtering and understanding.* We need to have sound techniques to filter out low-quality content from the *item pool* (i.e., the set of candidate items). Recommending low-quality content hurts user experience and the brand image of the website. The definition of low quality depends on the application. For a news recommendation problem, salacious content could be considered low quality by reputed publishers. An e-commerce site may not sell items from certain sellers with a low reputation rating. Defining and flagging low-quality content is typically a complex process that is addressed through a combination of methods, such as editorial labeling, crowdsourcing, and machine learning methods like classification. In addition to filtering low-quality content, it is important to analyze and understand the content of items that pass the quality bar. Creating item profiles (e.g., feature vectors) that capture the content with high fidelity is an effective approach. Features can be constructed using a variety of approaches, such as bag-of-words, phrase extraction, entity extraction, and topic extraction.
- *User profile modeling.* We also need to create user profiles that reflect the items that the users are likely to consume. These profiles could be based on demographics, user identity information submitted at the time of registration, social network information, or behavioral information about users.

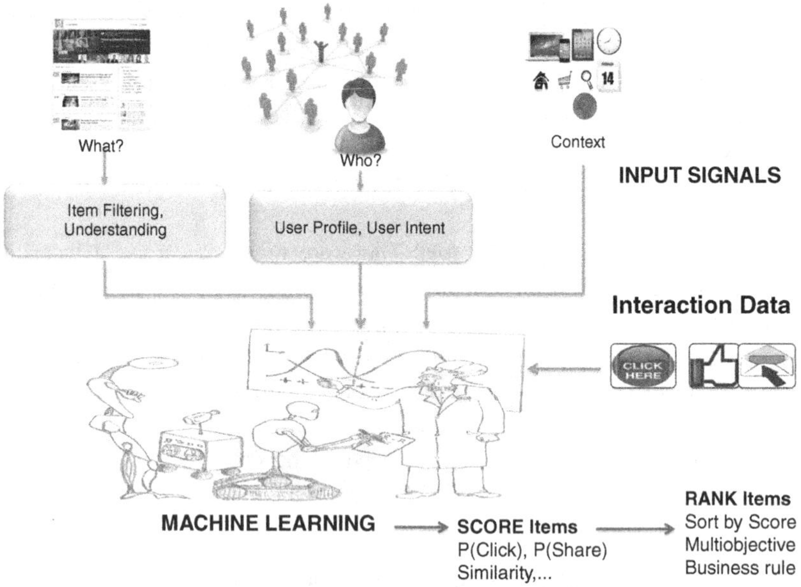

Figure 1.2. Overview of recommender system.

- *Scoring*. On the basis of user and item profiles, a scoring function needs to be designed to estimate the likely future "value" (e.g., CTRs, semantic relevance to the user's current goal, or expected revenue) of showing an item to a user in a given context (e.g., the page the user is viewing, the device being used, and the current location).
- *Ranking*. Finally, we need a mechanism to select a ranked list of items to recommend so as to maximize the expected value of the chosen objective function. In the simplest scenario, ranking may consist of sorting items based on a single score, such as the CTR of each item. However, in practice, ranking is more involved and is a blend of different considerations, such as semantic relevance, scores quantifying various utility measures, or diversity and business rules to ensure good user experience and preserve the brand image.

Figure 1.2 illustrates how the previously described algorithmic components are related. Input signals based on user information, item information, and historical user-item interaction data are used by machine-learned statistical models to produce scores that quantify users' affinity to items. The scores are combined by the ranking module to produce a sorted list of items based on descending order of priority obtained by considering single or multiple objectives.

Content filtering and understanding techniques depend to a large extent on the types of items to be recommended. For example, techniques for processing text are quite different from those used to process images. We do not intend to cover all such techniques, but we provide a brief review in Chapter 2. We also do not intend to cover a large variety of techniques for generating user profiles. However, we describe techniques that automatically "learn" both user and item profiles from historical user-item interaction data and that can also incorporate any existing profile information produced by some other existing techniques in a seamless fashion.

1.1.2 Metrics to Optimize

Among the considerations important to determining appropriate solutions for web recommendation problems, the first and foremost is to ascertain the metric(s) we want to optimize. In many applications, there is a single metric to optimize, for example, maximizing the total clicks or total revenue or total sales in a given time period. However, some applications may require simultaneous optimization of multiple metrics, for example, maximizing total clicks on content links subject to constraints on downstream engagement. An example constraint could be to ensure that the number of *bounce clicks* (clicks that do not materialize into a read) is less than some threshold. We may also want to balance other considerations, such as diversity (ensuring a user sees a range of topics over time) and serendipity (ensuring that we do not overfit our recommendations to the user, thereby limiting the discovery of new interests) to optimize long-term user experience.

Given the definition of metrics to optimize, the second consideration is to define scores that serve as the input to the optimization problem. For instance, if the goal is to maximize the total clicks, CTR is a good measure of the value of an item to a user. In the case of multiple objectives, one may have to use multiple scores, such as CTR and expected time spent. Statistical methods that can estimate the scores in a reliable fashion have to be developed. This is a nontrivial task that requires careful consideration. Once score estimates are available, they are combined in the ranking module based on the optimization problem under consideration.

1.1.3 The Explore-Exploit Trade-off

Reliably estimating scores is a fundamental statistical challenge in recommender systems. This often involves estimating expected rates of some positive response, such as click rate, explicit rating, share rate (probability of sharing an item), or like rate (probability of clicking the "like" button associated with an item). The expected response rates can be weighted according to the utility (or value) of each possible response. This provides a principled approach for ranking items based on expected utility. Response rates (appropriately weighted) are the primary scoring functions we consider in this book.

To accurately estimate response rates for each candidate item, we could *explore* each item by displaying it to some number of user visits to collect response data on all items in a timely manner. Then, we can *exploit* the items with high response rate estimates to optimize our objectives. However, exploration has an opportunity cost of not showing items that are empirically better (based on the data collected so far); balancing these two aspects constitutes the explore-exploit trade-off.

Explore-exploit is one of the main themes of this book. We provide an introduction in Chapter 3 and discuss the technical details in Chapter 6. The methods described in Chapters 7 and 8 are also developed to address this issue.

1.1.4 Evaluation of Recommender Systems

To understand whether a recommender system achieves its objectives, it is important to evaluate its performance at different stages during the development cycle. From the perspective of evaluation, we divide the development of a recommendation algorithm into two phases:

- *Predeployment phase* includes steps before the algorithm is deployed online to serve some fraction of user visits to the website. During this phase, we use past data to evaluate the performance of the algorithm. The evaluation is limited because it is *offline*; users' responses to items recommended by the algorithm are not available.
- *Postdeployment phase* starts when we deploy the algorithm *online* to serve users. It consists primarily of online bucket tests (also called A/B experiments) to measure appropriate metrics. Although this is far more close to reality, there is a cost to running such tests. A typical approach is to filter out algorithms with poor performance based on offline evaluation in the predeployment stage.

Different evaluation methods are used to evaluate various components of a recommender system:

- *Evaluation of scoring*. Scoring is usually done through statistical methods that predict how a user would respond to an item. Prediction accuracy is often used to measure the performance of such statistical methods. For example, if a statistical method is used to predict the numeric rating that a user would give to an item, we can use the absolute difference between the predicted rating and the true rating, averaged across users, to measure the error of the statistical method. The inverse of error is accuracy. Other ways of measuring accuracy are described in Section 4.1.2.

- *Evaluation of ranking*. The goal of ranking is to optimize for the objectives of a recommender system. In the postdeployment stage, we can evaluate a recommendation algorithm by directly computing the metrics of interest (e.g., CTR and time spent on recommended items) using data collected from online experiments. In Section 4.2, we discuss how to set up the experiments and analyze the results properly. However, in the predevelopment stage, we do not have data from users served by the algorithm – estimating the performance of the algorithm offline to mimic its online behavior is challenging. In Sections 4.3 and 4.4, we describe a couple of approaches to addressing this challenge.

1.1.5 Recommendation and Search: Push versus Pull

To set the scope of this book, we note that user intent is an important factor that differentiates various web applications. If the intent of a user is explicit and strong (e.g., query in web search), the problem of finding or "recommending" items that match the user's intent can be solved through a *pull* model – by retrieving items that are relevant to the explicit information needs of the user. However, in many recommendation scenarios, such explicit intent information is not available; at best, it can be inferred to some extent. In such cases, it is typical to follow the *push* model, where the system pushes information to the user – the goal is to serve items that are likely to engage the user.

Actual recommendation problems encountered in practice fall somewhere in the continuum of pull versus push. For instance, recommending news articles on a web portal is predominantly through a push model because explicit user intent is generally unavailable. Once the user starts reading an article, the system can recommend news stories related to the topic of the article that the user is reading, which provides some explicit intent information. Such a related news recommender system is usually based on a mix of pull and push models; we retrieve articles that are topically related to the article that the user is currently reading and then rank them to maximize user engagement.

We do not focus much on applications, such as web search, that require mostly a pull model and rely heavily on methods that estimate semantic similarity between a query and an item. Our focus is more on applications where

Figure 1.3. Today Module on the Yahoo! front page.

user intent is relatively weak and it is important to score items for each user based on response rates estimated through previous user-item interactions.

1.2 A Simple Scoring Model: Most-Popular Recommendation

To illustrate the basic idea of scoring, we consider the problem of recommending the most popular item (i.e., the item with the highest CTR) on a single slot of a web page to all users to maximize the total number of clicks. Although simple, this problem of *most-popular recommendation* includes the basic ingredients of item recommendation and also provides a strong baseline for the more sophisticated techniques that we describe in later chapters. We assume the number of items in the item pool is small relative to the number of visits and clicks. We do not make any assumption on the composition of the item pool; new items may get introduced and old ones may disappear over time.

Our example application is recommending new stories on the Today Module of Yahoo! front page (Figure 1.3 shows a snapshot). This application is used throughout the book for the purposes of illustration. The module is a panel with several slots, where each slot displays an item (i.e., story) selected from an item pool consisting of several items that are created through editorial oversight. For simplicity and ease of exposition, we focus on maximizing clicks on the single most prominent slot of the module, which gets a large fraction of the clicks.

Let p_{it} denote the instantaneous CTR of item i at time t. If we knew p_{it} for each candidate item i, we could simply serve the item with the highest instantaneous CTR to all user visits that occur at the given time point t. In other words, we select item $i_t^* = \arg\max_i p_{it}$ for visits at time t. However, instantaneous CTRs are not known; they have to be estimated from data. Let $\hat{p}_{it}$ denote the estimated CTR from data. Is it enough to serve the item with the highest estimated instantaneous CTR? Mathematically, is $\hat{i}_t^* = \arg\max_i \hat{p}_{it}$ a good approximation to i_t^*? This is clearly not always true because the statistical variance in the estimates varies across items. For instance, suppose there are two items and $\hat{p}_{1t} \sim \mathcal{D}$(mean=0.01, var=.005), $\hat{p}_{2t} \sim \mathcal{D}$(mean=0.015, var=.001), where $\mathcal{D}$ denotes some probability distribution that is approximately normal. Then, $P(\hat{p}_{1t} > \hat{p}_{2t}) = .47$, that is, there is a 47 percent chance of selecting the first item, although it is inferior to the second one. This happens because the variance in estimating the CTR of the first item is significantly larger than the variance in estimating the second because of the smaller sample size. Thus, it is clear that the naive scheme of selecting the item with the highest estimated CTR is likely to produce false positives (not selecting the true best item) in practice. Are there other schemes that can reduce such false positives on average? The answer is in the affirmative: there exist several such schemes (also called explore-exploit schemes) that perform better than the greedy scheme of selecting the item with the highest estimated CTR, especially in scenarios where CTR estimates have significant statistical variance when first introduced into the item pool.

The simplest explore-exploit scheme is to allocate a small fraction of visits chosen at random to a *randomized* serving scheme, which serves each item in the item pool with equal probability (1 / total number of items) for visits in this fraction. We refer to this fraction of visits as the *random bucket* of visits. Data collected from such a random bucket are used to estimate instantaneous CTRs of items, and visits outside the random bucket are served with the item that has the highest estimated CTR. We refer to the fraction of visits outside the random bucket as the *serving bucket*. The main idea here is to estimate the CTRs through a randomized design, which smooths out the sample size and disparity in variance across items. The random bucket also avoids the item "starvation" problem because every item in the item pool is guaranteed to receive a reasonable sample on a continuous basis. Instantaneous CTRs can be estimated using data in the random bucket through time series methods like moving averages and dynamic state-space models.

Figure 1.4 shows the CTR curves of items in the Today Module for a period of two days (the curves have been smoothed). Each curve represents the CTR of an item over time, which is estimated based on data collected from the random bucket. As is evident from the figure, the CTR of each item changes over time, and the lifetimes of items are usually short (from a few hours to a day). It is thus imperative to continuously update the CTR estimates of each item to adapt to changing CTR trends by giving more weight to recent data. A simple state-space model that can perform such smoothing for a given item entails running an exponentially weighted moving average (EWMA) separately for

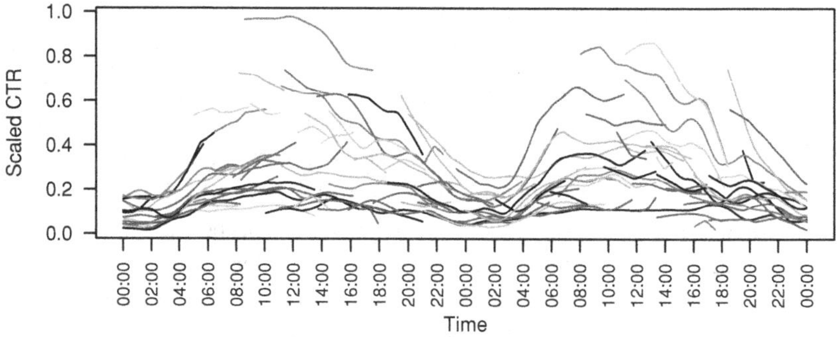

Figure 1.4. CTR curves of items in the Yahoo! Today Module over a period of two days. The y-axis is linearly scaled to conceal the actual CTR numbers.

clicks and views;[1] the ratio estimator provides the instantaneous item CTR. More specifically, we update the estimates after every ten-minute interval for this application. We chose ten minutes as our interval size because it takes time to get data from web servers to distributed computing clusters for offline processing. In general, keeping the interval size small ensures faster reaction to changes but requires more infrastructure cost. But reducing the interval size also reduces the sample size available per interval and may not give bang for the buck for the additional infrastructure investment. In our experience, we have not found significant gains in choosing interval sizes that are smaller than the interval size that would receive five clicks per item on average.

If the EWMA estimators for clicks and views for item i at the end of the tth interval are denoted by α_{it} and γ_{it}, respectively, they are given by

$$\begin{aligned} \alpha_{it} &= c_{it} + \delta\alpha_{i,t-1} \\ \gamma_{it} &= n_{it} + \delta\gamma_{i,t-1}, \end{aligned} \tag{1.1}$$

where c_{it} and n_{it} denote the number of clicks and views in the tth interval for item i, respectively, and $\delta \in [0, 1]$ is the EWMA smoothing parameter that can be selected via cross-validation to minimize predictive accuracy (typically, [.9, 1] is an appropriate range to search over). Note that $\delta = 1$ corresponds to an estimator that uses cumulative CTR with no time decay (i.e., the importance of the observed clicks and views does not decay over time), and $\delta = 0$ uses only the data in the current interval. We could interpret α and γ as pseudo-clicks and pseudo-views associated with an item. To complete the specification, we initialize $\alpha_{i0} = p_{i0}\gamma_{i0}$, where p_{i0} is an initial estimate of item i's CTR and γ_{i0} is the number of pseudo-views, which reflects the degree of confidence in the initial CTR estimate. Typically, in the absence of other information, we could

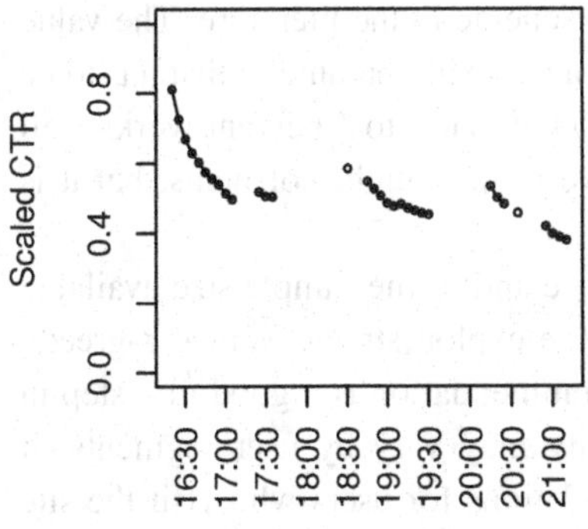

Figure 1.5. CTR of an item decays as a result of repeatedly showing the item.

set p_{i0} to some global system average and γ_{i0} to a small number like unity (or set γ_{i0} such that $p_{i0}\gamma_{i0}$ is unity).

Another important aspect that has to be kept in mind is the impact of repeatedly showing the same item to a given user. This is more likely to happen in the serving bucket and for users who visit more frequently. Figure 1.5 shows the relative CTR decay when the same item is shown to a user multiple times despite no prior clicks by the user. There is a significant drop in CTR of an item when it is shown to the same user multiple times. Hence the most-popular algorithm to display items in the serving bucket has to be modified to "discount" item CTRs based on the number of previous views by a user. In other words, the CTR of item i at time t for a user u is given by $\hat{p}_{it} f(v_{iu})$, where $\hat{p}_{it}$ is the estimated instantaneous CTR of item i using data in the random bucket and $f(v_{iu})$ is the discount applied based on the number of previous views v_{iu} on item i by user u. Typically, $f(v)$ can be estimated empirically for each value of v; one could also fit a parametric function like exponential decay.

We summarize our simple most-popular algorithm to maximize CTR as follows:

1. Create a small random bucket that shows an item at random to each visit.
2. Estimate the instantaneous CTR of each item through classical time series models using data in the random bucket. The CTRs are updated by collecting data in time intervals of some duration (e.g., ten minutes for time-sensitive applications).
3. Calculate the discounting factor to discourage repeated views of an item for each user based on prior exposure to the item by the user.
4. For each visit in the serving bucket, serve the item with the highest discounted CTR.

The scheme of using a random bucket to explore every candidate item and recommending the items with the highest estimated CTRs in the serving bucket is also called the ϵ-greedy explore-exploit scheme in the literature. The value of ϵ (i.e., the size of the random bucket) is a tweaking parameter that has to be chosen empirically. In practice, we have found that 1 to 5 percent works well when the number of clicks is large relative to the number of items, but it is application dependent.

When the number of items becomes large and/or the sample size available per item shrinks, more parsimonious explore-exploit strategies than ϵ-greedy are necessary. Although most-popular recommendation is a good first step in practice for several applications, popularity may vary by user segments. It is also desirable to personalize recommendations for users who visit the site frequently. The main challenge in dealing with these issues is data sparseness. Solutions to these issues are the focus of this book.

Exercises

1. Think of your favorite product that is powered by recommendation algorithms. How would you formulate the problem if you were to build this system from scratch using the framework described in this chapter?
2. Write down the probabilistic state-space model that provides the solution in Exercise 1.1. Also derive the variance of the estimate using the probabilistic model. Then derive the expression for the probability of an item being the best among a pool of K items. Can we use this expression to create a better explore-exploit scheme?

2

Classical Methods

A recommender system seeks to recommend a small set of items for each user visit to optimize one or more objectives in a given context. In this chapter, we review classical methods for making such recommendations.

In general, recommendations are made based on

- what we know about the items (Section 2.1)
- what we know about the user (Section 2.2)
- how users interacted with items (e.g., clicked or not) in the past

We represent information about a user i as a vector of user *features* and information about an item j as a vector of item features (examples of such feature vectors are given later). In this chapter, we review classical methods to compute a score $\hat{y}_{ij}$ for each (user i, item j) pair. The scores $\hat{y}_{ij}$ are usually computed in one of the following ways:

- similarity between feature vectors of user i and item j (Section 2.3)
- user i's past responses to items that are "similar" to item j and/or how other users "similar" to user i responded to item j in the past (Section 2.4)
- a combination of both of the preceding (Section 2.5)

Some methods leverage predefined similarity measures, whereas others seek to learn the similarity measure directly from data.

Classical methods serve as strong baselines for the more sophisticated methods described in later chapters. In this book, we only provide an overview of classical methods. For more details on classical methods, see Adomavicius and Tuzhilin (2005), Jannach et al. (2010), and Ricci et al. (2011).

Notation. We use i and j to denote a user and an item, respectively. Let y_{ij} denote the *rating* that user i gives to item j. Here we use the term *rating* in a general sense: it can be an explicit rating, such as a 5-star rating (on a movie,

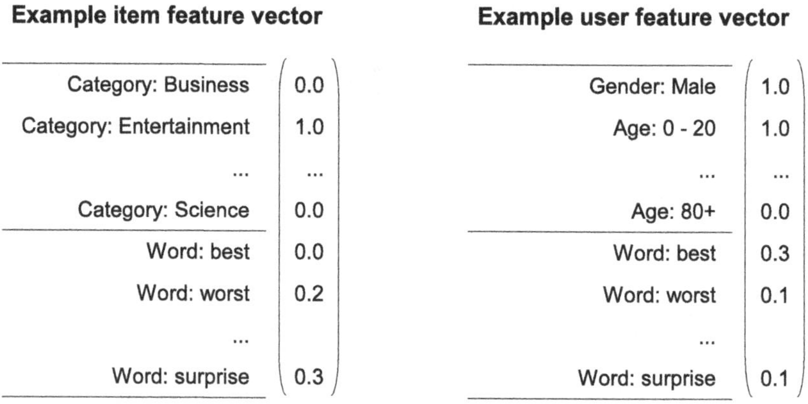
Example item feature vector
Category: Business
Category: Entertainment
...
Category: Science
Word: best
Word: worst
...
Word: surprise
0.0
1.0
...
0.0
0.0
0.2
0.3
Example user feature vector
Gender: Male
Age: 0 - 20
...
Age: 80+
Word: best
Word: worst
...
Word: surprise
1.0
1.0
...
0.0
0.3
0.1
0.1

Figure 2.1. Example feature vectors. The meaning of each dimension is noted to the left of the vector.

a book, or a product), or an implicit rating, such as a click (on a recommended item). We use $\boldsymbol{Y} = \{y_{ij} : \text{user } i \text{ rated item } j\}$ to denote a set of observed ratings and call it a *rating matrix*. Notice that many entries of this rating matrix are unobserved. We let $\boldsymbol{x}_i$ and $\boldsymbol{x}_j$ denote the vector of features of user i and the vector of features of item j, respectively. Although we use symbol $\boldsymbol{x}$ to denote both user and item feature vectors, it is important to note that $\boldsymbol{x}_i$ and $\boldsymbol{x}_j$ may consist of different features and may have different dimensionality. Figure 2.1 shows an example of an item feature vector $\boldsymbol{x}_j$ and an example of user feature vector $\boldsymbol{x}_i$. In the next section, we discuss how to construct such feature vectors.

2.1 Item Characterization

There are several ways to construct an item feature vector $\boldsymbol{x}_j$. The kinds of features that can be extracted depend on the nature of the item. A feature vector associated with a document can be very different from that of an image. We do not attempt to provide a detailed description of all the kinds of features that one might consider for various items. Instead, we give examples of commonly used item features for popular web recommender problems. However, as long as information about items can be represented as a vector of numbers for each item, the statistical methods described in this book can be applied.

Commonly used methods to create feature vectors for items are categorization (Section 2.1.1), bag of words (Section 2.1.2), and topic modeling (Section 2.1.3). We then discuss other item features in Section 2.1.4.

2.1.1 Categorization

In many application settings, items can be classified into a predefined taxonomy. For example, news articles on a website like Yahoo! News are usually classified into a news taxonomy that has "U.S.," "World," "Business," "Entertainment," "Sports," "Tech," "Politics," "Science," "Health," and so on, as first-level categories. Within these categories we may have subcategories. For instance, within the category "U.S.," there are subcategories "Education," "Religion," "Crimes and Trials," and so on. Similarly, product items on an e-commerce site are usually classified into a product taxonomy. For example, Amazon.com has "Books," "Movies, Music & Games," "Electronics & Computers," "Home, Garden & Tools," and so on, as first-level categories. Within the category "Books," there are subcategories such as "Arts & Photography," "Biographies & Memoirs," and "Business & Investing"; within the subcategory "Arts & Photography" are "Architecture Art & Design," "Business of Art," "Collections, Catalogs & Exhibitions," "Decorative Arts & Design," and so on; and within the sub-subcategory "Architecture Art & Design" are "Buildings," "Decoration & Ornament," "History," and "Individual Architects & Firms." An item may also belong to multiple categories with different degrees of membership.

The categorization of an item into a set of categories in the taxonomy can be done in several ways. The simplest method is, of course, through human labels. Many news websites categorize articles through an editorial process. For products, sellers usually categorize their items to facilitate discovery by potential buyers. Such a human labeling process works well with a small number of items; it is expensive for recommender problems where a large number of items are introduced at a rapid rate. When human labels are not available for all items, statistical methods can be used to automatically classify items into appropriate nodes in taxonomies. Such statistical methods learn a model from a set of labeled examples for each category using standard supervised learning methods. For a description of general supervised learning methods, see Hastie et al. (2009) and Mitchell (1997). For a survey of automated text categorization methods, see Sebastiani (2002).

Although classifying items into categories in a taxonomy is typically done to help users browse a website more efficiently to find items of interest, it may also provide useful semantic information about items. A common way of constructing a feature vector from this item-category relation is to define a vector space such that each dimension corresponds to a category. The ℓth dimension of the feature vector $\boldsymbol{x}_j$ of item j is 1 if item j belongs to the ℓth category; otherwise, it is 0. The top portion of the item feature vector in Figure 2.1 represents category features, where the example item belongs to the

"Entertainment" category. When information about the degree of membership to a category is available (usually when statistical methods are used to categorize items), the binary values (0 or 1) in the item feature vector can be replaced by these membership scores. It is also common to normalize the feature vector so that $||\boldsymbol{x}_j||_1 = 1$ or $||\boldsymbol{x}_j||_2 = 1$. However, the benefits of normalization are application – dependent and require empirical evaluation.

2.1.2 Bag of Words

For items that have associated text, the bag-of-words vector space model (Salton et al., 1975) is commonly used to construct item features. Even in applications where the primary content of an item may not be textual, there is usually some text associated with each item. For example, product items almost always have some textual descriptions; multimedia items usually have titles and sometimes textual descriptions and tags.

In the bag-of-words vector space model, a high-dimensional vector space is created by treating each word that appears in a reference *item corpus* as a dimension, where an item corpus is a large collection of typical items that may appear in the system. Each item j is represented as a point $\boldsymbol{x}_j$ in this bag-of-words vector space. We let $x_{j,\ell}$ denote the value of the ℓth dimension of vector $\boldsymbol{x}_j$. Three commonly used methods to map an item into this vector space are as follows:

1. *Unweighted version*: $x_{j,\ell} = 1$ if item j contains the ℓth word; otherwise, $x_{j,\ell} = 0$.
2. *Term frequency (TF) version*: We let $TF(j, \ell)$ denote the number of times the ℓth word appears in item j, then $x_{j,\ell} = TF(j, \ell)$.
3. *Term frequency – inverse document frequency (TF-IDF) version*: We let $DF(\ell) =$ the fraction of items (in a reference item corpus) that contain the ℓth word, and $IDF(\ell) = \log(1/DF(\ell))$, which represents how unique word ℓ is when it is used to describe an item. Then, $x_{j,\ell}$ is defined as $TF(j, \ell) \cdot IDF(\ell)$.

Finally, each vector $\boldsymbol{x}_j$ is normalized so that $||\boldsymbol{x}_j||_2 = 1$. In information retrieval, the inner product of a pair of normalized item vectors (which equals the cosine of the angle between the two vectors) provides a similarity measure between the two items. The bottom portion of the item feature vector in Figure 2.1 represents such bag-of-words features.

Sparse Format. Note that $\boldsymbol{x}_j$ is usually a sparse vector with zeros on a large fraction of dimensions. We can save memory by not storing all of the zeros.

Dense Format

Dimension	Vector
1	0.0
2	0.8
3	0.0
4	0.0
5	0.6
6	0.0

Sparse Format

Index	Value
2	0.8
5	0.6

Figure 2.2. Example vector in dense and sparse formats.

One way to store a sparse vector is by keeping a list of (index, value) pairs such that (i, v) is in the list if the ith dimension of the vector has value v, which is nonzero. Figure 2.2 shows an example vector in both dense and sparse formats. When reading the book, we can think of $\boldsymbol{x}_j$ as a high-dimensional vector with many zeros, with the understanding that $\boldsymbol{x}_j$ is actually stored in memory using a much smaller amount of space than the dimensionality of the vector.

Phrases and Entities. Although we refer to those features that capture textual information as "bag of words," we do not need to restrict ourselves to individual words when describing items with associated text. It is common to extend the vector space by including two-contiguous-words (bi-grams) or even three-contiguous-words (tri-grams) that correspond to phrases as additional dimensions. It is also often beneficial to focus on features corresponding to named entities such as people, organizations or locations. For a survey of named-entity recognition methods, see Nadeau and Sekine (2007).

Reducing Dimensionality. Even without considering phrases, the total number of words in an item corpus can be large, with several of them typically appearing in a small number of items. Also, it is typical for each item to contain only a small fraction of the total words in the corpus. Because the eventual goal is to use item feature vectors to estimate scores, increased dimensionality and data sparseness may add more noise relative to signal-to-score estimates. It is often useful to augment items with richer related information and/or to reduce noise by using dimensionality reduction procedures. We describe a few commonly used methods to reduce sparsity and dimensionality. These are mostly unsupervised methods that provide useful representations to be used as inputs to various supervised score estimation tasks in general. Direct methods to obtain representations that are optimal for an application-specific supervised learning problem are considered in Chapter 7 and Section 8.1.

1. *Synonym expansion*: A simple but useful method for expanding words in an item is by adding synonyms. For example, if an item contains the word "hardworking," we can also add synonyms like "dedicated" and "diligent" to the bag of words of the item so that the corresponding feature vector would have nonzero values on the dimensions corresponding to "dedicated" and "diligent." Synonyms can be found in thesauri or lexical databases such as the WordNet by Princeton University (2010).
2. *Feature selection*: Not all words are useful. Feature selection methods (Guyon and Elisseeff, 2003) can be applied to select top-K informative words. A very simple selection method is to prune words that appear too often or too infrequently, for example, by only considering words that appear in at least N items. This simple method often reduces the dimensionality and noise in the problem.
3. *Singular value decomposition*: Another way of reducing sparsity and dimensionality is through singular value decomposition (SVD). (See Golub and Van Loan, 2013, for details). Let $\boldsymbol{X}$ denote the $m \times n$ matrix such that the jth row is the feature vector $\boldsymbol{x}_j$ of each item j, where m is the number of items and n is the number of dimensions of a feature vector. The SVD of $\boldsymbol{X}$ is

$$\boldsymbol{X} = \boldsymbol{U}\boldsymbol{\Sigma}\boldsymbol{V}', \tag{2.1}$$

where $\boldsymbol{U}$ is an $m \times m$ orthogonal matrix, $\boldsymbol{V}$ is a $n \times n$ orthogonal matrix, and $\boldsymbol{\Sigma}$ is a rectangular diagonal matrix with descending nonnegative singular values on the diagonal (we have at most $\min(m, n)$ nonzero diagonal entries). To reduce dimensionality, we can choose to keep the top-d ($d \ll \min(m, n)$) projections corresponding to the largest d singular values. Let $\boldsymbol{\Sigma}_d$ denote the resulting $d \times d$ diagonal matrix obtained by retaining only the largest d singular values. Let $\boldsymbol{U}_d$ and $\boldsymbol{V}_d$ be the $m \times d$ and $n \times d$ matrices produced by keeping only the first d columns of $\boldsymbol{U}$ and $\boldsymbol{V}$, respectively. By the Eckart-Young theorem, $\boldsymbol{U}_d\boldsymbol{\Sigma}_d\boldsymbol{V}_d'$ is the *best* rank d matrix that approximates $\boldsymbol{X}$ in terms of minimizing the Frobenius norm (sum of squared element-wise differences) between the two matrices. Because $\boldsymbol{V}'$ is an orthonormal transformation (that only rotates the vector space), we can replace the original $m \times n$ feature matrix $\boldsymbol{X}$ with the new $m \times d$ feature matrix $\boldsymbol{U}_d\boldsymbol{\Sigma}_d = \boldsymbol{X}\boldsymbol{V}_d$; that is, we replace the original n-dimensional feature vector $\boldsymbol{x}_j$ for item j

with the new d-dimensional feature vector $V_d'x_j$, where V_d' projects x_j from an n-dimensional vector space into a d-dimensional one.

4. *Random projection*: Notice that the SVD method is based on a linear projection from a high-dimensional space to a low-dimensional one. A simple and sometimes effective alternative representation is to use a random linear projection (e.g., Bingham and Mannila, 2001). Let R_d be a $n \times d$ matrix with entries drawn from the standard normal distribution. Then, we use $R_d'x_j$ as our new d-dimensional feature vector for item j. The main idea is due to the Johnson-Lindenstrauss lemma that if d is sufficiently large, the Euclidean distance between two points in the original vector space is approximately preserved in the new d-dimensional vector space.

Empirical evaluations are usually required to determine which representations work best for a particular application setting. It is useful to construct multiple such representations and use them as inputs to supervised learning tasks for computing scores. New methods based on deep learning (e.g., Bengio et al., 2003) that can learn more non-linear representations is another alternative that may work well for certain applications. Because most modern-day supervised learning procedures use regularization techniques like L_2 or L_1 norm to avoid overfitting, they are effective at selecting the most informative features from a reasonable pool of input features. We defer the description of regularization to the end of Section 2.3.2.

2.1.3 Topic Modeling

In addition to hand-crafted categories, taxonomies, and the low-level bag-of-words representation of items, recent research has made good progress on unsupervised clustering of text-based items. Although several unsupervised clustering methods for documents are available, the latent Dirichlet allocation (LDA) model proposed by Blei et al. (2003) has emerged as a method of choice. Based on textual content, it assigns a membership score for each (item j, topic k) pair, which represents the probability that item j is about topic k. Note that topics here can be thought of as clusters.

The LDA model describes how each occurrence of words in each item is generated. It assumes that there are K topics in total in a corpus of items, where K is a prespecified number. Words and items are connected through these topics. Each topic is represented as a multinomial probability mass function over all of the words in the corpus. Let W denote the number of unique words in the corpus. The probability mass function of topic k can be represented as a W-dimensional vector $\boldsymbol{\Phi}_k$ of nonnegative numbers on the simplex (i.e., the numbers in the vector sum to 1) such that the wth element in the vector represents the probability of seeing word w in an item on topic k; that is, $\mathbf{\Phi}_{k,w} = \Pr(\text{word } w \mid \text{topic } k)$. Each item j is represented as a multinomial probability mass function over topics, which is a K-dimensional vector $\boldsymbol{\theta}_j$ such that the kth element in the vector represents the probability that item j is on topic k; that is, $\boldsymbol{\theta}_{j,k} = \Pr(\text{topic } k \mid \text{item } j)$. If $\mathbf{\Phi}_k$ and $\boldsymbol{\theta}_j$ are given, a word in item j can be generated by first sampling a topic k from $\boldsymbol{\theta}_j$ and then, given the topic k, sampling a word from $\mathbf{\Phi}_k$. To complete the Bayesian specification of the model, we add conjugate Dirichlet priors to the two multinomial probability mass vectors, $\mathbf{\Phi}_k$ and $\boldsymbol{\theta}_j$. The full specification of the generative model that prescribes how the words in each item are generated is as follows:

- For each topic k, draw a W-dimensional probability mass vector $\mathbf{\Phi}_k$ from a Dirichlet prior with hyperparameter $\boldsymbol{\eta}$.
- Then, for each item j,
  - first, draw a K-dimensional probability mass vector $\boldsymbol{\theta}_j$ from a Dirichlet prior with hyper-parameter $\boldsymbol{\lambda}$
  - then, for each occurrence of a word in item j,
    - draw a topic k from the probability mass vector $\boldsymbol{\theta}_j$
    - draw a word w from the probability mass vector $\mathbf{\Phi}_k$ corresponding to the topic k just picked

The preceding process describes how each occurrence of a word in each item is generated based on the LDA model. Now, given a set of items with their associated words as the observed data, we would like to estimate the parameters of the model. The posterior distribution of $\boldsymbol{\theta}_j$ for each item j and the posterior distribution of $\mathbf{\Phi}_k$ for each topic k can be estimated through variational approximation (Blei et al., 2003) or Gibbs sampling (Griffiths and Steyvers, 2004). The posterior mean of $\boldsymbol{\theta}_j$ is the Bayesian estimator of the probabilities that item j is about different topics, while the posterior mean of $\mathbf{\Phi}_k$ helps to interpret each topic k. By looking at the top-n words with the highest probability mass in $\mathbf{\Phi}_k$, many studies reported meaningful topics found in various article collections. We refer interested readers to Blei et al. (2003) and Griffiths and Steyvers (2004) for a detailed exposition of LDA. In Chapter 9, we discuss how to extend the LDA model to simultaneously model users' interactions with items and the topics of items with a detailed description of a parameter estimation method based on Gibbs sampling.

2.1.4 Other Item Features

Before we move on to user features, we briefly discuss some other types of item features that are available in different recommender problems. The following list is by no means exhaustive, and each application may have its own unique features:

- *Source*: The source of an item (e.g., author and publisher) can be a useful feature if users tend to prefer some sources more than others.
- *Location*: In some applications, items may be tagged with geographical locations. For example, pictures taken using a cell phone can be easily tagged with the location, and product items may be tagged with the locations of the stores that sell them. Such location information is important for applications of geographical interest. A location may be represented as two numbers, longitude and latitude, or as a node in a location taxonomy (with levels like Country, State/Province, Town).
- *Image features*: When items contain images or video clips, image features can provide useful information for recommendation. There is a large body of literature on this topic. See Datta et al. (2008) and Deselaers et al. (2008) for examples.
- *Audio features*: Similarly, when items contain audio clips, audio features are potentially useful. See Fu et al. (2011) and Mitrović et al. (2010) for examples.

Beyond the common ones, item features are usually application specific. Identification of good item features requires domain knowledge, experience, and insights into the application.

2.2 User Characterization

We now describe a number of methods for creating user features $\boldsymbol{x}_i$ for each user i. In general, user features can be derived from declared profiles (Section 2.2.1), users' past interaction with content (Section 2.2.2), and other user-related information available in a recommender system (Section 2.2.3).

2.2.1 Declared Profile

In many application settings, users provide basic information about themselves and sometimes even declare their interests in various topics when they sign up for services. It is common for the following user-declared features to be available in recommender systems:

- *Demographics*: As part of the registration process for a service, users are usually asked to provide their age, gender, profession, educational level, location, and other demographic information. Although some users do not provide all demographic information, many users do. It is likely that, for example, users with different genders, in different age groups or living in different locations, have different item preferences. Thus, it is usually useful to consider demographic features in recommender systems.

- *Declared interests*: Some recommender systems allow users to declare their interests by selecting from a set of predefined categories or topics or providing a set of keywords. Although many users do not bother to declare their interests, for users who do, these declared interests may serve as important features to provide better item recommendations. For recommender systems that allow users to declare interests, one important design problem is how to make this interest elicitation process natural, effortless, and even fun.

Feature vectors of user-declared information can be constructed in a way similar to item features. Categorical features such as gender, profession, education, and interest categories can be handled in a way similar to that described in Section 2.1.1. Keyword-based features can be handled by similar methods described in Section 2.1.2. Numerical features such as age can be treated as a single dimension in the feature vector or can be discretized into a number of bins (e.g., age groups), which are then treated as categories. Figure 2.1 (right) shows an example of a user feature vector.

2.2.2 Content-Based Profile

For users who have interacted with items in the past, one way of creating a feature vector for a given user is by aggregating the feature vector of items with which the user has interacted (A similar strategy can also be used to construct additional item features.) Let $\mathcal{J}_i$ denote the set of items that user i interacted with in the past. The kind of interaction depends on the application setting and may consist of clicking, sharing, reading (for article recommendation), buying (for product recommendation), or authoring (in systems where regular users also produce content items, e.g., comments). Recall that $\boldsymbol{x}_j$ denotes the feature vector of item j. The content-based feature vector of user i is then given by

$$\boldsymbol{x}_i = F(\{\boldsymbol{x}_j \,:\, j \in \mathcal{J}_i\}), \tag{2.2}$$

where F is an aggregator function that takes a set of vectors and returns a vector. One common choice of F is the average function. A simple extension is to make F a weighted average by giving more weight to items with which the user has interacted recently.

The set $\mathcal{J}_i$ of items with which user i interacted in the past can include items that are not candidates for recommendation. For example, a movie recommender system can use movie-related news articles that a user clicked on, read, and/or made comments on to construct content-based user features for the user, even though the recommender system does not recommend news articles or comments to users.

2.2.3 Other User Features

In addition to user-declared information and content-based user features, a recommender system may also have access to other kinds of user features. We list a few examples:

- *Current location*: Users may not always be at the declared locations that they provided when they signed up for a service. The current location of the user can usually be inferred based on the IP (Internet Protocol) address of the user's device or exactly determined if the user's device is equipped with GPS. This user location information is important when recommending geosensitive items such as stores and restaurants, for example, in an iPhone app used in a car.
- *Usage-based features*: Statistics on how a user interacts with a website (for which we are designing the recommender system) also provide a useful characterization of the user. Examples include the frequency of user visits to the website (e.g., number of times per month) and the frequency with which the user uses different devices, services, applications, or components of the website.
- *Search history*: If a recommender system is designed for a website that has a search capability, the search history of a user provides valuable information about the user's interests and recent intent. For example, if a user recently searched for an organization, then news articles about the organization may be of interest to the user. Usually the search history of a user can be represented using a bag-of-words vector in a way similar to that described in Section 2.1.2.
- *Item set*: A set of items in which a user showed interest (e.g., clicked, shared, liked) in the past can also be used to construct useful features. A feature vector can be constructed in a way that is similar to a bag-of-words approach whereby each item can be interpreted as "word."

2.3 Feature-Based Methods

Given user features and item features, one common scoring approach is to score items for a given user by designing a scoring function $s(\boldsymbol{x}_i, \boldsymbol{x}_j)$ that measures the affinity between user i and item j based on their feature vectors. Then, recommendations can be made to a user by ranking items based on their scores. The scoring function can be obtained by using either unsupervised methods (Section 2.3.1) or supervised methods (Section 2.3.2).

In general, finding good features is an elaborate task, but when done properly, it leads to significant improvements in performance. In Section 2.4.3, we also describe methods that automatically "learn" feature vectors for users and items based on past user-item interaction data. We shall call such "learned" features *factors* to distinguish them from the regular features generated without supervised learning.

2.3.1 Unsupervised Methods

Scoring functions for unsupervised methods are typically based on some similarity measure between a user feature vector $\boldsymbol{x}_i$ and an item feature vector $\boldsymbol{x}_j$. There are several ways to measure similarity between two vectors. We start with a simple setting where $\boldsymbol{x}_i$ and $\boldsymbol{x}_j$ are points in the same vector space; that is, both users and items are represented using the same set of features. A common example where this occurs is when both users and items are represented as bags of words from the same corpus. When items have associated text, it is natural to represent them as bags of words (as described in Section 2.1.2). The bag-of-words feature representation for a user in this case can be obtained from a content-based profile (see Section 2.2.2). Cosine similarity is a common choice of the scoring function:

$$s(\boldsymbol{x}_i, \boldsymbol{x}_j) = \frac{\boldsymbol{x}_i'\boldsymbol{x}_j}{||\boldsymbol{x}_i|| \cdot ||\boldsymbol{x}_j||}, \tag{2.3}$$

where $\boldsymbol{x}_i'$ is the transpose of column vector $\boldsymbol{x}_i$ and $\boldsymbol{x}_i'\boldsymbol{x}_j$ is the inner product of the two vectors. Other commonly used similarity functions for bag-of-words features include Okapi BM25 (Robertson et al., 1995), which is a popular TF-IDF-based similarity function used in information retrieval. For binary features, Jaccard similarity (Jaccard, 1901) is often used. The Jaccard similarity between two sets is the size of the intersection divided by the size of the union.

When $\boldsymbol{x}_i$ and $\boldsymbol{x}_j$ are normalized such that $||\boldsymbol{x}_i||_2 = ||\boldsymbol{x}_j||_2 = 1$, the inner product $\boldsymbol{x}_i'\boldsymbol{x}_j = \sum_k x_{i,k}x_{j,k}$ is the cosine similarity between the two vectors, where $x_{i,k}$ and $x_{j,k}$ are the values on the kth dimension of vectors $\boldsymbol{x}_i$ and $\boldsymbol{x}_j$. A simple extension is to associate different weights to dimensions; that is, $s(\boldsymbol{x}_i, \boldsymbol{x}_j) = \boldsymbol{x}_i'\boldsymbol{A}\boldsymbol{x}_j = \sum_k a_{kk}x_{i,k}x_{j,k}$, where $\boldsymbol{A}$ is a diagonal matrix and a_{kk}, the value of entry (k, k) of matrix $\boldsymbol{A}$, is the weight for the kth dimension. A

$$\boldsymbol{x}_i = \begin{pmatrix} x_{i1} \\ x_{i2} \\ x_{i3} \end{pmatrix} \qquad \boldsymbol{x}_j = \begin{pmatrix} x_{j1} \\ x_{j2} \end{pmatrix} \qquad A = \begin{pmatrix} a_{11} & a_{12} \\ a_{21} & a_{22} \\ a_{31} & a_{33} \end{pmatrix}.$$

$$\boldsymbol{x}_i\boldsymbol{x}_j' = \begin{pmatrix} x_{i1}x_{j1} & x_{i1}x_{j2} \\ x_{i2}x_{j1} & x_{i2}x_{j2} \\ x_{i3}x_{j1} & x_{i3}x_{j2} \end{pmatrix} \quad \boldsymbol{x}_{ij} = \begin{pmatrix} x_{i1}x_{j1} \\ x_{i2}x_{j1} \\ x_{i3}x_{j1} \\ x_{i1}x_{j2} \\ x_{i2}x_{j2} \\ x_{i3}x_{j2} \end{pmatrix} \quad \boldsymbol{\beta} = \begin{pmatrix} a_{11} \\ a_{21} \\ a_{31} \\ a_{12} \\ a_{22} \\ a_{32} \end{pmatrix}$$

Figure 2.3. Correspondence between the bilinear form and the regular linear form: $\boldsymbol{x}_i'\boldsymbol{A}\boldsymbol{x}_j = \boldsymbol{x}_{ij}'\boldsymbol{\beta}$.

further extension is to allow $\boldsymbol{A}$ to be a full matrix; that is, $s(\boldsymbol{x}_i, \boldsymbol{x}_j) = \boldsymbol{x}_i'\boldsymbol{A}\boldsymbol{x}_j = \sum_{k\ell} a_{k\ell}x_{i,k}x_{j,\ell}$, where $a_{k\ell}$ intuitively prescribes the similarity between the kth dimension of the user feature space and the ℓth dimension of the item feature space. With this extension, $\boldsymbol{x}_i$ and $\boldsymbol{x}_j$ can consist of different features and have different numbers of dimensions. However, how should we specify the matrix $\boldsymbol{A}$? It can be difficult when $\boldsymbol{x}_i$ and $\boldsymbol{x}_j$ are high dimensional. This provides us with motivation to use supervised methods.

2.3.2 Supervised Methods

Supervised methods use a set of observed *ratings* collected from past user-item interaction to learn a model that predicts the rating of any unobserved (user, item) pair based on their features. Recall that we use the term *rating* in a general sense to refer to any kind of response that a user gives to an item. This rating prediction problem is actually a standard supervised learning problem, and a variety of supervised learning methods can be directly used. Let $s_{ij} = s(\boldsymbol{x}_i, \boldsymbol{x}_j)$ denote the score of item j for user i. Here we illustrate the main ideas using a bilinear regression model:

$$s_{ij} = s(\boldsymbol{x}_i, \boldsymbol{x}_j) = \boldsymbol{x}_i'\boldsymbol{A}\boldsymbol{x}_j, \tag{2.4}$$

where $\boldsymbol{A}$ is a matrix of regression coefficients. It is straightforward to put this bilinear form into the regular linear form. Let $\boldsymbol{x}_{ij}$ be the vector constructed by concatenating the columns of matrix $\boldsymbol{x}_i\boldsymbol{x}_j'$ and $\boldsymbol{\beta}$ be the vector constructed by concatenating the columns of matrix $\boldsymbol{A}$. Then, we have $s_{ij} = \boldsymbol{x}_{ij}'\boldsymbol{\beta}$ in the regular linear form. See Figure 2.3 for an example.

Estimation methods of $\boldsymbol{A}$ depend on the type of observed ratings. In the following, we discuss four types of ratings and introduce a commonly used model for each type.

Binary Ratings (Logistic Model). We assume that the rating $y_{ij} \in \{+1, -1\}$ that user i gives item j (e.g., whether user i clicks item j) is generated based on a logistic response model:

$$y_{ij} \sim \text{Bernoulli}((1 + \exp\{-s_{ij}\})^{-1}). \tag{2.5}$$

Let Ω denote the set of observed (user i, item j) pairs and $\boldsymbol{Y} = \{y_{ij} : (i, j) \in \Omega\}$ denote the observed ratings. Then, the log-likelihood function is given by

$$\log \Pr(\boldsymbol{Y} \mid \boldsymbol{A}) = -\sum_{(i,j)\in\Omega} \log(1 + \exp\{-y_{ij}\, \boldsymbol{x}_i' \boldsymbol{A} \boldsymbol{x}_j\}). \tag{2.6}$$

See Section 4.4 of Hastie et al. (2009) for details on logistic regression.

Numeric Ratings (Gaussian Model). We assume that the numeric rating y_{ij} that user i gives item j (e.g., a numeric score or number of stars that user i gives item j) is generated based on a Gaussian response model:

$$y_{ij} \sim \text{Normal}(s_{ij},\ \sigma^2). \tag{2.7}$$

The log-likelihood function is given by

$$\log \Pr(\boldsymbol{Y} \mid \boldsymbol{A}) = -\frac{1}{2\sigma^2} \sum_{(i,j)\in\Omega} (y_{ij} - \boldsymbol{x}_i' \boldsymbol{A} \boldsymbol{x}_j)^2. \tag{2.8}$$

See Chapter 3 of Hastie et al. (2009) for details on Gaussian linear regression.

Ordinal Ratings (Cumulative Logit Model). For many applications, ratings are ordinal in nature expressed on some k-point scale. Although the Gaussian model in Equation (2.7) is commonly used for ordinal ratings (e.g., number of stars), this may not be the best theoretical solution. For instance, the difference between a 5-star and 4-star rating may not be the same as the difference between 3-star and 4-star ratings. In this case, ordinal regression (McCullagh, 1980) may be more appropriate. In this model, we assume the rating $y_{ij} \in \{1, \ldots, R\}$ that user i gives item j is generated according to a multinomial distribution:

$$y_{ij} \sim \text{Multinomial}(\pi_{ij,1}, \ldots, \pi_{ij,R}), \tag{2.9}$$

where $\pi_{ij,r}$ is the probability that user i would give item j rating r. Let Y_{ij} denote the random variable corresponding to observed rating y_{ij}. Then, we assume the log odds of $\Pr(Y_{ij} > r)$ is $s_{ij} - \theta_r$; that is,

$$\operatorname{logit}(\Pr(Y_{ij} > r)) = \log \frac{\Pr(Y_{ij} > r)}{1 - \Pr(Y_{ij} > r)} = s_{ij} - \theta_r \tag{2.10}$$

for $r = 1, \ldots, R-1$. By definition, $\Pr(Y_{ij} > R) = 0$, and we need $\theta_1 \leq \cdots \leq \theta_{R-1}$. Here we can think of θ_r as representing the cut point between level r and $r+1$. Consider two items j and ℓ such that $s_{ij} > s_{i\ell}$. Then, we have

$$\Pr(Y_{ij} > r) > \Pr(Y_{i\ell} > r)$$

for all levels $r = 1, \ldots, R-1$, meaning that user i likes item j more than item ℓ. It can be easily seen that

$$\begin{aligned} \Pr(Y_{ij} > r) &= \sum_{q=r+1}^{R} \pi_{ij,q} = (1 + \exp\{-(s_{ij} - \theta_r)\})^{-1} \\ &= (1 + \exp\{-(\boldsymbol{x}_i' \boldsymbol{A} \boldsymbol{x}_j - \theta_r)\})^{-1}. \end{aligned} \tag{2.11}$$

Let $f_{ij}(r, \boldsymbol{\theta}, \boldsymbol{A}) = \Pr(Y_{ij} > r)$, where $\boldsymbol{\theta}$ denotes the vector of θ_rs. Note that $f_{ij}(0, \boldsymbol{\theta}, \boldsymbol{A}) = 1$ and $f_{ij}(R, \boldsymbol{\theta}, \boldsymbol{A}) = 0$. The log-likelihood function is given by

$$\log \Pr(\boldsymbol{Y} \mid \boldsymbol{A}, \boldsymbol{\theta}) = \sum_{(i,j)\in\Omega} \log(f_{ij}(y_{ij} - 1, \boldsymbol{\theta}, \boldsymbol{A}) - f_{ij}(y_{ij}, \boldsymbol{\theta}, \boldsymbol{A})). \tag{2.12}$$

Pairwise Preference Scores. In some application settings, we may observe that a user prefers one item over another item. Or, we can choose to turn user response into such pairwise preferences (e.g., a clicked item is better than an unclicked item for the same user) (Fürnkranz and Hüllermeier, 2003). To model such preference data, we begin by making a slight change in our notation. Let $y_{ij\ell} \in \{+1, -1\}$ denote whether user i prefers item j over item ℓ. Let Ω denote the set of observed (i, j, ℓ) triples. We assume that the propensity (in fact, log odds) that user i likes item j more than item ℓ is proportional to $s_{ij} - s_{i\ell}$; that is,

$$y_{ij\ell} \sim \operatorname{Bernoulli}((1 + \exp\{-(s_{ij} - s_{i\ell})\})^{-1}). \tag{2.13}$$

The log-likelihood function is given by

$$\log \Pr(\boldsymbol{Y} \mid \boldsymbol{A}) = - \sum_{(i,j,\ell)\in\Omega} \log(1 + \exp\{-y_{ij\ell}\, \boldsymbol{x}_i' \boldsymbol{A}(\boldsymbol{x}_j - \boldsymbol{x}_\ell)\}). \tag{2.14}$$

Regularized Maximum Likelihood Estimation. For the scoring methods described so far, we have to estimate the unknown parameters $\boldsymbol{A}$ to obtain our scoring function. When $\boldsymbol{x}_i$ and $\boldsymbol{x}_j$ are high dimensional, the number of unknown regression coefficients in $\boldsymbol{A}$ is large. Adding a regularization term $r(\boldsymbol{A})$ to the log-likelihood function makes the regression more stable and reduces the impact of overfitting. Common choices of the regularization terms include the L_2 norm and the L_1 norm. Let a_{ij} denote the value of entry (i, j) in matrix $\boldsymbol{A}$. The L_2 norm is $r(\boldsymbol{A}) = \sum_{ij} a_{ij}^2$ and the L_1 norm is $r(\boldsymbol{A}) = \sum_{ij} |a_{ij}|$. Now, given a set of observed ratings $\boldsymbol{Y}$, we can determine the unknown parameter $\boldsymbol{A}$ of the scoring function by

$$\arg\max_{\boldsymbol{A},\boldsymbol{\theta}}(\log \Pr(\boldsymbol{Y} \mid \boldsymbol{A}, \boldsymbol{\theta}) - \lambda\, r(\boldsymbol{A})), \tag{2.15}$$

where λ is a tuning parameter specifying the strength of regularization and $\boldsymbol{\theta}$ is the cut-point vector in the cumulative logit model (in Equation (2.10)) and is empty for the logistic, Gaussian, and pairwise preference models. The optimization problem in Equation (2.15) can be solved by standard optimization methods such as L-BFGS (Zhu et al., 1997), coordinate descent, and stochastic gradient descent (Bottou, 2010).

2.3.3 Contextual Information

So far, we have only considered how to predict the rating y_{ij} that user i would give to item j. However, such a rating is usually context dependent. For example, consider that y_{ij} (whether user i would click item j) usually depends on the position of the item on the web page; a prominent position has a higher click probability than a not-so-prominent position for the same item. The click probability could also depend on the time of day, weekday versus weekend, the device (desktop versus mobile), other items displayed on the same web page, and so on. If we represent such contextual information as a feature vector z_{ij}, which characterizes the context in which user i interacts with item j, then the supervised methods in Section 2.3.2 can easily incorporate contextual information by redefining the predicted rating or score as

$$s_{ij} = s(\boldsymbol{x}_i, \boldsymbol{x}_j, z_{ij}) = \boldsymbol{x}_i' \boldsymbol{A} \boldsymbol{x}_j + \boldsymbol{b}' z_{ij}. \tag{2.16}$$

This is still a linear model with features $\boldsymbol{x}_i$, $\boldsymbol{x}_j$, and z_{ij}, regression coefficient matrix $\boldsymbol{A}$, and regression coefficient vector b. All of the discussions in Section 2.3.2 apply to this model in a straightforward way.

Notation. For notational simplicity, we would like to use $\boldsymbol{x}$ to denote features. Thus, in later chapters, we use $\boldsymbol{x}_{ij}$ to denote context features, instead of z_{ij}. Also, the current notation assumes that each user i only interacts with any item j at most once. When user i interacts with item j multiple times (each of which is in a different context), we need to extend our notation to $\boldsymbol{x}_{ij}^{(k)}$, representing the feature vector of the kth interaction between user i and item j.

For succinctness, we will mostly use $\boldsymbol{x}_{ij}$ in later chapters. Extension from $\boldsymbol{x}_{ij}$ to $\boldsymbol{x}_{ij}^{(k)}$ is straightforward.

2.4 Collaborative Filtering

The ratings that a user gives to different items is usually indicative of his or her preferences. Two users who rate items similarly are likely to have similar taste in items. Based on this intuition, for a given user i, we can obtain a set of other users that are similar to i in terms of their rating behavior. The score of an item j for user i can then be obtained by using the average rating given to j by users who are similar to i. Such an approach usually predicts how much a user prefers an item based only on users' past ratings on items and does not rely on any user or item features. This approach treats item ratings by users as a collaborative process in which users help one another to identify interesting items (although they are not aware of the collaboration), thus called *collaborative filtering*.[1]

2.4.1 Methods Based on User-User Similarity

We start with collaborative filtering methods that predict the rating (or score) s_{ij} that user i would give to an unrated item j based on the ratings that other users similar to user i have given to item j. One common choice of the scoring function is the average of the ratings of the similar users; this can also be a weighted average that assigns larger weights to users who are more similar to user i.

Let $\mathcal{I}_j(i)$ denote the set of users who rated item j and are similar to user i. We discuss how to construct this set later in this section. Let $w(i, \ell)$ denote the weight we assign to the rating of user ℓ when it is used to predict how user i would rate item j. Let $\bar{y}_{i\cdot}$ denote the average rating of user i. Given these notations, the predicted rating s_{ij} that user i would give item j is

$$s_{ij} = \bar{y}_{i\cdot} + \frac{\sum_{\ell \in \mathcal{I}_j(i)} w(i, \ell)\,(y_{\ell j} - \bar{y}_{\ell\cdot})}{\sum_{\ell \in \mathcal{I}_j(i)} |w(i, \ell)|}, \tag{2.17}$$

which averages over the "centered" ratings to mitigate users' individual rating bias (because the same rating value can represent different degrees of satisfaction for different users). In addition to centering, we can further standardize a user's ratings by dividing the centered rating by the standard deviation of the user's ratings. See Herlocker et al. (1999) for an example.

Similarity Functions. One popular choice for the similarity function between users is the Pearson correlation as used in Resnick et al. (1994), where the similarity between user i and ℓ is defined as

$$sim(i, \ell) = \frac{\sum_{j \in \mathcal{J}_{i\ell}} (y_{ij} - \bar{y}_{i\cdot})(y_{\ell j} - \bar{y}_{\ell\cdot})}{\sqrt{\sum_{j \in \mathcal{J}_{i\ell}} (y_{ij} - \bar{y}_{i\cdot})^2} \sqrt{\sum_{j \in \mathcal{J}_{i\ell}} (y_{\ell j} - \bar{y}_{\ell\cdot})^2}}. \tag{2.18}$$

$\mathcal{J}_{i\ell}$ denotes the set of items rated by both users i and ℓ. Notice that correlations can be negative. We may choose to set negative correlations to zero. See Desrosiers and Karypis (2011) for more similarity functions.

Neighborhood Selection. The set $\mathcal{I}_j(i)$ of similar users can be constructed in several different ways. We can choose simply to include all users who rated item j and use the similarity between users i and ℓ to define the weight $w(i, \ell)$ when predicting ratings for user i. For items rated by many users, such averaging over many users may incur a high computational cost. Other choices include selecting the top n users who are most similar to user i or selecting users whose similarity to user i passes some threshold. Empirical evaluation is typically needed to make a good choice for a given application.

Weighting. The most common weighting method is to set $w(i, \ell) = sim(i, \ell)$. When $sim(i, \ell)$ is computed based on a small set $\mathcal{J}_{i\ell}$ of items rated both by user i and ℓ, this can become unreliable due to small sample size. One way of addressing this small sample size problem is to give unreliable similarity values lower weights. For example, Herlocker et al. (1999) used the formula

$$w(i, \ell) = \min\{|\mathcal{J}_{i\ell}|/\alpha \ , 1\} \cdot sim(i, \ell) \tag{2.19}$$

and found that $\alpha = 50$ gave the best results on their data. When $\mathcal{I}_j(i)$ selects only the top n most similar users, we can also set $w(i, \ell) = 1$ to perform an unweighted average of the ratings from the most similar users. Again, empirical evaluation is often needed to make a good choice.

2.4.2 Methods Based on Item-Item Similarity

In Section 2.4.1, we discussed how to measure similarity between users. We can also leverage similarity between items to predict scores. In this case, we predict the ratings that user i would give to item j by averaging the user's own ratings on items that are similar to item j.

Let $\mathcal{J}_i(j)$ denote the set of items that were rated by user i and are similar to item j. Let $w(j, \ell)$ denote the weight we assign to the rating that user i gives item ℓ when we use it to predict user i's rating on item j. Let $\bar{y}_{\cdot j}$ denote the average rating on item j. The predicted rating s_{ij} that user i would give item j is

$$s_{ij} = \bar{y}_{\cdot j} + \frac{\sum_{\ell \in \mathcal{J}_i(j)} w(j, \ell)(y_{i\ell} - \bar{y}_{\cdot \ell})}{\sum_{\ell \in \mathcal{J}_i(j)} |w(j, \ell)|}. \tag{2.20}$$

$\mathcal{J}_i(j)$ and $w(j, \ell)$ can be determined in a way similar to the method described in Section 2.4.1.

2.4.3 Matrix Factorization

Classical user-user and item-item similarity-based methods predict the rating that a user would give to an item based on a predetermined similarity function. The choice of similarity function and weighting method practiced for these methods, although intuitive, is may not capture all important structure in the data. A more flexible approach is to directly learn the scoring function from the rating data. Matrix factorization has emerged as the method of choice to predict unobserved ratings from a partially observed rating matrix without any features by using a model that relies on a low-rank matrix decomposition. We call a matrix $\boldsymbol{Y}$ a rating matrix if its (i, j) entry Y_{ij} is the rating that user i gives to item j. In practice, several entries of a rating matrix are unobserved because, typically, a large fraction of users rate a small fraction of items.

Let s_{ij} denote the affinity (i.e., score) between user i and item j, which can be thought of as the predicted rating that user i would give to item j (the actual interpretation of rating of course depends on the response model). The matrix factorization method assumes that

$$s_{ij} = \boldsymbol{u}_i' \boldsymbol{v}_j, \tag{2.21}$$

where $\boldsymbol{u}_i$ and $\boldsymbol{v}_j$ are two L-dimensional vectors associated with user i and item j, respectively. They have to be estimated from a given rating matrix $\boldsymbol{Y}$. We refer to the vectors $\boldsymbol{u}_i$ and $\boldsymbol{v}_j$ as *latent factors* for user i and item j, respectively, and call L the number of latent dimensions, which is usually much smaller than the number M of users and the number N of items. For the sake of succinctness, we shall also refer to $\boldsymbol{u}_i$ and $\boldsymbol{v}_j$ as factors. Intuitively, this model maps each user i and each item j as points, $\boldsymbol{u}_i$ and $\boldsymbol{v}_j$, in the same L-dimensional latent vector space and then uses the inner product in this vector space to measure the affinity between user i and item j. The space is "latent" because the positions of users and items in this space is not observed. Throughout this book, *features* refer to information about users or items that is known or given before any supervised learning based on ratings is applied, whereas *factors* can be thought of as unobserved user or item features that are actually model parameters to be learned from the ratings data using supervised learning.

In the rest of this section, we use the Gaussian response model to illustrate estimation of factors in the matrix factorization approach. We assume that the rating y_{ij} that user i would give to item j is generated according to a Gaussian distribution with mean s_{ij} and some unknown fixed variance σ^2 (as in Equation (2.7)). Other response models, such as those defined by Equations (2.5), (2.10), and (2.13), can be applied in a similar manner. The maximum likelihood estimate (MLE) of $\boldsymbol{u}_i$ and $\boldsymbol{v}_j$ for the Gaussian model can be found by solving the following problem:

$$\arg\min_{\boldsymbol{u}_i, \boldsymbol{v}_j, \forall i \forall j} \sum_{(i,j)\in\Omega} (y_{ij} - \boldsymbol{u}_i'\boldsymbol{v}_j)^2. \tag{2.22}$$

Let $\boldsymbol{U}$ and $\boldsymbol{V}$ denote the matrices such that the ith row of $\boldsymbol{U}$ is row vector $\boldsymbol{u}_i'$ and the jth row of $\boldsymbol{V}$ is row vector $\boldsymbol{v}_j'$. Let $(\boldsymbol{Y})_{ij}$ denote the value of the (i, j) entry of matrix $\boldsymbol{Y}$. Then, the optimization problem in Equation (2.22) can also be written as

$$\arg\min_{\boldsymbol{U}, \boldsymbol{V}} \sum_{(i,j)\in\Omega} ((\boldsymbol{Y})_{ij} - (\boldsymbol{U}\boldsymbol{V}')_{ij})^2. \tag{2.23}$$

Recall that $\boldsymbol{Y}$ is the partially observed rating matrix. Maximum likelihood estimation corresponds to approximating or factorizing matrix $\boldsymbol{Y}_{M\times N}$ using the product of two low-rank matrices $\boldsymbol{U}_{M\times L}$ and $\boldsymbol{V}'_{L\times N}$, where the subscripts show the sizes of the matrices and L is much smaller than M and N. While the connotation matrix factorization is inspired by the preceding decomposition, it is important to note that such a decomposition for a partially observed matrix is not the same as for a complete matrix.

Regularization. Although the total number of factors $(L(M + N))$ that needs to be estimated is much smaller than the size of the entire rating matrix (MN), it may not be small compared to the number of observed ratings. Such over parameterization may lead to unreliable maximum likelihood estimates and poor out-of-sample predictive accuracy. For users (or items) who rated (or were rated by) less than L items (or users), the corresponding user (or item) factors cannot be determined even if all of the item (or user) factors are known. To alleviate this situation, one commonly used method is to regularize by adding an L_2 penalty to the objective function; that is,

$$\arg\min_{\boldsymbol{u}_i, \boldsymbol{v}_j, \forall i \forall j} \sum_{(i,j)\in\Omega} (y_{ij} - \boldsymbol{u}_i'\boldsymbol{v}_j)^2 + \lambda_1 \sum_i ||\boldsymbol{u}_i||^2 + \lambda_2 \sum_j ||\boldsymbol{v}_j||^2, \tag{2.24}$$

where λ_1 and λ_2 are tuning parameters. The intuition behind this regularization is that the factor estimates of users or items with little observed rating data should be constrained in magnitude by "shrinking" them toward zero, the mean of the residual distribution.

Optimization Methods. The optimization problem in Equation (2.24) can be solved in multiple ways. First, notice that the optimal solution is not unique. For example, changing the signs of all factors does not change the value of the objective function. In practice, the lack of uniquely identified factors is not a concern as long as we do not try to interpret the meaning of factors. In the following, we briefly describe two popular optimization methods:

1. *Alternating least squares*: Fixing the $\boldsymbol{u}_i$s as constants for all users i, the objective function is convex with respect to $\boldsymbol{v}_j$ for all j and, in fact, corresponds to a set of least squares linear regression problems with L_2 regularization for each item. The same holds for the $\boldsymbol{u}_i$s when we fix the $\boldsymbol{v}_j$s as constant for all items j. Let $\mathcal{I}_j$ denote the set of users who rated item j and $\mathcal{J}_i$ denote the set of items that user i rated. Let I be the identity matrix. The algorithm works as follows: we first randomly initialize $\boldsymbol{u}_i$ and $\boldsymbol{v}_j$ for all i and j. Then, we repeat the following two steps until convergence:
   - Fix the $\boldsymbol{u}_i$s as constants for all i and solve the least squares problem to obtain the new estimate of $\boldsymbol{v}_j$ for each j:
$$\boldsymbol{v}_j^{\text{new}} = \left(\lambda_2 I + \textstyle\sum_{i \in \mathcal{I}_j} \boldsymbol{u}_i \boldsymbol{u}_i'\right)^{-1} \left(\textstyle\sum_{i \in \mathcal{I}_j} \boldsymbol{u}_i \, y_{ij}\right). \tag{2.25}$$
   - Fix the $\boldsymbol{v}_j$s as constants for all j and solve the least squares problem to obtain the new estimate of $\boldsymbol{u}_i$ for each i:
$$\boldsymbol{u}_i^{\text{new}} = \left(\lambda_1 I + \textstyle\sum_{j \in \mathcal{J}_i} \boldsymbol{v}_j \boldsymbol{v}_j'\right)^{-1} \left(\textstyle\sum_{j \in \mathcal{J}_i} \boldsymbol{v}_j \, y_{ij}\right). \tag{2.26}$$
2. *Stochastic gradient descent*: One simple gradient descent method that has gained popularity in recent years is stochastic gradient descent (SGD). Let
$$f_{ij}(\boldsymbol{u}_i, \boldsymbol{v}_j) = (y_{ij} - \boldsymbol{u}_i'\boldsymbol{v}_j)^2 + \frac{\lambda_1}{|\mathcal{J}_i|}||\boldsymbol{u}_i||^2 + \frac{\lambda_2}{|\mathcal{I}_j|}||\boldsymbol{v}_j||^2. \tag{2.27}$$
   Equation (2.24) can also be written as
$$\arg\min_{\boldsymbol{u}_i, \boldsymbol{v}_j, \forall i \forall j} \sum_{(i,j)\in\Omega} f_{ij}(\boldsymbol{u}_i, \boldsymbol{v}_j). \tag{2.28}$$
   The SGD method performs gradient descent by taking a small gradient step for each $(i, j) \in \Omega$, where the gradient is taken over $f_{ij}(\boldsymbol{u}_i, \boldsymbol{v}_j)$. The algorithm works as follows: first, randomly initialize $\boldsymbol{u}_i$ and $\boldsymbol{v}_j$ for all i and

j. Then, for each observed rating $(i, j) \in \Omega$ in a random order, update $\boldsymbol{u}_i$ and $\boldsymbol{v}_j$ as follows:

$$\begin{aligned}\boldsymbol{u}_i^{\text{new}} &= \boldsymbol{u}_i - \alpha \nabla_{\boldsymbol{u}_i} f_{ij}(\boldsymbol{u}_i, \boldsymbol{v}_j) \\ \boldsymbol{v}_j^{\text{new}} &= \boldsymbol{v}_j - \alpha \nabla_{\boldsymbol{v}_j} f_{ij}(\boldsymbol{u}_i, \boldsymbol{v}_j),\end{aligned} \tag{2.29}$$

where α is a small step size that needs to be tuned and $\nabla_{\boldsymbol{u}_i} f_{ij}(\boldsymbol{u}_i, \boldsymbol{v}_j)$ and $\nabla_{\boldsymbol{v}_j} f_{ij}(\boldsymbol{u}_i, \boldsymbol{v}_j)$ are the gradient of $f_{ij}(\boldsymbol{u}_i, \boldsymbol{v}_j)$ with respect to $\boldsymbol{u}_i$ and $\boldsymbol{v}_j$, respectively:

$$\begin{aligned}\nabla_{\boldsymbol{u}_i} f_{ij}(\boldsymbol{u}_i, \boldsymbol{v}_j) &= 2(y_{ij} - \boldsymbol{u}_i'\boldsymbol{v}_j)\boldsymbol{v}_j + 2\frac{\lambda_1}{|\mathcal{J}_i|}\boldsymbol{u}_i \\ \nabla_{\boldsymbol{v}_j} f_{ij}(\boldsymbol{u}_i, \boldsymbol{v}_j) &= 2(y_{ij} - \boldsymbol{u}_i'\boldsymbol{v}_j)\boldsymbol{u}_i + 2\frac{\lambda_2}{|\mathcal{I}_j|}\boldsymbol{v}_j.\end{aligned} \tag{2.30}$$

We repeat the preceding gradient steps by going through each observed rating multiple times until convergence. Instead of choosing a fixed step size, it is also typical to choose the step size in an adaptive fashion (Duchi et al., 2011). One would typically start with a relatively large step size that is gradually reduced over iterations.

2.5 Hybrid Methods

Collaborative filtering and feature-based methods have their strengths and weaknesses. Feature-based methods typically require effort to define, analyze, and generate predictive features, whereas collaborative filtering does not use any features and can outperform feature-based methods for users and items that have more than certain number of ratings in the training data. For example, Pilászy and Tikk (2009) showed that just ten ratings for a new movie can provide better predictive accuracy than an extensive set of movie features for a movie recommendation problem. Such scenarios are usually referred to as *warm-start* situations because users and items in these scenarios have enough past rating data to warm up the recommender system. However, for users and items that have little or no past rating data (i.e., in *cold-start* situations), collaborative filtering methods do not perform well. For instance, for a new user who has not yet rated any item, collaborative filtering methods would have a hard time assigning scores to items. In such *cold-start* situations, feature-based methods generally outperform collaborative filtering because new users and new items make no difference to feature-based methods as long as feature values are available. For example, most websites record basic profile information for new users as part of the registration process, and content features can be extracted when new items are put into the system.

Collaborative filtering works well for warm-start scenarios but fails in cold-start scenarios, whereas feature-based methods work better in cold-start scenarios in the presence of predictive features but are usually not as accurate as collaborative filtering in warm-start scenarios. To combine the best of both methods, hybrid methods have been developed. We give a few examples of such hybrid methods:

- *Ensemble*: One straightforward hybrid approach is to implement a few different methods separately (e.g, collaborative filtering and feature based) and combine the outputs or predicted ratings from these methods through a linear combination or a voting scheme. See Claypool et al. (1999) for an illustration.
- *Treating collaborative filtering as features*: Another simple way of integrating collaborative filtering into feature-based methods is by treating the score of a (user, item) pair obtained from a collaborative filtering method as a new feature associated with each (user, item) pair.
- *Using feature-based similarity in similarity-based collaborative filtering*: For collaborative filtering methods based on user-user or item-item similarity, we can define a new similarity function that combines two components, one based on similarity in ratings and the other based on similarity in their feature vectors, and combine them using a linear combination (Balabanović and Shoham, 1997).
- *Collaborative filtering augmented by artificial feature-based ratings*: To address the cold-start problem, ratings of new users or new items can be *imputed* artificially. For a new item, we can add a few artificial users who rate every item (including the new one) using the predicted ratings from a feature-based model. Then, classical collaborative filtering methods can be applied to this augmented rating data to recommend new items. Such artificial users are called "filterbots" by Konstan et al. (1998). Similarly, we can also add a few artificial items that are rated by every user (including new users) using the predicted ratings from a feature-based model.

Early hybrid methods reported in the literature were mostly based on heuristics and lacked a flexible underlying framework. We introduce hybrid methods in Chapter 8 that can seamlessly combine various aspects through rich probabilistic models.

2.6 Summary

We discussed various methods to construct user and item features along with strategies to estimate user-item affinity scores using classical feature-based, collaborative, and hybrid methods. However, the focus of most of this line of research has been to improve the out-of-sample predictive accuracy on retrospective data. Although this is an important component in building recommender systems, it is only one aspect. Constructing good serving schemes to maximize overall objectives, such as maximizing clicks or revenue or sales, requires attention to aspects beyond improving predictive accuracy. One has to pay attention to how to collect training data on a continuous basis to optimize performance. This involves blending some of the techniques described in this chapter with explore-exploit methodologies. It is also important to develop a framework that works well for various kinds of applications with different degrees of available feature information, sizes of item pools, item lifetime distributions, data sparsity, and degree of cold start in the system. We focus on these in subsequent chapters.

Exercises

1. Familiarize yourself with probabilistic latent semantic indexing (PLSI). What are the differences between LDA and PLSI? Which of these has more unknown parameters?
2. In several applications, user demographic information is missing for a subset of users. How would you incorporate demographic information to estimate scores in this scenario?
3. Familiarize yourself with the Okapi BM25 similarity function.
4. Derive alternating least squares and stochastic gradient descent for matrix factorization with binary response.

3
Explore-Exploit for Recommender Problems

In Chapter 2, we reviewed classical methods to score an item for a user in a given context. In this chapter, we describe scoring methods based on modern techniques, particularly those that are based on explore-exploit methods.

Scoring involves estimating the "value" of an item according to some criteria. Because explicit user intent in most modern-day recommender problems is at best partially observed and often weak, scoring items based on the predicted value of some rating or response is a popular mechanism. For ease of exposition, our response is binary, and the "positive" label corresponds to a certain positive user interaction with the item, such as click, like, or share, whereas "negative" indicates lack of any such positive interaction. For instance, in a news recommender problem, user click on a recommended item is the primary response variable. The score of an item is given by the *response rate*, which is the expected value of user response. For instance, response rate for a binary variable by this definition will translate to the probability of a positive response. For ease of exposition, throughout this chapter, we use click to refer to a positive response and CTR to refer to the corresponding response rate.

Often the goal in recommender problems is to maximize the total number of positive response, such as clicks on recommended items. For instance, in a news recommender problem, maximizing the total clicks on the recommended news articles is an important objective. With known item response rates, this is easy to accomplish by always recommending the item with the highest response rate. However, because response rates are not known, a key task is to accurately estimate them for items in the item pool. In Sections 2.3 and 2.4, we considered various supervised learning methods to estimate response rates through feature-based models and collaborative filtering. In this chapter, we show that scoring items in a recommender problem is not purely a supervised learning problem but more importantly an *explore-exploit* problem. We need to achieve a good balance between *exploring* or experimenting with items that are new or have a small sample size by displaying them in certain numbers of user visits, versus *exploiting* items that are known to have high response rates with high statistical certainty. Exploration has an opportunity cost of not showing items that are empirically better based on the data collected so far; balancing these two aspects constitutes the explore-exploit trade-off.

Because recommender problems are explore-exploit problems, one might argue that we can ignore all supervised learning techniques and instead focus only on explore-exploit methods. Such an assertion is not true because combining both explore-exploit and supervised learning provides a more efficient solution in practice. Explore-exploit techniques benefit from supervised learning because a good supervised model reduces the intrinsic dimensionality of the problem and makes exploration more economical. The impact of such a reduction can be significant in high-dimensional settings.

In the rest of this chapter, we motivate the explore-exploit problem (Section 3.1), review classical explore-exploit methods (Section 3.2), discuss the challenges of explore-exploit in recommender systems (Section 3.3), and introduce the main ideas used to address these challenges (Section 3.4). Detailed solutions are presented in Part II of the book. In Chapter 6, we develop explore-exploit methods for most-popular recommendation in which both the set of candidate items and the popularity of each item change over time. In Chapters 7 and 8, we develop methods to address the challenges in personalized recommendation where the amount of data available to explore-exploit an individual user's preferences to different items is sparse.

3.1 Introduction to the Explore-Exploit Trade-off

For an intuitive understanding of the explore-exploit problem, it is convenient to consider a recommendation problem with two items. We recommend a single item for each user visit, and the goal is to develop an optimal recommendation algorithm for the next one hundred user visits to maximize the expected total number of clicks. The solution space here consists of 2^{100} (more than 2 trillion!) different possible recommendation sequences since we can make two choices for each of the 100 user visits. This is similar in spirit to the classical multi-armed bandit problem that dynamically allocates a single resource to alternate projects (Robbins, 1952). Remarkably, an optimal solution exists and involves adaptively changing future decisions based on past feedback (Gittins, 1979).

The name multiarmed bandit has its root in a casino setting where a gambler is playing a slot machine with multiple arms and needs to decide which arm to pull next. The probability of obtaining a reward from pulling each arm is different and unknown to the gambler. The multiarmed bandit problem illustrates the fundamental explore-exploit trade-off – the gambler may choose to *explore* a potentially good arm to obtain a more accurate estimate of its reward probability or *exploit* an arm that appears to be performing well with high certainty. Mapping to our recommender setting, the system is the gambler, pulling an arm corresponds to displaying an item to a user, and the reward of an arm corresponds to user interaction with the item (click or no click). The CTR of an item is the reward probability.

The reason we have the explore-exploit trade-off is due to the uncertainty in CTR estimates. Suppose after twenty user visits, the estimated CTRs for item 1 and item 2 are 1/3 (five clicks out of fifteen visits) and 1/5 (one click out of five visits), respectively. It is tempting to abandon item 2 and persist with item 1 for the remaining eighty visits, but that may not be optimal because the true CTR for item 2 could be higher than the noisy estimate obtained using a small sample. The explore-exploit problem in the case of two items was published by Thompson (1933) long before the optimal solution to the multiarmed bandit was formulated. The algorithm proposed was simple and involves serving an item with the probability that the item is the best among all candidate items. We take a closer look at this algorithm in Section 3.2.3.

Although the explore-exploit trade-off in recommender problems has a strong resemblance to the multiarmed bandit problem, several assumptions that are required to obtain the optimal solution are violated in practice. In many web applications, the item pool changes over time; the response rates can be nonstationary and the response feedback is usually delayed (due to delay by users in responding to an item after display and delay in data transmission from web servers to the backend machines). However, the most difficult issue is perhaps the curse of dimensionality introduced by the need to provide personalized recommendation with a large or dynamic item pool and hence the dearth of experimental budget to estimate item response rates at fine resolutions. Therefore, web recommendation problems cannot be solved satisfactorily through classical multiarmed bandit schemes.

3.2 Multiarmed Bandit Problem

Before we address the explore-exploit problem in recommender systems, we review the multiarmed bandit (MAB) problem in this section, a popular variant of the explore-exploit problem. Consider again the gambler's choice of the arm to pull next. Let p_i denote the *unknown* reward probability of arm i; that is, by pulling arm i, the gambler obtains a unit reward with probability p_i and no reward with probability $1 - p_i$. The set of arms and their reward probabilities is assumed not to change over time. The gambler's goal is to pull the arms sequentially to maximize the total expected reward.

Let $\boldsymbol{\theta}_t$ denote all the information that the gambler obtained by pulling arms before time t. Vector $\boldsymbol{\theta}_t$ is called the *state parameter* or simply the *state* at time t, which includes, for each arm i, the number of pulls γ_i and total reward α_i obtained so far. A *bandit scheme* is a decision function π that takes $\boldsymbol{\theta}_t$ as input and returns the next arm to pull as its output. It is also referred to as an *explore-exploit scheme* or a *policy*. A bandit scheme can be either a deterministic function or a stochastic function of the state parameter.

In the rest of this section, we give an overview of different kinds of explore-exploit schemes in the *classical bandit* setting as defined earlier. They are classified into three categories: Bayesian methods (Section 3.2.1), minimax methods (Section 3.2.2), and heuristic methods (Section 3.2.3).

3.2.1 Bayesian Approach

From the Bayesian perspective, the MAB problem can be formulated as a Markov decision process (MDP) and the optimal solution can be obtained through dynamic programming. Although the optimal solution exists, solving the problem is computationally expensive.

MDP is a flexible framework to study sequential decision problems. An MDP defines a sequential problem through the space of states, a reward function, and transition probabilities. The Bayesian approach seeks to obtain the Bayes optimal solution to the MDP that corresponds to the MAB problem. We now define a Beta-binomial MDP for the classical bandit problem.

State. To maximize the reward, the gambler needs to estimate the reward probability of each arm. The state $\boldsymbol{\theta}_t$ at time t represents the gambler's knowledge based on experimental data collected prior to t. Specifically, this knowledge is represented by a two-parameter Beta distribution for each arm; that is, $\boldsymbol{\theta}_t = (\boldsymbol{\theta}_{1t}, \ldots, \boldsymbol{\theta}_{Kt})$, where $\boldsymbol{\theta}_{it}$ is the state of arm i at time t, and $\boldsymbol{\theta}_{it} = (\alpha_{it}, \gamma_{it})$ consists of the two parameters of the Beta distribution for arm i; γ_{it} denotes the number of times the gambler pulled arm i before time t, and α_{it} denotes the total reward obtained from pulling arm i before time t. The Beta(α_{it}, γ_{it}) distribution for arm i has

$$\begin{aligned} \text{mean} &= \alpha_{it}/\gamma_{it} \\ \text{variance} &= (\alpha_{it}/\gamma_{it})(1 - \alpha_{it}/\gamma_{it})/(\gamma_{it} + 1). \end{aligned} \tag{3.1}$$

The mean is the gambler's empirical estimate of the reward probability based on the data collected so far. The variance represents the uncertainty in his empirical estimate.

State Transition. After the gambler pulls an arm i and observes the outcome, he gains additional information about arm i that can be used to update his knowledge by transitioning from the current state $\boldsymbol{\theta}_t$ to a new state $\boldsymbol{\theta}_{t+1}$. There are two possible outcomes, obtaining a reward or not, and thus two possible new states.

- With probability α_{it}/γ_{it} (which is our current estimate of the probability of obtaining a reward from pulling arm i), the gambler obtains a reward and updates the state of arm i from $\boldsymbol{\theta}_{it} = (\alpha_{it}, \gamma_{it})$ to $\boldsymbol{\theta}_{i,t+1} = (\alpha_{it} + 1, \gamma_{it} + 1)$.
- With probability $1 - \alpha_{it}/\gamma_{it}$, the gambler does not obtain a reward and updates the state of arm i from $\boldsymbol{\theta}_{it} = (\alpha_{it}, \gamma_{it})$ to $\boldsymbol{\theta}_{i,t+1} = (\alpha_{it}, \gamma_{it} + 1)$.

The states of all the other arms j remain the same; that is, $\boldsymbol{\theta}_{j,t+1} = \boldsymbol{\theta}_{j,t}$, for all $j \neq i$. This is an important characteristic of the classical bandit problem. We use $p(\boldsymbol{\theta}_{t+1} \mid \boldsymbol{\theta}_t, i)$, called the *transition probability*, to denote the probability of transitioning from state $\boldsymbol{\theta}_t$ to state $\boldsymbol{\theta}_{t+1}$ after pulling arm i. Because there are only two possible new states given the current state, the transition probabilities to other states are all zero.

The preceding state transition follows the Beta-binomial conjugacy. Let $c_i \in \{0, 1\}$ denote whether the gambler obtains a reward by pulling arm i. If we assume

$$\begin{aligned} c_i &\sim \text{Binomial}(\text{probability} = p_i, \quad \text{size} = 1) \\ p_i &\sim \text{Beta}(\alpha_{it}, \gamma_{it}), \end{aligned} \tag{3.2}$$

where p_i is the reward probability, then the posterior distribution of p_i after incorporating c_i is

$$(p_i \mid c_i) \sim \text{Beta}(\alpha_{it} + c_i, \gamma_{it} + 1). \tag{3.3}$$

This shows that the state transition rule is consistent with the interpretation that the state of each arm follows a Beta distribution given all the past observations.

Reward. The reward function $R_i(\boldsymbol{\theta}_t, \boldsymbol{\theta}_{t+1})$ specifies the expected immediate reward obtained when arm i is pulled and the state transitions from $\boldsymbol{\theta}_t$ to $\boldsymbol{\theta}_{t+1}$. The classical bandit problem has a simple reward function. The gambler obtains a unit reward if the state of arm i transitions from $(\alpha_{it}, \gamma_{it})$ to $(\alpha_{it} + 1, \gamma_{it} + 1)$; otherwise, there is no reward.

When we consider maximizing future rewards, if the gambler can pull arms an infinite number of times, it is useful to discount rewards in the far future. For such *discounted-reward* settings, it is common to discount future rewards in an exponential manner; that is, the reward obtained t steps in the future is discounted by a factor d^t, where $0 < d < 1$. For *fixed-reward* settings, it is common to maximize the total reward of the next T steps for a given T value.

Optimal Policy. An explore-exploit policy π is a function that takes a state $\boldsymbol{\theta}_t$ as its input and returns an arm $\pi(\boldsymbol{\theta}_t)$ to pull next. Assume that there are K arms; $\boldsymbol{\theta}_t$ is a $2K$-dimensional vector of nonnegative integers, and π needs to map each of such $2K$-dimensional vectors to an arm $\in \{1, \ldots, K\}$. As we shall see later, finding the optimal policy is challenging. Deriving the optimal solution is also out of the scope of this book.

Somewhat surprisingly, the optimal solution to the discounted-reward K-armed bandit problem can be obtained by solving K independent one-armed bandit problems. In each one-armed bandit problem, pulling the only arm incurs some cost, and we need to decide whether to pull or stop. This landmark result was first given by Jones and Gittins (1972) and Gittins (1979) and is generally referred to as Gittins index. One intuitive interpretation is that Gittins index $g(\boldsymbol{\theta}_{it})$ for an arm with state $\boldsymbol{\theta}_{it}$ is the fixed charge per pull for the one-armed bandit problem such that the charge makes the Bayesian optimal scheme generate zero net reward. The charge $g(\boldsymbol{\theta}_{it})$ depends on the two-dimensional state $\boldsymbol{\theta}_{it}$ of the arm and is independent of other arms. Then, at any point, we simply pull the arm having the highest Gittins index; that is,

$$\pi(\boldsymbol{\theta}_t) = \arg\max_i \; g(\boldsymbol{\theta}_{it}). \tag{3.4}$$

We note that computing Gittins index for an arm is still expensive. We refer interested readers to Varaiya et al. (1985), Katehakis and Veinott (1987), and Niño-Mora (2007) for more details. Whittle (1988) extended the classical bandit problem to allow the reward probabilities of the arms to change over time. However, the optimal solution has not been found.

A Look into the Optimization Problem. In the rest of this section, we discuss how to find the optimal solution for the fixed-reward K-armed bandit problem. Our goal is to determine the policy that maximizes the expected total reward in the next T pulls. We call T the budget. The solution is computationally expensive and even infeasible for modest K and T values. Readers not interested in the analysis of this problem can jump to Section 3.2.2.

Let $V(\pi, \boldsymbol{\theta}_0, T)$ denote the expected sum of rewards obtained by using scheme π to pull arms T times, starting from initial state $\boldsymbol{\theta}_0$. We shall call this the value of the scheme π. The value of π can be recursively defined as follows:

$$\begin{aligned} V(\pi, \boldsymbol{\theta}_0, T) &= E_{\boldsymbol{\theta}_1}\left[R_{\pi(\boldsymbol{\theta}_0)}(\boldsymbol{\theta}_0, \boldsymbol{\theta}_1) + V(\pi, \boldsymbol{\theta}_1, T-1)\right] \\ &= \sum_{\boldsymbol{\theta}_1} p(\boldsymbol{\theta}_1 \mid \boldsymbol{\theta}_0, \pi(\boldsymbol{\theta}_0)) \cdot \left[R_{\pi(\boldsymbol{\theta}_0)}(\boldsymbol{\theta}_0, \boldsymbol{\theta}_1) + V(\pi, \boldsymbol{\theta}_1, T-1)\right], \end{aligned} \tag{3.5}$$

where $R_{\pi(\boldsymbol{\theta}_0)}(\boldsymbol{\theta}_0, \boldsymbol{\theta}_1)$ is the immediate reward and $V(\pi, \boldsymbol{\theta}_1, T-1)$ is the future value if we start from the next state $\boldsymbol{\theta}_1$ and use π to pull arms $T-1$ times. Note that $\pi(\boldsymbol{\theta}_0)$ is the arm i picked by π at state $\boldsymbol{\theta}_0$ and $\boldsymbol{\theta}_1$ is the random variable that we take expectation over, because we do not know exactly what the next state is.

The Bayesian optimal scheme π^* is the scheme that maximizes the value; that is,

$$\pi^* = \arg\max_{\pi} V(\pi, \boldsymbol{\theta}_0, T). \tag{3.6}$$

The optimal arm to pull also depends on the total budget T of future pulls. In this setting, a bandit scheme π is a function that takes a state $\boldsymbol{\theta}_t$ and the budget T and returns an arm $\pi(\boldsymbol{\theta}_t, T)$ to be pulled next. When T is small, the Bayesian optimal scheme can be obtained exactly. Let $V(\boldsymbol{\theta}_0, T) = V(\pi^*, \boldsymbol{\theta}_0, T)$ denote the value of the optimal solution. It is easy to see that the value is 0 when $T = 0$; that is, $V(\boldsymbol{\theta}_t, 0) = 0$ for any state $\boldsymbol{\theta}_t$. When $T = 1$ with initial state $\boldsymbol{\theta}_0$, we can find $\pi^*(\boldsymbol{\theta}_0, 1)$ by solving

$$\begin{aligned} \pi^*(\boldsymbol{\theta}_0, 1) &= \arg\max_i E_{\boldsymbol{\theta}_1}\left[R_i(\boldsymbol{\theta}_0, \boldsymbol{\theta}_1) \mid \text{pulling } i\right] \\ &= \arg\max_i \{\alpha_{i0}/\gamma_{i0}\}, \end{aligned} \tag{3.7}$$

because, in this case, the expected reward of pulling arm i is its reward probability α_{i0}/γ_{i0}. We can also compute

$$V(\boldsymbol{\theta}_0, 1) = \max_i \{\alpha_{i0}/\gamma_{i0}\} \tag{3.8}$$

for any starting state $\boldsymbol{\theta}_0$. When $T = 2$ with initial state $\boldsymbol{\theta}_0$, we can find $\pi^*(\boldsymbol{\theta}_0, 2)$ by solving

$$\pi^*(\boldsymbol{\theta}_0, 2) = \arg\max_i E_{\boldsymbol{\theta}_1}\left[R_i(\boldsymbol{\theta}_t, \boldsymbol{\theta}_1) + V(\boldsymbol{\theta}_1, 1) \mid \text{pulling } i\right], \tag{3.9}$$

which can be solved by enumerating all possible next states $\boldsymbol{\theta}_1$. In fact, we only have two possible next states for each arm in this Beta-binomial MDP. That is $2K$ next states to be evaluated in total, where K is the number of arms. Note that the total number of possible states is linear in the number of arms K because the state of arms that are not pulled remains unchanged. Let $\boldsymbol{\theta}_1^{(i,0)} = \boldsymbol{\theta}_0$, except that the new state of arm i is $(\alpha_{i0}, \gamma_{i0} + 1)$ (corresponding to pulling arm i without a reward), and $\boldsymbol{\theta}_1^{(i,1)} = \boldsymbol{\theta}_t$, except that the new state of arm i is $(\alpha_{i0} + 1, \gamma_{i0} + 1)$ (corresponding to pulling arm i with a reward). The optimal solution can be obtained by solving

$$\pi^*(\boldsymbol{\theta}_0, 2) = \arg\max_i \left[\frac{\alpha_{i0}}{\gamma_{i0}} (1 + V(\boldsymbol{\theta}_1^{(i,1)}, 1)) + \left(1 - \frac{\alpha_{i0}}{\gamma_{i0}}\right)(0 + V(\boldsymbol{\theta}_1^{(i,0)}, 1)) \right], \tag{3.10}$$

where $V(\cdot, 1)$ have been solved in Equation (3.8). It should be easy to see that, for $T \geq 2$, the optimal solution can be obtained by solving

$$\pi^*(\boldsymbol{\theta}_0, T) = \arg\max_i \left[\frac{\alpha_{i0}}{\gamma_{i0}} (1 + V(\boldsymbol{\theta}_1^{(i,1)}, T-1)) + \left(1 - \frac{\alpha_{i0}}{\gamma_{i0}}\right) V(\boldsymbol{\theta}_1^{(i,0)}, T-1) \right]. \tag{3.11}$$

However, computing $V(\cdot, T-1)$ is expensive. If we simply compute it based on the recursive definition, the total number of states that have to be evaluated can grow in the order of $(2K)^{T-1}$. It shows the computational challenges in the Bayesian approach. See Puterman (2009) for detailed analysis of the optimal solution.

3.2.2 Minimax Approach

Explore-exploit schemes can also be developed based on a minimax approach. The central idea is to find schemes whose worst-case performance can be bounded by a reasonable rate. In this approach, the performance of a scheme is typically measured through the notion of *regret*. Assuming stationary reward probabilities for arms, the arm with the highest reward probability is the *best arm* (unknown to the scheme). The regret of a scheme after T pulls is the difference between the expected total reward of pulling the best arm T times and the reward obtained from the scheme.

In the minimax approach, UCB1 proposed by Auer et al. (2002) is a popular scheme, where UCB stands for upper confidence bound. At any point in time, UCB1 gives each arm i a priority score:

$$\frac{\alpha_i}{\gamma_i} + \sqrt{\frac{2 \ln n}{\gamma_i}}, \tag{3.12}$$

where α_i is the total reward obtained from pulling arm i so far, γ_i is the number of times arm i has been pulled, and n is the total number of arm pulls. Then, we simply pull the arm with the highest priority score. At the beginning, when $\gamma_i = 0$, we pull every arm once. Notice that $\frac{\alpha_i}{\gamma_i}$ is our current estimate of the reward probability of arm i and the second term represents the uncertainty of our current estimate. Based on Chernoff-Hoeffding bound, Auer proved that the regret of UCB1 after T pulls is at most $O(\ln T)$, which is quite significant, because Lai and Robbins (1985) showed that the regret of any scheme for the classical bandit problem after T pulls is at least of order $O(\ln T)$.

We note that Auer's result does not imply that UCB1 can achieve the best performance in practice because the constants involved in the big-O notation can make a difference. To be more precise, the exact regret bound of UCB1 after T pulls is

$$\left(8 \sum_{i:\mu_i<\mu^*} \frac{\ln T}{\Delta_i}\right) + \left(1 + \frac{\pi^2}{3}\right)\left(\sum_{i=1}^{K} \Delta_i\right), \tag{3.13}$$

where μ_i is the unobserved reward probability of arm i, $\mu^* = \max_i \mu_i$, and $\Delta_i = \mu^* - \mu_i$. In practice, if we care more about the average performance, UCB1 usually explores more to guarantee its worst case performance.

The minimax approach has also been applied to bandit problems in adversarial settings where the reward probability of each arm is not stationary over time and can change arbitrarily even in a way that tries to minimize rewards. Auer et al. (1995) studied this problem and developed the EXP3 algorithm that incurs bounded regret. We refer interested readers to Auer et al. (1995).

3.2.3 Heuristic Bandit Schemes

A number of heuristic bandit schemes have also been proposed. In the following, we review some of them. Let $\hat{p}_i = \alpha_i/\gamma_i$ denote our current estimate of the reward probability of arm i:

- *ϵ-Greedy*: This policy pulls an arm uniformly at random with probability ϵ, and with probability $1 - \epsilon$ it pulls the arm with the highest estimated reward probability, that is, $\arg\max_i \hat{p}_i$. One extension to reduce excessive exploration is to shrink ϵ over time. For instance, if n is the total number of pulls, we can set $\epsilon_n = \min\{1, \delta/n\}$ for some constant δ. Auer et al. (2002) showed that a logarithmic regret bound can be obtained when δ is set appropriately.
- *SoftMax*: Given a "temperature" parameter τ, we pull arm i with probability

$$\frac{e^{\hat{p}_i/\tau}}{\sum_j e^{\hat{p}_j/\tau}}. \tag{3.14}$$

Notice that when the temperature τ is high, $e^{\hat{p}_i/\tau} \to 1$, and each arm has almost an equal chance of being selected. Conversely, when τ is low, the probability mass will concentrate on the arm having the highest estimated reward probability.

- *Thompson sampling*: Suppose we use a Bayesian approach to estimate the reward probability of each arm. Let $\mathcal{P}_i$ denote the posterior distribution of the reward probability for arm i. To select an arm to pull, we first draw a random number p_i according to the distribution $\mathcal{P}_i$ for each arm i and then pull the arm with the highest p_i. This approach was first proposed by Thompson (1933). The Beta-binomial model in Equations (3.2) and (3.3) can be used to derive the posterior distributions of the arms.
- *k-deviation UCB*: The UCB method can also be applied in a heuristic way. Let $E[p_i]$ and $\text{Dev}[p_i]$ denote the mean and standard deviation of the posterior distribution $\mathcal{P}_i$ of the reward probability of arm i. Then, we pull the arm i with the highest score $s_i = E[p_i] + k \cdot \text{Dev}[p_i]$, where k is selected heuristically. The mean and variance of a Beta posterior distribution are described in Equation (3.1).

3.2.4 Remarks

In general, the Bayesian approach is computationally expensive, but when the modeling assumptions are reasonable, the performance is relatively better. Conversely, the minimax approach can achieve best performance in the worst case but usually explores more in the average case. Methods based on heuristic are often used in practice. They do not necessarily have proven guarantees for either the worst case or the average case, but they are simple to implement and can achieve reasonable performance when tuned properly.

3.3 Explore-Exploit in Recommender Systems

We now discuss the explore-exploit problem in the context of recommender systems and describe the main challenges.

3.3.1 Most-Popular Recommendation

We begin with the problem of recommending the most popular item on a single slot to all users to maximize the total number of positive responses, where we recommend a single item to each user visit without leveraging any information about the user (i.e., no personalization). Although simple, this problem of *most-popular recommendation* includes the basic ingredients of item recommendation (as described in Section 1.2) and also provides a strong baseline for more sophisticated techniques.

Estimating item popularity (response rate) involves several nuances. Ideally, popularity for each item should be estimated by displaying the item to a representative sample of the current user population. For instance, serving the most popular items at night with popularity estimated using data from the morning may not work well because of differences in user populations. Several other factors can also bias popularity estimates when using retrospective data collected from existing systems. To protect against such bias, it is useful to update popularity estimates rapidly in an adaptive fashion through procedures like a Kalman filter (Pole et al., 1994) or the simple exponentially weighted moving average (EWMA) introduced in Section 1.2, using data obtained through randomization, that is, randomly assigning some fraction of visits in a given time interval to each item in the pool. Because both the set of candidate items and the response rate of an item change over time, the optimality results of classical bandit schemes do not apply to the most-popular recommendation problem. The ϵ-greedy scheme described in Section 3.2.3 equally randomizes over all items and is simple to implement and thus is a good starting point. However, it may be far from optimal for web applications where the sample size available per item in each time interval is small. Fortunately, a near-optimal amount of randomization for each item can still be computed by using extensions of the bandit schemes. We describe these extensions in Chapter 6.

3.3.2 Personalized Recommendation

A natural extension to most-popular recommendation is to classify users into coarse segments based on attributes like demographics and geographic location and then to apply most-popular recommendation techniques to each segment. Such an approach works well if segments are coarse and item affinities for users within a segment are relatively homogeneous. Techniques like clustering and decision trees (see Chapters 9 and 14 of Hastie et al. 2009) can be used to identify such segments.

However, this *segmented most-popular recommendation* approach only works when the number of user visits per segment available to explore each candidate item is "sufficiently" large to ensure reliable identification of the items with the highest response rates. It is challenging to provide personalized recommendations from a large pool of items, because it may not even be possible to show each item to any user even once!

In practice, depending on the sample size available per item in each interval, applying segmented most-popular recommendation by controlling the granularity of segments is a simple but reasonable approach. It is also possible to increase the granularity of segments by increasing the size of each interval to accumulate more samples. The trade-off between the size of an interval and segment coarseness has to be determined empirically for an application.

3.3.3 Data Sparsity Challenge

Data sparsity is the main challenge in many recommender systems. Major factors that contribute to data sparsity include the following:

- *Need to personalize*: User visit distributions tend to be heavy-tailed. A large fraction of users are sporadic (even first-time) visitors, whereas a small fraction of users visit more frequently. An ideal approach would personalize deeply for users with many visits and back off to segmented most-popular recommendation for those who are sporadic visitors. It is nontrivial to devise explore-exploit schemes to perform personalization in the presence of such heterogeneity in sample sizes.
- *Large and/or dynamic content pool*: To satisfy the unique interests of each user, the item pool has to be sufficiently large. Items are often time sensitive and user interest in an item usually decays over time. Thus, the amount of data available to estimate the response rate of each item at each time point could be small in practice.

3.4 Explore-Exploit with Data Sparsity

In this section, we provide the key ideas used to develop statistical methods in this book to address the challenges of data sparsity. We first reduce dimensionality by creating homogeneous groups through user and item features (in Section 3.4.1) and then couple dimension reduction with explore/exploit (in Section 3.4.2). Although it is ideal to couple dimension reduction with explore-exploit techniques, obtaining an optimal solution is difficult. Heuristics are often used in practice. For time-sensitive items, it is also important to update model parameters in an online fashion using most recent user feedback and initialize online models to facilitate fast model convergence (Section 3.4.3).

3.4.1 Dimension Reduction Techniques

We cover a few representative approaches to dimension reduction that are commonly used in practice for recommender problems.

Grouping through Hierarchies. In some scenarios, users and/or items are hierarchically organized. For instance, the city in which a user lives is nested

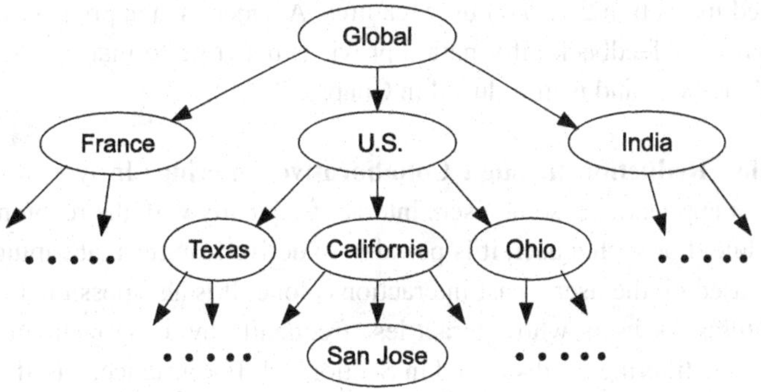

Figure 3.1. Example geographical hierarchy.

within a state, which in turn is nested within a country (Figure 3.1). If such hierarchies do not exist, hierarchical clustering or decision tree learning (see Chapters 9 and 14 of Hastie et al. (2009)) may be applied to automatically create hierarchies from data.

Instead of exploring-exploiting individual items for each individual user, one can start with exploring-exploiting coarse content categories for coarse user segments and gradually transition to fine-grained user segments and items as we obtain more data. See Kocsis and Szepesvari (2006) and Pandey et al. (2007) for examples.

Dimension Reduction through Linear Projections. Another popular approach is to work in a generalized linear model framework (Nelder and Wedderburn, 1972). In many applications, we have a rich set of user features, such as demographics, geolocation, and behavioral activities such as searches. Let us denote the feature vector for user i by $\boldsymbol{x}_i = (x_{i1}, \ldots, x_{iM})$. The number M of such features is typically large (thousands or even millions). A generalized linear model assumes that the response rate of item j for user i is a monotone function of a linear combination of features $\boldsymbol{x}_i'\boldsymbol{\beta}_j$, and the unknown coefficient vector $\boldsymbol{\beta}_j$ for each item j is estimated by using item interaction data across users. Notice that each item j has its own coefficient vector $\boldsymbol{\beta}_j$ to model the unique behavior of each item. Although such a model reduces the estimation problem from estimating a response rate for each (user, item) pair to estimating M coefficients for each item, it is still daunting when M is large. One approach is to project $\boldsymbol{\beta}_j$ into a low-dimensional space through a linear projection matrix B; that is, $\boldsymbol{\beta}_j = B\boldsymbol{\theta}_j$, where $\boldsymbol{\theta}_j$ is low dimensional. The projection B can be estimated in an unsupervised fashion by using principal component analysis (PCA) (see Chapter 14 of Hastie et al. (2009)) or singular value decomposition (discussed in Section 2.1.2) on user features. A supervised approach that uses additional click feedback information provides better performance than unsupervised methods and is introduced in Chapter 7.

Dimension Reduction through Collaborative Filtering. In typical recommendation applications, some users interact frequently with the recommendation module. For such a user, it is possible to derive features that capture item affinity based on the user's past interactions alone. It is also possible to derive such features for users who interact less frequently by using techniques like collaborative filtering, as discussed in Section 2.4. For instance, based on data from the entire user population, one can estimate associations of the form "users who like item *A* also like item *B*." The stronger these associations, the smaller the effective dimensionality, because they induce soft constraints on the joint distributions of response rates of all user-item pairs. Such approaches work well in practice even in the absence of other user and item features (Pilászy and Tikk, 2009; Das et al., 2007).

Collaborative filtering approaches based on factor models currently provide state-of-the-art performance (Koren et al., 2009). The idea is to map user i and item j into two points $\boldsymbol{u}_i$ and $\boldsymbol{v}_j$ in the same Euclidean space. Points $\boldsymbol{u}_i$ and $\boldsymbol{v}_j$ need to be learned from data and are called the vector of *user factors* and the vector of *item factors*, respectively. User-item affinity is then given by the inner product $\boldsymbol{u}_i'\boldsymbol{v}_j$ of $\boldsymbol{u}_i$ and $\boldsymbol{v}_j$, which is a measure of similarity between the two. We can think of each dimension of vectors $\boldsymbol{u}_i$ and $\boldsymbol{v}_j$ as a "group," and the values on the kth dimension in vectors $\boldsymbol{u}_i$ and $\boldsymbol{v}_j$ represent propensities that the user and the item belong to the the kth group. Unlike explicit interest categories, these groups are latent and are estimated from retrospective data; a small number (few tens to hundreds) of factors usually provide good performance in applications.

3.4.2 Explore-Exploit with Dimension Reduction

It is challenging to obtain an optimal explore-exploit solution to personalized recommendation with dimension reduction. The heuristic schemes described in Section 3.2.3 are often used in practice. A slight revision needs to be made. The predicted response rate $\hat{p}_i$ (i.e., the reward probability in the bandit problem) of item i for a user is no longer computed by counting the responses to the item but by a personalized model described in Section 3.4.1. With this change, ϵ-greedy and SoftMax can be easily applied to personalized recommendations. See Langford and Zhang (2007) and Kakade et al. (2008) for a few examples. If the personalized model can also estimate the posterior distribution of the response rate of each item for each user given the observed data, Thompson sampling and k-deviation UCB can also be applied. See Li et al. (2010) for an example.

In practice, Thompson sampling and k-deviation UCB are more desirable than ϵ-greedy and SoftMax because they incorporate the uncertainty in response rate estimation into explore-exploit, while ϵ-greedy and SoftMax do not. For Thompson sampling and k-deviation UCB, the key to success is accurate estimation of the posterior distributions (not just the mean) of response rates through appropriate statistical models.

3.4.3 Online Models

In several recommender problems, items are time sensitive with short lifetimes. For instance, in a news recommender problem, articles about breaking news become stale and irrelevant in a few hours. Models to estimate response rates for such time-sensitive items need to be updated frequently using the most recent user feedback. Such *online models* start with an initial estimate of the model parameters and continuously update parameters as new data become available. For instance, in the factor model, we can assume user factor estimates $\boldsymbol{u}_i$ are more stable than those of items $\boldsymbol{v}_j$; thus, we only need to update $\boldsymbol{v}_j$ in an online manner. From a Bayesian perspective, without any click feedback on item j, we postulate a prior distribution for $\boldsymbol{v}_j$ with mean $\boldsymbol{\mu}_j$ and some variance. After receiving feedback (click or no click), we update the prior to obtain the posterior distribution of $\boldsymbol{v}_j$; the resulting posterior serves as the prior for subsequent updates. See Section 7.3 for details. For applications where items are not time sensitive (e.g., movie recommendations), such frequent online updates may not provide additional benefits.

For an item j that is new or has received little click feedback, predicting response rate depends crucially on the prior mean $\boldsymbol{\mu}_j$, which is the initial estimate. We could naively set $\boldsymbol{\mu}_j$ of all items to the same value for all users, say, $\mathbf{0}$. This can be improved by initializing item factors $\boldsymbol{v}_j$ through feature vector $\boldsymbol{z}_j$ for item j as $\boldsymbol{v}_j = D'\boldsymbol{z}_j + \boldsymbol{\eta}_j$, where D is a matrix of regression coefficients and $\boldsymbol{\eta}_j$ are correction terms learning item-specific idosyncracies not captured through item features. Intuitively, the vector of item factors $\boldsymbol{v}_j$ is first predicted by a regression $D'\boldsymbol{z}_j$ based on item features $\boldsymbol{z}_j$. Because the output $\boldsymbol{v}_j$ of this regression is a vector (instead of a number), the regression coefficients are in a matrix D (instead of a vector). For new items that receive little click feedback, we mainly use this feature-based regression to obtain item factors. However, item features are not always predictive. For items with more click feedback, their item factors can be estimated more accurately by using the correction term $\boldsymbol{\eta}_j$ to capture the signal that the features cannot capture.

Similar treatment can also be applied to user factors. A detailed description is provided in Chapter 8.

3.5 Summary

To summarize this chapter, the goal in most web recommender problems is to maximize some metric that is indicative of positive user interaction with items. Although much of the focus in the literature has been on methods that improve the predictive accuracy of such metrics via supervised learning techniques, recommender problems are not just a supervised learning problem. In fact, this is an explore-exploit problem. However, supervised learning techniques help in reducing the dimensionality of such explore-exploit problems and aid rapid convergence to the best items for a given user in a given context. Simple heuristics that combine supervised learning methods with classical multiarmed bandit schemes work well in practice. Obtaining better methods for such high-dimensional explore-exploit problems is still an active research area.

Exercise

1. Consider a most-popular recommendation problem with two items that have CTRs of p_1 and $p_1 + \delta(> 0)$, respectively. Assume that the items have been shown n and kn times, respectively ($k > 0$). Using a Beta-binomial distribution with a uniform prior, compute the posterior probability of the first item being better than the second one as a function of k and δ for $n = 5, 10, 15, \ldots, 100$. Summarize your observations.

4
Evaluation Methods

After developing statistical methods for recommender systems, it is important to evaluate their performance to assess performance metrics in different application settings. Broadly speaking, there are two kinds of evaluation, depending on whether a recommendation algorithm, or more precisely, the model used in the algorithm, has been deployed to serve users:

1. *Predeployment offline evaluation*: A new model must show strong signs of performance improvement over existing baselines before being deployed to serve real users. To ascertain the potential of a new model before testing it on real user visits, we compute various performance measures on retrospective (historical) data. We refer to this as *offline evaluation*. To perform such offline evaluation, we need to log data that record past user-item interactions in the system. Model comparison is performed by computing various offline metrics based on such data.
2. *Postdeployment online evaluation*: Once the model performance looks promising based on offline metrics, we test it on a small fraction of real user visits. We refer to this as *online evaluation*. To perform online evaluation, it is typical to run randomized experiments online. A randomized experiment, also referred to as an A/B test or a bucket test in web applications, compares a new method to an existing baseline. It is conducted by assigning two random user or visit populations to the *treatment bucket* and the *control bucket*, respectively. The treatment bucket is typically smaller than the control because it serves users according to the new recommendation model that is being tested, whereas the control bucket serves users using the status quo. After running such a *bucket test* for a certain time period, we gauge model performance by comparing metrics that are computed using data collected from the corresponding buckets.

In this chapter, we describe several ways to measure the performance of recommendation models and discuss their strengths and weaknesses. We start in Section 4.1 with traditional offline evaluation metrics that measure out-of-sample predictive accuracy on retrospective ratings data. Our use of the term *rating* is generic and refers to both explicit ratings like star ratings on movies and implicit ratings (also called responses) like clicks on recommended items (we use ratings and responses interchangeably). In Section 4.2, we discuss online evaluation methods, describing both performance metrics and how to set up online bucket tests in a proper way. Improving online performance of a model is our ultimate goal; however, performing online evaluation has an associated cost because a poor model could significantly impact user experience. Can we use offline evaluation to approximate online performance metrics? Unfortunately, the answer is not always affirmative. In Sections 4.3 and 4.4, we describe two offline methods that can bridge this gap in some scenarios through simulation and replay.

4.1 Traditional Offline Evaluation

For recommendation models that predict user i's rating on item j, because they are predictive models, one natural evaluation metric is to measure out-of-sample predictive accuracy for *unseen ratings*, that is, ratings on unseen or unobserved user-item pairs. For other recommendation models such as the unsupervised methods discussed in Section 2.3.1, the goal is not to predict ratings. Metrics that measure a model's ranking performance are useful for these models. In fact, such ranking metrics are useful in a much broader setting, because the goal of many recommendation problems (no matter whether predictive models or unsupervised methods are used) is to rank items according to some score – we do not necessarily have to accurately predict users' absolute ratings, as long as we can appropriately rank items on a relative scale.

Offline evaluation methods are based on users' ratings on items observed in the past. We use the term *observed ratings* to distinguish them from unseen ratings and predicted ratings. To measure a model's out-of-sample accuracy or ranking performance, we first need appropriate methods to split the observed ratings into a training set and a test set and use the ratings in the test set to "simulate" unseen ratings for various application settings. After introducing data-splitting methods, we describe commonly used accuracy metrics in Section 4.1.2 and commonly used ranking metrics in Section 4.1.3.

4.1.1 Data-Splitting Methods

In this section, we describe ways of splitting the observed ratings into two parts: a training set and a test set. All unknown model parameters must be estimated using only data in the training set. The estimated model is used to compute test set accuracy by aggregating predicted ratings or rankings in the test set. For ease of exposition, in the rest of this section, we assume that we want to compute an accuracy metric. Applying the following data-splitting methods to computation of ranking metrics is straightforward. Because we have not yet precisely defined accuracy and ranking metrics, for now, we can think of them as functions that return a number that measures the performance of a recommendation model based on a training set and a test set.

Splitting Methods. Although splitting data into training and test sets is routinely used to assess model performance for supervised learning tasks, methods to perform this split depend on the properties of our recommendation model. In the following, we describe a number of ways to split the data, and we discuss their properties.

- *Random splitting*: We randomly select P percent of the observed ratings to create the training set and the remaining $(100 - P)$ percent observed ratings from to create the test set. Random splitting is a standard way to measure the predictive accuracy of a statistical model. However, it may not be appropriate for estimating the expected performance of a recommendation model in a real system. In particular, old ratings of a user (or an item) may be included in the test set, whereas new ratings of the user (or the item) may be in the training set. In this case, some models may end up using future ratings to predict past ratings, which does not correspond to any real application setting. However, if we only want to measure the predictive accuracy of a statistical model, then random splitting can be a suitable method. One advantage of random splitting is that we can easily perform random splitting multiple times and compute the variance of the accuracy numbers obtained from different training-test splits.
- *Time-based splitting*: If we record the time when a user rates an item, we can split the data by using observed ratings before a certain time point to form the training set and the rest to form the test set. Time-based splitting eliminates the problem of using future data to predict the past and is perhaps a better splitting method for understanding the performance of a model in a real application setting. Unlike random splitting, we cannot use time-based splitting to generate multiple training-test splits with the same percentage of training (or test) data because each splitting time point corresponds to a unique training-test split. Nonetheless, bootstrap sampling (Efron and Tibshirani, 1993) can be used to estimate the variance of model accuracy for this splitting method. For example, after creating a training-test split, we can

obtain multiple versions of training and test data by random sampling with replacement from the original training set and test set.

- *User-based splitting*: If the goal is to understand the accuracy of a model on *new users* who have not yet rated any item, we can randomly select P percent users and their ratings to form the training set, and the ratings by the remaining $(100 - P)$ percent users form the test set. User-based splitting simulates a scenario where users in the test set do not have any past ratings that a model can use. Thus, the test set accuracy measures the ability of the model to predict ratings for new users. Similar to the random splitting method, we can easily generate multiple training-test splits to assess the variance of model accuracy for this splitting method.
- *Item-based splitting*: If the goal is to understand the accuracy of a model on *new items* that have not yet received any ratings, we can split items into a set of training items and a set of test items. All the ratings on training items belong to the training set, and all the ratings on test items belong to the test set. Again, multiple training-test splits can be easily generated.

Cross-validation. When we need to generate multiple training-test splits, n-fold cross-validation is a useful method for ensuring that each observed rating is used exactly once in the computation of test set accuracy. We describe cross-validation for random splitting and note that the method applies to user-based splitting and item-based splitting in a similar manner. The n-fold cross-validation works as follows:

- We randomly split the observed ratings into n roughly equally sized partitions.
- For k from 1 to n, do the following:
  - Treat the kth partition as the test set and the union of the other $n - 1$ partitions as the training set.
  - Train the model using the training set and compute the accuracy metric using the test set.
- Average the n partition-specific accuracy numbers to obtain the final accuracy estimate. Variance or standard deviation can also be computed from the n partition-specific accuracy numbers.

Tuning Set. It is common for a model-fitting algorithm to have a few *tuning parameters* that are not estimated by the algorithm but important inputs to the algorithm. These tuning parameters often affect how the fitting algorithm determines regular model parameters. For example, regularization parameters (e.g., λ in Equation 2.15 and λ_1 and λ_2 in Equation 2.24) are usually treated as tuning parameters. The number of latent dimensions in matrix factorization is another example. The step size (e.g., α in Equation 2.29) in the SGD method is yet another one. In general, it is not a good practice to compare many different settings of tuning parameters based on the accuracy on the test set and report the test set accuracy of the best setting. This best test set accuracy obtained after estimating the tuning parameter using the test set will always be optimistic and overestimate the actual accuracy of the model on unseen ratings. Consider the simple example of a model that predicts ratings randomly. If we run this model several times on the test set and report the best test set accuracy over all trials, the model performance will get better with increasing number of trials. Each trial here can be thought of as a tuning parameter setting that has no real effect on model performance at all. If the test set is large and the number of tuning parameter settings is small, this overestimation may not be a serious issue. Nevertheless, it is a good practice to further split the training set into two parts. We call one part the tuning set and still call the other part the training set. Now, the training set is used to determine model parameters, and the tuning set is used to select a good setting of tuning parameters. Finally, after fixing all unknown quantities obtained without using the test set, we apply the model with the best setting to the test set and measure its accuracy. The process works as follows:

- For each setting s of tuning parameters, we do the following:
  - Fit the model using tuning parameter setting s and the training set.
  - Measure the accuracy of the fitted model using the tuning set.
- Let s^* denote the best setting of tuning parameters that has the highest tuning set accuracy.
- Fit the model using tuning parameter setting s^* and the training set (or the union of the training set and tuning set).
- Measure the accuracy of the fitted model using the test set.

Cross-validation is not used in the preceding process. It is straightforward to apply cross-validation to create training-tuning splits and find the best setting of tuning parameters.

4.1.2 Accuracy Metrics

Let $\mathbf{\Omega}^{\text{test}}$ denote the set of (user i, item j) pairs in the test set. Recall that y_{ij} denotes the observed rating that user i gives to item j and $\hat{y}_{ij}$ denotes the predicted rating by a model. Accuracy can be measured in a variety of ways.

- *Root mean squared error*: For numeric ratings, root mean squared error (RMSE) between predicted ratings and observed ratings is a frequently used accuracy metric:

$$\text{RMSE} = \sqrt{\frac{\sum_{(i,j)\in\mathbf{\Omega}^{\text{test}}}(y_{ij} - \hat{y}_{ij})^2}{|\mathbf{\Omega}^{\text{test}}|}}. \tag{4.1}$$

  The fact that RMSE was chosen as the accuracy metric for the Netflix contest has made it particularly popular in recent years.
- *Mean absolute error*: Another frequently used metric for numeric ratings is mean absolute error (MAE):

$$\text{MAE} = \frac{\sum_{(i,j)\in\mathbf{\Omega}^{\text{test}}}|y_{ij} - \hat{y}_{ij}|}{|\mathbf{\Omega}^{\text{test}}|}. \tag{4.2}$$

- *Normalized L_p norm*: MAE and RMSE are two special cases of the normalized L_p norm with $p = 1$ and 2, respectively:

$$\text{Normalized } L_p \text{ norm} = \left(\frac{\sum_{(i,j)\in\mathbf{\Omega}^{\text{test}}}|y_{ij} - \hat{y}_{ij}|^p}{|\mathbf{\Omega}^{\text{test}}|}\right)^{1/p}. \tag{4.3}$$

  Larger values of p put more penalty on (user, item) pairs with larger errors. At one extreme, $L_\infty = \max_{(i,j)\in\mathbf{\Omega}^{\text{test}}}|y_{ij} - \hat{y}_{ij}|$. In practice, MAE and RMSE are widely used.
- *Log-likelihood*: For a model that predicts the probability that a user would respond to an item positively (e.g., click or not), the log-likelihood of the model on the test set (not the training set) is a useful accuracy metric. Let $\hat{p}_{ij}$ denote the predicted probability that user i responds to item j positively and $y_{ij} \in \{1, 0\}$ denote whether user i actually responds to item j positively. Then, we have

$$\begin{aligned}\text{Log-likelihood} &= \sum_{(i,j)\in\mathbf{\Omega}^{\text{test}}} \log \Pr(y_{ij} \mid \hat{p}_{ij}) \\ &= \sum_{(i,j)\in\mathbf{\Omega}^{\text{test}}} y_{ij}\log(\hat{p}_{ij}) + (1 - y_{ij})\log(1 - \hat{p}_{ij}).\end{aligned} \tag{4.4}$$

Accuracy metrics are basic evaluation measures for predictive models. When comparing a new predictive model with an existing one, ensuring that the new model is more accurate than the old one on retrospective data is a good start. However, we should not rely solely on accuracy metrics because they have the following limitations:

- *Unsuitable for measuring ranking performance*: In most systems, only the top few items are recommended to users. Accuracy on items that are likely to be ranked higher is relatively more important than accuracy on lower-ranked items. For instance, in a binary response problem, large errors in estimating low response rates may not affect the performance by much because there could be a large margin between items with low and high response rates. Classical accuracy metrics do not weight errors appropriately to take the ordering of items into consideration.

- *Difficult to translate accuracy improvements to real system performance improvements*: Being able to improve model accuracy is typically an encouraging sign. However, offline accuracy improvements do not necessarily translate to performance improvements in real online systems. For example, it is difficult to say how much we can expect a recommender system to improve if we improve a model's RMSE from 0.9 to 0.8 or how many more additional clicks we can obtain on recommended items if we improve the model's log-likelihood by 10 percent.

4.1.3 Ranking Metrics

As discussed before, recommendation problems are usually ranking problems. It is useful to evaluate a model based on how well it can rank highly rated items relative to the rest. Let s_{ij} denote the score that the model gives to a (user i, item j) pair. As long as the scores can be used to order items according to their affinities to a user, the actual score values need not be on the same scale as the ratings. As before, we use y_{ij} to denote the observed rating that user i gives to item j and split the observed ratings (more precisely, user-item pairs for which we have observed ratings) into a training set and a test set and measure ranking metrics using the test set.

We first consider *global ranking metrics*, where the entire test set is ranked according to the predicted scores from a model and we measure the extent to which user-item pairs with high ratings are ranked above those with low ratings. Then, we discuss *local ranking metrics*, where we rank items for each individual user separately and measure the extent to which highly rated items are ranked above those with lower ratings for that user, and then average across users.

Global Ranking Metrics. We start with problem settings where the observed ratings y_{ij} are binary (e.g., clicks) or can be made binary (e.g., treating rating values above a threshold as positive and the rest as negative). Let Ω_{+}^{test} denote the test (user i, item j) pairs with positive ratings and Ω_{-}^{test} denote those with negative ratings. Given a threshold θ, we call (i, j) pairs with score $s_{ij} > \theta$ the *predicted positive* pairs, and (i, j) pairs with score $s_{ij} \leq \theta$ the *predicted*

Table 4.1. *Definitions of TP, TN, FP, and FN*

$$
\begin{aligned}
TP(\theta) &= |\{(i,j) \in \Omega_{+}^{\text{test}} : s_{ij} > \theta\}|, \\
&\quad \text{which is the number of true positive user-item pairs} \\
TN(\theta) &= |\{(i,j) \in \Omega_{-}^{\text{test}} : s_{ij} \le \theta\}|, \\
&\quad \text{which is the number of true negative user-item pairs} \\
FP(\theta) &= |\{(i,j) \in \Omega_{-}^{\text{test}} : s_{ij} > \theta\}|, \\
&\quad \text{which is the number of false positive user-item pairs} \\
FN(\theta) &= |\{(i,j) \in \Omega_{+}^{\text{test}} : s_{ij} \le \theta\}|, \\
&\quad \text{which is the number of false negative user-item pairs}
\end{aligned}
$$

negative pairs. We define $TP(\theta)$, $TN(\theta)$, $FP(\theta)$, and $FN(\theta)$ in Table 4.1. A few commonly used metrics based on these quantities are as follows:

- *Precision-recall (P-R) curve*: The P-R curve of a model is a two-dimensional curve generated by varying θ from negative infinity to positive infinity. A point on the curve for a given θ is (Recall(θ), Precision(θ)), where

$$
\begin{aligned}
\text{Precision}(\theta) &= \frac{TP(\theta)}{TP(\theta) + FP(\theta)} \\
\text{Recall}(\theta) &= \frac{TP(\theta)}{TP(\theta) + FN(\theta)}.
\end{aligned}
\tag{4.5}
$$

- *Receiver operating characteristic curve*: The receiver operating characteristic (ROC) curve of a model is also a two-dimensional curve generated by varying θ from negative infinity to positive infinity. The point on the curve for a given θ is ($FPR(\theta)$, $TPR(\theta)$), where

$$
\begin{aligned}
TPR(\theta) &= \frac{TP(\theta)}{TP(\theta) + FN(\theta)} \quad \text{(i.e., true positive rate)} \\
FPR(\theta) &= \frac{FP(\theta)}{FP(\theta) + TN(\theta)} \quad \text{(i.e., false positive rate).}
\end{aligned}
\tag{4.6}
$$

  It is easy to see that for a *random model* that outputs random s_{ij} scores, the ROC curve is a straight line from (0,0) to (1,1).
- *Area under the ROC curve (AUC)*: P-R curves and ROC curves are both two-dimensional plots. Sometimes it is useful to summarize the performance of a model using a single number. AUC is a commonly used metric that summarizes an ROC curve by computing the area under the curve. The range is from 0 to 1 – the higher, the better. A random model has an AUC of 0.5.

Another way to measure the ranking performance of a model is rank correlation, which compares a ranked list of test user-item pairs sorted by model scores s_{ij} to the *ground-truth* ranked list of test user-item pairs sorted by the observed ratings y_{ij}. The more similar the two ranked lists are, the better the performance of the model is. Two commonly used rank correlation metrics for measuring the similarity of two ranked lists are Spearman's ρ and Kendall's τ:

- *Spearman's ρ* is the Pearson correlation between rank values of elements in the two lists. Let s^*_{ij} and y^*_{ij} denote the ranks of (user i, item j) pair in the ranked list according to s_{ij} and the ranked list according to y_{ij}, respectively. For example, if s_{ij} is the kth highest score among all user-item pairs in the test set, then $s^*_{ij} = k$. Ties are handled in the following way. If there are n user-item pairs with the same rating (or score) value y and there are m user-item pairs with rating (or score) values $> y$, then ranks of those n user-item pairs are all equal to the average rank = $\sum_{i=m+1}^{m+n} i/n$. Let $\bar{s}^*$ and $\bar{y}^*$ denote the average of s^*_{ij} and the average of y^*_{ij} over all test (i, j) pairs, respectively. Then, we compute the Pearson correlation coefficient as follows:

$$\frac{\sum_{(i,j)\in\Omega^{\text{test}}}(s^*_{ij} - \bar{s}^*)(y^*_{ij} - \bar{y}^*)}{\sqrt{\sum_{(i,j)\in\Omega^{\text{test}}}(s^*_{ij} - \bar{s}^*)^2}\sqrt{\sum_{(i,j)\in\Omega^{\text{test}}}(y^*_{ij} - \bar{y}^*)^2}}. \tag{4.7}$$

- *Kendall's τ* measures the propensity that two user-item pairs would be ordered in the same way in the two ranked lists. Consider any two user-item pairs in the test set: (i_1, j_1) and (i_2, j_2). We define two indicator functions as follows:

$$\begin{aligned}
&\text{Concordant}((i_1, j_1), (i_2, j_2))\\
&\quad = I((s_{i_1 j_1} > s_{i_2 j_2} \text{ and } y_{i_1 j_1} > y_{i_2 j_2}) \text{ or } (s_{i_1 j_1} < s_{i_2 j_2} \text{ and } y_{i_1 j_1} < y_{i_2 j_2}))\\
&\text{Discordant}((i_1, j_1), (i_2, j_2))\\
&\quad = I((s_{i_1 j_1} > s_{i_2 j_2} \text{ and } y_{i_1 j_1} < y_{i_2 j_2}) \text{ or } (s_{i_1 j_1} < s_{i_2 j_2} \text{ and } y_{i_1 j_1} > y_{i_2 j_2})).
\end{aligned}$$

  Let n_c and n_d denote the numbers of concordant and discordant pairs:

$$\begin{aligned}
n_c &= \frac{1}{2} \sum_{(i_1,j_1)\in\Omega^{\text{test}}} \sum_{(i_2,j_2)\in\Omega^{\text{test}}} \text{Concordant}((i_1, j_1), (i_2, j_2))\\
n_d &= \frac{1}{2} \sum_{(i_1,j_1)\in\Omega^{\text{test}}} \sum_{(i_2,j_2)\in\Omega^{\text{test}}} \text{Discordant}((i_1, j_1), (i_2, j_2)).
\end{aligned} \tag{4.8}$$

  Then, Kendall's τ is defined as follows:

$$\tau = \frac{n_c - n_d}{n(n-1)/2}, \tag{4.9}$$

where $n = |\Omega^{\text{test}}|$ is the total number of test user-item pairs. Rank correlation metrics naturally handle nonbinary ratings. Several variants to deal with ties are also available (e.g., τ_b, τ_c).

Local Ranking Metrics. Let $\mathcal{J}_i^{test}$ denote the set of items rated by user i. We first compute a ranking metric for each user i based on $\mathcal{J}_i^{test}$ and then average over all users. We focus on binary ratings; otherwise, we either convert multivalue ratings to binary ones based on a threshold or compute average rank correlation over users. A number of commonly used metrics are as follows:

- *Precision at rank K (P@K)*: For each user i, we rank items in $\mathcal{J}_i^{test}$ according to their scores (from high to low) predicted by a model. P@K is the fraction of positive items among the first K items. After computing P@K for each user, we average those numbers over all users. Usually, we consider a few K values (e.g., 1, 3, 5). A good model should outperform baseline models consistently for all K values.
- *Mean average precision*: One way to summarize P@K for all K values is the average precision, which is computed as follows. As before, we rank items in $\mathcal{J}_i^{test}$ according to the predicted scores, for each user i. Average precision is defined as the average of P@K over only the rank positions K at which the items have positive ratings. Mean average precision (MAP) is then the mean of average precisions over all users.
- *Normalized discounted cumulative gain (nDCG)*: Again, for each user i, we rank items in $\mathcal{J}_i^{test}$ according to the predicted scores. Let $p_i(k) = 1$ if the item at rank position k has a positive rating by user i; otherwise, $p_i(k) = 0$. Let $n_i = |\mathcal{J}_i^{test}|$ and n_i^+ denote the number of items in $\mathcal{J}_i^{test}$ that are rated positively by user i. Then, discounted cumulative gain (DCG) is defined as follows:

$$\text{DCG}_i = p_i(1) + \sum_{k=2}^{n_i} \frac{p_i(k)}{\log_2 k}. \tag{4.10}$$

nDCG is DCG normalized by the maximal achievable DCG value for user i:

$$\text{nDCG}_i = \frac{\text{DCG}_i}{1 + \sum_{k=2}^{n_i^+} \frac{1}{\log_2 k}}, \tag{4.11}$$

where the denominator is the maximal achievable DCG value for user i and is 1 if $n_i^+ = 1$. Finally, we average nDCG_i over all users i who have at least one positive rating.

Remarks. Most ranking metrics were originally defined to measure the performance of information retrieval (IR) systems. In those settings, the goal is to measure whether an IR model can rank documents "relevant" to a given query higher than the documents "irrelevant" to the query. Usually, a set of queries is sampled based on the goal of an IR task, and for each query, a set of documents is sampled according to a desired distribution. Then, human evaluators judge whether a document is relevant or irrelevant to the query.

When applying global ranking metrics to a recommendation model, there is no notion of a query and no clear correspondence to the usage in IR. In fact, global ranking metrics obtained by evaluating ratings on (user, item) pairs do not directly measure the ability of a ranking model to rank items for each user; instead, they should be treated in a way similar to accuracy metrics in a classification task in supervised learning. Hence, all the limitations of accuracy metrics also apply to global ranking metrics.

For local ranking metrics, each user corresponds to a query, the items rated by the user in the test data correspond to documents, and a positive rating corresponds to a "relevant" judgment. Local ranking metrics are useful for measuring the ability of a model to rank items for users. However, they are limited by selection bias and by difficulties in translating ranking metrics to online performance.

Unlike a properly defined IR task where documents are sampled according to certain desired distribution, the set of items used to compute a local ranking metric are subject to selection bias. For explicit ratings, users select the items they want to rate. In many systems, users are more likely to rate items they like. Thus, the item distribution of the test data (which consists of rated items, many of which are liked by users) can be quite different from the item distribution obtained with a new model used to serve real users (where most of the items are unseen by the user before). For implicit ratings, such as clicks on recommended items, the test data are usually collected from an existing recommender system. In this case, the model used by the system during the data collection period decides the item distribution for the test data. If a new model that is to be tested tends to select items that do not appear in the test data, we cannot measure its performance accurately.

Measuring online model performance is the ultimate goal of experimentation. Ranking metrics provide a useful indicator of whether a new model may rank items better than an old model. However, it is difficult to use offline metrics to obtain performance gains for online user engagement metrics like clicks on recommended items. For instance, it is difficult to predict the online performance gain that corresponds to a 10 percent improvement in a ranking metric.

4.2 Online Bucket Tests

To measure the true performance of a recommendation model, we should use the model to serve a fraction of randomly selected users and observe how those users respond to the recommended items. We call such experiments *online bucket tests* or just *bucket tests*. In this section, we first discuss how to properly set up an online bucket test, then we introduce a number of commonly used metrics, and finally, we discuss how to analyze bucket test results.

4.2.1 Bucket Setup

For ease of exposition, we describe bucket tests that compare two recommendation models: model A and model B. We first create two disjoint random samples of users or "requests" (user visits) and then use model A to serve one sample while model B is used to serve the other for a certain period of time. Here each sample is called a *bucket*. Two types of buckets are commonly used:

1. *User-based bucket*: A bucket is a set of users selected at random. One simple way to assign users to a bucket is to apply a hash function to each user ID and assign users with hash values in a prespecified range into a single bucket. An MD5 hash designed by Ron Rivest is a good example.
2. *Request-based bucket*: In this case, a bucket is a set of requests selected at random. A simple way to create a request-based bucket is to generate a random number for each request and assign requests with random numbers in a prespecified range into the bucket. Note that in such a bucket, different visits by the same user during the experiment may belong to different buckets.

User-based buckets typically provide cleaner separation between buckets than request-based buckets. For example, when request-based buckets are used, a user's response to a request served using model A can be influenced by model B if the user's previous requests were served using model B. This is not the case with user-based buckets. Also, impact on any long-term user behavior due to a model can only be measured with user-based buckets. However, when a poor model is applied to a user-based bucket, the users in the bucket would see inferior results, and this may lead to poor user experience. Request-based buckets are less sensitive to this issue, because it is unlikely that all requests by a user would be assigned to the same bucket. In general, user-based buckets are more preferable.

In controlled experiments, the settings of the buckets should be exactly the same, except for the treatment assigned to each bucket; that is, model A is used to serve one bucket, while model B is used to serve the other. In particular, it is important to ensure that we apply the same selection criterion to the two buckets. For example, if one bucket consists of only logged-in users, the other bucket also needs to do the same.

When user-based buckets are used, it is useful to have "independent" hash functions for different tests to ensure orthogonality. For example, suppose we have two recommendation modules on a web page and each module has two models to be tested. There are two tests that correspond to the two modules: test 1 and test 2. Each test i has two buckets corresponding two recommendation models: A_i and B_i. If we use the same hash function for both tests and assign users with hash values below a threshold to model A_i and the rest to model B_i for both modules, then model A_1 is always used with model A_2 and model B_1 is always used with model B_2; this may lead to invalid comparison between models A_1 and B_1 due to interactions with A_2 and B_2. One way of addressing this issue is to ensure that the probability of a user being assigned to A_1 is independent of the user being assigned to A_2 or B_2 in test 2. This can easily be achieved if the mapping from user IDs to hash values used in test 1 is statistically independent of that used in test 2. Using independent hash functions can also help to control dependencies between current and previous tests.

Another useful practice is to use the same model to serve two buckets and check whether the performance metrics of these buckets are statistically similar. Such tests are commonly referred to as A/A tests. Not only do they provide a good estimate of inherent statistical variability, they also help detect obvious errors in the experimental setup. Yet another useful practice is to run a bucket test for at least one or two weeks because user behavior typically differs by time of day and day of week. Also, when a new recommendation model recommends items that are different from those recommended by the previous model, users may tend to click more aggressively in the initial stages due to the *novelty effect*. To reduce the potential bias caused by this, it is often useful to discard test results from the first few days of a test when monitoring test metrics over time.

Beyond the preceding practical suggestions, standard experimental design methods can be used to determine the required size of a bucket to reach statistical significance. Bootstrap sampling methods are useful in determining the variances of performance metrics, which in turn help in sample size computation for buckets. These methods are out of the scope of this book. We refer interested readers to Montgomery (2012) and Efron and Tibshirani (1993).

4.2.2 Online Performance Metrics

The performance metrics that a recommender system should use depend on the objectives of the application. For most systems, the main objective is to improve user engagement. We describe a number of commonly used engagement metrics in the following:

- *Click-through rate*: The click-through rate (CTR) of a recommendation module is the average number of clicks for each display of the module. This is empirically obtained by dividing the total clicks on the module with the total number of times the module was shown to users. Clicks on module items are usually a good indicator of user interest in the recommended items. However, there are some clicks that are not valuable in measuring user engagement and should be removed. Examples of such clicks include those from software robots and other forms of spam, clicks that bounce back quickly (which usually happens when the content of an item is inconsistent with the description provided on the recommendation module) and clicks on dead links (because users usually click such links multiple times). It is also useful to remove multiple clicks on the same item by the same user, to limit the weight on each (user, item) pair. In this case, the numerator of CTR becomes the number of unique (user, item) pairs for which the user clicked the item.
- *Average number of clicks per user*: Good recommendations usually encourage repeat user visits to the website. This increase in user visit frequency indicates increased user engagement; however, it also increases the denominator of the CTR and may decrease a model's CTR. One way to address this problem is to replace the denominator by the total number of users in the model's bucket. The resulting metric is the average number of clicks per user, that is, the number of clicks divided by the number of users. This metric is more useful for user-based buckets than request-based buckets, because a user can be served via multiple models across visits in request-based buckets.
- *Fraction of clickers*: Some users never click on recommended items. A good model may be able to entice such users to click. A metric that quantifies this aspect is the fraction of clickers, which is the number of users who click on any recommended items in a bucket divided by the total number of users in the bucket.
- *Actions beyond clicks*: Clicks are just one type of positive user action. Some systems provide a list of buttons on each recommended item to allow users to share, like, and comment. Different kinds of action rates, such as share rate, like rate, and comment rate, can be defined in a way similar to CTR. Number of actions per user and fraction of action takers are also similarly defined as in the case of clicks.
- *Time spent*: Beyond actions, the amount of time that a user spends on the site after clicking or taking an action on a recommended item is also a useful engagement metric. However, accurate estimation of time spent can

be difficult. For instance, in a news article recommender system, although it is relatively easy to measure the time between when a user opens an article page and leaves the page, it is difficult to know whether the user was actually reading or left the page open while doing other things.

In typical applications, it is useful to compute all or most of the engagement metrics described earlier to obtain a complete picture of model performance.

4.2.3 Test Result Analysis

Before computing performance metrics, it is good practice to perform some "sanity checks" to verify the validity of experimental setup.

Sanity Checks. Several statistics are expected to be the same across buckets. Checking these statistics can ensure that the buckets were set up correctly. A few useful statistics are described in the following:

- *Histograms of user attributes*: Histograms of user demographics (e.g., age, gender, geographical location, profession), user tenures (i.e., time difference between user registration time and now), user-declared interests, and so on, should have the same distribution across buckets.
- *Impression statistics*: When CTR is used as a main performance metric, it is useful to check if the numbers of times we show the recommendation module (also called the number of impressions) in different equally sized buckets are roughly similar (for unequally sized buckets, we normalize by the bucket size).
- *Numbers of impressions, clicks, and users in a bucket over time*: Such time series plots can show whether the bucket is set up as expected. Time series anomalies in any of these statistics may indicate issues that should be investigated.
- *User visits by frequency*: Distribution of user visits by frequency should be same across buckets; differences can be detected through statistical tests like chi-squared. Any difference may indicate some error in experimental setup or data issues.

Monitoring a system through these metrics is important to have confidence in experimental results, because most end-to-end recommender systems are complex.

Metrics Split by Segments. A single metric that averages over all users during the entire test period may not reveal the complete story when testing a new model online. To better understand the performance of a model, we can compute the metric for different types of segments.

- *Breakdown by user attributes*: When comparing two models, it is useful to check whether one model is consistently better than the other over all or most user segments defined based on some known attributes (e.g., by age, gender, geographical location).
- *Breakdown by user activity levels*: Some classes of models are good at making recommendations for heavy users but may lack the ability to serve light users well. Some other classes of models may provide similar performance for both heavy and light users. It is useful to compute performance metrics over different activity-based user segments to better understand user segments that benefit the most from the model. For instance, one can create such activity-based user segments based on the average number of visits or actions by a user on a monthly basis.
- *Breakdown by time*: Looking at the performance of models over time can reveal if factors like time of day and weekday versus weekend have an impact on model performance. It is also useful in detecting temporal effects like novelty (at the beginning of the experiment) and trends (when running long longitudinal tests).

4.3 Offline Simulation

Online bucket tests are relatively expensive compared to offline tests because they require experimentation with real users, whose experience may be negatively impacted if they are subjected to a poor serving scheme. Hence, it is difficult to simultaneously test many model variations online. Although offline tests are cheaper to run, they may fail to provide accurate estimates of online model performance. We discuss two offline evaluation methods that can help close the gap when certain assumptions are satisfied. We begin by describing the offline simulation method in this section, followed by the offline replay method in Section 4.4.

The basic idea of simulation is to build a *ground-truth model* that can simulate users' response to items in an offline fashion. One could argue that if such a model exists, it should be used to recommend items and that there is no need to evaluate other models. But of course, such a model is difficult to build in practice. Thus, instead of building a simulation model that captures all nuances of user behavior when interacting with items, we select a class of models that are simpler and have the advantage of accessing test data when estimating parameters. The models that are to be evaluated do not have this crucial advantage of being able to see the test data. We illustrate with some examples.

Simulation for Most-popular Recommendation. We start with the simple most-popular recommendation setting as described in Section 3.3.1. Our goal is to select the most-popular item at each time point. Assume that the popularity of an item is measured by the overall positive response rate (e.g., CTR). In this setting, a ground-truth model consists of the following components:

- The response rate p_{jt} of each item j at each time point t. It is typical to create equally spaced time intervals (e.g., bucketing the time line into ten-minute intervals) and let t refer to the tth interval.
- The number n_t of user visits in interval t.
- The set $\mathcal{J}_t$ of candidate items in interval t.

We can usually collect data from the online system to estimate p_{jt}, n_t, and $\mathcal{J}_t$ and treat them as the ground truth for evaluation purposes. Given a data collection period, n_t can be easily estimated by looking at the total number of user visits in interval t, and $\mathcal{J}_t$ is the candidate set of items during that interval. One useful way to collect data to estimate p_{jt} is to create a randomized bucket in which each candidate item has a positive probability of being shown to every user visit in that bucket. Based on data collected from this bucket, we can obtain p_{jt} through time series smoothing or estimation (for details, see Pole et al., 1994). Note that $\{p_{jt}\}_{\forall t}$ is a time series of the response rate of item j. If there are too many items in our pool, it may become difficult to obtain reliable response rate estimates for each item due to small sample sizes. One simple solution that works well in practice for the purpose of evaluation is to restrict the candidate set $\mathcal{J}_t$ by only including the top K items according to some baseline recommendation model. The estimation of $\{p_{jt}\}$ for the ground-truth model can be obtained by using the entire time series, that is, estimate of p_{jt} can be influenced by data both before and after time point t.

To perform simulation, we need to make an assumption about the *ground-truth distribution*. If a model recommends item j to m_{jt} user visits at time t, the number c_{jt} of clicks on this item is generated according to a distribution with mean $p_{jt}m_{jt}$. Two commonly used distributions for c_{jt} are the binomial distribution and the Poisson distribution if we allow a user to click multiple times on an item; that is,

$$\begin{aligned} c_{jt} &\sim \text{Binomial}(\text{probability} = p_{jt},\ \text{size} = m_{jt}) \text{ or} \\ c_{jt} &\sim \text{Poisson}(\text{mean} = p_{jt}m_{jt}). \end{aligned} \tag{4.12}$$

We consider a probabilistic most-popular recommendation model $\mathcal{M}$, which works in the following way: for each time interval t, before the interval begins, it decides a serving plan for the interval, which consists of the fraction x_{jt} of user visits in the interval to be recommended with item j for each candidate item j. The performance metric is the overall response rate of the items recommended by $\mathcal{M}$. To test $\mathcal{M}$, we use the following procedure:

1. For each time interval t, do the following:
   1.1. Use model $\mathcal{M}$ to decide the fraction x_{jt} of user visits to be recommended item $j \in \mathcal{J}_t$ at time t, such that $\sum_j x_{jt} = 1$ and $x_{jt} \geq 0$, for each item j. Let $m_{jt} = n_t x_{jt}$ be the number of user visits to be recommended item j. This decision is based on data observed before time t; that is, $\{(c_{j\tau}, m_{j\tau})\}_{\forall j, \tau < t}$.
   1.2. For each item j, draw the number c_{jt} of clicks from the ground-truth distribution based on p_{jt} and m_{jt}.
2. Compute the response rate of model $\mathcal{M}$ as $(\sum_t \sum_j c_{jt})/(\sum_t n_t)$.

Simulation for Segmented Most-popular Recommendation. A simple extension of most-popular recommendation is obtained by partitioning users into different segments. Given fixed segments (we do not seek to compare different ways of segmenting users), we can evaluate a model for segmented most-popular recommendation in a way similar to the method for nonsegmented most-popular recommendation. Let $\mathcal{U}$ denote the set of user segments; p_{ujt} and n_{ut} denote the CTR of item j for users in segment $u \in \mathcal{U}$ at time t and the number of user visits in segment u at time t, respectively. The segments cannot be too fine grained; otherwise, estimates of p_{ujt} and n_{ut} will be too noisy and unsuitable to be treated as the ground truth.

Given a set $\mathcal{U}$ of user segments, to test a segmented most-popular recommendation model $\mathcal{M}_s$, we use the following procedure:

1. For each time interval t, do the following:
   1.1. Use model $\mathcal{M}_s$ to decide the fraction x_{ujt} of user visits in segment u to be recommended item $j \in \mathcal{J}_t$ at time t, such that $\sum_j x_{ujt} = 1$, for all u. This decision is based on data observed before time t; that is, $\{(c_{uj\tau}, m_{uj\tau})\}_{\forall u, j, \tau < t}$, where $c_{uj\tau}$ denotes the number of clicks and $m_{ujt} = n_{ut} x_{jt}$.
   1.2. Draw the number c_{ujt} of clicks from the ground-truth distribution based on p_{ujt} and m_{ujt}.
2. Compute the response rate of model $\mathcal{M}_s$ as $(\sum_u \sum_t \sum_j c_{ujt})/(\sum_u \sum_t n_{ut})$.

For simple problem settings, simulation is a useful method to compare models. However, when the problem setting becomes complex (e.g., how to create good user segments, how to decide whether factorization is better than similarity-based models), it is difficult to obtain a good ground-truth model. More precisely, when comparing different classes of models, the choice of the ground-truth model is likely to cause a bias because it favors recommendation models similar to the chosen ground-truth model.

4.4 Offline Replay

In this section, we address the issue of conducting offline evaluation for general problem settings by "replaying" historical recommendations on logged data. We begin with a simplified setting in Section 4.4.1, where we only recommend a single item from a fixed set of items to each user visit, and then we discuss how to handle other scenarios in Section 4.4.2. We use "reward" to refer to the performance metric that we want to maximize. For instance, a click or some positive action on an item is a reward. In some cases, a positive action like a click can be weighted by some downstream utility like advertising revenue or time spent on the landing page (the page that provides detailed information about the item and is shown after a user clicks the recommended item) to obtain a weighted click reward. Our goal is to estimate the expected reward of a new recommendation model using data collected in the past.

4.4.1 Basic Replay Estimator

Consider a scenario where we recommend a single item for each user visit from a fixed item pool. We let $\boldsymbol{x}$ denote all the information available at the time when we make a recommendation. In particular, $\boldsymbol{x}$ includes

- the user ID and associated user features
- a set of candidate items, their IDs, and their features
- context features, for example, display format, layout, time of day, day of week

Let $\boldsymbol{r}$ denote a vector of reward values, where $r[j]$ is the reward if item j is recommended. Let $\mathcal{P}$ denote the joint probability distribution of $(\boldsymbol{x}, \boldsymbol{r})$. Our goal is to estimate the expected reward of a new recommendation model h, which is a function $h(\boldsymbol{x})$ that returns one item from a fixed candidate set of items based on $\boldsymbol{x}$. The function h could depend on features and may also include some randomization. For instance, h may select an item uniformly at random from the item pool with probability ϵ, and with probability $(1-\epsilon)$ it selects the item with the highest response rate estimated through a regression model. The expected reward is given by

$$E_{(\boldsymbol{x},\boldsymbol{r})\sim\mathcal{P}}\left[\sum_j r[j]\cdot \Pr(h(\boldsymbol{x})=j\mid \boldsymbol{x})\right], \tag{4.13}$$

where $E_{(\boldsymbol{x},\boldsymbol{r})\sim\mathcal{P}}$ denotes expectation taken over the joint distribution $\mathcal{P}$ of $(\boldsymbol{x},\boldsymbol{r})$ and $\Pr(h(\boldsymbol{x})=j\mid\boldsymbol{x})$ is the conditional probability that model h selects item j given features $\boldsymbol{x}$. To estimate the expected reward, we log past user-item interactions with their associated rewards. These logged data are obtained through a historical serving model s, which is a function $s(\boldsymbol{x})$ that returns one item from a fixed candidate set of items based on $\boldsymbol{x}$. Different from Section 4.3, where t is used to index time intervals, we now use t to index each individual user visit. Let $\boldsymbol{x}_t$ denote the features of the tth logged user visit. Let $i_t=s(\boldsymbol{x}_t)$ denote the item selected by the historical serving model s for the tth logged user visit. Then, the logged data have the following form:

$$\boldsymbol{D}=\{(\boldsymbol{x}_t,\ i_t,\ r_t[i_t])\}_{t=1}^{T}, \tag{4.14}$$

where T denotes the total number of logged user visits. Note that we only observe a single element of the reward vector $\boldsymbol{r}_t$ for each user visit t in the logged data, which is the reward of the item i_t returned from $s(\boldsymbol{x}_t)$.

Now, consider the following replay procedure to evaluate the new recommendation function h:

1. For $t=1$ to T, we obtain the record $(\boldsymbol{x}_t,\ i_t,\ r_t[i_t])$ and do the following:
   1.1. Use h to select a candidate item. Let j_t denote the selected item; that is, $j_t=h(\boldsymbol{x}_t)$.
   1.2. If $j_t=i_t$, we count reward $r_t[i_t]\cdot w_{jt}$, where w_{jt} is the weight for this record, which will be determined later.
   1.3. If $j_t\neq i_t$, we ignore this record.
2. Return the sum of all the accrued rewards divided by T.

We call the output of this procedure the *replay estimator*:

$$\frac{1}{T}\sum_{t=1}^{T}\sum_j r_t[j]\cdot \mathbf{1}\{h(\boldsymbol{x}_t)=j \text{ and } s(\boldsymbol{x}_t)=j\}\cdot w_{jt}, \tag{4.15}$$

where $\mathbf{1}\{X\}$ returns 1 if statement X is true, and 0 otherwise, and w_{jt} are importance weights (to be determined) of item j for the tth user visit. Notice that

$$(h(\boldsymbol{x}_t) = j \text{ and } s(\boldsymbol{x}_t) = j) \iff j_t = i_t. \tag{4.16}$$

Unbiased Estimator of Expected Reward. We now determine importance weights w_{jt} for the replay estimator to obtain an unbiased estimator for the expected reward. Assume the logged data $\{(\boldsymbol{x}_t, \boldsymbol{r}_t)\}_{\forall t}$ consist of *iid* samples of $(\boldsymbol{x}, \boldsymbol{r})$ from $\mathcal{P}$.

The expectation of the replay estimator is

$$\frac{1}{T}\sum_{t=1}^{T} E_{(\boldsymbol{x}_t,\boldsymbol{r}_t)}\left[\sum_j r_t[j]\cdot \Pr(h(\boldsymbol{x}_t) = j \text{ and } s(\boldsymbol{x}_t) = j \mid \boldsymbol{x}_t)\cdot w_{jt}\right].$$

If we set

$$w_{jt} = \frac{1}{\Pr(s(\boldsymbol{x}_t) = j \mid h(\boldsymbol{x}_t) = j,\ \boldsymbol{x}_t)}, \tag{4.17}$$

then by the definition of conditional probability, the expectation of the replay estimator becomes

$$\frac{1}{T}\sum_{t=1}^{T} E_{(\boldsymbol{x}_t,\boldsymbol{r}_t)}\left[\sum_j r_t[j]\cdot \Pr(h(\boldsymbol{x}_t) = j \mid \boldsymbol{x}_t)\right],$$

which is exactly the expected reward, because $(\boldsymbol{x}_t, \boldsymbol{r}_t)$ is *iid* as $(\boldsymbol{x}, \boldsymbol{r})$.

In Equation (4.17), the probability is defined over stochastic functions h and s conditioned on $\boldsymbol{x}_t$. In practice, the randomization of these two functions (i.e., the new recommendation model and the historical serving model) is generated based on independent random seeds and can be treated as independent. Thus, we can simply set

$$w_{jt} = \frac{1}{\Pr(s(\boldsymbol{x}_t) = j \mid \boldsymbol{x}_t)}. \tag{4.18}$$

To see this independence, we rewrite $h(\boldsymbol{x}_t)$ as $h^*(\boldsymbol{x}_t, \xi_t)$ and $s(\boldsymbol{x}_t)$ as $s^*(\boldsymbol{x}_t, \eta_t)$, where h^* and s^* are deterministic functions and ξ_t and η_t are the random seeds. By definition, as long as ξ_t and η_t are independent given $\boldsymbol{x}_t$, $h(\boldsymbol{x}_t)$ and $s(\boldsymbol{x}_t)$ are independent given $\boldsymbol{x}_t$.

The new recommendation model h can be a deterministic function but the historical serving model s cannot be. In particular, for each user visit t and each item j, the historical serving model s must have a nonzero probability of selecting item j; otherwise, the importance weight w_{jt} will be undefined. A simple choice of the historical serving model s is to pick an item uniformly at random from the item pool for each user visit. This can be done for a small bucket of users to minimize the potential negative impact on users. For such a historical serving model, the replay estimator has a simple interpretation – it is the precision at rank 1 on historical logged data obtained through uniform randomization. The uniform randomization across the item pool and user visits facilitates the comprehensive evaluation of any new recommendation model h in different scenarios in a reliable fashion.

The basic replay estimator can be used to evaluate online learning and explore-exploit methods, where $h(\boldsymbol{x}_t)$ depends on the rewards obtained from previously selected items by h. However, it has a few limitations. Because the replay method only uses the rewards when $h(\boldsymbol{x}_t) = s(\boldsymbol{x}_t)$, it can only estimate the expected reward for online learning and explore-exploit methods with a reduced traffic volume. The traffic volume (in number of user visits per unit time) is reduced to the original volume times the probability that $h(\boldsymbol{x}_t) = s(\boldsymbol{x}_t)$. Also, when the set of candidate items is large, the probability that $h(\boldsymbol{x}_t) = s(\boldsymbol{x}_t)$ will be small, hence the variance of the estimator will be large.

4.4.2 Extensions of Replay

The basic replay estimator is an unbiased estimator of the expected reward for evaluating a recommender system that recommends a single item for each user visit from a fixed set of candidates, where the reward distribution of each item does not change over time. We now discuss how to extend to more general settings.

Varying Item Pools Across User Visits. Consider an application scenario where each user visit may have a different item pool. For example, in a recommender system like Facebook/LinkedIn Newsfeed that recommends a user the status updates and shares from his or her friends, every user is likely to have a different item pool due to differences in their friend circles. In some applications that recommend time-sensitive items, such as news, the lifetimes of items are short and the item pool changes frequently over time.

Let $\mathcal{J}_\tau(\boldsymbol{x})$ denote the set of candidate items at time τ for a user visit with features $\boldsymbol{x}$. Let $\mathcal{D}$ denote the distribution of τ and $\mathcal{P}_\tau$ denote the distribution of $(\boldsymbol{x}, \boldsymbol{r})$ at time τ. We assume that $\mathcal{P}_\tau$ does not change rapidly over time. The expected reward in this case is

$$E_{\tau\sim D}\, E_{(\boldsymbol{x},\boldsymbol{r})\sim\mathcal{P}_\tau} \left[\sum_{j\in\mathcal{J}_\tau(\boldsymbol{x})} r[j] \cdot \Pr(h(\boldsymbol{x}) = j,\ | \boldsymbol{x}) \right] \tag{4.19}$$

Then, the replay estimator for this setting is

$$\frac{1}{T}\sum_{t=1}^{T}\sum_{j\in\mathcal{J}_t(\boldsymbol{x}_t)} r_t[j]\cdot\mathbf{1}\{h(\boldsymbol{x}_t)=j \text{ and } s(\boldsymbol{x}_t)=j\}\cdot w_{jt}, \tag{4.20}$$

which is unbiased.

Multiple Slots. In some application scenarios, we have more than one slot to display recommended items for each user visit. Assume there are K_t slots to display recommendations for user visit t. Let $r_t^{(k)}[j]$ denote the reward of item j displayed at slot k for user visit t. Let $h_k(\boldsymbol{x}_t)$ denote the item that model h recommends at slot k and $s_k(\boldsymbol{x}_t)$ denote the item that the historical serving model s displayed at slot k. Then, a useful replay estimator for this setting is

$$\frac{1}{T}\sum_{t=1}^{T}\sum_{k=1}^{K_t}\sum_{j\in\mathcal{J}_t(\boldsymbol{x}_t)} r_t^{(k)}[j]\cdot\mathbf{1}\{h_k(\boldsymbol{x}_t)=j \text{ and } s_k(\boldsymbol{x}_t)=j\}\cdot w_{jt}^{(k)}. \tag{4.21}$$

This estimator assumes that the reward of an item at a slot is independent of the items shown concurrently at other slots. This may not be true in practice for many applications. For instance, in a news recommender system, recommending a news story in politics with two other political news stories may reduce the reward. In general, this is not an unbiased estimator. Obtaining an unbiased replay metric for multiple slot recommendation with a large item pool, in the presence of dependencies in ranking, is still an open research problem.

4.5 Summary

Evaluation is an important component in the development process of a recommender system. Before we deploy a new recommendation model to serve real users, it is useful to conduct offline evaluation to ensure the new model does not have obvious problems and also to understand what to expect. Unbiased offline evaluation that accurately predicts the model performance on real users after deployment can be difficult. Fortunately, if we can collect data in a controlled, randomized manner, the offline replay method can be used to produce unbiased estimates of model performance for some simplified settings (e.g., recommending a single item for each user visit from a relatively small set of candidate items). Unbiased offline evaluation for general settings is still an open problem.

After we deploy a new recommendation model to serve real users, we should conduct online evaluation to verify model performance. Treatment (new model) and control (baseline) buckets need to be set up properly to ensure correct comparison. It is also useful to consider metrics by using different ways of segmenting the users or data records, to obtain a more detailed understanding of model behavior.

Good recommender systems are usually obtained by continuous model improvements. Continuous model improvements require sufficient attention to model evaluation and careful choice and implementation of appropriate evaluation methods and metrics.

Exercise

1. Given a time series $\{(c_t, n_t) : t = 1, \ldots, T\}$ of clicks and views on an item, suggest methods to estimate the time series of CTR $\{p_t\}$. Is there an advantage of using methods that also provide an estimate of uncertainty in the estimates ? If so, indicate the strategy you would use to modify the simulation method when both mean and uncertainty estimates for the ground-truth model are available.

PART II

Common Problem Settings

5

Problem Settings and System Architecture

Recommender systems have to select items for users to optimize for one or more objectives. We introduced several possible objectives in Chapter 1, reviewed classical methods in Chapter 2, described the explore-exploit trade-off and the key ideas to reduce dimensionality of the problem in Chapter 3, and discussed how to evaluate recommendation models in Chapter 4. In this and the five subsequent chapters of the book, we discuss various statistical methods used in some commonly encountered scenarios. In particular, we focus on problem settings where the main objective is to maximize some positive user response to the recommended items. In many application scenarios, clicks on items are the primary response. To maximize clicks, we have to recommend items with high click-through rates (CTRs). Thus, CTR estimation is our main focus. Although we use click and CTR as our primary objectives, other types of positive response (e.g., share, like) can be handled in a similar way. We defer the discussion of multiobjective optimization to Chapter 11.

The choice of statistical methods for a recommendation problem depends on the application. In this chapter, we provide a high-level overview of techniques to be introduced in the next four chapters. We start with an introduction to a variety of different problem settings in Section 5.1 and then describe an example system architecture in Section 5.2 to illustrate how web recommender systems work in practice, along with the role of statistical methods in such systems.

5.1 Problem Settings

A typical recommender system is usually implemented as a *module* on a web page. In this section, we introduce some common recommendation modules, provide details of the application settings, and conclude with a discussion of commonly used statistical methods for these settings.

Table 5.1. *Websites and recommendation modules*

Website category	Examples	Typical recommendation modules	
General portals	www.yahoo.com www.msn.com www.aol.com	Home page	Featured module (FM: general and domain specific)
Personal portals	my.yahoo.com igoogle.com	Home page	Featured module (FM: personalized)
Domain-specific sites	sport.yahoo.com	Home page	Featured module (FM: domain specific)
	money.msn.com music.aol.com	Detail page	Related content module (RM)
Social network sites	facebook.com	Home page	Network update module (NM)
	linkedin.com twitter.com	Detail page	Related content module (RM)

Note: Following Agarwal et al. (2013).

5.1.1 Common Recommendation Modules

We classify websites into the following four categories: general portals, personal portals, domain-specific sites, and social network sites. Table 5.1 provides a summary.

General portals are websites that provide a wide range of different content. The home pages of content networks like Yahoo!, MSN, and AOL are examples of general portals.

Personal portals are websites that allow users to customize their home pages with desired content. For example, users of My Yahoo! customize their home pages by selecting content feeds from different sources or publishers and arranging the feeds on the pages according to their preferences.

Domain-specific sites are websites that provide content from a specific domain, for example, sports, finance, music, or movies. At a very high level, there are two kinds of pages on a domain-specific site: a home page that provides the highlights of the site and many detail pages that provide detailed content. Examples of detail pages include article pages, movie pages, and product pages.

Social network sites are websites that allow users to connect to one another and disseminate information through their networks. LinkedIn, Facebook, and Twitter are examples of such sites. As we did for domain-specific sites, we distinguish two kinds of pages, in this case, a personal home page for each user

Figure 5.1. Today Module (general FM) on the Yahoo! home page.

that summarizes all the information about the user's interests (usually updates from other users connected to that user) and many detail pages that provide detailed content for individual entities (e.g., users, companies, articles).

Recommendation modules on these websites broadly fall into three categories: featured modules, network-update modules, and related-content modules.

Featured modules (FMs) recommend interesting or "featured" recent content to users. The Today Module on the Yahoo! home page shown in Figure 5.1 is an example of a *general* FM. Such FMs show heterogeneous content with links to items hosted across the content network (e.g., sports, finance) and serve as a distribution channel sending users to different domain-specific sites in the content network. General portals also have a set of *domain-specific* FMs that only recommend items from specific domains. Figure 5.2 shows three domain-specific FMs for news, sports, and entertainment on MSN. On personal portals,

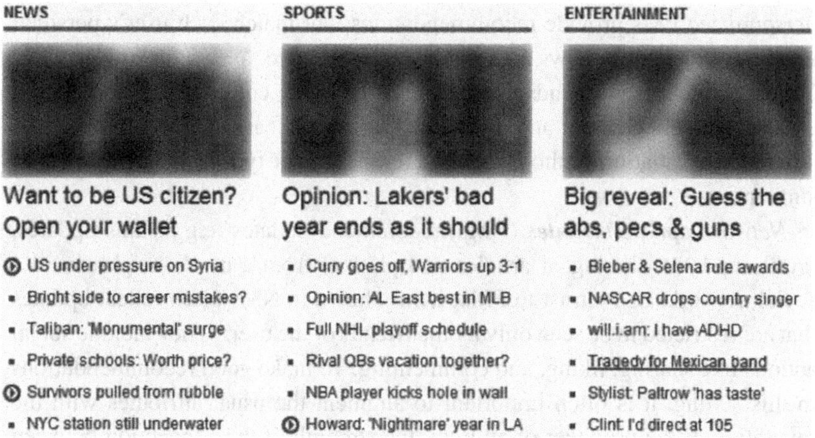

Figure 5.2. Domain-specific FMs on MSN.

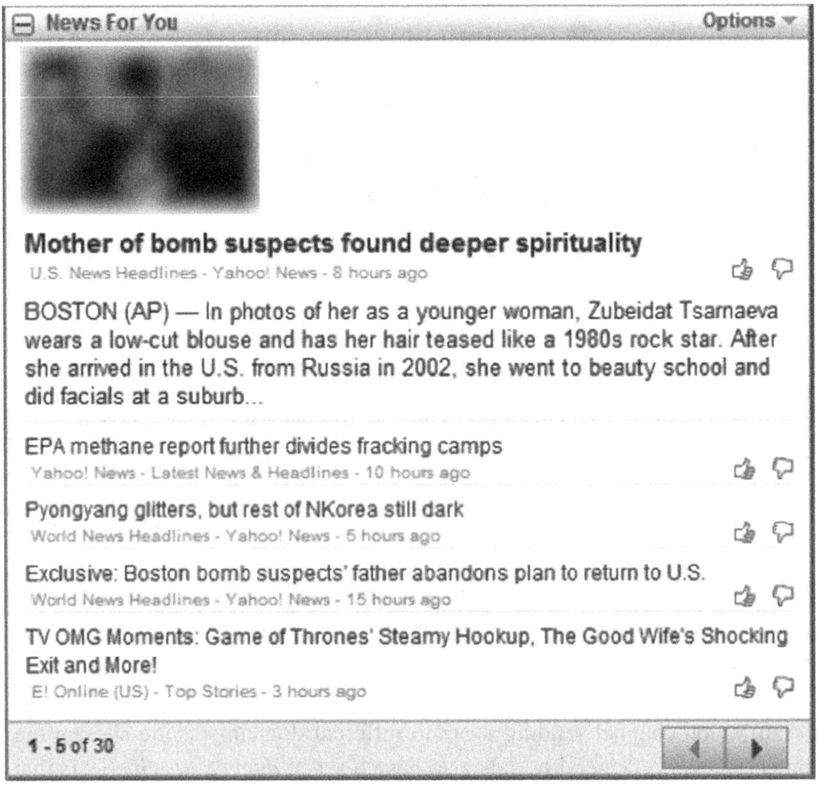

Figure 5.3. News-for-You module (personalized FM) on My Yahoo!

personalized FMs provide recommendations that match each user's personal interests. Figure 5.3 shows a personalized FM called "News for You" on My Yahoo!, which recommends content items from the content feeds to which a user subscribes. General and domain-specific FMs can also be personalized. The recommendation methods required for these three types of FMs have strong similarities.

Network-update modules (NMs) recommend updates (e.g., status updates, profile updates, sharing of articles and photos) from a user's neighbors in a social network. In contrast to FMs, items shown in NMs often reflect updates that are restricted to be seen only by the friends of the user.[1] They include social actions like sharing, liking, and commenting. To make good recommendations in this setting, it is often important to augment the usual attributes with the reputation of the producer of an item, the strength of the connection between the producer and the recipient, and the nature of the social actions involved.

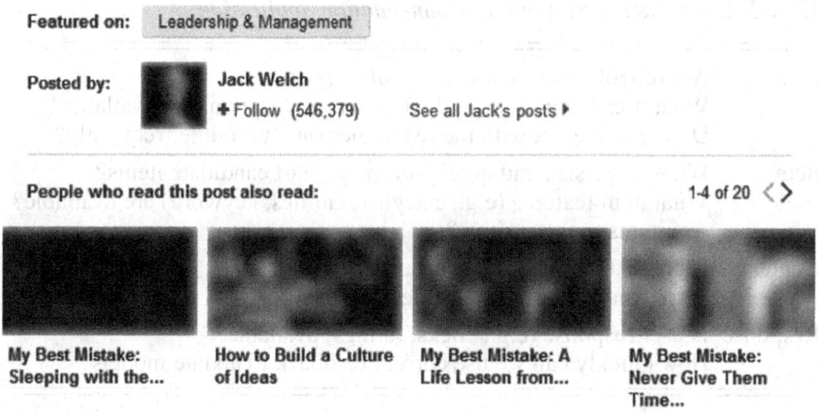

Figure 5.4. Related-content module on LinkedIn.

Related-content modules (RMs) usually appear on a detail page and recommend items "related" to the primary content (e.g., an article) of the detail page. In contrast to FMs and NMs, a RM has an additional piece of information: the context. The detail page provides the context, and the recommendations must be relevant to that context. Figure 5.4 shows an example RM on LinkedIn published on the article page "The Six Deadly Sins of Leadership" posted by Jack Welch, a well-recognized thought leader in leadership and management. Good recommendations are usually made by leveraging users' coviewing behavior (e.g., users who read item A also read item B), semantic relevance, item popularity, and how closely an item matches the user's personal interests.

5.1.2 Application Settings

To choose an appropriate recommendation method for an application, we need to consider the characteristics of the application. A set of typical questions used to characterize a recommendation application is summarized in Table 5.2.

User-related Characteristics. The ability to provide personalized recommendations depends on whether reliable user identifiers are available. Personalized portal and social network sites usually require users to log in to consume content and thus obtain reliable user identifiers. General and domain-specific portals usually do not require users to log in and may not have reliable user identifiers. Browser cookies (bcookies) can be used to keep track of users and provide identifiers for users who do not log in. More precisely, bcookies are identifiers for web browsers, instead of users. Thus, bcookies can only serve as

Table 5.2. *Characteristics of a recommendation application*

User	Are reliable user identifiers available? What user features (e.g., demographics, location) are available? Do users interact with the recommendation module frequently?
Item	What is the size and quality of the pool of candidate items? What item features (e.g., category, entities, keyword) are available? Are items time sensitive?
Context	Is contextual information available? If so, what features of a context are available?
Response	Is user response (e.g., clicks, ratings) available? How quickly can we use current feedback to update models?

noisy identifiers because multiple users can use the same browser, a user can use multiple browsers, and bcookies can also be cleared by users. After we are able to identify users, we look at what user features are available and whether users frequently interact with the recommendation module. When user features are available, we can use them to predict user response. However, when user features are not available, we can still personalize recommendations for *heavy* users through collaborative filtering methods. Also, not all recommendation modules require personalization. For example, FMs on general and domain-specific portals may not need to be deeply personalized.

Item-related Characteristics. The choice of a recommendation method depends on the size and quality of the item pool. Ranking a small set of high-quality items requires different considerations than ranking a large set of low-quality items. Whereas the challenge in the former scenario is to quickly and accurately estimate the CTR of each item through efficient explore-exploit methods without incurring significant opportunity cost, the latter requires removal of low-quality items before we even observe any user response. Also, when the item pool is small and the user visit volume is large, item features are not very important, because we may have sufficient user response data for each item to accurately estimate the CTRs of items. When the item pool is large, we can reduce the exploration cost by using good item features to set up an informative prior for each item. Another important consideration is whether items are time sensitive. For example, news articles are ephemeral and become obsolete in a day or two, whereas educational articles written by luminaries in the field are evergreen and may not depend much on article age. Users' response rates for different kinds of items may also change over time. Hence it is often important to keep track of changes through online models that update parameters frequently.

Context-related Characteristics. Some recommendation applications like RMs on an article detail page require the recommended items to be relevant to an explicit context (e.g., the article on the page), whereas others, such as FMs, do not. However, even for applications without an explicit context, there are implicit contexts like time of day, weekday versus weekend, and mobile device versus desktop computer. When context information is available, recommendation problems extend from modeling response in a user-by-item matrix to modeling response in a three-dimensional tensor spanned by user, item, and context. We discuss this in Chapter 10.

Response-related Characteristics. An important assumption we make in this book is the availability of some user response for modeling. However, we may not have any past responses from some users and for some items. Also, availability of a one-time snapshot of user response for modeling versus availability of continuous stream of user response in real time makes a significant difference to modeling. The latter is an essential requirement for recommending time-sensitive items. Applicability of explore-exploit schemes also depends on the supply of continuous user response data in near–real time. Another consideration is the interpretation of user response when users provide multiple types of feedback (e.g., click, share, like, comment). The choice of the response model (see Section 2.3.2) depends on how we interpret user response. Multivariate response modeling is useful when users generate responses of multiple types.

5.1.3 Common Statistical Methods

In the next four chapters, we focus on three kinds of statistical methods – offline models, online models, and explore-exploit schemes. We consider these methods for the following three common application settings.

Most-popular Recommendation. We have discussed this type of recommendation in Sections 1.2 and 3.3.1. The goal is to quickly identify the items that have the highest CTR and recommend them to all users. We assume that items are time sensitive and user response is available in near–real time. We begin with methods that estimate popularity (i.e., CTR) for a small pool of high-quality items through explore-exploit schemes and then extend the methods to tackle a large item pool by modeling the prior distribution of each item through item features. Light personalization can be achieved within this class of methods through segmented most-popular recommendation. This is achieved by segmenting the user population into subpopulations and estimating item popularity separately for each segment, as discussed in Section 3.3.2. Although conceptually simple, most-popular recommendation is often a useful method for FMs on general or domain-specific portals and provides a strong baseline for more sophisticated modeling techniques. We introduce the following statistical methods for most-popular recommendation in Chapter 6:

Online models: Dynamic Beta-binomial and Gamma-Poisson models to track the CTR of items over time

Offline models: Maximum likelihood estimation of prior parameters used in the Beta-binomial and Gamma-Poisson models to initialize online models for estimating the CTR of new items through item features

Explore-exploit: A variety of multiarmed bandit schemes to achieve a good explore-exploit trade-off with a special focus on an approximate Bayes optimal solution obtained through Lagrange relaxation

Personalized Recommendation. The goal is to achieve deeper personalization by accurately predicting how each individual user would respond to a particular item. We assume some user identifier is available. Some of the methods we consider could also work when the only available information about users is their features. We will start out with offline models that do not address time sensitivity. The main issue here is how to simultaneously model users or items with a large number of past responses as well as those with few or no past responses. We then extend to online models for time-sensitive items. Personalized recommendation can be applied to a wide range of application settings, including FMs and NMs, on most websites. We introduce the following statistical methods in Chapters 7 and 8:

Offline models: Matrix factorization (which gives state-of-the-art performance in many application settings) with flexible regression priors that use features to predict user and item latent factors in cold-start situations

Online models: Reduced-rank regression to reduce dimensionality for faster model convergence, and Bayesian state-space models to incrementally update regression models by leveraging most recent response data

Explore-exploit: Thompson sampling, upper confidence bound (UCB) methods, and soft max

Context-dependent Recommendation. The goal is to accurately predict CTR in a three-dimensional tensor spanned by user, item, and context; that is, how a user would respond to an item when the user is in a given context (e.g., an article page to which the recommended items are supposed to be related). We assume that features of the context and the item are available and that different kinds of similarity and relatedness can be measured through the features.

Context-dependent recommendation is useful for building RMs on the detail pages of most websites. One of the main modeling challenges is extreme sparsity of observed user response in the three-dimensional tensor. We focus on offline models, such as tensor factorization with regression priors and hierarchical smoothing to address the sparsity issue, in Chapter 10. Online models and explore-exploit schemes are similar to those introduced in personalized recommendation.

5.2 System Architecture

Before we dive deeper into the statistical methods, it is useful to understand how they interact with web systems. In this section, we first describe the main components of typical web recommender systems and then describe a concrete example system for personalized recommendation of time-sensitive items.

5.2.1 Main Components

Figure 5.5 shows the architecture of a typical web recommender system. There are four main components:

1. *Recommendation service*: This service takes recommendation requests from a web server and returns the recommended items.
2. *Storage systems*: These systems store user features (and latent factors), item features (and factors), and model parameters and also index items for efficient retrieval.
3. *Offline learner*: This component learns model parameters (and latent factors) from user response data and pushes the parameters (and factors) to online storage systems periodically (e.g., daily). Because learning is usually a time-consuming process, especially when the number user response data are large, this component is usually in an offline environment separate from the online systems that serve user requests with subsecond latency.
4. *Online learner*: This component continuously updates some model parameters in real time to adjust the models using the most recent user response data.

5.2.2 Example System

We make the discussion concrete by way of an extended example.

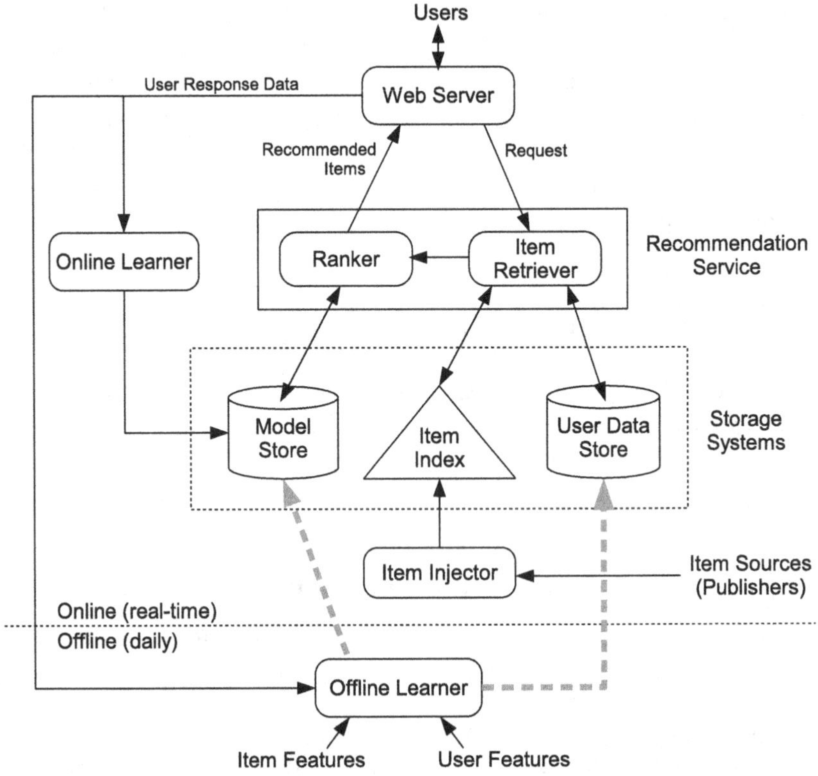

Figure 5.5. Architecture of a typical web recommender system.

Application Setting. Consider the problem of building a personalized recommendation service for a FM on a portal for time-sensitive items (e.g., news articles). The pool of candidate items changes over time and may consist of a large number of candidate items at any given point. User features are available from profile data (e.g., demographics, declared interests). Whereas item features (e.g., bag of words) are extracted from items. Assume user response data are continuously collected with latency of at most a few minutes in most cases and that our goal is to maximize the number of clicks on the recommended items.

Model. We consider the following model for CTR prediction. Let $\boldsymbol{x}_i$ denote the feature vector of user i and $\boldsymbol{x}_j$ denote the feature vector of item j, where $\boldsymbol{x}_i$ and $\boldsymbol{x}_j$ may include different features and have different lengths. Let $\boldsymbol{u}_i$ denote the latent factor vector of user i and $\boldsymbol{v}_j$ denote the latent factor vector of item j, both to be learned from data. We predict the CTR when user i interacts with item j by $1/(1+\exp(-s_{ij}))$, as in the logistic response model, where the score s_{ij} is

$$s_{ij} = \boldsymbol{x}_i' \boldsymbol{A} \boldsymbol{x}_j + \boldsymbol{u}_i' \boldsymbol{v}_j. \tag{5.1}$$

$\boldsymbol{A}$ is a regression coefficient matrix (for interactions between each pair of a user feature and an item feature), to be learned from data. We assume that it is acceptable to update $\boldsymbol{A}$ and $\boldsymbol{u}_i$ daily because regression coefficients do not change significantly over time and user interests usually do not change much within a day. However, because items are time sensitive, it is important to update $\boldsymbol{v}_j$ as soon as new user response data become available.

Storage Systems. Candidate items, features, and models are stored in the storage systems.

- *Item index*: In this example, an item injector service monitors a number of item sources (e.g., publishers) for new items. When a new item j becomes available, the item injector extracts item features $\boldsymbol{x}_j$ and puts the item and its features into the item index to support fast retrieval of items by features. For an example of such an item index, see Fontoura et al. (2011).
- *User data store*: User features $\boldsymbol{x}_i$ are stored in a user data store, which is a key-value store (e.g., a Voldemort[2] store) designed to support fast retrieval of values (i.e., user features) by a given key (i.e., user ID). Because user latent factors $\boldsymbol{u}_i$ are also keyed by the user ID, they are also stored in the user data store.
- *Model store*: The regression coefficient matrix $\boldsymbol{A}$ is stored in a model store and updated daily by the offline learner. We also store item factors $\boldsymbol{v}_j$ in the model store because they are the model parameters of online models that are continuously updated by the online learner. The model store is also a key-value store. Item factors are keyed by item IDs, and a special key is reserved for storing the regression coefficient matrix.

Offline Learner. Given user and item features ($\boldsymbol{x}_i$ and $\boldsymbol{x}_j$) and user response data, the offline learner estimates model parameters and latent factors (A, $\boldsymbol{u}_i$ and $\boldsymbol{v}_j$) from the data that are collected from web server logs. Offline learning can easily take several hours. In this example, we execute the offline learning process once a day and push the learned model parameters and factors to the corresponding online storage systems daily. When the user response data are numerous, a parallel computation infrastructure is usually required. MapReduce is a common choice for many web applications, and Hadoop[3] is a popular and widely used open-source implementation.

Online Learner. Given user and item features $\boldsymbol{x}_i$ and $\boldsymbol{x}_j$, user factors $\boldsymbol{u}_i$, the regression coefficient matrix $\boldsymbol{A}$, and a continuous stream of user response data coming from web server logs in real time, the online learner updates item factors $\boldsymbol{v}_j$ continuously to keep track of the most recent behavior of each item. When $\boldsymbol{x}_i$, $\boldsymbol{x}_j$, $\boldsymbol{A}$, and $\boldsymbol{u}_i$ are given, this learning problem reduces to estimating a large number of independent regression problems, one for each item j. Each regression estimates the coefficient vector $\boldsymbol{v}_j$ by treating $\boldsymbol{u}_i$ as the feature vector and $\boldsymbol{x}_i'\boldsymbol{A}\boldsymbol{x}_j$ as the offset (a constant to be added to the bias or intercept term of the regression model). More details can be found in Chapters 7 and 8. Here we note that because the item-specific regression models are independent of one another and the number of user response data for an individual item is relatively small, item factors can be learned much more quickly than the offline learning process.

Synchronization between Offline and Online Learners. It is important to note offline learning takes time. When the offline learner finishes its daily job and pushes the newly learned $\boldsymbol{A}$, $\boldsymbol{u}_i$, and $\boldsymbol{v}_j$ to the storage systems, the item factors $\boldsymbol{v}_j$ learned offline may not be up to date because the data collected after the start time of offline learning have not yet been used to estimate $\boldsymbol{v}_j$. To ensure a smooth model transition during the time around the push of offline models, we can keep two versions of model parameters $\boldsymbol{A}$, $\boldsymbol{u}_i$, and $\boldsymbol{v}_j$. After the push, we still use the old version of model parameters to serve users and keep updating the old version of parameters until the new version is ready. Once the new version of $\boldsymbol{A}$, $\boldsymbol{u}_i$, and $\boldsymbol{v}_j$ (learned offline) is pushed to the storage systems, we start to update the new version of item factors $\boldsymbol{v}_j$ online using the data that have not yet been used in offline learning. Once the new version of $\boldsymbol{v}_j$ incorporates all of the online data, we switch to using the new version to serve users and stop updating the old version of $\boldsymbol{v}_j$ online.

Recommendation Service. Once features, factors, and models are put in the storage systems and updated, the recommendation service works as follows.

- *Item retrieval*: For each request, the item retriever uses the user ID i to query the user data store, to obtain the user feature vector $\boldsymbol{x}_i$ and latent factor vector $\boldsymbol{u}_i$. Based on user features, the item retriever queries the item index to obtain a set of candidate items for the user. If needed, we can reduce computation by limiting to the top-k candidate items returned from the index by using some simple criteria or model. Then, the candidate items, together with user features and factors, are sent to the ranker.

- *Ranking*: On receiving the candidate items for user i, the ranker computes the mean and variance of the predicted response rate for each item j. The mean is some monotone function of $\boldsymbol{x}_i'\boldsymbol{A}\boldsymbol{x}_j + \boldsymbol{u}_i'\boldsymbol{v}_j$; the variance computation is introduced in Chapter 7. Finally, an explore-exploit scheme based on the means and/or variances of the response rates of all candidate items is applied to avoid item starvation and ensure rapid convergence to best items for users.

6

Most-Popular Recommendation

In Chapter 3, we provided a theoretical overview of the explore-exploit problem and its importance in scoring items for recommender systems, in particular, the connection to the classical multiarmed bandit (MAB) problem. We discussed the Bayesian and the minimax approaches to the MAB problem, including some popular heuristics that are used in practice. However, several additional nuances that arise in recommender systems violate assumptions made in the MAB problem. These include dynamic item pool, nonstationary CTR, and delay in feedback. This chapter develops new solutions that work well in practice.

For many recommender systems, it is appropriate to score items based on some positive action rate, such as click probabilities (CTR). Such an approach maximizes the total number of actions on recommended items. A simple approach that is often used in practice is to recommend the top-k items with the highest CTR. We shall refer to this as the most-popular recommendation approach, where popularity is measured through item-specific CTR. Although conceptually simple, the most-popular approach is technically nontrivial because the CTR of items have to be estimated. It also serves as a good baseline for applications where nonpersonalized recommendation is an acceptable solution. Hence we begin in this chapter by developing explore-exploit solutions for the most-popular recommendation problem.

In Section 6.1, we introduce an example application and show the characteristics of most-popular recommendation in this real-life application. We then mathematically define the explore-exploit problem for most-popular recommendation in Section 6.2 and develop a Bayesian solution from first principles in Section 6.3. A number of popular non-Bayesian solutions are reviewed in Section 6.4. Through a series of extensive experiments in Section 6.5, we show that, when the system can be properly modeled using a Bayesian framework, the Bayesian solution performs significantly better than other solutions. Finally,

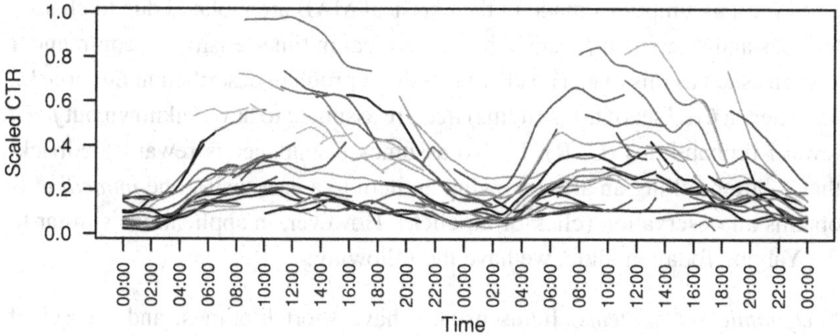

Figure 6.1. CTR curves of items in the Yahoo! Today module over a period of two days. The y-axis is linearly scaled to conceal the actual CTR numbers.

in Section 6.6, we discuss how to address the data sparsity challenge when the set of candidate items is large.

6.1 Example Application: Yahoo! Today Module

In Section 5.1.1, we introduced feature modules that are commonly shown on the home pages of web portals. The Today Module on the Yahoo! home page (see Figure 5.1 for a snapshot) is a typical example. The goal for this module is to recommend items (mostly news stories of different types) to maximize user engagement on the home page, usually measured by the total number of clicks. The module is a panel with several slots, where each slot displays an editorially programmed item (i.e., a story) selected from a content pool of several items. For simplicity and ease of exposition, we focus on maximizing clicks on the most prominent slot of the module, which gets a large fraction of module clicks.

To better understand the characteristics of this application, we look at the CTR curves of items in the Today module over a period of two days. In Figure 6.1, each curve represents the CTR of an item over time, estimated based on data collected from a randomized experiment. The experiment was conducted by randomly selecting a set of users (on the order of hundreds of thousands to a few millions). When a user from this set visits the Yahoo! home page, we serve the user by selecting an item uniformly at random from the content pool. As evident from the figure, the CTR of each item changes over time, and the lifetimes of items are usually short (from a few hours to a day). The lifetime of an item starts when the item is editorially introduced into the content pool and ends when it is removed to keep the content in the module fresh and timely.

Several assumptions made in the classical MAB are violated due to characteristics and system constraints that are typical in time-sensitive recommender systems such as this one. The classical bandit problem described in Section 3.2 considers a *fixed* set of arms (items) that are assumed to have unknown but *fixed* reward probabilities (CTR). It also assumes instantaneous reward feedback; that is, after pulling an arm (showing an item to a user visit), one *immediately* obtains an observation (click or no click). However, in applications similar to the Yahoo! Today module, we have the following:

- *Dynamic set of items*: Items usually have short lifetimes, and the set of available ones changes over time. Short lifetimes make the regret bounds of classical bandit schemes less useful, because when the number of pulls is small, the constants in the big-O notation cannot be ignored for practical purposes.
- *Nonstationary CTR*: The CTR of each item changes over time. The high point of the CTR curve of an item can be 400 percent higher than its low point in our example application. However, CTR curves are usually smooth over time and can be modeled through appropriate time series models. Although adversarial bandit schemes like Auer et al. (1995) do consider nonstationarity in CTR, this characteristic is quite different from those settings.
- *Batch serving*: Click and view observations are delayed because of system performance constraints and delayed user feedback. The latter occurs due to the time lag between an item view (i.e., display of the item produced by the recommender system) and subsequent user click (usually within minutes). A common way to handle this delay is to discretize time into intervals (e.g., n-minute intervals) and let the explore-exploit scheme decide a sampling plan that specifies the fraction of views to be allocated to each item in the next interval, instead of making decisions for each individual user visit.

6.2 Problem Definition

We now provide a rigorous mathematical formulation of the most-popular recommendation approach based on the characteristics observed for the Yahoo! Today module example. The goal is to find a *serving scheme* that decides what fraction of user visits is to be allocated to each item in the next time interval to maximize the expected total number of clicks in the future.

Throughout this chapter, index i and index t denote item i and interval t, respectively. Let p_{it} denote the *unobserved* time-varying CTR of item i at time t, N_t denote the total number of user visits (i.e., pageviews), and $\mathcal{I}_t$ denote the set of available items during interval t. The available item pool is dynamic,

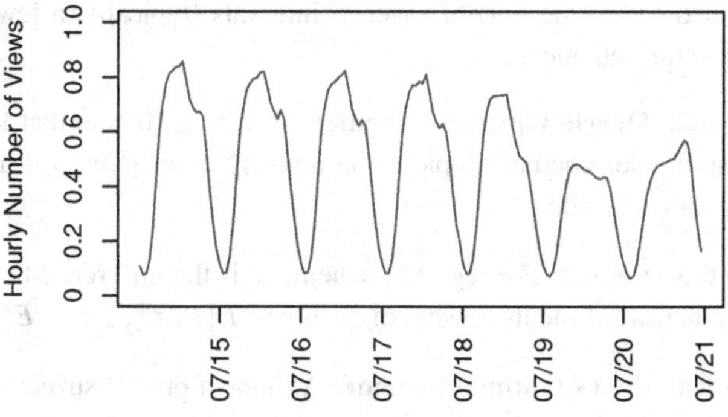

Figure 6.2. Hourly number of user visits to the Yahoo! Today module during a week. The y-axis is linearly rescaled to conceal the actual traffic volume.

hence the suffix t on $\mathcal{I}$. If the CTRs p_{it} were known, the optimal solution would be to serve all N_t user visits to item $i_t^* = \arg\max_i p_{it}$ at t. Because the CTRs p_{it} are unknown, they need to be estimated by showing item i to some user visits. We assume the number of user visits N_t in each interval t is known. In practice, we typically obtain it through a forecasting model. For example, Figure 6.2 shows N_t over a period of one week for the Yahoo! Today module. The traffic pattern is regular, with pronounced day of week and hour of day effects that can be easily modeled using standard time series methods.

Definition 6.1. Serving Scheme: A serving scheme π (also referred to as a policy) is an algorithm that, for each interval t, decides what fraction of user visits should be allocated to each item based on all data observed before t. Let x_{it}^π denote the fraction of user visits that π allocates to item i in interval t, where $\sum_i x_{it}^\pi = 1$, for each t, and $x_{it}^\pi \geq 0$. We call the set of x_{it}^π for all items i the *serving plan* or *allocation plan* for interval t.

It is easy to see that $x_{it}^\pi N_t$ denotes the number of user visits that π allocates to item i in interval t. These schemes are different from standard multiarmed bandit ones where feedback is assumed instantaneous and item states change after each user visit. In subsequent discussions, we may drop superscript π and subscript i when they are clear from the context.

Let c_{it}^π denote the number of clicks that we observe after serving $x_{it}^\pi N_t$ user visits to item i in interval t, where c_{it}^π is a random variable. Based on the findings reported in the appendix of Agarwal et al. (2009), we assume $c_{it}^\pi \sim \text{Poisson}(p_{it} x_{it}^\pi N_t)$, which we have also found to be reasonable in several other web applications.[1] Let $R(\pi, T) = \sum_{t=1}^{T} \sum_{i \in \mathcal{I}_t} c_{it}^\pi$ denote the total number of clicks (also called the *reward*) over T intervals (typically, a few months) obtained through scheme π.

Definition 6.2. Oracle Optimal Scheme: Assume an oracle that knows p_{it} exactly. The oracle scheme π^+ picks the item ($i_t^* = \arg\max_i p_{it}$) having the highest p_{it} for each time t.

Definition 6.3. Regret: The regret of scheme π is the difference between the oracle optimal reward and the reward of π; that is, $E[R(\pi^+, T)] - E[R(\pi, T)]$.

Definition 6.4. Bayes Optimal Scheme: Assume a prior distribution $\mathcal{P}$ over p_{it}. Given N_t and $\mathcal{I}_t$ (for $1 \leq t \leq T$), a serving scheme π^* is Bayes optimal under $\mathcal{P}$ if $E_{\mathcal{P}}[R(\pi^*, T)] = \max_\pi E_{\mathcal{P}}[R(\pi, T)]$, where $E_{\mathcal{P}}$ denotes expectation computed under $\mathcal{P}$.

Our goal is to find a Bayes optimal scheme. Note that Bayes optimal schemes have nonzero regrets because they need to explore items to estimate item CTRs, while the oracle optimal scheme does not explore at all.

Most of the known optimality results for explore-exploit schemes assume that arms (or items) are always available and regret is defined based on the "optimal scheme" that plays the *single* best arm *at all times* (e.g., Gittins, 1979; Lai and Robbins, 1985; Auer, 2002). For many common web applications, we are in a different setting, where arms have short lifetimes and different start times (e.g., news, advertising). Thus, we define regret based on the oracle optimal scheme that plays the best available arm at each time point. Because the best available arms at different time points may change, optimal bounds for this regret are not well studied and require further research. Instead of deriving such optimal regret bounds for the most-popular recommendation problem, we discuss adaptations of classical bandit solutions that work well in practice. These approaches are based on appropriately modeling the characteristics of applications, developing Bayes optimal solutions in simplified scenarios and near-optimal solutions to the general case by appropriate approximations, and then empirically evaluating a large number of schemes using real log data. We also discuss online bucket test results on the Yahoo! Today module, comparing a few explore-exploit schemes in a real-world application. Such an evaluation is rare. We were able to conduct such a study during our tenure at Yahoo!

6.3 Bayesian Solution

In this section, we describe a Bayesian explore-exploit scheme with approximations that ensure computational feasibility. We develop this Bayesian solution in stages, beginning with optimal solutions for simple scenarios that assume a fixed set of items. This is followed by a near-optimal solution to the general case similar to an index policy (solving a K-dimensional problem through K one-dimensional problems).

To simplify notation, we consider a single item and drop index i. The item CTR in interval t has prior $p_t \sim \mathcal{P}(\boldsymbol{\theta}_t)$, where vector $\boldsymbol{\theta}_t$ is the *state* or parameter of the distribution. After we serve the item $x_t N_t$ times to obtain c_t clicks, we obtain the posterior (updated prior) at time $t+1$, $p_{t+1} \sim \mathcal{P}(\boldsymbol{\theta}_{t+1})$. Note that c_t is a random variable; to emphasize that $\boldsymbol{\theta}_{t+1}$ is a function of c_t and x_t, we sometimes write $\boldsymbol{\theta}_{t+1}(c_t, x_t)$. We consider the Gamma-Poisson model, assuming a stationary CTR. Dynamic models are discussed in Section 6.3.3.

Gamma-Poisson Model (GP). Following Agarwal et al. (2009), we assume, at time t, the prior distribution $\mathcal{P}(\boldsymbol{\theta}_t)$ is Gamma(α_t, γ_t) with mean α_t/γ_t and variance α_t/γ_t^2. Suppose we serve $x_t N_t$ user visits with the item and get c_t clicks, where the click count distribution is $(c_t \mid p_t, x_t N_t) \sim \text{Poisson}(p_t x_t N_t)$. By conjugacy, $\mathcal{P}(\boldsymbol{\theta}_{t+1}) = \text{Gamma}(\alpha_t + c_t, \gamma_t + x_t N_t)$. Note that α_t and γ_t intuitively represent the numbers of clicks and views (respectively) observed so far. When computing the fraction of user visits to be allocated to the item in interval t, item state $\boldsymbol{\theta}_t = [\alpha_t, \gamma_t]$ is known. However, $\boldsymbol{\theta}_{t+1}(c_t, x_t)$ is a function of random variable c_t, because we have *not* observed c_t, the number of clicks that would be obtained with an allocation of $x_t N_t$ user visits.

One-step Look-ahead. We consider the optimal scheme with only one remaining interval (call this interval 1; that is, we want to find x_{i1}s that maximize the expected total number of clicks,

$$\max_{x_{i1}} E\left[\sum_{i \in \mathcal{I}_1} x_{i1} N_1 p_{i1}\right] = \max_{x_{i1}} \sum_{i \in \mathcal{I}_1} x_{i1} N_1 E[p_{i1}],$$

subject to $\sum_{i \in \mathcal{I}_1} x_{i1} = 1$ and $0 \le x_{i1} \le 1$, for all i. It is easy to see that the maximum is attained if we assign 100 percent of user visits to the item with the highest expected CTR; that is, $x_{i^*1} = 1$ if $E[p_{i^*1}] = \max_i E[p_{i1}]$, and $x_{i1} = 0$ otherwise.

6.3.1 2×2 Case: Two Items, Two intervals

Now, we consider another simplified scenario for which the optimal solution can be computed efficiently. We call this the 2×2 case; that is, we have two items and two remaining intervals to optimize over. The two-armed bandit case has been studied in the literature before (e.g., DeGroot, 2004; Sarkar, 1991), but under different assumptions that are not germane for the most-popular recommendation problem. To simplify the discussion further, let us also assume we know the CTR of one item without any uncertainty. We use 0 and 1 as time indices for the two intervals. Because we only have two items in this scenario, we simplify our notation:

- N_0 and N_1 are the number of user visits in interval 0 and interval 1, respectively.
- q_0 and q_1 are the CTR of the *certain* item in interval 0 and interval 1, respectively.
- $p_0 \sim \mathcal{P}(\boldsymbol{\theta}_0)$ and $p_1 \sim \mathcal{P}(\boldsymbol{\theta}_1)$ are the CTR distribution of the *uncertain* item in interval 0 and interval 1, respectively.
- x and x_1 are the fraction of user visits allocated to the uncertain item in interval 0 and interval 1, respectively; $(1 - x)$ and $(1 - x_1)$ are the fractions allocated to the certain item.
- c is a random variable representing the number of clicks obtained by the uncertain item in interval 0.
- $\hat{p}_0 = E[p_0]$ and $\hat{p}_1(x, c) = E[p_1 \mid x, c]$; for the GP model, $\hat{p}_0 = \alpha/\gamma$ and $\hat{p}_1(x, c) = (c + p_0\gamma)/(\gamma + xN_0)$.

The current state $\boldsymbol{\theta}_0 = [\alpha, \gamma]$ is known, but $\boldsymbol{\theta}_1$ is a function of c, hence random. The decision x_1 is a function of c. To emphasize this, we write $x_1(c)$ and let $\mathcal{X}_1$ denote the set of all such functions. Our goal is to find $x \in [0, 1]$ and $x_1 \in \mathcal{X}_1$ that maximize the expected total number of clicks in the two intervals given by

$$\begin{aligned} &E[N_0(xp_0 + (1 - x)q_0) + N_1(x_1 p_1 + (1 - x_1)q_1)] \\ &\quad = E[N_0 x(p_0 - q_0) + N_1 x_1(p_1 - q_1)] + q_0 N_0 + q_1 N_1. \end{aligned}$$

Because $q_0 N_0$ and $q_1 N_1$ are constants, we only need to maximize the expectation term. That is, we find x and x_1 that maximize

$$\text{Gain}(x, x_1) = E[N_0 x(p_0 - q_0) + N_1 x_1(p_1 - q_1)], \tag{6.1}$$

$\text{Gain}(x, x_1)$ is the difference in the expected number of clicks between (1) a scheme that distributes user visits between two items (xN_0 and $x_1 N_1$ are allocated to the uncertain item at time 0 and 1) and (2) a scheme that always serves the certain item. Intuitively, it quantifies the gain obtained by exploring the uncertain item because that this item is *potentially* better than the certain one.

Proposition 6.5. *Given* $\boldsymbol{\theta}_0$, q_0, q_1, N_0, *and* N_1,

$$\max_{x\in[0,1],x_1\in\mathcal{X}_1} \text{Gain}(x, x_1) = \max_{x\in[0,1]} \text{Gain}(x),$$

where $\text{Gain}(x) = \text{Gain}(x, \boldsymbol{\theta}_0, q_0, q_1, N_0, N_1) =$

$$N_0 x(\hat{p}_0 - q_0) + N_1 E_c[\max\{\hat{p}_1(x, c) - q_1\ ,\ 0\}].$$

Note that $\hat{p}_0$ ($= \alpha/\gamma$ for Gamma) and $\hat{p}_1(x, c)$ ($= (c + p_0\gamma)/(\gamma + xN_0)$ for Gamma) are functions of $\boldsymbol{\theta}_0$ ($= [\alpha, \gamma]$ for Gamma). The tail expectation $E_c[\max\{\hat{p}_1(x, c) - q_1\ ,\ 0\}]$ with respect to the *marginal* distribution of c appears in the expression because interval 1 is the last interval, and from the one-step look-ahead case, when the gain is maximized, $x_1(c)$ is either 1 or 0, depending on whether $\hat{p}_1(x, c) - q_1 > 0$.

Optimal Solution. The expression $\max_{x\in[0,1]} \text{Gain}(x)$ is the optimal number of clicks in the 2×2 case. For a given class of distribution $\mathcal{P}$, the optimal x can be obtained numerically. For computational efficiency, we use a normal approximation. Assume $\hat{p}_1(x, c)$ is approximately normal. Here we only approximate the posterior $(p_1 \mid x, c)$ by a normal distribution; the prior p_0 is still assumed to be Gamma. Let σ_0^2 denote the variance of p_0; $\sigma_0^2 = \alpha/\gamma^2$ for the Gamma distribution. By a derivation using iterated expectations with respect to distributions $(c \mid p_1)$ and p_1, we obtain

$$E_c[\hat{p}_1(x, c)] = \hat{p}_0 = \alpha/\gamma$$

$$\text{Var}_c[\hat{p}_1(x, c)] = \sigma_1^2(x) = \frac{xN_0}{\gamma + xN_0}\sigma_0^2.$$

Using the normal approximation, the tail expectation is obtained in a closed form.

Proposition 6.6. (Normal Approximation) *Let* ϕ *and* Φ *denote the density and distribution functions of the standard normal:*

$$\text{Gain}(x, \boldsymbol{\theta}_0, q_0, q_1, N_0, N_1) \approx N_0 x(\hat{p}_0 - q_0)$$
$$+ N_1\left[\sigma_1(x)\phi\left(\frac{q_1 - \hat{p}_0}{\sigma_1(x)}\right) + \left(1 - \Phi\left(\frac{q_1 - \hat{p}_0}{\sigma_1(x)}\right)\right)(\hat{p}_0 - q_1)\right].$$

The normal approximation makes $\text{Gain}(x)$ a differentiable function with some nice properties. Figure 6.3(a) shows three Gain functions with different prior means. In particular, $\text{Gain}(x)$ has at most one minimum and at most one maximum (excluding the boundaries). It can also be shown that $\frac{d^2}{dx^2}\text{Gain}(x) = 0$ has at most one solution for $0 < x < 1$. Let C denote the solution, if it exists. One can also show that $\frac{d^2}{dx^2}\text{Gain}(x) > 0$ for $0 < x < C$, and $\frac{d^2}{dx^2}\text{Gain}(x) < 0$;

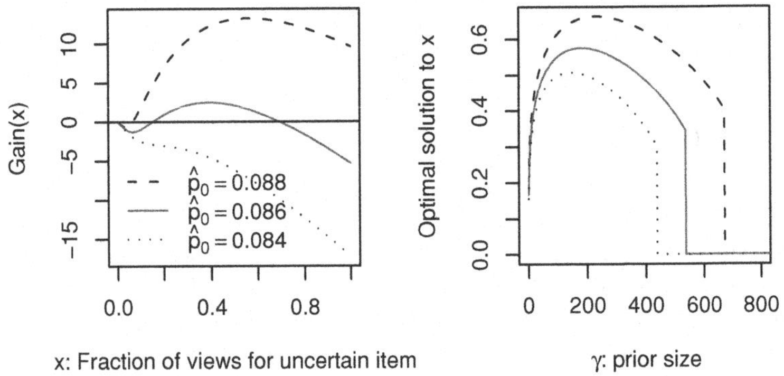

(a) Gain function (b) Optimal solution

Figure 6.3. (a) Gain(x) for different $\hat{p}_0$ when $\gamma = 500$, $N_0 = 2K$, $N_1 = 40$K, $q_0 = q_1 = 0.1$. (b) Optimal solution to x ($\arg\max_x$ Gain(x)) as a function of γ.

thus, $\frac{d}{dx}\text{Gain}(x)$ is decreasing for $C < x < 1$. Now, binary search can be used to efficiently find $C < x^* < 1$ such that $\frac{d}{dx}\text{Gain}(x) = 0$, if it exists. Then, the optimal solution is $x = 0$, x^*, or 1.

Proposition 6.7. *Let x^* denote the optimal solution to the normal approximation. The time complexity of finding solution x such that $|x - x^*| < \epsilon$ is $O(\log 1/\epsilon)$.*

This follows easily from the observation that the optimal solution can be obtained through a bisection algorithm.

Properties of the Gain Function. Figure 6.3(b) shows the optimal amount of exploration as a function of uncertainty (small γ means high uncertainty) for different mean values of the uncertain item. Contrary to what one might expect, the amount of exploration is not monotonically decreasing as uncertainty goes down (i.e., γ goes up); we in fact should not explore too much when the degree of uncertainty is too high (i.e., small γ). The scheme is cautious and does not allocate too many observations to items that have a high degree of uncertainty. This occurs because we only consider a two-interval look-ahead.

6.3.2 $K \times 2$ Case: K Items, Two Intervals

We now consider the case of K items but still use two intervals. The optimal solution to this problem is computationally hard. Thus, we apply the Lagrange relaxation technique to find a near-optimal solution in a way that is similar to Whittle (1988).

Recall that $p_{it} \sim \mathcal{P}(\boldsymbol{\theta}_{it})$ denotes the CTR of item i at time $t \in \{0, 1\}$. Let $\mu(\boldsymbol{\theta}_{it}) = E[p_{it}]$. To simplify notation, we use vectors: $\boldsymbol{\theta}_t = [\boldsymbol{\theta}_{1t}, \ldots, \boldsymbol{\theta}_{Kt}]$, $\mathbf{x_t} = [x_{1t}, \ldots, x_{Kt}]$, and $\mathbf{c_0} = [c_{10}, \ldots, c_{K0}]$, where x_{it} is the fraction of views allocated to item i at time $t \in \{0, 1\}$ and c_{i0} denotes the random number of clicks item i obtained at time 0. Our goal is 0 obtain $\mathbf{x_0}$ and $\mathbf{x_1}$ that maximize the total expected number of clicks in the two intervals. When we make this decision, $\boldsymbol{\theta}_0$ is known and $\boldsymbol{\theta}_1 = \boldsymbol{\theta}_1(\mathbf{x_0}, \mathbf{c_0})$ depends on $\mathbf{x_0}$ and $\mathbf{c_0}$. Also, $\mathbf{x_0}$ is a vector of numbers, but $\mathbf{x_1} = \mathbf{x_1}(\boldsymbol{\theta}_1)$ is a function of $\boldsymbol{\theta}_1$. Let $\mathbf{x} = [\mathbf{x_0}, \mathbf{x_1}]$.

Now, the expected total number of clicks is

$$R(\mathbf{x}, \boldsymbol{\theta}_0, N_0, N_1) = N_0 \sum_i x_{i0}\mu(\boldsymbol{\theta}_{i0}) + N_1 \sum_i E_{\boldsymbol{\theta}_1}[x_{i1}(\boldsymbol{\theta}_1)\mu(\boldsymbol{\theta}_{i1})].$$

Our goal is to find

$$R^*(\boldsymbol{\theta}_0, N_0, N_1) = \max_{0 \le \mathbf{x} \le 1} R(\mathbf{x}, \boldsymbol{\theta}_0, N_0, N_1), \text{ subject to}$$

$$\sum_i x_{i0} = 1 \text{ and } \sum_i x_{i1}(\boldsymbol{\theta}_1) = 1, \text{ for all possible } \boldsymbol{\theta}_1.$$

Lagrange Relaxation. To make the preceding optimization computationally feasible, we relax the constraints on interval 1. Instead of requiring $\sum_i x_{i1}(\boldsymbol{\theta}_1) = 1$ *for all possible* $\boldsymbol{\theta}_1$, we only require $\sum_i x_{i1}(\boldsymbol{\theta}_1) = 1$ on average. Thus, the optimization problem becomes

$$R^+(\boldsymbol{\theta}_0, N_0, N_1) = \max_{0 \le \mathbf{x} \le 1} R(\mathbf{x}, \boldsymbol{\theta}_0, N_0, N_1), \text{ subject to}$$

$$\sum_i x_{i0} = 1 \text{ and } E_{\boldsymbol{\theta}_1}\left[\sum_i x_{i1}(\boldsymbol{\theta}_1)\right] = 1.$$

Next, we define the value function V as

$$V(\boldsymbol{\theta}_0, q_0, q_1, N_0, N_1) = \max_{0 \le \mathbf{x} \le 1} \{R(\mathbf{x}, \boldsymbol{\theta}_0, N_0, N_1) - q_0 N_0(\Sigma_i\, x_{i0} - 1) - q_1 N_1(E[\Sigma_i\, x_{i0}] - 1)\},$$

where q_0 and q_1 are the Lagrange multipliers. Under mild conditions,

$$R^+(\boldsymbol{\theta}_0, N_0, N_1) = \min_{q_0, q_1} V(\boldsymbol{\theta}_0, q_0, q_1, N_0, N_1).$$

We now state two important properties of the V function that simplify computation.

Proposition 6.8. (Convexity) *$V(\boldsymbol{\theta}_0, q_0, q_1, N_0, N_1)$ is convex in (q_0, q_1).*

Because V is convex in (q_0, q_1), standard convex optimization tools can be used to find the minimum solution. However, we need to compute V efficiently given (q_0, q_1). Fortunately, this can be done because of the separability property stated in the following.

Proposition 6.9. (Separability)

$$V(\boldsymbol{\theta}_0, q_0, q_1, N_0, N_1) = \sum_i \left(\max_{0 \le x_{i0} \le 1} \text{Gain}(x_{i0}, \boldsymbol{\theta}_{i0}, q_0, q_1, N_0, N_1) \right) + q_0 N_0 + q_1 N_1, \tag{6.2}$$

where Gain is defined in Proposition 6.5.

Owing to separability, the V function can be computed by maximization (over x_{i0}) for each item i *independently*. This independent maximization reduces to the gain maximization of Proposition 6.5 and can be solved efficiently using Proposition 6.6. Thus, we are able to solve a *joint* maximization (over $x_{10}, \ldots, x_{K0}$) problem in a K-dimensional space through K independent one-dimensional optimization. This *decoupling* is similar in spirit to Gittins (1979) index policy calculation.

Near-optimal Solution. To compute the fraction of user visits allocated to each item i in the immediate interval (interval 0), we use a standard convex optimizer to compute $\min_{q_0, q_1} V(\boldsymbol{\theta}_0, q_0, q_1, N_0, N_1)$. Let q_0^* and q_1^* be the minimum solution. Then,

$$x_{i0}^* = \arg \max_{0 \le x_{i0} \le 1} \text{Gain}(x_{i0}, \boldsymbol{\theta}_{i0}, q_0^*, q_1^*, N_0, N_1)$$

is the fraction to be given to item i. The Langrange relaxation technique was first applied by Whittle (1988) to bandit problems. Studies of several related (but different) problems suggest that Lagrange relaxation usually provides near-optimal solutions, as noted by Glazebrook et al. (2004, 57) "A developing body of empirical evidence testifies to the strong performance of Whittle's index [Lagrange relaxation–based] policies."

6.3.3 General Solution

We now describe the solution to the general most-popular recommendation problem, in which we have many future intervals and a dynamic set of candidate items with nonstationary CTRs. We start with a two-stage approximation to address the case of more than two future intervals and then extend to a dynamic set of candidate items. Finally, we discuss how to use a dynamic Gamma-Poisson model to handle nonstationary item CTRs.

Two-Stage Approximation

Suppose we have K items and $T+1$ future intervals ($t = 0, \ldots, T$). We first assume that all K items are available in every future interval. Similar to the $K \times 2$ case, after we apply Lagrange relaxation, the convexity and separability properties still hold (with slightly modified formulae). However, the computation complexity increases exponentially in T. For efficient computation, we approximate the $T+1$ interval case by only considering two stages: the first stage (indexed by 0) contains interval 0 with N_0 user visits, whereas the second stage (indexed by 1) contains the rest of the T intervals with $\Sigma_{t \in [1,T]} N_t$ user visits. We then treat the second stage as the second interval in the $K \times 2$ case. Thus, we obtain the approximate solution by solving the $K \times 2$ case where N_1 is replaced by $\Sigma_{t \in [1,T]} N_t$.

Dynamic Set of Candidate Items

We extend the near-optimal solution for the $K \times 2$ case to a dynamic set of items with multiple future intervals. Now, the set $\mathcal{I}_t$ of items is allowed to change over time. Let $s(i)$ and $e(i)$ denote the start time and end time of item i, respectively. The end time of an item may be stochastic; this can be incorporated into our framework by marginalizing over the value function. Here we assume a deterministic $e(i)$ for ease of exposition. $\mathcal{I}_0$ is the set of items i such that $s(i) \leq 0$ and $e(i) \geq 0$, called *live items*, which start before the current time $t = 0$. Let $T = \max_{i \in \mathcal{I}_0} e(i)$ denote the end time of the live item having the longest remaining lifetime. Let $\mathcal{I}^+$ be the set of items i with $1 \leq s(i) \leq T$, called *future items*. Let $T(i) = \min\{T, e(i)\}$.

After we apply Lagrange relaxation, the convexity and separability properties still hold (with slightly modified formulae), but computational complexity increases exponentially in the number of intervals. For efficiency, we apply the two-stage approximation to each item i: the first interval of the item ($\max\{0, s(i)\}$) is the exploration stage, whereas the remaining intervals ($\max\{0, s(i)\} + 1$ to $T(i)$) of the item are the exploitation stage. These two stages correspond to $t = 0$ and $t = 1$ in the $K \times 2$ case, respectively. The two-stage approximation is only used to compute the serving plan for interval $t = 0$ – we do not actually do pure exploitation for $t = 1, \ldots, T(i)$. At $t = 1$, we consider $\max\{1, s(i)\}$ the exploration stage for item i and compute the serving plan for it based on the data observed at $t = 0$ and before.

After this two-stage approximation, the objective function V (in Proposition 6.9) becomes

$$
\begin{aligned}
& V(\boldsymbol{\theta}_0, q_0, q_1, N_0, \ldots, N_T) \\
& = \sum_{i \in \mathcal{I}_0} \max_{0 \le x_{i0} \le 1} \text{Gain}\left(x_{i0}, \boldsymbol{\theta}_{i0}, q_0, q_1, N_0, \sum_{t=1}^{T(i)} N_t\right) \\
& \quad + \sum_{i \in \mathcal{I}^+} \max_{0 \le y_i \le 1} \text{Gain}\left(y_i, \boldsymbol{\theta}_{i0}, q_1, q_1, N_{s(i)}, \sum_{t=s(i)+1}^{T(i)} N_t\right) \\
& \quad + q_0 N_0 + q_1 \sum_{t \in [1,T]} N_t.
\end{aligned}
\tag{6.3}
$$

We apply standard convex minimization techniques to find q_0^* and q_1^* that minimize the V function. The x_{i0} that maximizes the preceding Gain function (on the second line) with $q_0 = q_0^*$ and $q_1 = q_1^*$ is the fraction of user visits to be given to item i in the next interval.

We now explain Equation (6.3). Live items $\mathcal{I}_0$ (on the second line) require a different treatment from future items $\mathcal{I}^+$ (on the third line). For each item, we apply the two-stage approximation. For live item $i \in \mathcal{I}_0$, the first stage is time 0 having N_0 views, whereas the second stage is from 1 to $T(i)$ having $\sum_{t \in [1,T(i)]} N_t$ views. For future item $i \in \mathcal{I}^+$, the first stage is $s(i) > 0$, and the second stage is from $s(i) + 1$ to $T(i)$. Because our goal is to decide how to serve live items at time 0 (i.e., x_{i0}), we use different variables y_i for future items i that enter the system later than time 0.

In Equation (6.3), the Lagrange multipliers q_0 and q_1 are used to ensure that the optimizer-allocated number of views matches the specified total number of views. In fact, q_0 ensures $\sum_i x_{i0} N_0 = N_0$, for time 0; and q_1 ensures $E[\sum_{t \in [1,T]} \sum_i x_{it} N_t] = \sum_{t \in [1,T]} N_t$, for time 1 to T. Future items $\mathcal{I}^+$ only occur in time 1 to T. Thus, their Gain functions on the third line of Equation (6.3) have two occurrences of q_1 and no q_0.

Variable $\boldsymbol{\theta}_{i0}$ represents our current belief about the CTR of item i. For live item $i \in \mathcal{I}_0$, $\boldsymbol{\theta}_{i0}$ is the current state of the item's CTR model. For future item $i \in \mathcal{I}^+$, $\boldsymbol{\theta}_{i0}$ is the prior belief of the item's CTR (possibly predicted using item features).

Definition 6.10. BayesGeneral Scheme: We call the solution to Equation (6.3) the BayesGeneral scheme.

The BayesGeneral scheme requires solving a two-dimensional convex, nondifferentiable minimization problem for q_0 and q_1. To ensure the constraints are satisfied, the minimization needs high precision, which leads to long execution time. To achieve better efficiency, we consider the following approximation.

Definition 6.11. Bayes 2×2 Scheme: The Bayes 2×2 scheme works by approximating q_0 and q_1 by the CTR of item i^* that has the highest estimated CTR $\max_i \mu(\boldsymbol{\theta}_{i,0})$ and then finding the optimal solution to each x_{i0} with fixed q_0, q_1. The intuition is that we compare each item i with the best item i^* using the 2×2 case, assuming we are certain about the CTR of i^*. Because $\sum_i x_{i0}$ may not sum to unity, we set the fraction allocated to item i as $\rho\, x_{i0}$, where ρ is a global tuning parameter. Also, because comparing i^* to itself is not appropriate (which makes x_{i^*0} always 1), we set the fraction given to i^* to be $\max\{1 - \sum_{i \neq i^*} \rho\, x_{i0},\ 0\}$.

In Section 6.5, we show that the performance of Bayes 2×2 is close to BayesGeneral. We note that ρ is tuned based on simulations, and we find the performance of Bayes 2×2 not to be very sensitive to the setting of ρ.

Nonstationary CTR

We incorporate nonstationarity into our solution by using time series models to update the distribution of item CTR over time. In general, any model that estimates the predictive distribution of CTR accurately can be plugged in to our Bayesian solution. Following Agarwal et al. (2009), we use the *dynamic Gamma-Poisson* (DGP) model. Assume CTR $p_{i,t-1}$ of item i at time $t-1$ follows Gamma(α, γ). We capture temporal variation in CTR by giving more weight to recent data. One simple way is to down-weight the effective sample size γ after each interval; that is, the prior at t is centered around the posterior mean at $t-1$ with variance obtained by inflating the posterior variance at $t-1$ through a "discounting" factor w (the variance depends on the effective sample size). See West and Harrison (1997) for details on the discounting concept for state-space models. More specifically, after observing c clicks and v views for item i at time t, the prior at time t is $p_{i,t} \sim \text{Gamma}(w\alpha + c,\ w\gamma + v)$, where $w \in (0, 1]$ is a prespecified discount factor, tuned on training data. Incorporating the DGP model into the solution for the 2×2 case is straightforward. When computing the Gain function, we down-weight α and γ for the second interval by w. Specifically, in the normal approximation, we redefine

$$\text{Var}_c[\hat{p}_1(x, c)] = \sigma_1(x)^2 \equiv \frac{x N_0}{w\gamma + x N_0}\sigma_{0w}^2, \quad \text{where } \sigma_{0w}^2 = \frac{\alpha}{w\gamma^2}. \tag{6.4}$$

6.4 Non-Bayesian Solutions

In this section, we adapt a number of non-Bayesian schemes (UCB, POKER, and Exp3) from the standard multiarmed bandit literature to recommendation problems with a dynamic set of items, nonstationary CTR, and batch serving (as discussed in Section 6.1). We also describe baseline methods to which we will empirically compare the Bayesian solution in Section 6.5. For ease of exposition, let $\hat{p}_{it} = E[p_{it}]$ be estimated by the DGP model.

B-UCB1. The UCB1 scheme, proposed by Auer (2002), is a popular scheme designed for one-at-a-time serving – it serves an incoming pageview with item i that has the highest *priority*; the item priorities are updated after each feedback (assumed to be instantaneous). The priority for item i is given by

$$\hat{p}_{it} + \sqrt{\frac{2 \ln n}{n_i}}, \tag{6.5}$$

where n_i is the total number of views given to item i so far and $n = \sum_i n_i$. This does not work in our scenario. We modify the scheme as follows:

- To incorporate nonstationary CTR, we use the DGP model with state $[\alpha_{it}, \gamma_{it}]$ for item i to estimate $\hat{p}_{it} = \alpha_{it}/\gamma_{it}$ and replace n_i with the effective sample size γ_{it}.
- To adapt to time-varying $\mathcal{I}_t$, we replace n with $\sum_{i \in \mathcal{I}_t} \gamma_{it}$.
- For batch serving, we propose a *hypothetical run* technique to incorporate the impact of delayed feedback. The main idea is to hypothetically run UCB1 to serve every pageview in the next interval one by one. Because we do not actually serve any page, we do not observe any reward after each "hypothetical" serve (which is required to run UCB1). Instead, we assume the reward of serving item i to be its current CTR estimate. After hypothetically running through all the user visits in the next interval, the fraction of views allocated to item i is the fraction of hypothetical serves we made to item i.

Putting it all together, we sequentially go through each of the N_t user visits in the next interval as follows. For $k = 1$ to N_t, we hypothetically give the kth pageview to item i^* that has the highest priority: let m_i be a counter that tracks the number of views that have been given to item i during the hypothetical run. At a current value of k during the hypothetical run, we update sample sizes as $n_i = \gamma_{it} + m_i$ and $n = \sum_{i \in \mathcal{I}_t} n_i$; the priority for item i is

$$\begin{aligned} &\text{Untuned:} \quad \hat{p}_{it} + \sqrt{\frac{2 \ln n}{n_i}} \quad \text{or} \\ &\text{Tuned:} \quad \hat{p}_{it} + \left(\frac{\ln n}{n_i} \min \left\{ \frac{1}{4},\ \text{Var}(i) + \sqrt{\frac{2 \ln n}{n_i}} \right\} \right)^{\frac{1}{2}}, \end{aligned} \tag{6.6}$$

where $\mathrm{Var}(i) = \hat{p}_{it}(1 - \hat{p}_{it})$. After the hypothetical run finishes, m_i is the number of user visits allocated to item i during interval t. Thus, we set $x_{it} = m_i / \Sigma_j m_j$. We call this scheme Batch-UCB1 or B-UCB1. The tuned version uniformly outperforms the untuned version in our experiments.

B-POKER. The POKER scheme, proposed by Vermorel and Mohri (2005), is similar to UCB1 but has a different priority function. Let $K = |\mathcal{I}_t|$. Without loss of generality, assume $\hat{p}_{1t} \geq \cdots \geq \hat{p}_{Kt}$. We adapt POKER to our setting by following the B-UCB1 procedure and only replace the priority function with

$$\hat{p}_{it} + \Pr(p_{it} \geq \hat{p}_{1t} + \delta)\, \delta H,$$

where $\delta = (\hat{p}_{1t} - \hat{p}_{\sqrt{K},t})/\sqrt{K}$, H is a tuning parameter and the tail probability is computed by assuming $p_{it} \sim \mathcal{P}(\alpha_{it} + m_i \hat{p}_{it},\ \gamma_{it} + m_i)$, where $\mathcal{P}$ is Gamma.

Exp3. Proposed by Auer et al. (1995), Exp3 is designed for adversarial, nonstationary reward distributions. Let G_i (initially 0) denote the total number of "adjusted" clicks that item i has received so far. Let $\epsilon \in (0, 1]$ and $\eta > 0$ be two tuning parameters. For each time interval t, we do the following:

1. Give item i fraction x_{it} of the user visits at time t, where $x_{it} = (1 - \epsilon)r_{it} + \epsilon/|\mathcal{I}_t|$ and $r_{it} \propto e^{\eta G_i}$.
2. At the end of interval t, assuming item i receives c_{it} clicks, update G_i by $G_i = G_i + c_{it}/x_{it}$.

Baseline Heuristic Schemes. *ϵ-Greedy* is a simple scheme that, for each interval, allocates a fixed fraction ϵ of user visits to explore all live items uniformly and gives the rest of traffic to the item having the highest estimated CTR. *SoftMax* is another simple scheme that sets $x_{it} \propto e^{\hat{p}_{it}/\tau}$, where the *temperature* parameter τ is a tuning parameter.

For comparison, we also include nonbatch UCB1 and POKER, called *WTA-UCB1* and *WTA-POKER*, where WTA stands for "winner takes all," which means we allocate all traffic in an interval to the single item that has the highest priority value.

6.5 Empirical Evaluation

In this section, we provide an empirical evaluation for the explore-exploit schemes discussed earlier in this chapter. We start by evaluating the schemes for the Yahoo! Today module, which has roughly twenty live items to choose from at any point in time during the data collection period. We then evaluate hypothetical scenarios where the number of live items ranges from ten to one thousand, followed by analysis that demonstrates the benefit of applying multiarmed bandit schemes on user segments. This is followed by results obtained from online bucket tests conducted on a small random fraction of traffic from the Yahoo! Today module.

6.5.1 Comparative Analysis

The Yahoo! Today Module Scenario. This application selects the most-popular item from a set of roughly twenty live items in each five-minute interval. To set up our simulation experiments, we retrospectively collected four months of past data to obtain the set of live items and the number of user visits for each interval. We estimated the *ground-truth* CTR of each item in each interval through a *loess* fit with bandwidth selected to minimize the autocorrelations in the residuals, as proposed in Agarwal et al. (2009). Our data were collected from a *random bucket,* which consists of a set of randomly selected users to whom we show every live item in our content pool with equal probability. The number of visits in this bucket was large enough to reliably estimate the CTR of *every* live item in *every* interval. The estimated item CTR at t obtained retrospectively by using data both before and after time t is more accurate than estimating CTR prospectively by only looking at data before time t.

To evaluate the performance of schemes under different sample size scenarios, we set $N_t' = a \cdot N_t$ and vary the value of a. Here N_t is the actual number of views observed in the data in interval t. The number of clicks c_{it} on item i at time t for an allocation volume N_{it}' calculated through the scheme is simulated from Poisson($p_{it} N_{it}'$) using retrospective CTR estimates. All schemes, except Exp3, use the posterior mean estimate from the DGP model to estimate the nonstationary CTR prospectively; the Bayesian schemes, B-UCB1 (where n_i is the effective sample size from the model that is equivalent to knowing the variance), WTA-UCB1, B-POKER, and WTA-POKER also use the variance estimate from the model. We set aside the first month's data to determine the tuning parameters for schemes (if they have some) and test all schemes on the remaining three months. To tune the parameters for a scheme, we tried ten to twenty parameter settings; for each of the settings, we ran a simulation over the first-month data and then selected the setting that gave the best performance. Figure 6.4(a) shows the percentage regret of each scheme as a function of the amount of traffic (in terms of the average number of user visits per interval).

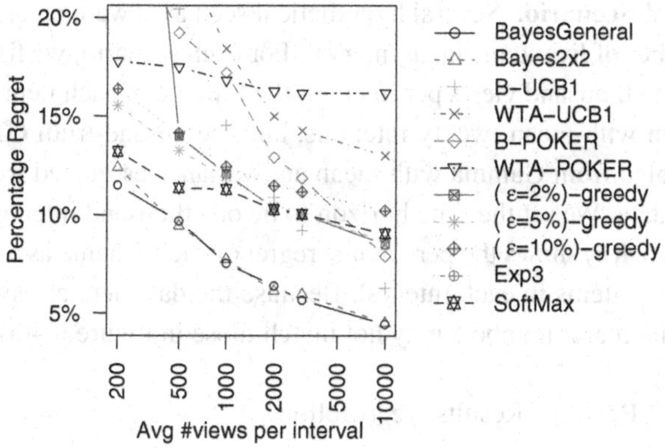

(a) Yahoo! Today module scenario

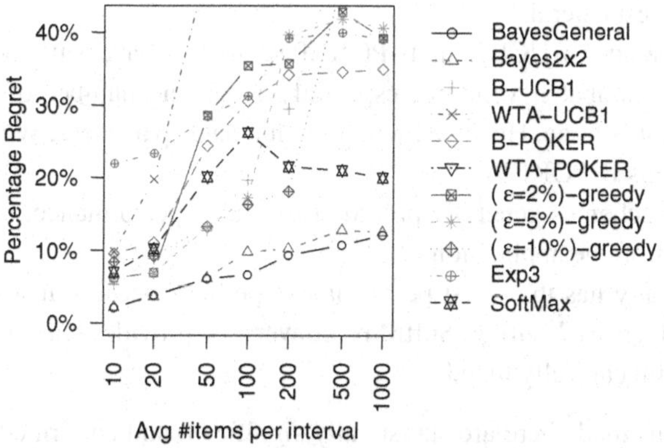

(b) Hypothetical scenario

Figure 6.4. Empirical comparison of explore-exploit schemes; x-axes are log-scaled. Note that, in (a), WTA-UCB1 and Exp3 have regrets more than 20 percent. In (b), WTA-POKER has regrets more than 40 percent.

The percentage regret of a scheme S is defined as

$$\frac{\#\text{Clicks(Opt)} - \#\text{Clicks}(S)}{\#\text{Clicks(Opt)}}, \tag{6.7}$$

where Opt is the oracle optimal scheme assuming the ground truth is completely known. Opt may pick different items in different intervals and provides a stronger notion of regret than the optimal scheme used in standard bandit problems that select a single best item for all intervals (for more details, see Auer et al., 1995).

Hypothetical Scenario. Several hypothetical scenarios were created by varying the number of live items in an interval. For each scenario, we fix the traffic volume to one thousand views per interval, the lifetime of each item is sampled from Poisson with mean twenty intervals, and the ground-truth CTR of each item is sampled from Gamma with mean and variance estimated from the real application data. We set the time horizon to be one thousand intervals with ten runs. Figure 6.4(b) shows the percentage regret of each scheme as a function of number of live items in each interval. Because the data here are synthetically generated, the regret numbers may not match those in Figure 6.4(a).

Summary of Results. Results are as follows:

- BayesGeneral and Bayes 2×2 are uniformly better than all other schemes; differences in performance get larger with increasing data sparseness. The more computationally efficient Bayes 2×2 (with tuned ρ) closely approximates BayesGeneral.
- Batch schemes (B-UCB1 and B-POKER) generally have better performance than their nonbatch versions, especially when the number of user visits per interval is large. However, with extreme data sparseness, WTA-POKER outperforms B-POKER.
- ϵ-Greedy schemes generally provide reasonable performance, but the right ϵ depends on the application.
- Exp3 usually has the worst performance, perhaps because it was designed for the adversarial setting; SoftMax, conversely, provides reasonable performance with carefully tuned τ.

All assertions made here are statistically significant and confirmed by experiments on several additional data sets with several replications on each.

6.5.2 Scheme Characterization

More intuition on the explore-exploit properties of each scheme helps us understand why some schemes perform better than others. A scheme that tends to be greedy would allocate more user visits to the item with highest posterior mean quickly and is likely to lose clicks over a larger time horizon. Conversely, a scheme that is cautious in allocating a large fraction of user visits to the higher posterior mean items may converge slowly to the best ones.

To quantify this explore-exploit trade-off for bandit schemes, we characterize a bandit scheme using three criteria. At a given time point, let us call the item having the highest estimated CTR under a given scheme the estimated most-popular (EMP) item for that scheme. Different schemes may pick different

EMP items at the same time point even with the same statistical estimation technique because of differences in sample size allocated to each item. Let n_{it} denote the number of views that the scheme allocates to item i at time t. Let p_{it} denote the true CTR of item i at time t, and $p_t^* = \max_i p_{it}$. Without loss of generality, assume $i = 1$ denotes the EMP item determined by the scheme.

We define the following three metrics to characterize a scheme:

1. *Fraction of EMP display:* $\sum_t n_{1t} / \sum_t \sum_i n_{it}$ is the fraction of views where the scheme displays EMP items. This number quantifies the amount of traffic for which the scheme *exploits* its current knowledge about the items.
2. *EMP regret:* $\sum_t n_{1t} (p_t^* - p_{1t}) / \sum_t n_{1t}$ is the regret of displaying the EMP item. This number quantifies a scheme's ability to identify the optimal item (or a good item) to exploit. When a scheme explores less than necessary, its EMP regret is likely to be high because it does not have enough observations to identify the best item.
3. *Non-EMP regret:* $\sum_t \sum_{i \neq 1} n_{it} (p_t^* - p_{it}) / \sum_t \sum_{i \neq 1} n_{it}$ is the regret of displaying all the non-EMP items. This number quantifies the cost of exploration because when the scheme knows the CTRs of items exactly, it should always display the EMP item.

Figure 6.5(a) shows EMP regret versus non-EMP regret for each scheme. We ran three simulations (corresponding to three points in the figure) for each scheme with twenty, one hundred, and one thousand items per interval. The simulation setup is the same as that of the hypothetical scenarios in Section 6.5.1. In this plot, good schemes are at the bottom left corner. Figure 6.5(b) shows EMP regret versus fraction of EMP display for each scheme. Good schemes are at the bottom right corner.

The Bayesian scheme is among the best in both plots; even when the number of items is large, its performance is still good. Nonbatch schemes (WTA-UCB1 and WTA-POKER) usually are not able to identify the best items because they only show a *single item* for each interval; when item lifetimes are only twenty intervals on average, they are not able to collect enough observations to identify good items before the items expire. B-UCB1 has low EMP regret, illustrating its property of identifying good items without much error. However, this scheme typically explores more than necessary. The three ϵ-greedy schemes have very similar characteristics. Their fractions of EMP display are fixed at $1 - \epsilon$. Their non-EMP regrets are large because of complete randomization. As the number of items becomes large, their ability to identify good items deteriorates. SoftMax is quite competitive, especially when the number of items is small; however, its overall performance is significantly worse than the Bayesian scheme for all simulation settings. Moreover, we found this scheme

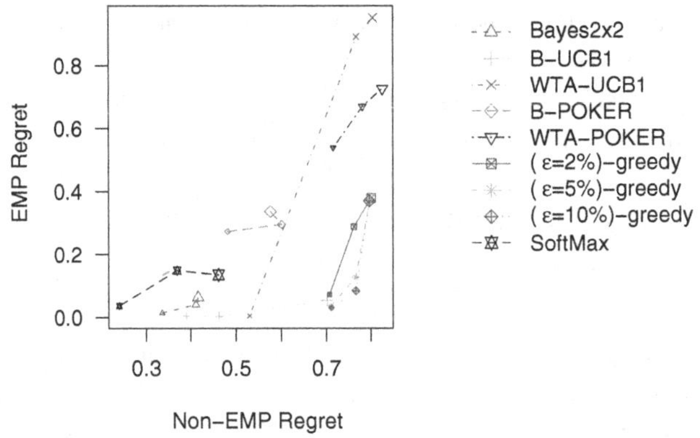

(a) Regret: EMP vs. non-EMP

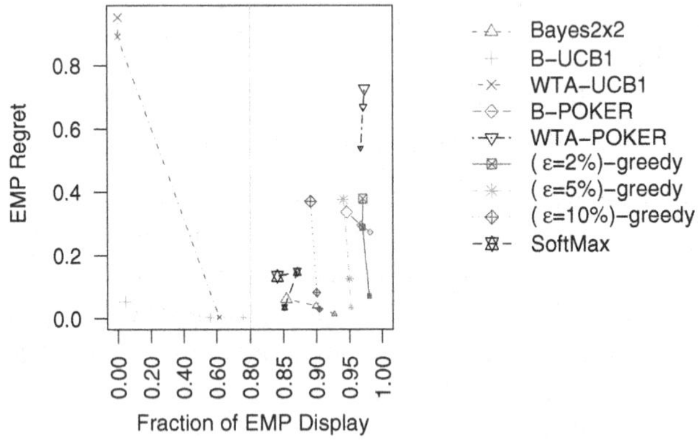

(b) EMP regret vs. fraction of EMP

Figure 6.5. Characteristics of bandit schemes. Each point represents a simulation of a scheme. For each scheme, we ran three simulations with twenty (small point), one hundred (medium point), and one thousand (large point) items per interval. BayesGeneral is omitted because it has almost the same characteristics as Bayes 2×2. In (b), we provide a zoom-in view for x-axis ≥ 0.8.

to be overly sensitive to the temperature parameter, which has to be tweaked carefully. But SoftMax does have the advantage of not requiring estimates of uncertainty.

6.5.3 Segmentation Analysis

We demonstrate performance of our schemes for personalized recommendations by running them separately on user segments that were created using

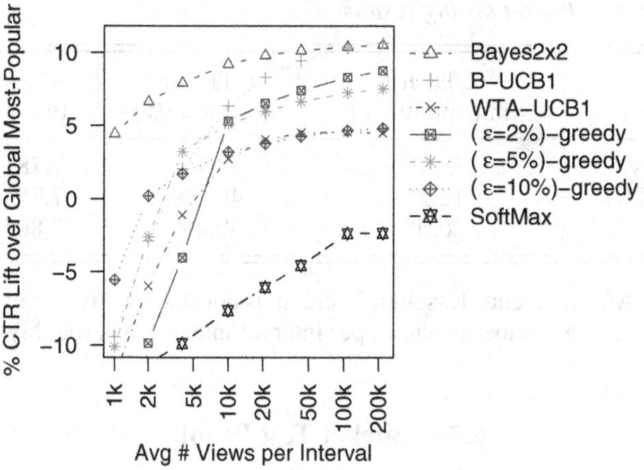

Figure 6.6. Segmentation analysis.

known user features such as age, gender, geolocation, and browse behavior (search history, pages visited, ads clicked, etc.). Several other features were evaluated, but we found them to be weakly predictive. Each item was hand-labeled and assigned to one of the C content categories. Using a large number of retrospective data, we generated user segments as follows.

Let y_{uit} denote the response (click or no click) for user u on item i at time t and $\boldsymbol{x}_{ut}$ denote the user features (browse behavior is dynamic, hence the suffix t). Then, we fit a logistic regression model $y_{uit} \mid p_{uit} \sim$ Bernoulli(p_{uit}), where $\log(p_{uit}/(1 - p_{uit})) = \boldsymbol{x}'_{ut}\boldsymbol{\beta}_{c(i)}$; $\boldsymbol{\beta}_k$s are latent factors for category k and $c(i)$ denote the category of item i. Using the estimated $\boldsymbol{\beta}_k$s, we project each user with feature $\boldsymbol{x}_{ut}$ into the category space as $[\boldsymbol{x}'_{ut}\boldsymbol{\beta}_1, \ldots, \boldsymbol{x}'_{ut}\boldsymbol{\beta}_C]$. We cluster these projections and select five user segments (cluster) after careful analysis. The segments were also analyzed and interpreted by editors who *program* stories for the Yahoo! Today module application. Segmentation provides better interpretability for editors than the regression model for programming targeted content items. In Figure 6.6, we show the CTR lift relative to the oracle optimal scheme without segmentation for each scheme. The maximum achievable lift is about 13 percent. The Bayesian scheme is uniformly better than all other schemes and provides positive lift for all traffic volumes. B-UCB1 and ϵ-greedy perform reasonably well for large traffic volumes, but they deteriorate rapidly with low traffic volume. Surprisingly, SoftMax does not perform well in this experiment. This is because we used a single τ for all the segments. Because τ is sensitive to the scale of item CTRs and the segments have very different item CTR distributions, a single τ value for all segments leads to poor performance.

Table 6.1. *Bucket testing results*

Serving scheme	CTR lift in explore (%)	CTR lift in exploit (%)	#Views in two weeks
Bayes 2×2	35.7%	38.7%	7,781,285
B-UCB1	12.2%	40.1%	7,753,184
ϵ-greedy	0.0%	39.4%	7,805,165

Note. Any difference less than 5 percent is not statistically significant. The average number of views per interval in explore is roughly 270.

6.5.4 Bucket Test Results

We now report results of experiments that were conducted on a fraction of live traffic from the Yahoo! Today module.

Experimental Setup. To set up an experiment, we create a number of equally sized random samples (i.e., buckets) of users. Each user is identified by an identifier (cookie) saved in the user's web browser by the website. We exclude users who do not accept cookies; the size of this user population is relatively small and does not affect the validity of our experiments. In each bucket, we run a different serving scheme and compare the performance of multiple schemes over the same time period. We consider three schemes, Bayes 2×2, B-UCB1, and ϵ-greedy, and use the overall CTR of a bucket over a two-week period as our performance measure for all methods. Ideally, we would like a scheme to have full control over all the traffic in its allocated bucket. However, owing to concerns regarding user experience with excessive exploration, each scheme was allowed a maximum of 15 percent of the bucket to explore at any given time (the *explore traffic*). The remaining 85 percent of the bucket has to show the current EMP as determined by the scheme (the *exploit traffic*). We report the performance of the explore traffic and of the exploit traffic separately. Both Bayes 2×2 and B-UCB1 assign 85 percent of views to the item having the highest estimated CTR and allocate the remaining 15 percent using the scheme after incorporating feedback from 85 percent views that have already been allocated to the highest-CTR item. For ϵ-greedy, we use 15 percent to explore every available item randomly. For confidentiality reasons, we do not disclose the actual CTRs of the buckets and only report CTR lift relative to a bucket that serves every available item randomly.

Table 6.1 shows the results. All the schemes have almost the same CTR lift in the exploit traffic. However, in the explore traffic, it is clear that Bayes 2×2

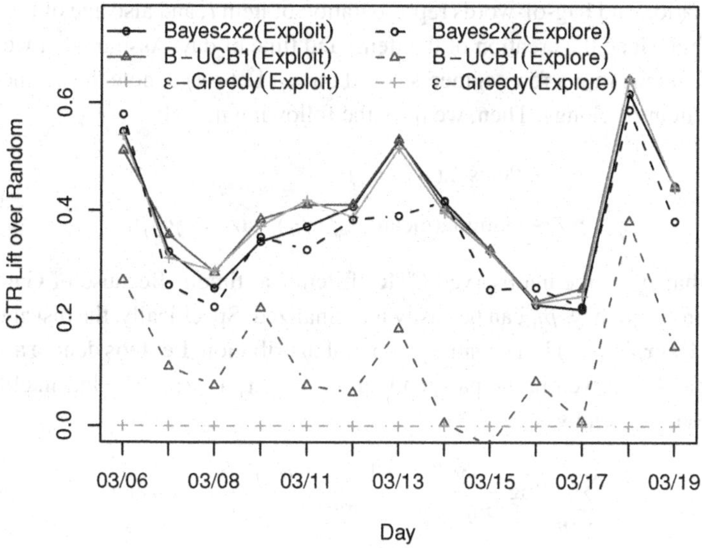

Figure 6.7. Online bucket test results over a two-week period.

is significantly better than B-UCB1, which is significantly better than random. With roughly 270 views per five-minute interval to explore roughly twenty items, all schemes can easily find the current best item, but Bayes 2×2 finds it more economically. Figure 6.7 shows the same results on a daily basis. Bayes 2×2 dominates others uniformly across days in the explore bucket.

6.6 Large Content Pools

So far, we have analyzed the most-popular recommendation with a modestly sized content pool, where the number of candidate items is relatively small compared to the number of user visits. In some application settings, the size of the content pool may be prohibitively large to explore each item even a small number of times. In these scenarios, it is important to obtain some a priori estimates of item CTRs before we recommend them to any user to reduce exploration cost. One natural approach is to use item features to obtain an informative prior distribution for each item at the beginning of its lifetime. This CTR prior is then continuously updated once views and clicks are observed, and it is also used by explore-exploit schemes to compute serving plans.

We continue using the Gamma-Poisson model. Let c_{it} and n_{it} denote the number of clicks and the number of views for item i at time t. Let $\boldsymbol{x}_{it}$ denote the features associated with item i and time t, which may include the category information and bag-of-words representation of item i, and also age of the item (i.e., time since the creation of the item) and time of day. Assume that we also classify items into a few segments based on $\boldsymbol{x}_{it}$. Let $s(i)$ denote the segment to which item i belongs. Then, we have the following model:

$$\begin{aligned} c_{it} &\sim \text{Poisson}(p_{it} \cdot n_{it}) \\ p_{it} &\sim \text{Gamma}(\text{mean} = f(\boldsymbol{x}_{it}),\ \text{size} = \gamma_{s(i)}). \end{aligned} \tag{6.8}$$

Note that p_{it} is the unobserved CTR of item i at time t. Because of Gamma-Poisson conjugacy, p_{it} can be easily marginalized. Specifically, the distribution of $(c_{it} \mid f(\boldsymbol{x}_{it}), \gamma_{s(i)})$ is a negative-binomial distribution. Let **Obs** denote a set of (i, t) pairs observed in the past, and let $\alpha_{it} = f(\boldsymbol{x}_{it}) \cdot \gamma_{s(i)}$. The log-likelihood function is given by

$$\sum_{(i,t)\in\textbf{Obs}} \log \frac{(\gamma_{s(i)})^{\alpha_{it}} \cdot \Gamma(c_{it} + \alpha_{it})}{(n_{it} + \gamma_{s(i)})^{(c_{it}+\alpha_{it})} \cdot \Gamma(\alpha_{it})} + \text{ constant}, \tag{6.9}$$

where $\Gamma(\cdot)$ is the Gamma function. Because the mean of the Gamma distribution is positive, one common choice of the prediction function is $f(\boldsymbol{x}_{it}) = \exp(\boldsymbol{\beta}'\boldsymbol{x}_{it})$, where $\boldsymbol{\beta}$ is the regression coefficient vector. The maximum likelihood estimate can be obtained by maximizing log-likelihood function (6.9) (e.g., using gradient descent). To stabilize model fitting, L2 regularization $\lambda \cdot \|\boldsymbol{\beta}\|^2$ is commonly added to the loss function (i.e., negative log-likelihood), where λ is a tuning parameter.

6.7 Summary

The simplest problem of recommending the most-popular item in web recommender problems is an explore-exploit problem. Although it has strong connections to the classic multiarmed bandit problems studied for a long time in the literature, several crucial assumptions do not hold. This requires developing a new set of methods. We presented a Bayesian decision-theoretic approach that attacked the problem from first principles and also described some adaptations of classical techniques. Our empirical evaluation shows that when the system can be modeled properly using a Bayesian framework, the Bayesian solution is significantly better than others. However, if proper modeling requires significant work, using simple heuristics that are adaptations of classical bandit schemes is a good approach. Of these heuristics, we recommend B-UCB1, SoftMax (with proper tweaking), and the simplest of them all: ϵ-greedy (with proper tweaking).

Exercises

1. Provide a detailed proof of Propositions 6.5 and 6.6. Also, verify the properties of the Gain function stated immediately following Proposition 6.6.
2. Provide detailed proofs of Propositions 6.8 and 6.9. Also, derive the formula in Equation (6.3).

7
Personalization through Feature-Based Regression

It is important to recommend items that are tailored to the personal interests and information needs of each individual user. Recommending items based on global popularity is often not sufficient. Some personalization may be achieved through an easy extension to most-popular recommendation by creating user segments based on attributes such as age, gender and geolocation (e.g., male users between twenty and forty years old living on the East Coast may form a segment) and serving the most-popular items within each segment. However, such a strategy has limitations. When the number of user segments is large, obtaining a reliable estimate of the popularity of items for each segment is difficult because of data sparsity. Also, user visits tend to follow a power law type of distribution – a small fraction of active users tends to visit the site very often, while the rest are sporadic. It is desirable to build custom models for active users who have visited the site several times in the past. For instance, if Mary visited the Yahoo! front page one hundred times in the last week and clearly indicated her preference for baseball news over everything else, a baseball article in our content pool should get precedence for Mary's next visit. For users who visit sporadically, personalization is usually accomplished by pooling data across users who are similar. Defining similarity is the crux of the problem, and it is often done by looking at user features such as demographics, behavioral attributes, and social network information, among other sources of signals. Combining these signals in an accurate fashion is challenging. In addition, many users are in the gray area of being superactive versus sporadic visitors. We need a methodology that can automatically determine the appropriate amount of weighting we should provide to a user's own past interactions and those of similar users.

For recommender systems where users, items, and their behavior do not change over time, offline models that are trained based on a one-time dump of historical data may be sufficient. See Chapter 2 for such models. However, in many application settings, new items are frequently added, and user behaviors and interests also change over time. It is important to update recommendation models frequently to capture such nonstationarity.

In this chapter, we focus on feature-based regression, which personalizes recommendations of time-sensitive items by capturing similarities through a regression approach. In Chapter 8, we improve these feature-based models through matrix factorization methods that can appropriately weight the signals derived using similarity and users' past actions.

Two standard approaches that are often used are based on offline feature-based regression and standard online regression. Although they are simple to implement, both have limitations: in offline feature-based regression, user i and item j are characterized by feature vectors $\boldsymbol{x}_i$ and $\boldsymbol{x}_j$, respectively. An *offline* regression model is trained using $\boldsymbol{x}_i$ and $\boldsymbol{x}_j$ as features to predict expected response s_{ij} when user i interacts with item j. Such models are effective when the behavior of users, items, and their interaction can be completely captured by their features. However, finding such an exhaustive set of predictive features is challenging. We often find that items with very similar features have different popularity for a given user segment, simply because the constrained set of features is not able to capture all the heterogeneity in the data. Also, addition of new items and users adds to the heterogeneity and requires constant revision of features in the model. Another routine approach is to build an online regression model for each user or item. Consider a scenario where we want to learn an item-specific regression for a set of the user features. We can model the expected response s_{ij} (or some monotone transformation) using a generalized linear model $f(s_{ij}) = \boldsymbol{x}_i'\boldsymbol{\beta}_j$, where $\boldsymbol{\beta}_j$ is the regression coefficient vector of item j on the user features $\boldsymbol{x}_i$. This is an attractive approach when the dimension of user feature vector is small; a large-dimensional $\boldsymbol{\beta}_j$ will generally lead to slow convergence and inferior performance in online scenarios. Also notice that $\boldsymbol{\beta}_j$ needs to be trained through user response data on item j. For applications with many items in the content pool, we may not have sufficient user response to accurately learn $\boldsymbol{\beta}_j$ before item j expires.

The goal of this chapter is to provide methods that have the following characteristics:

- *Fast learning of item-specific or user-specific behavior*: To overcome the limitations of feature-based regression, we want to model user-item interaction at the individual item or user level. This is achieved by extending feature-based models with item-specific or user-specific *factors*, that is, a set of regression coefficients for individual items or users. The factors are not known for new items or users and have to be learned rapidly in an online manner to provide good personalized recommendations in a timely fashion.

- *Effective cold-start handling*: Good recommendations should be provided for new items and users when no response data are available to determine item or user factors.
- *Scalability*: It is routine to have applications with large item pools and a high frequency of visits. Hence the online learning methods should be computationally efficient and scalable.

In this chapter, we discuss models that have either item-specific factors or user-specific factors, but not both. For ease of exposition, we consider models that leverage user *features* and learn item-specific *factors*. It is straightforward to switch the roles of users and items when needed. Models with factors for both users and items are discussed in Chapter 8.

Although a model with item-specific factors is a special case of that with both item- and user-specific factors, the former is computationally simpler and easier to scale. In application scenarios where a large fraction of visits are from sporadic visitors, it is computationally simple to use models that only use item factors. Given the cost to serve associated with complex models in real-world recommendation systems, studying simpler alternatives is important. A simpler model that sacrifices accuracy by a small amount but significantly reduces the engineering cost to serve is typically more attractive in applications.

7.1 Fast Online Bilinear Factor Model

In this section, we introduce our main model, the Fast Online Bilinear Factor Model (FOBFM). We give an overview in Section 7.1.1 and develop it fully in Section 7.1.2.

7.1.1 Overview of FOBFM

Conceptually, FOBFM consists of two main components: (1) a feature-based function to initialize online models using historical data and (2) a dimension reduction step for the online component where we learn only the reduced parameters online. We present a simplified version of FOBFM in this overview.

We use a feature-based regression model to predict the expected response s_{ij} of user i to item j:

$$\boldsymbol{x}_i' \boldsymbol{A} \boldsymbol{x}_j + \boldsymbol{x}_i' \boldsymbol{v}_j, \text{ where } \boldsymbol{v}_j = \boldsymbol{B} \boldsymbol{\delta}_j,$$

where $\boldsymbol{x}_i$ is the feature vector associated with user i; $\boldsymbol{x}_j$ is the feature vector for item j; $\boldsymbol{A}$ is a regression weight matrix (to be learned in an offline training process) that models the interaction between $\boldsymbol{x}_i$ and $\boldsymbol{x}_j$, as described in Section 2.3.2; and $\boldsymbol{v}_j$ is the item factor vector of item j. See Chapter 2 for examples of user and item features. The dimensionality of $\boldsymbol{v}_j$ is the same as $\boldsymbol{x}_i$, which is typically large. Thus, we decompose it into a *global* linear projection matrix $\boldsymbol{B}$ that is shared by all items and a low-dimensional item-specific factor vector $\boldsymbol{\delta}_j$ for each item. We learn $\boldsymbol{B}$ and $\boldsymbol{\delta}_j$ through an offline and an online training process, respectively. The four main ideas of this model are as follows.

Feature-based Initialization. The offline bilinear feature-based regression model $\boldsymbol{x}_i'\boldsymbol{A}\boldsymbol{x}_j$ provides a good offset (or initial point) for online learning of $\boldsymbol{\delta}_j$ based on features $\boldsymbol{x}_i$ and $\boldsymbol{x}_j$; the online model only needs to learn the "correction" over this offset. Before we observe any online data (when $\boldsymbol{\delta}_j = 0$), the response is actually predicted by this offline regression model. For instance, if click rates for males on sports articles are four times higher than those for females, the offline part will use this knowledge for a new sports article and expedite convergence of the online item factor estimates. In applications where feature-based components capture most of the signal in the data, the online component is not needed. This is rarely the case in web recommendation problems.

Dimensionality Reduction. Vector $\boldsymbol{v}_j$ is the regression coefficient vector on user factors (with one coefficient per individual user feature) for each item j (each item has its own coefficient vector). In practice, the dimensionality of $\boldsymbol{v}_j$ (i.e., the dimensionality of the user feature space) needs to be reasonably large to model the data well. However, $\boldsymbol{v}_j$ also needs to be learned online. For faster convergence, some form of dimension reduction is called for, especially during the early part of an item's lifetime. In the context of regression, this can be achieved through shrinkage estimation techniques that constrain the degrees of freedom in $\boldsymbol{v}_j$ by estimating an informative prior through retrospective data. Such an approach, although attractive, is computationally expensive, because it still requires updates of a large number of parameters in an online setting. To achieve both "shrinkage" and "fast updates," we appeal to an old technique known as reduced-rank regression (Anderson, 1951) to reduce the dimension of parameter space when estimating a large set of related regressions through a lower-dimensional projection. Thus, $\boldsymbol{v}_j = \boldsymbol{B}\boldsymbol{\delta}_j$, and $\boldsymbol{B}$ is learned offline. Then, only the small-dimensional vector $\boldsymbol{\delta}_j$ needs to be learned online per item. In fact, rank reduction is equivalent to putting linear constraints on the parameter vector $\boldsymbol{v}_j$, thus reduced rank imposes "hard" constraints on the parameters, as opposed to "soft" constraints that are imposed through a prior on $\boldsymbol{v}_j$ by shrinkage methods.

Table 7.1. *Fast Online Bilinear Factor Model*

Observation	$y_{ijt} \sim \text{Normal}(s_{ijt}, \sigma^2)$ or $y_{ijt} \sim \text{Bernoulli}(p_{ijt}),\ s_{ijt} = \log \frac{p_{ijt}}{1-p_{ijt}}$
Offline model	$s_{ijt} = \boldsymbol{x}'_{ijt}\boldsymbol{b} + \boldsymbol{x}'_{it}\boldsymbol{A}\boldsymbol{x}_j + \boldsymbol{x}'_{it}\boldsymbol{v}_{jt}$ $\boldsymbol{v}_{jt} = \boldsymbol{B}\boldsymbol{\delta}_j$ $\boldsymbol{\delta}_j \sim N(\boldsymbol{0}, \sigma_v^2\boldsymbol{I})$
Online model	$s_{ijt} = \boldsymbol{x}'_{ijt}\boldsymbol{b} + \boldsymbol{x}'_{it}\boldsymbol{A}\boldsymbol{x}_j + \boldsymbol{x}'_{it}\boldsymbol{B}\boldsymbol{\delta}_{jt}$ Only $\boldsymbol{\delta}_{jt}$ is learned through online regression

Rapid Online Regression. Because the dimensionality of $\boldsymbol{\delta}_j$ is small, we can obtain reliable online estimates for each item even with a relatively smaller sample size. Also, each $\boldsymbol{\delta}_j$ can be learned independently. Thus, the models for different items can be fitted in parallel.

Online Model Selection. A rank reduction parameter $k = \text{rank}(\boldsymbol{B})$ is crucial and needs to be estimated properly. We do so by simultaneously fitting k online models for each item j for k different rank values and selecting the model with the current best predictive log-likelihood.

7.1.2 Details of FOBFM

The details of FOBFM are summarized in Table 7.1. We denote by (i, j) the pair corresponding to user i and item j. Let y_{ijt} denote the response (rating or click) observed after item j is displayed to user i at time t. Following our convention, let $\boldsymbol{x}_{it}$, $\boldsymbol{x}_j$ and $\boldsymbol{x}_{ijt}$ denote feature vectors for user i (at time t), item j and pair (i, j) (at time t) respectively. Vector $\boldsymbol{x}_{it}$ may include user demographics, geolocation, browse behavior, and so on; $\boldsymbol{x}_j$ may include content category, tokens extracted from the title or body when items have textual description, and so on. Although item features may also be time sensitive, in most of our examples we do not have such features, hence there is no subscript t for item features $\boldsymbol{x}_j$ in our notation. Finally, $\boldsymbol{x}_{ijt}$ is a vector of features that are not entirely attributable to either user or item; examples include position on a page where an item is displayed, time of day when an item is displayed, and so on. We may drop the time index t when it is not required.

Response Model

Let s_{ijt} denote the *unobserved true score* that user i would give item j at time t. Our goal is to estimate s_{ijt}, for any given (i, j) pair, based on the observed response, y_{ijt} (which may be noisy), and features, $\boldsymbol{x}_{it}, \boldsymbol{x}_j$, and $\boldsymbol{x}_{ijt}$. Any response model described in Section 2.3.2 can be used. Here we only discuss two.

- *Gaussian model for numeric response*: For a numeric response (or ratings), it is common to assume that:

$$y_{ijt} \sim N(s_{ijt}, \sigma^2), \tag{7.1}$$

  where σ^2 is the variance of noise in user response, to be estimated from data. Here s_{ijt} represents the mean of the numeric rating that user i would give j.
- *Logistic model for binary response*: When users respond to items in a binary manner (e.g., click or not, like or not, share or not), it is common to assume that:

$$y_{ijt} \sim \text{Bernoulli}(p_{ijt}) \text{ and } s_{ijt} = \log \tfrac{p_{ijt}}{1-p_{ijt}}, \tag{7.2}$$

  where p_{ijt} is the probability that user i would respond to item j positively at time t (e.g., click probability).

Online Regression + Feature-based Offset

The key modeling challenge is to estimate the s_{ijt}s that capture interaction between user i and item j over time. FOBFM models s_{ijt} as a combination of feature-based regression and per-item regression:

$$s_{ijt} = (\boldsymbol{x}'_{ijt}\boldsymbol{b} + \boldsymbol{x}'_{it}\boldsymbol{A}\boldsymbol{x}_j) + \boldsymbol{x}'_{it}\boldsymbol{v}_{jt}. \tag{7.3}$$

In the feature-based regression term $(\boldsymbol{x}'_{ijt}\boldsymbol{b} + \boldsymbol{x}'_{it}\boldsymbol{A}\boldsymbol{x}_j)$, $\boldsymbol{b}$ and $\boldsymbol{A}$ are unknown regression weights that can be estimated from large number of historical data. Note that we do not consider item IDs to be features. Although this regression provides a good baseline, the predictive performance can be significantly improved by adding the per-item regression term $\boldsymbol{x}'_{it}\boldsymbol{v}_{jt}$, where $\boldsymbol{v}_{jt}$ is the item-specific factor vector and incorporates heterogeneity at the individual item level. Because new items do not appear in historical data, their $\boldsymbol{v}_{jt}$s need to be learned online.

The feature-based regression term $\boldsymbol{x}'_{ijt}\boldsymbol{b} + \boldsymbol{x}'_{it}\boldsymbol{A}\boldsymbol{x}_j$ provides a strong *offset* for online learning of item-specific factors. In particular, we only need to learn the "correction" to this offset online. When the features are reasonably predictive, the variation in corrections is small and the online model converges more quickly.

In general, $\boldsymbol{x}_{it}$ and $\boldsymbol{x}_j$ can be high-dimensional; hence, the regression weight matrix $\boldsymbol{A}$ can be large. However, $\boldsymbol{x}_{it}$ and $\boldsymbol{x}_j$ are also typically sparse; many learning methods (e.g., Lin et al., 2008) can exploit this sparsity to obtain estimates of $\boldsymbol{A}$ in a scalable fashion.

Having item-specific factors $\boldsymbol{v}_{jt}$ increases the complexity of the model and makes parameter estimation challenging. For instance, if the user feature vector $\boldsymbol{x}_{it}$ has a few thousand elements, one may have to estimate millions of parameters with a modest inventory pool of a few thousand items using a fairly small number of observations (because new items have small sample size).

Reduced Rank Regression

By imposing linear constraints on item regression parameters, we obtain a significant reduction in computational complexity in the online phase by sharing parameters across items. We assume the $\boldsymbol{v}_{jt}$s belong to a k-dimensional linear subspace spanned by the columns of an unknown projection matrix $\boldsymbol{B}_{r\times k}$ $(k \ll r)$; that is,

$$\boldsymbol{v}_{jt} = \boldsymbol{B}\boldsymbol{\delta}_{jt} \tag{7.4}$$

for all items j. All of the items share the same projection matrix $\boldsymbol{B}$. Given $\boldsymbol{B}$, we only need to learn a k-dimensional vector $\boldsymbol{\delta}_{jt}$ online for each item j.

To avoid numerical ill-conditioning during computations, we assume $\boldsymbol{\delta}_{jt} \sim \text{MVN}(\boldsymbol{0}, \sigma_\delta^2 \boldsymbol{I})$, where MVN denotes the multivariate normal distribution. Marginalizing over $\boldsymbol{\delta}_{jt}$, it is easy to see that $\boldsymbol{v}_{jt} \sim \text{MVN}(\boldsymbol{0}, \sigma^2 \boldsymbol{B}\boldsymbol{B}')$. Because $\text{rank}(\boldsymbol{B}) = k < r$, this puts all probability mass in a lower-dimensional subspace spanned by the columns of $\boldsymbol{B}$. It is generally better to work with a more robust model that assumes $\boldsymbol{v}_{jt} = \boldsymbol{B}\boldsymbol{\delta}_{jt} + \boldsymbol{\epsilon}_{jt}$, where $\boldsymbol{\epsilon}_{jt} \sim \text{MVN}(\boldsymbol{0}, \tau^2 \boldsymbol{I})$ is a white-noise process that captures idiosyncracies leftover after the k-dimensional linear projection. This removes the rank deficiency and the marginal distribution of $\boldsymbol{v}_{jt} \sim \text{MVN}(\boldsymbol{0}, \sigma^2 \boldsymbol{B}\boldsymbol{B}' + \tau^2 \boldsymbol{I})$. Although it is easy to work with this model for Gaussian response, it adds significant computational complexity for the logistic model; hence, we assume $\tau^2 = 0$.

7.2 Offline Training

The model-fitting algorithms that we use for FOBFM consist of an offline training algorithm (described in this section) and an online learning algorithm (described in Section 7.3). The offline training algorithm is based on the expectation-maximization (EM) algorithm to estimate parameters $\boldsymbol{\Theta} = (\boldsymbol{b}, \boldsymbol{A}, \boldsymbol{B}, \sigma^2, \sigma_v^2)$ using response data observed in the past. For succinctness, we drop the time index t and let $\boldsymbol{y} = \{y_{ij}\}$ denote the set of the observations. These "incomplete" data are augmented with unobserved item factors $\boldsymbol{\Delta} = \{\boldsymbol{\delta}_j\}_{\forall j}$ to obtain the *complete data*. The goal of the EM algorithm is to find the parameter $\boldsymbol{\Theta}$ that maximizes the "incomplete" data likelihood $\Pr(\boldsymbol{y}|\boldsymbol{\Theta}) = \int \Pr(\boldsymbol{y}, \boldsymbol{\Delta}|\boldsymbol{\Theta}) d\boldsymbol{\Delta}$ obtained after marginalization over the distribution of $\boldsymbol{\Delta}$

(because they are not observed). Such a marginalization is computationally expensive. Hence, we take recourse to the EM algorithm.

7.2.1 EM Algorithm

The complete data log-likelihood $L(\boldsymbol{\Theta}; \boldsymbol{y}, \boldsymbol{\Delta})$ for the Gaussian model is given by

$$
\begin{aligned}
L(\boldsymbol{\Theta}; \boldsymbol{y}, \boldsymbol{\Delta}) &= \log \Pr(\boldsymbol{y} \mid \boldsymbol{\Theta}, \boldsymbol{\Delta}) \\
&= -\frac{1}{2\sigma^2} \sum_{ij} (y_{ij} - \boldsymbol{x}_{ij}'\boldsymbol{b} - \boldsymbol{x}_i'\boldsymbol{A}\boldsymbol{x}_j - \boldsymbol{x}_i'\boldsymbol{B}\boldsymbol{\delta}_j)^2 - \frac{D}{2}\log\sigma^2 \\
&\quad - \frac{1}{2\sigma_v^2} \sum_j \boldsymbol{\delta}_j'\boldsymbol{\delta}_j - \frac{Nk}{2}\log\sigma_v^2,
\end{aligned} \tag{7.5}
$$

where D is the number of observations, N is the number of items, and $\boldsymbol{\delta}_j$ is a k-dimensional vector. For the logistic model ($y_{ij} \in \{0, 1\}$), we have

$$
\begin{aligned}
&L(\boldsymbol{\Theta}; \boldsymbol{y}, \boldsymbol{\Delta}) \\
&= -\sum_{ij} \log\left(1 + \exp\{-(2y_{ij} - 1)(\boldsymbol{x}_{ij}'\boldsymbol{b} + \boldsymbol{x}_i'\boldsymbol{A}\boldsymbol{x}_j + \boldsymbol{x}_i'\boldsymbol{B}\boldsymbol{\delta}_j)\}\right) \\
&\quad - \frac{1}{2\sigma_v^2} \sum_j \boldsymbol{\delta}_j'\boldsymbol{\delta}_j - \frac{Nk}{2}\log\sigma_v^2.
\end{aligned} \tag{7.6}
$$

Let $\boldsymbol{\Theta}^{(h)}$ denote the estimated parameter setting at the hth iteration. The EM algorithm iterates through the following two steps until convergence:

1. *E-step*: Compute $q_h(\boldsymbol{\Theta}) = E_{\boldsymbol{\Delta}}[L(\boldsymbol{\Theta}; \boldsymbol{y}, \boldsymbol{\Delta}) \mid \boldsymbol{\Theta}^{(h)}]$ as a function of $\boldsymbol{\Theta}$, where the expectation is taken over the posterior distribution of $(\boldsymbol{\Delta} \mid \boldsymbol{\Theta}^{(h)}, \boldsymbol{y})$. Here $\boldsymbol{\Theta} = (\boldsymbol{b}, \boldsymbol{A}, \boldsymbol{B}, \sigma^2, \sigma_v^2)$ is the input variable of function q_h, but $\boldsymbol{\Theta}^{(h)}$ consists of known quantities determined in the previous iteration. Let $\hat{\boldsymbol{\delta}}_j$ and $\hat{V}[\boldsymbol{\delta}_j]$ denote the posterior mean and variance given $\boldsymbol{y}$ and $\boldsymbol{\Theta}^{(h)}$. For the Gaussian model, we have

$$
\begin{aligned}
q_h(\boldsymbol{\Theta}) &= E_{\boldsymbol{\Delta}}[L(\boldsymbol{\Theta}; \boldsymbol{y}, \boldsymbol{\Delta}) \mid \boldsymbol{\Theta}^{(h)}] \\
&= -\frac{1}{2\sigma^2} \sum_{ij} \left((y_{ij} - \boldsymbol{x}_{ij}'\boldsymbol{b} - \boldsymbol{x}_i'\boldsymbol{A}\boldsymbol{x}_j - \boldsymbol{x}_i'\boldsymbol{B}\hat{\boldsymbol{\delta}}_j)^2 + \boldsymbol{x}_i'\boldsymbol{B}\hat{V}[\boldsymbol{\delta}_j]\boldsymbol{B}'\boldsymbol{x}_i \right) \\
&\quad - \frac{D}{2}\log\sigma^2 - \frac{1}{2\sigma_v^2} \sum_j \left(\hat{\boldsymbol{\delta}}_j'\hat{\boldsymbol{\delta}}_j + \mathrm{tr}(\hat{V}[\boldsymbol{\delta}_j]) \right) - \frac{Nk}{2}\log\sigma_v^2.
\end{aligned} \tag{7.7}
$$

The logistic model is described in Section 7.2.2. We compute the sufficient statistics of $q_h(\boldsymbol{\Theta})$ (i.e., $\hat{\boldsymbol{\delta}}_j$ and $\hat{V}[\boldsymbol{\delta}_j]$, for all item j) in the E-step.

2. *M-step*: Find the $\boldsymbol{\Theta}$ that maximizes the expectation computed in the E-step:

$$\boldsymbol{\Theta}^{(h+1)} = \arg\max_{\boldsymbol{\Theta}} q_h(\boldsymbol{\Theta}). \tag{7.8}$$

For the Gaussian model, we find $(\boldsymbol{b}, \boldsymbol{A}, \boldsymbol{B}, \sigma^2, \sigma_v^2)$ that maximizes Equation (7.7) with $\hat{\boldsymbol{\delta}}_j$ and $\hat{V}[\boldsymbol{\delta}_j]$ computed in the previous E-step.

We now look at the details of the E-step and the M-step.

7.2.2 E-Step

The goal of the E-step is to compute the posterior mean $\hat{\boldsymbol{\delta}}_j$ and variance $\hat{V}[\boldsymbol{\delta}_j]$ of the factor vector for each item j. Let $o_{ij} = \boldsymbol{x}'_{ij}\boldsymbol{b} + \boldsymbol{x}'_i\boldsymbol{A}\boldsymbol{x}_j$ and $\boldsymbol{z}_i = \boldsymbol{B}'\boldsymbol{x}_i$.

Gaussian Model. We rewrite the Gaussian model as

$$\begin{aligned} y_{ij} &\sim N(o_{ij} + \boldsymbol{z}'_i\boldsymbol{\delta}_j,\ \sigma^2) \\ \boldsymbol{\delta}_j &\sim N(\boldsymbol{0},\ \sigma_v^2\boldsymbol{I}). \end{aligned} \tag{7.9}$$

This is a standard form of Bayesian linear regression with (linearly transformed) feature vector $\boldsymbol{z}_i$ and offset o_{ij}. By Gaussian conjugacy, we have

$$\begin{aligned} \hat{V}[\boldsymbol{\delta}_j] &= \left(\frac{1}{\sigma_v^2}\boldsymbol{I} + \sum_{i \in \mathcal{I}_j} \frac{\boldsymbol{z}_i\boldsymbol{z}'_i}{\sigma^2}\right)^{-1} \\ \hat{\boldsymbol{\delta}}_j &= \hat{V}[\boldsymbol{\delta}_j]\left(\sum_{i \in \mathcal{I}_j} \frac{(y_{ij} - o_{ij})\boldsymbol{z}_i}{\sigma^2}\right). \end{aligned} \tag{7.10}$$

Logistic Model. We can also rewrite the logistic model in a similar way:

$$\begin{aligned} y_{ij} &\sim \text{Bernoulli}(p_{ij}) \text{ with } \log\frac{p_{ij}}{1 - p_{ij}} = o_{ij} + \boldsymbol{z}'_i\boldsymbol{\delta}_j \\ \boldsymbol{\delta}_j &\sim N(\boldsymbol{0},\ \sigma_v^2\boldsymbol{I}). \end{aligned} \tag{7.11}$$

This is a standard Bayesian logistic regression with a Gaussian prior. Unfortunately, the posterior mean and variance of $\boldsymbol{\delta}_j$ are not available in closed form. One way to estimate them is by Laplace approximation. In particular, the posterior density of $\boldsymbol{\delta}_j$ is

$$\begin{aligned} p(\boldsymbol{\delta}_j \mid \boldsymbol{y}) &= p(\boldsymbol{\delta}_j, \boldsymbol{y})/p(\boldsymbol{y}) \\ \propto\ p(\boldsymbol{\delta}_j, \boldsymbol{y}) &= \sum_i \log f((2y_{ij} - 1)(o_{ij} + \boldsymbol{z}_i'\boldsymbol{\delta}_j)) - \frac{1}{2\sigma_v^2}\|\boldsymbol{\delta}_j\|^2, \end{aligned} \tag{7.12}$$

where $f(x) = (1 + e^{-x})^{-1}$ is the sigmoid function. We approximate the posterior mean by the posterior mode, that is,

$$\hat{\boldsymbol{\delta}}_j \approx \arg\max_{\boldsymbol{\delta}_j} p(\boldsymbol{\delta}_j, \boldsymbol{y}), \tag{7.13}$$

and we approximate the posterior variance through second-order Taylor series expansion evaluated at the mode, that is,

$$\hat{V}[\boldsymbol{\delta}_j] \approx \left[(-\nabla^2_{\boldsymbol{\delta}_j} p(\boldsymbol{\delta}_j, \boldsymbol{y}))|_{\boldsymbol{\delta}_j = \hat{\boldsymbol{\delta}}_j}\right]^{-1}. \tag{7.14}$$

Let $g_{ij}(\boldsymbol{\delta}_j) = f((2y_{ij} - 1)(o_{ij} + \boldsymbol{z}_i'\boldsymbol{\delta}_j))$. Then, $\hat{\boldsymbol{\delta}}_j$ can be found using any gradient methods, where the gradient and Hessian are given by

$$\begin{aligned} \nabla_{\boldsymbol{\delta}_j} p(\boldsymbol{\delta}_j, \boldsymbol{y}) &= \textstyle\sum_i (1 - g_{ij}(\boldsymbol{\delta}_j))(2y_{ij} - 1)\boldsymbol{z}_i - \frac{1}{\sigma_v^2}\boldsymbol{\delta}_j \\ \nabla^2_{\boldsymbol{\delta}_j} p(\boldsymbol{\delta}_j, \boldsymbol{y}) &= -\textstyle\sum_i g_{ij}(\boldsymbol{\delta}_j)(1 - g_{ij}(\boldsymbol{\delta}_j))\boldsymbol{z}_i\boldsymbol{z}_i' - \frac{1}{\sigma_v^2}\boldsymbol{I}. \end{aligned} \tag{7.15}$$

7.2.3 M-step

In the M-step, the goal is to find $\boldsymbol{\Theta}$ that maximizes

$$q_h(\boldsymbol{\Theta}) = E_{\boldsymbol{\Delta}}[L(\boldsymbol{\Theta}; \boldsymbol{y}, \boldsymbol{\Delta}) \mid \boldsymbol{\Theta}^{(h)}].$$

Gaussian Model. $q_h(\boldsymbol{\Theta})$ for the Gaussian model is defined in Equation (7.7). The steps as follows:

1. *Estimate regression coefficients* $(\boldsymbol{b}, \boldsymbol{A}, \boldsymbol{B})$: For computational efficiency, we make the following approximation:

$$\begin{aligned} &E[\textstyle\sum_{ij}(y_{ij} - \boldsymbol{x}_{ij}'\boldsymbol{b} - \boldsymbol{x}_i'\boldsymbol{A}\boldsymbol{x}_j - \boldsymbol{x}_i'\boldsymbol{B}\boldsymbol{\delta}_j)^2] \\ &\approx \textstyle\sum_{ij}(y_{ij} - \boldsymbol{x}_{ij}'\boldsymbol{b} - \boldsymbol{x}_i'\boldsymbol{A}\boldsymbol{x}_j - \boldsymbol{x}_i'\boldsymbol{B}\hat{\boldsymbol{\delta}}_j)^2. \end{aligned} \tag{7.16}$$

   Approximating the exact formula using plug-in estimates is a common practice to speed up computation (e.g., Mnih and Salakhutdinov, 2007; Celeux and Govaert, 1992). This means that we ignore covariance components

$x_i' B \hat{V}[\delta_j] B' x_i$ in our optimization. Now, we have a standard least squares regression problem:

$$\arg\max_{b,A,B} \sum_{ij} (y_{ij} - x_{ij}' b - x_i' A x_j - x_i' B \hat{\delta}_j)^2$$
$$+ \lambda_1 \|b\|^2 + \lambda_2 \|A\|^2 + \lambda_3 \|B\|^2. \tag{7.17}$$

Here we add L_2 regularization to make estimation robust, and any regularization and fitting methods can be applied to this standard least squares problem. We use $\hat{b}$, $\hat{A}$ and $\hat{B}$ to denote the estimated regression coefficients.

2. *Estimate observation variance* σ^2: By setting the gradient of $q_h(\Theta)$ with respect to σ^2 to zero, we obtain

$$\hat{\sigma}^2 = \frac{1}{D} \sum_{ij} \left((y_{ij} - x_{ij}' b - x_i' A x_j - x_i' B \hat{\delta}_j)^2 + x_i' B \hat{V}[\delta_j] B' x_i \right). \tag{7.18}$$

3. *Estimate prior variance* σ_v^2: By setting the gradient of $q_h(\Theta)$ with respect to σ_v^2 to zero, we obtain

$$\frac{1}{Nk} \sum_j \left(\hat{\delta}_j' \hat{\delta}_j + \text{tr}(\hat{V}[\delta_j]) \right). \tag{7.19}$$

Logistic Model. This is similar to the Gaussian model. We make the following approximation:

$$E[\textstyle\sum_{ij} \log \left(1 + \exp\{-(2y_{ij} - 1)(x_{ij}' b + x_i' A x_j + x_i' B \delta_j)\}\right)]$$
$$\approx \textstyle\sum_{ij} \log \left(1 + \exp\{-(2y_{ij} - 1)(x_{ij}' b + x_i' A x_j + x_i' B \hat{\delta}_j)\}\right). \tag{7.20}$$

Now, estimation of (b, A, B) is a standard logistic regression problem. Any regularization and fitting method can be used. It is also easy to see that estimation of σ_v^2 is the same as for the Gaussian model.

7.2.4 Scalability

The E-step consists of solving one independent Bayesian regression problem for each item. Because of this independence, we can easily split the response data by items and solve all the regression problems in parallel. The number of data for an individual problem is usually small. Even when the number of data is large, because the dimensionality of δ_j is small, using a random subsample usually does not cause much loss in precision. The main computation of the M-step is the estimation of (b, A, B), which is a standard least squares or logistic regression problem. Any scalable fitting methods such as stochastic gradient descent (SGD) or conjugate gradient (CG) can be used.

7.3 Online Learning

The output from the offline training that will be used in online learning consists of the regression coefficients ($\boldsymbol{b}$, $\boldsymbol{A}$, $\boldsymbol{B}$) and the prior variance σ_v^2. The online model for item j is given in Table 7.1, which we can rewrite as

$$\begin{aligned} s_{ijt} &= \boldsymbol{x}_{ijt}'\boldsymbol{b} + \boldsymbol{x}_{it}'\boldsymbol{A}\boldsymbol{x}_j + \boldsymbol{x}_{it}'\boldsymbol{B}\boldsymbol{\delta}_{jt} \\ &= o_{ijt} + \boldsymbol{z}_{it}'\boldsymbol{\delta}_{jt}, \end{aligned}$$

where $o_{ijt} = \boldsymbol{x}_{ijt}'\boldsymbol{b} + \boldsymbol{x}_{it}'\boldsymbol{A}\boldsymbol{x}_j$ is the offset, $\boldsymbol{z}_{it} = \boldsymbol{B}'\boldsymbol{x}_{it}$ is the dimension-reduced user feature vector, and $\boldsymbol{\delta}_{jt}$ is the regression coefficient vector. Because the online models (one for each item j) are independent and the dimensionality of $\boldsymbol{\delta}_j$ is small, the model update is very efficient, is scalable, and can be computed in parallel. In general, one can use the standard Kalman filter (West and Harrison, 1997) to sequentially update the model by setting the prior mean and variance of $\boldsymbol{\delta}_j$ to be 0 and σ_v^2, respectively. In the following, we provide the details of online learning for the Gaussian and logistic models and then discuss explore-exploit and online selection of the dimensionality of $\boldsymbol{\delta}_j$.

7.3.1 Gaussian Online Model

For any item j, we set $\boldsymbol{\mu}_{j0} = \boldsymbol{0}$ and $\boldsymbol{\Sigma}_{j0} = \sigma_v^2\boldsymbol{I}$ as the initial prior mean of variance of $\boldsymbol{\delta}_j$. Suppose we receive the response data from a set $\mathcal{I}_{jt}$ consisting of users i who interact with item j at time t (time t usually denotes a certain time period). The Gaussian online model is given by

$$\begin{aligned} y_{ijt} &\sim N(o_{ijt} + \boldsymbol{z}_{it}'\boldsymbol{\delta}_{jt},\ \sigma^2), \quad \text{for all } i \in \mathcal{I}_{jt} \\ \boldsymbol{\delta}_{jt} &\sim N(\boldsymbol{\mu}_{j,t-1},\ \rho\boldsymbol{\Sigma}_{j,t-1}), \end{aligned} \tag{7.21}$$

where $\rho \geq 1$ (usually close to 1) dilates the prior variance over time to give more recent observations higher weights. By Gaussian conjugacy, we have

$$\begin{aligned} \boldsymbol{\Sigma}_{jt} &= \left(\frac{1}{\rho}\boldsymbol{\Sigma}_{j,t-1}^{-1} + \sum_{i\in\mathcal{I}_{jt}} \frac{1}{\sigma^2}\boldsymbol{z}_{it}\boldsymbol{z}_{it}'\right)^{-1} \\ \boldsymbol{\mu}_{jt} &= \boldsymbol{\Sigma}_{jt}\left(\boldsymbol{\Sigma}_{j,t-1}^{-1}\boldsymbol{\mu}_{j,t-1} + \sum_{i\in\mathcal{I}_{jt}} \frac{(y_{ijt} - o_{ijt})\boldsymbol{z}_{it}}{\sigma^2}\right). \end{aligned} \tag{7.22}$$

7.3.2 Logistic Online Model

The logistic online model is given by

$$
\begin{aligned}
y_{ijt} &\sim \text{Bernoulli}(p_{ijt}), \\
\log \frac{p_{ijt}}{1 - p_{ijt}} &= o_{ijt} + z_{it}'\delta_{jt}, \quad \text{for all } i \in \mathcal{I}_{jt}, \\
\delta_{jt} &\sim N(\mu_{j,t-1},\ \rho\Sigma_{j,t-1}).
\end{aligned} \tag{7.23}
$$

As with the logistic model in Section 7.2.2, the posterior mean and variance of δ_{jt} are not available in closed form, and we use the Laplace approximation:

$$
\begin{aligned}
p(\delta_{jt}, y) = &\textstyle\sum_{i \in \mathcal{I}_{jt}} \log f((2y_{ijt} - 1)(o_{ijt} + z_{it}'\delta_{jt})) \\
&- \tfrac{1}{2\rho}(\delta_{jt} - \mu_{j,t-1})'\Sigma_{j,t-1}^{-1}(\delta_{jt} - \mu_{j,t-1}),
\end{aligned} \tag{7.24}
$$

where $f(x) = (1 + e^{-x})^{-1}$ is the sigmoid function. We approximate the posterior mean by the posterior mode, that is,

$$
\mu_{jt} \approx \arg\max_{\delta_{jt}} p(\delta_{jt}, y), \tag{7.25}
$$

and we approximate the posterior variance through second-order Taylor series expansion evaluated at the mode, that is,

$$
\Sigma_{jt} \approx \left[(-\nabla^2_{\delta_{jt}} p(\delta_{jt}, y))|_{\delta_{jt}=\mu_{jt}}\right]^{-1}. \tag{7.26}
$$

Let $g_{ijt}(\delta_{jt}) = f((2y_{ijt} - 1)(o_{ijt} + z_{it}'\delta_{jt}))$. Then, μ_{jt} can be found using any gradient methods, where the gradient and Hessian are given by

$$
\begin{aligned}
\nabla_{\delta_{jt}} p(\delta_{jt}, y) &= \textstyle\sum_i (1 - g_{ijt}(\delta_{jt}))(2y_{ijt} - 1)z_{it} - \tfrac{1}{\rho}\Sigma_{j,t-1}^{-1}(\delta_{jt} - \mu_{j,t-1}) \\
\nabla^2_{\delta_j} p(\delta_j, y) &= -\textstyle\sum_i g_{ij}(\delta_j)(1 - g_{ij}(\delta_j))z_i z_i' - \tfrac{1}{\rho}\Sigma_{j,t-1}^{-1}.
\end{aligned} \tag{7.27}
$$

7.3.3 Explore-Exploit Schemes

To estimate the factor vector δ_{jt} of item j, we need to obtain users' responses on the item. An explore-exploit scheme is needed to explore items with uncertain factor estimates, especially for new items. Although Bayesian explore-exploit schemes outperform many other schemes in the most-popular recommendation scenario, they are not easy to extend to personalized models because of high computational cost. The following explore-exploit schemes are commonly used in practice:

- *ϵ-Greedy*: Allocate a small fraction ϵ of users (or visits, for certain positions in the recommendation module) to random exploration of items that have not received some number of observations. For the rest of the users, recommend items with the highest predicted response rates.

- *SoftMax*: For each user visit i, we pick item j with probability

$$\frac{e^{\hat{s}_{ijt}/\tau}}{\sum_j e^{\hat{s}_{ijt}/\tau}}, \tag{7.28}$$

where the temperature parameter τ can be empirically tuned and s_{ijt} is the predicted score from the model.

- *Thompson sampling*: For each user visit i, for each candidate item j, draw $\boldsymbol{\delta}_{jt}$ from $N(\boldsymbol{\mu}_{jt}, \boldsymbol{\Sigma}_{jt})$ and compute the score s_{ijt} based on this sampled factor vector. Then, rank items based on the scores.
- *d-deviation UCB*: For each user visit i, for each candidate item j, compute the d-deviation UCB score

$$o_{ijt} + \boldsymbol{z}'_{it}\boldsymbol{\mu}_{jt} + d(\boldsymbol{z}'_{it}\boldsymbol{\Sigma}_{jt}\boldsymbol{z}_{it})^{\frac{1}{2}} \tag{7.29}$$

and rank items based on these scores, where d can be empirically tuned.

7.3.4 Online Model Selection

The number of factors k per item (the length of vector $\boldsymbol{\delta}_j$) can have an impact on model performance; this is especially true in the early part of an item's lifetime. For instance, when we only have a small number of users' responses (i.e., observations) to an item, it is difficult to learn a model with a large number of parameters; thus, models with small values of k are expected to perform better. However, models with small values of k are less flexible and usually do not have the capacity to capture the detailed behavior of users' interactions with the item; thus, with an increasing number of observations on the item, models with large values of k are expected to perform better.

To select the best k, we take the approach of online model selection. Specifically, for each item, we maintain multiple models, one for each preselected k value (e.g., $k = 1, \ldots, 10$). We assume that the best k value for an item is a function of the number n of observations that the item has received, denoted by $k^*(n)$. To determine $k^*(n)$, we use the predictive log-likelihood as the selection criterion. Let $\ell(k, n, j)$ denote the log-likelihood of predicting the $(n+1)$th observations of item j using the model for the item with k factors trained with the item's first n observations. Let $\mathcal{J}(n)$ denote the set of candidate items that have received n observations. $\mathcal{J}(n)$ changes over time because both the set of candidate items and the number of observations received by each item change over time. The average log-likelihood of the models with k factors trained with n observations is

$$\ell(k, n) = \frac{\sum_{j \in \mathcal{J}(n+1)} \ell(k, n, j)}{|\mathcal{J}(n+1)|}. \tag{7.30}$$

For any given item with n observations, we could pick the k that has the largest $\ell(k, n)$; that is, $k^*(n) = \arg\max_k \ell(k, n)$. However, when $|\mathcal{J}(n+1)|$ is small, $\ell(k, n)$ would be noisy. We can use a simple exponential weighting scheme to smooth $\ell(k, n)$. Let $0 < w \leq 1$ be a prespecified weight. The smoothed average log-likelihood $\ell^*(k, n)$ is obtained through the following rules:

$$\begin{aligned} &\ell^*(k, 1) = \ell(k, 1) \\ &\ell^*(k, n) = w\,\ell(k, n) + (1 - w)\,\ell^*(k, n-1), \quad \text{for } n > 1. \end{aligned} \tag{7.31}$$

7.4 Illustration on Yahoo! Data Sets

In this section, we demonstrate FOBFM on two data sets collected from a selected set of server logs of user visits to the Yahoo! front page and My Yahoo!, respectively. Each observation represents either a *positive event*, in which a user clicked an item (article link), or a *negative event*, in which a user viewed an item but did not click. In particular, we show that online models using a large number of features without proper initialization may have poor performance in cold-start situations; principal component regression (PCR) models without proper initialization could also suffer. On the contrary, FOBFM effectively accelerates online learning and significantly outperforms other baseline models in our application scenarios.

We partition each data set into two disjoint sets of events:

1. *Training set*: Offline model parameters (e.g., $\boldsymbol{\Theta} = (\boldsymbol{b}, \boldsymbol{A}, \boldsymbol{B}, \sigma^2)$ in FOBFM) are estimated using the training set. Whenever necessary, we further subdivide the training set to create a tuning set to tweak parameters of some baseline models. We note that no such tweaking is required for FOBFM; all parameters are estimated using the training data through the EM algorithm.
2. *Test set*: Model performance metrics are computed using data in the test set. After a model makes a prediction for a test event, the event is available to the model for online learning (e.g., updating parameter estimates $\boldsymbol{\delta}_{jt}$ and selecting the model rank k in FOBFM).

To report model performance over time, we sort the events in our test set by time stamps and allocate the first n events for each item to bucket 1, the subsequent n events for each item into bucket 2, and so on (in most plots, we use $n = 10$). We then compute performance metrics for each bucket. For instance, events in bucket b are evaluated by a model through parameter estimates obtained using observations for all events prior to bucket b. Let p_c denote the predicted click probability of the cth test event in bucket b. Let S^+ denote the set of p_cs that correspond to positive events and S^- denote the set of p_cs that correspond to negative events. We look at two performance metrics:

1. *Test-set log-likelihood*: $\sum_{p_c \in S^+} \log p_c + \sum_{p_c \in S^-} \log(1 - p_c)$. It quantifies how likely the test events are under the model (intuitively, it represents how accurately the model predicts click probability).
2. *Test-set rank correlation*: Because we use model scores to rank articles in both applications, comparing models based on Kendall's τ rank correlation between the y_cs (the true label) and the p_cs is a useful metric to consider. See Section 4.1.3 for the definition of Kendall's τ.

The methods that we compare are as follows:

- *FOBFM*: Here the FOBFM includes *automatic* estimation of model rank k in an online fashion. No parameter tweaking is required for FOBFM.
- *Offline*: A bilinear regression model is trained using retrospective data based only on offline features; that is, $s_{ijt} = \boldsymbol{x}'_{ijt}\boldsymbol{b} + \boldsymbol{x}'_{it}A\boldsymbol{x}_j$. No online learning is done for this model.
- *No-init*: This is a saturated item-level online regression model without initialization; that is, $s_{ijt} = \boldsymbol{x}'_{it}\boldsymbol{v}_j$, where $\boldsymbol{v}_j$ is learned in an online manner with prior $MVN(0, \sigma^2 I)$. The variance component σ^2 is estimated using the tuning set, and we only report the performance for the best σ^2. This model has a large number of parameters to be estimated online – one parameter for each (item ID, user feature) pair.
- *PCR*: This is a principal component regression model without offline bilinear regression; that is, $s_{ijt} = \boldsymbol{x}'_{it}B\boldsymbol{\delta}_j$, where B consists of the top-m principal components for user features. B is determined based only on the $\boldsymbol{x}_{it}$s in the training set, and m is tuned based on the tuning set; we only report the performance for the best m value.
- *PCR-B*: This is a principal component regression model that also includes offline bilinear regression; that is, $s_{ijt} = \boldsymbol{x}'_{ijt}\boldsymbol{b} + \boldsymbol{x}'_{it}A\boldsymbol{x}_j + \boldsymbol{x}'_{it}B\boldsymbol{\delta}_j$, where B consists of the top-k principal components of the user features. B is determined based only on the $\boldsymbol{x}_{it}$s, but A is estimated in a supervised manner based on the y_{ijt}s in the training set. Again, we only report the performance of the best k estimated from the tuning set.

7.4.1 My Yahoo! Data Set

My Yahoo! (http://my.yahoo.com/) is a personalized news reading service. Personalization is based on RSS feeds to which users explicitly explicitly subscribe.

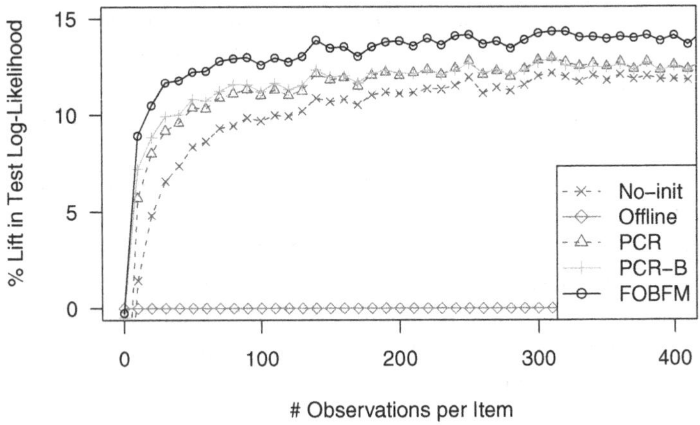

Figure 7.1. Test-set log-likelihood of different models on the My Yahoo! data set (the log-likelihood of the Offline model is approximately -0.64).

In this section, we consider the problem of how to provide personalized recommendation of articles from all My Yahoo! feeds (not just the articles from the feeds that a user subscribed to) based on users' interaction with recommended articles. Because the application is time sensitive and the users would like to see articles as soon as they are published, recommendations have to be made in cold-start situations.

The data were collected during August and September 2009 and consist of 13,808 items (articles) and approximately 3 million users. Item features include top keywords and top URL hosts. User features include age, gender, user interest categories, and user's activity levels on different Yahoo! sites (Chen et al., 2009). When a user clicks an item, we record a positive event; all the items in the same module that are ranked above the clicked item at the time of click and are not clicked by the user are negative events. The training set consists of all the events that are associated with the first eight thousand items (based on item publication time), and the remaining data comprise the test set.

In Figures 7.1 and 7.2, we evaluate the performance of a model as a function of the number of observations that have been used to update the model for each item (in the x-axis) and compare different models in terms of the test-set log-likelihood and rank correlation, respectively. We report the lift in log-likelihood (and rank correlation) of each model relative to the Offline model. As evident from the figures, FOBFM significantly outperforms all the other models; the lift obtained is uniformly better than other methods over all time bins. For this data set, the item features are not very predictive, as evident from the poor log-likelihood and rank correlation of the Offline model. In fact, this poor performance of the Offline model contributes to the large lifts we obtain from online models.

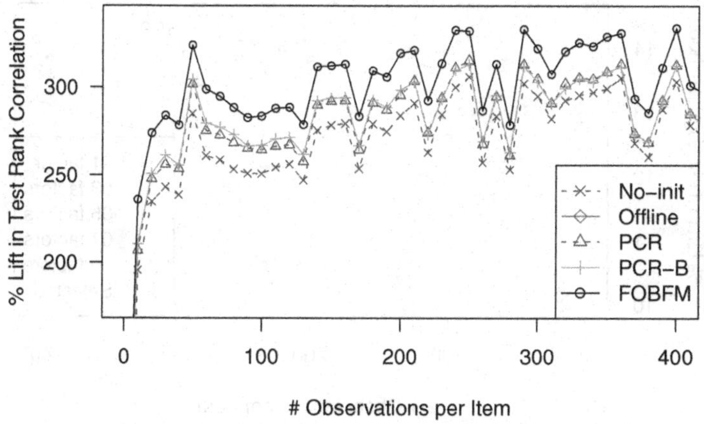

Figure 7.2. Test-set rank correlation of different models on the My Yahoo! data set (the rank correlation of the Offline model is approximately 0.12).

Effectiveness of Online Model Selection. To investigate the effectiveness of online model selection (to select the rank k) in FOBFM, we plot log-likelihood lift curves for our reduced-rank regression model, but with different values of the rank parameter k in Figure 7.3. Similar behavior is observed for rank correlation lift curves. Intuitively, increasing the rank increases the number of observations required for online convergence. Roughly speaking, before an item gets one hundred observations for online learning, the model with rank 1 per item outperforms all others. Subsequently, the model with rank 3 per item catches up, and then the model with rank 5 per item catches up, and so on. For this data set, the rank 1 model dominates during the initial part of the curve, and then the rank 3 model dominates the rest. From this figure, we also see that the online model selection scheme provides uniformly better performance.

7.4.2 Yahoo! Front Page Data Set

In this section, we look at the Yahoo! front page data set. The Today Module on the Yahoo! home page (http://www.yahoo.com; the top center module) is a module that displays four recent stories for every user visit to the page. We focus on an application scenario where we personalize the recommendations based on user features.

We collected six months of data from November 2008 to April 2009, consisting of 4,396 items and approximately 13.5 million events. Each item in this application is labeled by an editor with a set of categories. The user features are the same as those in the My Yahoo! data set. An event is positive if a user clicked on an item at the first position of the module. An event is negative if

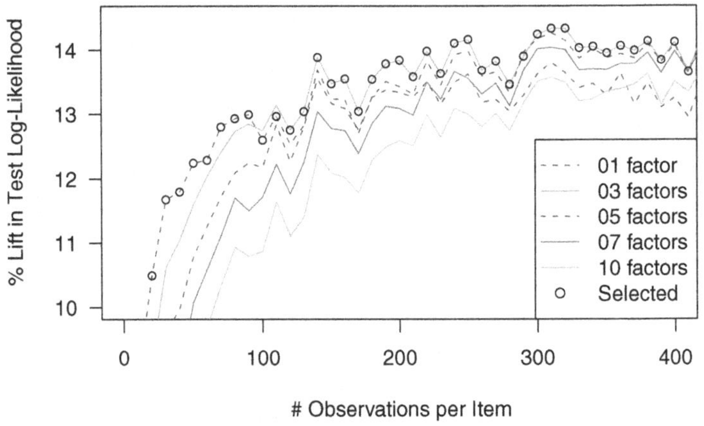

Figure 7.3. Test-set log-likelihood for different number of factors on the My Yahoo! data set.

an item was shown to a user at the first position of the module and not clicked, and it was not clicked by the user at any other position. We use the first four months of data as the training set and the last two months of data as the test set.

Figures 7.4 and 7.5 show the performance of different models in terms of the test-set log likelihood and rank correlation. We report the lift in log-likelihood (and rank correlation) of each model relative to the Offline model. As in the My Yahoo! data set, FOBFM outperforms all the other models uniformly across time. Because item features for the Yahoo! front page data set are more predictive (e.g., editorially labeled categories), the No-init model and the PCR

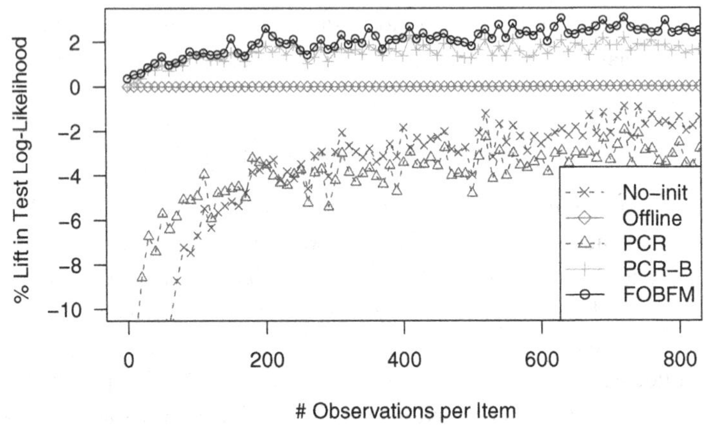

Figure 7.4. Test-set log-likelihood of different models on the Yahoo! front page data set (the log-likelihood of the Offline model is approximately −0.39).

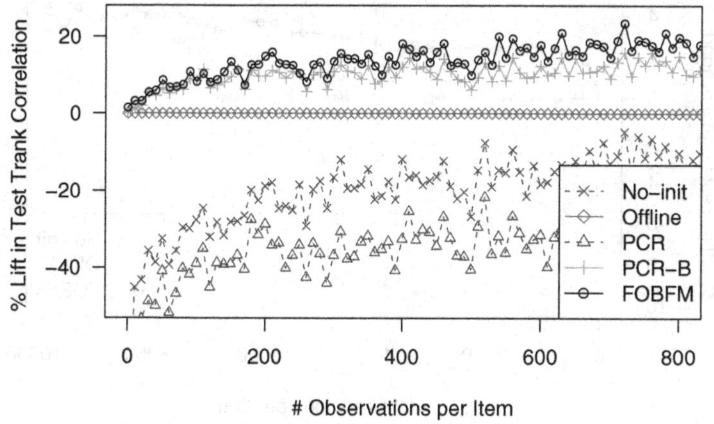

Figure 7.5. Test-set rank correlation of different models on the Yahoo! front page data set (the rank correlation of the Offline model is approximately 0.34).

model, which are not based on item features, perform poorly compared to models based on item features. Also, since the baseline (the Offline model) that is based on predictive item features is stronger than that in My Yahoo!, the lift numbers are smaller.

Figure 7.6 shows the effectiveness of our online model selection scheme. The curves in this case have higher variability than Figure 7.3; nonetheless, FOBFM is still uniformly better for almost all time batches, again illustrating the usefulness of the online model selection scheme.

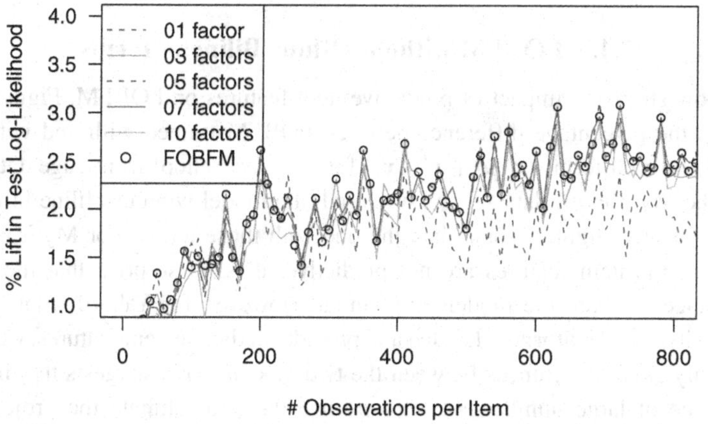

Figure 7.6. Test-set log-likelihood for different numbers of factors on the Yahoo! front page data set.

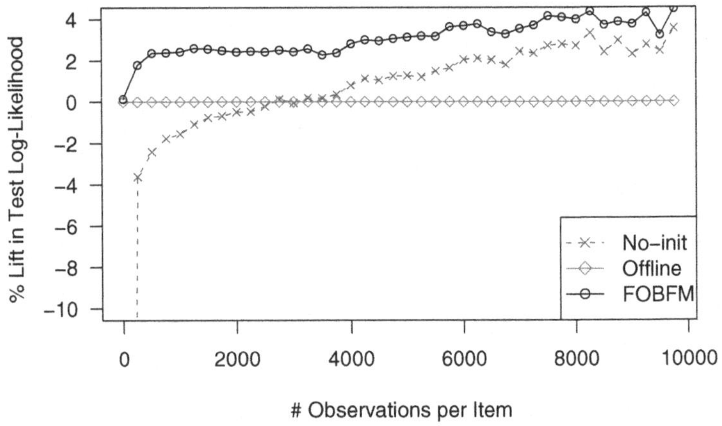

Figure 7.7. The No-init model catches up when it gets a large number of observations.

Because the traffic volume on Yahoo! front page is large and we deal with a relatively small pool of items, we are able to study model performance for a longer time horizon (more observations for each item to do online learning). One would expect the saturated No-init model to outperform other models with a large number of observations in an online scenario; it is interesting to see the point at which this transition happens. Figure 7.7 shows that although the gap between No-init and FOBFM reduces over time, the former does not outperform the latter even after ten thousand observations per item. This suggests the presence of redundancies in item coefficients; when exploited (as in FOBFM), it leads to rapid convergence for online per-item models.

7.4.3 FOBFM without Offline Bilinear Terms

We now study the impact of predictive item features on FOBFM. Figure 7.8 shows the percentage difference between FOBFM trained with and without offline bilinear terms ($\boldsymbol{x}'_{ijt}\boldsymbol{b} + \boldsymbol{x}'_{it}A\boldsymbol{x}_j$) for both the Yahoo! front page data set and the My Yahoo! data set. As observed, the model without offline bilinear terms is only slightly worse than the one with those terms. For My Yahoo!, because the item features are not predictive, it is no surprise that the performances of both the models are similar. However, for Yahoo! front page, where items are editorially labeled and provide predictive item features, we still see only small differences between the two models. This suggests that in the presence of large numbers of retrospective data, to estimate the projection matrix B, the additional cost incurred to construct predictive item features may not provide a significant benefit in recommender systems.

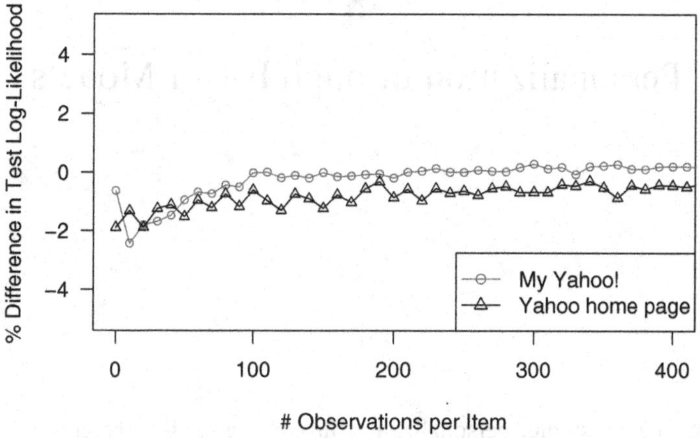

Figure 7.8. Percentage difference between the FOBFM model with offline bilinear terms and the model without offline bilinear terms.

7.5 Summary

To conclude this chapter, we summarize the insights gained through the set of experiments. A rank reduction technique used in FOBFM is effective in providing a strong initialization for rapidly learning per-item online models. We also see that the performance depends on the model rank k; small values of k are better early on during an item's lifetime, but larger values provide better performance with increasing number of observations. Our online model selection criteria based on maximizing out-of-sample predictive log-likelihood provides an effective model selection strategy. Interestingly, a saturated model with all item coefficients has slower convergence compared to reduced-rank models. It is also interesting to see the small additional benefit obtained by initializing FOBFM through predictive item features in our Yahoo! front page application. If such a phenomenon generalizes to a wide range of web applications, we can significantly reduce the cost that is often incurred while collecting item metadata in recommender applications for the web.

Exercise

1. Consider the alternate formulation that assumes $\boldsymbol{v}_{jt} \sim N(B\boldsymbol{\delta}_{jt}, \tau^2 I)$ instead of $\boldsymbol{v}_{jt} = B\boldsymbol{\delta}_{jt}$. Dercribe the fitting algorithm for this model.

8

Personalization through Factor Models

In Chapter 7, we studied personalization through feature-based regression models. We reviewed models based on item-item similarity, user-user similarity, and matrix factorization in Chapter 2. In practice, matrix factorization has better prediction accuracy in *warm-start* scenarios, that is, when predicting responses for (user, item) pairs where both the user and the item have large numbers of observations in the training data. However, prediction accuracy deteriorates for users (or items) with meagre or no response in the training data. Such cases are often referred to as *cold-start* scenarios. In Section 8.1, we describe the regression-based latent factor model (RLFM) that extends matrix factorization to leverage available user and item features simultaneously. Such a strategy helps to improve the performance of both cold-start and warm-start scenarios in a single framework. We then develop the model-fitting algorithms in Section 8.2 and illustrate the performance of RLFM on a number of data sets in Section 8.3. Finally, in Section 8.4, we discuss model-fitting strategies to train RLFM on the very large data that are typical in modern web recommendation systems, and we evaluate their performance in Section 8.5.

8.1 Regression-Based Latent Factor Model (RLFM)

RLFM extends matrix factorization to leverage features and users' past responses to items within a single modeling framework (Agarwal and Chen, 2009; Zhang et al., 2011). It provides a principled framework to combine the pros of collaborative filtering and content-based methods. When past response data are not sufficient to determine the latent factors of a user or an item, RLFM estimates them through a regression model based on features; otherwise, the latent factors are estimated as in matrix factorization. The key aspect of RLFM is the ability to seamlessly transition, in the continuum, from cold start to warm start.

Data and Notation. As usual, we use i to denote a user and j to denote an item. Let y_{ij} denote the response that user i gives item j. This response can be of various types, as described in Section 2.3.2, including numeric response (e.g., numeric ratings) modeled using the Gaussian response model and binary response (e.g., click or not) modeled using the logistic response model.

In addition to response data, we also have features available for each user and item. Let $\boldsymbol{x}_i$, $\boldsymbol{x}_j$, and $\boldsymbol{x}_{ij}$ denote feature vectors for user i, item j, and pair (i, j), respectively. The feature vector $\boldsymbol{x}_i$ for user i may include user demographics, geolocation, and browse behavior. The item feature vector $\boldsymbol{x}_j$ may include content categories and tokens extracted from the title or body when items have textual description. Vector $\boldsymbol{x}_{ij}$ is a vector of features for the situation when item j is recommended (or to be recommended) to user i; examples include the position of the item displayed on a page, the time of day when an item is displayed, and any feature capturing the interaction or similarity between user i and item j. Vectors $\boldsymbol{x}_i$, $\boldsymbol{x}_j$, and $\boldsymbol{x}_{ij}$ contain different features and have different numbers of dimensions. See Chapter 2 for more examples of features in recommendation problems.

8.1.1 From Matrix Factorization to RLFM

In matrix factorization, we predict y_{ij} using $\boldsymbol{u}_i'\boldsymbol{v}_j$, where $\boldsymbol{u}_i$ and $\boldsymbol{v}_j$ are two r-dimensional vectors of latent factors (see Section 2.4.3 for details). We call $\boldsymbol{u}_i$ the factor vector of user i and $\boldsymbol{v}_j$ the factor vector of item j. We shall refer to r as the number of latent dimensions, which is much smaller than the number of users and the number of items. We have an r-dimensional parameter vector associated with each user and item. Owing to data heterogeneity across users and items and noise in response data, it is often attractive to use a relatively large value of r (from tens to hundreds) to accurately estimate factors for heavy users and items but to regularize the factors to avoid overfitting for users and items with few data. The most common regularization method is to "shrink" the factors toward zero. For example, when we have few or no past response data for user i, the factor vector $\boldsymbol{u}_i$ is constrained to be close to a neutral value $\boldsymbol{0}$. This method is equivalent to assuming that $\boldsymbol{u}_i$ has a Gaussian prior with mean $= \boldsymbol{0}$, for all i, and it is referred to as probabilistic matrix factorization (PMF). Notice that a new user i who does not have any past response data would have $\boldsymbol{u}_i = \boldsymbol{0}$, meaning $\boldsymbol{u}_i'\boldsymbol{v}_j = 0$ for all item j. Thus, matrix factorization alone cannot be used to recommend items to new users.

The idea of RLFM is conceptually simple. Instead of shrinking $\boldsymbol{u}_i$ toward zero, we shrink it toward a nonzero value that depends on user features through an r-dimensional regression function $G(\boldsymbol{x}_i)$. More precisely, instead of assuming the prior mean of $\boldsymbol{u}_i$ to be zero, we assume the prior mean of $\boldsymbol{u}_i$ to be $G(\boldsymbol{x}_i)$. The factors $\boldsymbol{u}_i$ and the regression function G are learned simultaneously as part of model-fitting process. The same idea also applies to $\boldsymbol{v}_j$. Although the modeling idea underlying RLFM is simple, estimation is nontrivial and challenging.

Intuitively, RLFM *anchors* each user (or item) factor vector at a point estimated by using features and allows the factor vector to deviate from this point in a smooth fashion. In fact, the amount of deviation depends on the sample size and correlations among observations. In particular, users (or items) with few data shrink aggressively to the feature-based point. Thus, user and item factors are initialized based on features, but they get refined with the availability of more data. This ability to move from coarse to fine resolutions in a smooth fashion after accounting for differing sample sizes, correlation, and heterogeneity is a key aspect providing for an accurate, scalable, and general-purpose predictive method for personalized recommendations.

Consider a one-dimensional latent factor space; that is, $r = 1$. In this case, $\boldsymbol{u}_i$ is a scalar. Figure 8.1 shows the distribution of user latent factors estimated separately for a sample of heavy and light users on the Yahoo! front page using the following three models:

1. *RLFM:* $\boldsymbol{u}_i$ has a prior with mean $= G(\boldsymbol{x}_i)$.
2. *FactorOnly:* $\boldsymbol{u}_i$ has a prior with mean $= 0$, which is the same as PMF.
3. *FeatureOnly:* $\boldsymbol{u}_i = G(\boldsymbol{x}_i)$; that is, y_{ij} is predicted by $G(\boldsymbol{x}_i)'H(\boldsymbol{x}_j)$, which depends only on features without any deviation from the feature-based points. We use H to denote the regression function for items.

For light users, FactorOnly "shrinks" the factors close to zero and fails to exploit information available in user and item features. RLFM, conversely, mitigates data sparseness by falling back on the feature-based points. For heavy users, FactorOnly tends to overfit the data. RLFM, conversely, deviates from the prior mean in a smooth way and provides better regularization.

8.1.2 Model Specification

Response Model. Let s_{ij} denote the *unobserved true score* that quantifies user i's response to item j. Our goal is to estimate s_{ij} for any given (i, j) pair based on all observed responses y_{ij} and features $\boldsymbol{x}_i$, $\boldsymbol{x}_j$, and $\boldsymbol{x}_{ij}$:

- *Gaussian model for numeric response*: For numeric responses (or ratings), it is common to assume (sometimes after transforming the response)

$$y_{ij} \sim N(s_{ij}, \sigma^2), \tag{8.1}$$

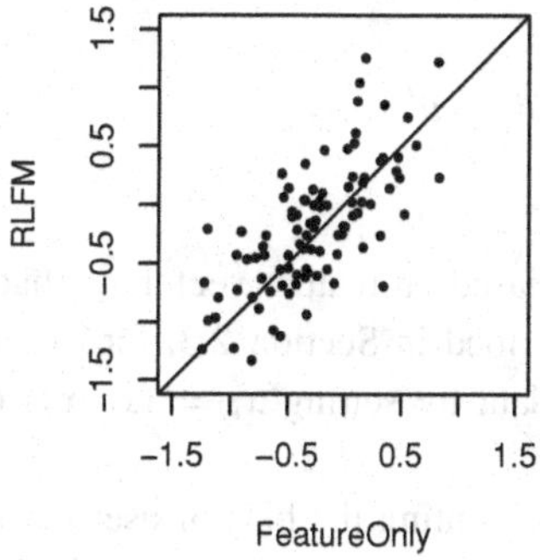

(a) RLFM for heavy users

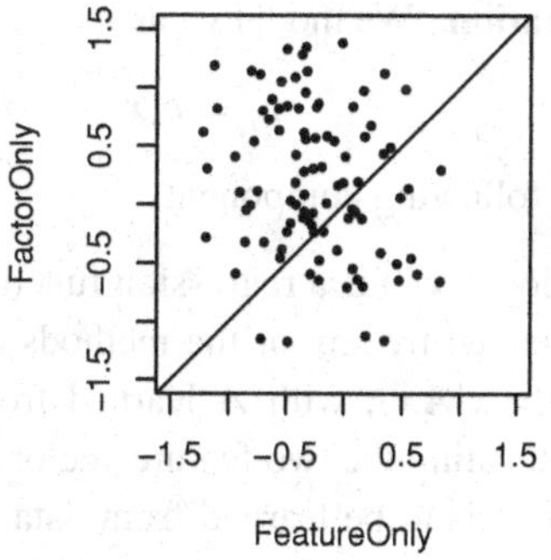

(b) FactorOnly for heavy users

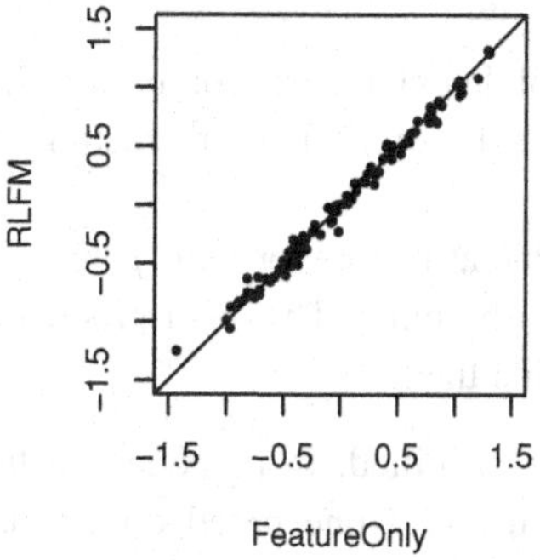

(c) RLFM for light users

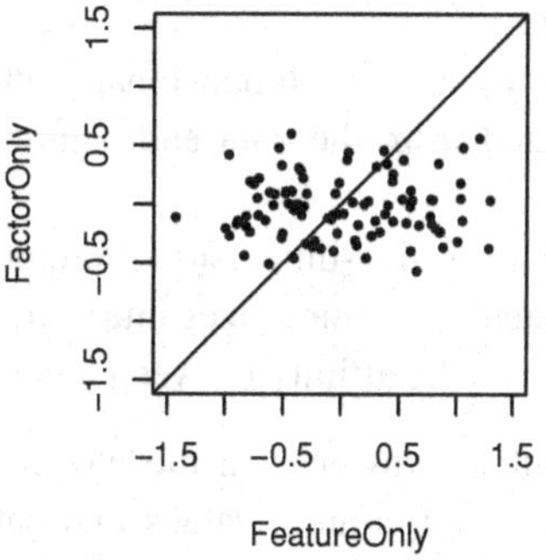

(d) FactorOnly for light users

Figure 8.1. Comparing latent factors estimated through RLFM, FactorOnly, and FeatureOnly. Each point (x, y) in a plot reports the estimated values, x and y, of the first latent factor of a user using the two methods indicated in the plot. For light users, FactorOnly collapses to zero; RLFM, conservely, collapses to FeatureOnly.

where σ^2, the variance of the noise in users' responses, needs to be estimated from data. Here s_{ij} represents the mean of the response that user i provides item j.

- *Logistic model for binary response*: When users' responses are binary (e.g., click or not, like or not, share or not), it is common to assume

$$y_{ij} \sim \text{Bernoulli}(p_{ij}) \text{ and } s_{ij} = \log \frac{p_{ij}}{1 - p_{ij}}, \tag{8.2}$$

where p_{ij} is the probability that user i would respond to item j positively.

Factorization. We model s_{ij} as

$$s_{ij} = b(\boldsymbol{x}_{ij}) + \alpha_i + \beta_j + \boldsymbol{u}_i'\boldsymbol{v}_j \tag{8.3}$$

with the following components:

- Function $b(\boldsymbol{x}_{ij})$ is a regression function based on feature vector x_{ij} that can be obtained by any of the methods described in Section 2.3, for example, $b(\boldsymbol{x}_{ij}) = \boldsymbol{x}_i'\boldsymbol{A}\boldsymbol{x}_j$, with $\boldsymbol{A}$ learned from data by setting $\boldsymbol{x}_{ij} = (\boldsymbol{x}_i, \boldsymbol{x}_j)$ (i.e., concatenating the two feature vectors).
- Scalar α_i is to be learned from data, representing the bias of user i caused by the fact that some users tend to respond to items more positively (or negatively) than others.
- Scalar β_j is also to be learned from data, representing the popularity of item j.
- Vector $\boldsymbol{u}_i$ is an r-dimensional vector of latent factors for user i that is estimated from the data and summarizes the user's past interactions with items.
- Vector $\boldsymbol{v}_j$ is an r-dimensional vector of latent factors for item j that is also estimated and summarizes interactions with item j. The inner product $\boldsymbol{u}_i'\boldsymbol{v}_j$ represents the affinity between the user and the item.

The latent dimension r in the model is prespecified. In practice, we fit the model with different r values and select the best one based on evaluation methods described in Chapter 4. Intuitively, we can interpret user factors $\boldsymbol{u}_i = (u_{i1}, \ldots, u_{ir})$ as user i's affinity to r different latent "topics" and item factors $\boldsymbol{v}_j = (v_{j1}, \ldots, v_{jr})$ as item j's affinity to the same set of "topics." Because users and items are both mapped to the same latent vector space, the inner product $\boldsymbol{u}_i'\boldsymbol{v}_j = \sum_{k=1}^{r} u_{ik}v_{jk}$ represents the similarity between the user and the item.

Overfitting Problem. In addition to the parameters in b, the number of additional parameters that need to be estimated from the data is $(r+1)(M+N)$, where M is the number of users and N is the number of items. In practice, $(r+1)(M+N)$ may be larger than the number of observations; this can lead to severe overfitting. It is a common practice to shrink the factors toward zero, that is, to put zero-mean Gaussian priors on the latent factors. However, shrinking toward zero is restrictive and may not generalize well, especially in cold-start scenarios. Furthermore, because the distribution of the number of responses that a user (or item) has is usually skewed, it may be difficult to achieve good predictive accuracy with small values of r (e.g., within ten). Hence, allowing for large values of r (e.g., tens to hundreds) but regularizing the parameters to reduce the effective degrees of freedom is important. Although the approach of shrinking toward zero reasonably addresses the overfitting problem through variance reduction, the resulting model *fails to provide accurate predictions in cold-start scenarios*. For example, users or items with no past observations would inherit the same factor estimates of zero. With availability of features on users or items, one should be able to do better. For instance, observing a large number of users from New York and California in the training data may clearly discriminate the average factor estimates in these two regions; leveraging this information while predicting factors for a new user may help to reduce the bias significantly.

Regression Priors. The key idea of RLFM is to shrink the factors of different users and items to different means based on their features, instead of always shrinking the factors toward zero. To add this flexibility, we need to do both the regressions and factor estimation simultaneously. Specifically, we put the following priors on α_i, β_j, $\boldsymbol{u}_i$, and $\boldsymbol{v}_j$:

$$\begin{aligned} \alpha_i &\sim N(g(x_i),\ \sigma_\alpha^2), \quad \boldsymbol{u}_i \sim N(G(x_i),\ \sigma_u^2 I), \\ \beta_j &\sim N(h(x_j),\ \sigma_\beta^2), \quad \boldsymbol{v}_j \sim N(H(x_j),\ \sigma_v^2 I), \end{aligned} \tag{8.4}$$

where g and h are any choices of regression functions that return scalars and G and H are regression functions that return r-dimensional vectors. Adding these regression functions to the priors presents formidable computational challenges that are addressed in Section 8.2. In general, we can specify the full variance-covariance matrix for the priors of $\boldsymbol{u}_i$ and $\boldsymbol{v}_j$. For simplicity, we only focus on the uncorrelated priors, which have diagonal variance-covariance matrices $\sigma_u^2 I$ and $\sigma_v^2 I$, respectively. In our experience, nondiagonal covariance matrices usually do not provide significant improvements over diagonal ones.

Regression Functions. Setting b, g, h, G, H to linear regression functions corresponds to the models proposed by Agarwal and Chen (2009) and Stern et al. (2009). Zhang et al. (2011) generalizes this approach to other regression functions, allowing us to leverage a large body of work on nonlinear regression models. For example, one can use a decision tree for b, a nearest-neighbor model for g, a random forest for h, a sparse LASSO regression model for G, and a gradient-boosted tree ensemble for H.

G and H are functions that return vectors. One can either use multivariate regression models to predict all the values in a vector jointly or use regular univariate regression models to predict each value in the vector separately. The former may leverage the correlation between the components in the vector and potentially provide better accuracy, whereas the latter provides simplicity and more scalable model fitting. For the latter, we define $G(x_i) = (G_1(x_i), \ldots, G_r(x_i))$, where each $G_k(x_i)$ is an independent univariate regression function.

Likelihood Function. Let $\boldsymbol{\Theta} = (b, g, h, G, H, \sigma_\alpha^2, \sigma_u^2, \sigma_\beta^2, \sigma_v^2)$ be the set of prior parameters (also referred to as hyperparameters); b, g, h, G, and H are the model parameters that need to be estimated in the corresponding regression function. Let $\boldsymbol{\Delta} = \{\alpha_i, \beta_j, \boldsymbol{u}_i, \boldsymbol{v}_j\}_{\forall i,j}$ be the set of factors (also referred to as random effects). Let $\boldsymbol{y}$ denote the observed response. In the Gaussian model, where observed response follows the normal distribution, the *complete data log-likelihood* (the probability of jointly observing $\boldsymbol{y}$ and a given setting of $\boldsymbol{\Delta}$) is given by

$$\begin{aligned}\log L(\boldsymbol{\Theta}; \boldsymbol{\Delta}, \boldsymbol{y}) = \log \Pr(\boldsymbol{y}, \boldsymbol{\Delta} \mid \boldsymbol{\Theta}) = &\text{ constant} \\ &- \frac{1}{2}\sum_{ij}\left(\frac{1}{\sigma^2}(y_{ij} - b(\boldsymbol{x}_{ij}) - \alpha_i - \beta_j - \boldsymbol{u}_i'\boldsymbol{v}_j)^2 + \log \sigma^2\right) \\ &- \frac{1}{2\sigma_\alpha^2}\sum_i(\alpha_i - g(\boldsymbol{x}_i))^2 - \frac{M}{2}\log\sigma_\alpha^2 \\ &- \frac{1}{2\sigma_\beta^2}\sum_j(\beta_j - h(\boldsymbol{x}_j))^2 - \frac{N}{2}\log\sigma_\beta^2 \\ &- \frac{1}{2\sigma_u^2}\sum_i\|\boldsymbol{u}_i - G(\boldsymbol{x}_i)\|^2 - \frac{Mr}{2}\log\sigma_u^2 \\ &- \frac{1}{2\sigma_v^2}\sum_j\|\boldsymbol{v}_j - H(\boldsymbol{x}_j)\|^2 - \frac{Nr}{2}\log\sigma_v^2,\end{aligned} \tag{8.5}$$

where the second line specifies the prediction error in terms of the sum of squared differences and the next four lines specify L_2 regularization shrinking the corresponding factors toward values predicted by regression functions. The $\log\sigma_\star^2$ terms result from the assumption of normal distributions; $\sigma^2/\sigma_\alpha^2, \sigma^2/\sigma_\beta^2$, σ^2/σ_u^2, and σ^2/σ_v^2 can be interpreted as the strength of the corresponding regularization terms, with higher values indicating more regularization.

Model Fitting and Prediction. Given observed response data $\boldsymbol{y}$ and features associated with observed (user, item) pairs, the goal of model fitting is to first find the maximum likelihood estimate (MLE) of the prior parameters $\boldsymbol{\Theta}$; that is,

$$\begin{aligned}\hat{\boldsymbol{\Theta}} &= \arg\max_{\boldsymbol{\Theta}} \log \Pr(\boldsymbol{y} \mid \boldsymbol{\Theta}) \\ &= \arg\max_{\boldsymbol{\Theta}} \log \int \Pr(\boldsymbol{y}, \boldsymbol{\Delta} \mid \boldsymbol{\Theta})\, d\,\boldsymbol{\Delta}.\end{aligned} \tag{8.6}$$

Unlike the complete data log-likelihood in Equation (8.5), the log-likelihood in Equation (8.6) is marginal, with the unobserved latent factors $\boldsymbol{\Delta}$ integrated out, which is more appropriate because $\mathbf{\Delta}$ is not observed. Here we only define the output of model fitting; the actual algorithm is described in Section 8.2. After obtaining the MLE $\hat{\mathbf{\Theta}}$ of the prior parameters, we take the *empirical Bayes* approach and compute the posterior mean of the factors given the MLE:

$$\begin{aligned} \hat{\alpha}_i &= E[\alpha_i \mid \boldsymbol{y}, \hat{\mathbf{\Theta}}], & \hat{\boldsymbol{u}}_i &= E[\boldsymbol{u}_i \mid \boldsymbol{y}, \hat{\mathbf{\Theta}}], \\ \hat{\beta}_j &= E[\beta_j \mid \boldsymbol{y}, \hat{\mathbf{\Theta}}], & \hat{\boldsymbol{v}}_j &= E[\boldsymbol{v}_j \mid \boldsymbol{y}, \hat{\mathbf{\Theta}}]. \end{aligned} \tag{8.7}$$

To predict the response of an unobserved (i, j) pair, we use the following posterior mean:

$$\begin{aligned} \hat{s}_{ij} &= b(\boldsymbol{x}_{ij}) + \hat{\alpha}_i + \hat{\beta}_j + E[\boldsymbol{u}_i'\boldsymbol{v}_j \mid \boldsymbol{y}, \hat{\mathbf{\Theta}}] \\ &\approx b(\boldsymbol{x}_{ij}) + \hat{\alpha}_i + \hat{\beta}_j + \hat{\boldsymbol{u}}_i'\hat{\boldsymbol{v}}_j, \end{aligned} \tag{8.8}$$

where the approximation, $E[\boldsymbol{u}_i'\boldsymbol{v}_j \mid \boldsymbol{y}, \hat{\mathbf{\Theta}}] \approx \hat{\boldsymbol{u}}_i'\hat{\boldsymbol{v}}_j$, reduces the computational cost of prediction. If user i does not appear in the training data $\boldsymbol{y}$, her factors should equal the prior mean predicted using features; that is, $\hat{\alpha}_i = g(\boldsymbol{x}_i)$ and $\hat{\boldsymbol{u}}_i = G(\boldsymbol{x}_i)$. The same applies to new items.

8.1.3 Stochastic Process of RLFM

To get intuition into the class of predictor functions induced by RLFM, we look at the marginal prior distribution of y_{ij} for Gaussian response:

$$\begin{aligned} E[y_{ij} \mid \Theta] &= b(\boldsymbol{x}_{ij}) + g(\boldsymbol{x}_i) + h(\boldsymbol{x}_j) + G(\boldsymbol{x}_i)'H(\boldsymbol{x}_j) \\ \mathrm{Var}[y_{ij} \mid \Theta] &= \sigma^2 + \sigma_\alpha^2 + \sigma_\beta^2 + \sigma_u^2\sigma_v^2 \\ &\quad + \sigma_u^2 H(\boldsymbol{x}_j)'H(\boldsymbol{x}_j) + \sigma_v^2 G(\boldsymbol{x}_i)'G(\boldsymbol{x}_i) \\ \mathrm{Cov}[y_{ij_1}, y_{ij_2} \mid \Theta] &= \sigma_\alpha^2 + \sigma_u^2 H(\boldsymbol{x}_{j_1})'H(\boldsymbol{x}_{j_2}) \\ \mathrm{Cov}[y_{i_1 j}, y_{i_2 j} \mid \Theta] &= \sigma_\beta^2 + \sigma_v^2 G(\boldsymbol{x}_{i_1})'G(\boldsymbol{x}_{i_2}). \end{aligned} \tag{8.9}$$

$E[y_{ij} \mid \Theta]$ is the prediction function for a new user i on a new item j. With state-of-the-art regression functions, the function class induced is rich; for example, if G and H are decision trees, the predictive function is now a cross-product of trees.

Equation (8.9) can be used to define the covariance (or kernel) function of a Gaussian process. Although the marginal distribution of y_{ij} is not Gaussian (because of the inner product of two r-dimensional Gaussian random variables), looking at the Gaussian process defined using this covariance structure provides insights into the behavior of RLFM. Given a vector of observed response $\boldsymbol{y}$, the predicted response of an unobserved response y_{ij} can be represented as a weighted sum of the observed response values. Based on Equation (8.9), we define $\boldsymbol{\mu}$ and $\boldsymbol{\Sigma}$ as the mean and variance-covariance matrix of the observed response $\boldsymbol{y}$ and vector $\boldsymbol{c}_{ij} = \text{Cov}[y_{ij}, \boldsymbol{y}]$ as the covariance between the unobserved responses y_{ij} and each of the observed response $\boldsymbol{y}$. Then, the posterior mean of y_{ij} is given by

$$E[y_{ij} \mid \Theta] + \boldsymbol{c}'_{ij}\boldsymbol{\Sigma}^{-1}(\boldsymbol{y} - \boldsymbol{\mu}). \tag{8.10}$$

Note that $\boldsymbol{c}_{ij}$ is nonzero only for entries in the training data across the ith row and jth column. Thus, intuitively, RLFM predicts y_{ij} by adding an *adjustment* to the feature-based predictor; the adjustment is a weighted average of row and column residuals, with weights depending on the induced correlations based on features. Hence, if item j is correlated with other items and/or user i has correlations with others, the stochastic process will exploit them to provide an additional adjustment term that will improve performance. In practice, it is computationally infeasible to work directly with the stochastic process defined through Equation (8.9). Our model-fitting strategy works by augmenting observed data through latent factors to scale computation. In fact, the stochastic process defined through Equations (8.9) and (8.10) shows the role played by regression parameters in inducing correlations among observations. It also provides the invariant parameters that matter in prediction, namely, $G(\boldsymbol{x}_i)'H(\boldsymbol{x}_j)$, $G(\boldsymbol{x}_i)'G(\boldsymbol{x}_i)$, and $H(\boldsymbol{x}_j)'H(\boldsymbol{x}_j)$. While working directly with the latent factor model (instead of the marginalized one), this invariance is manifested in the nonestimability of $\boldsymbol{u}_i$ and $\boldsymbol{v}_j$ individually; only the product $\boldsymbol{u}'_i\boldsymbol{v}_j$ can be uniquely identified from the data.

8.2 Fitting Algorithms

In this section, we provide a detailed description of fitting algorithms. We first describe the expectation-maximization (EM) algorithm for the Gaussian model in Section 8.2.1 and then discuss how to fit the logistic models using adaptive rejection sampling (ARS) in Section 8.2.2 and variational approximation in Section 8.2.3.

Problem Definition. Recall that $\boldsymbol{\Theta} = (b, g, h, G, H, \sigma_\alpha^2, \sigma_u^2, \sigma_\beta^2, \sigma_v^2)$ denotes the set of prior parameters, $\boldsymbol{\Delta} = \{\alpha_i, \beta_j, \boldsymbol{u}_i, \boldsymbol{v}_j\}_{\forall i,j}$ denotes the set of latent factors, and $\boldsymbol{y}$ denotes the set of observed response. Our goal is to obtain the MLE $\hat{\boldsymbol{\Theta}}$ of the prior parameters defined in Equation (8.6) and estimate the posterior mean of the factors $E[\boldsymbol{\Delta} \mid \boldsymbol{y}, \hat{\boldsymbol{\Theta}}]$.

This formulation differs from the regular optimization formulation in two ways. First, marginalizing over the factors usually provides better generalization. Second, except for the number r of latent dimensions, no tuning is needed in our formulation because the regularization weights (i.e., the prior variances) are obtained automatically from our fitting procedure. This is different from a typical optimization formulation of this problem, where the regularization weights are often tuned through a separate tuning data set, and such tuning is difficult because the optimal values of the regularization parameters are functions of the rank parameter r. Indeed, our empirical observation clearly demonstrates that larger values of r automatically induce more regularization and support using a large rank with more regularization.

8.2.1 EM Algorithm for Gaussian Response

The EM algorithm proposed by Dempster et al. (1977) is well suited to fit factor models. The factors in this case form the missing data that are augmented to the observed data. The EM algorithm iterates between an E-step and an M-step until convergence. Let $\hat{\mathbf{\Theta}}^{(t)}$ denote the current estimated value of $\mathbf{\Theta}$ at the beginning of the tth iteration.

- *E-step*: We take the expectation of complete data log-likelihood with respect to the posterior of missing data $\mathbf{\Delta}$ conditional on observed data $\boldsymbol{y}$ and the current estimate of $\mathbf{\Theta}$; that is, compute

$$q_t(\mathbf{\Theta}) = E_{\mathbf{\Delta}}[\log L(\mathbf{\Theta}; \mathbf{\Delta}, \boldsymbol{y}) \mid \hat{\mathbf{\Theta}}^{(t)}]$$

  as a function of $\mathbf{\Theta}$, where the expectation is taken over the posterior distribution of $(\mathbf{\Delta} \mid \hat{\mathbf{\Theta}}^{(t)}, \boldsymbol{y})$.
- *M-step*: We maximize the expected complete data log-likelihood from the E-step to obtain updated values of $\mathbf{\Theta}$; that is, we find

$$\hat{\mathbf{\Theta}}^{(t+1)} = \arg\max_{\mathbf{\Theta}} \; q_t(\mathbf{\Theta}).$$

The actual computation in the E-step is to generate sufficient statistics for computing $\arg\max_{\mathbf{\Theta}} q_t(\mathbf{\Theta})$, so we do not need to scan the raw data every time we need to evaluate $q_t(\mathbf{\Theta})$. At each iteration, the EM algorithm is guaranteed not to deteriorate the value of $\int L(\mathbf{\Theta}; \mathbf{\Delta}, \boldsymbol{y})\, d\,\mathbf{\Delta}$.

The major computational bottleneck is in the E-step because the posterior of factors is not available in closed form. Hence, we follow the Monte Carlo EM (MCEM) algorithm developed by Booth and Hobert (1999) by drawing samples from this posterior and approximating the expectation in the E-step by taking the Monte Carlo mean.

Alternatively, one can apply variational approximation to derive a closed-form formula for the expectation or apply the iterated conditional modes (ICM) algorithm (Besag, 1986), in which the expectation computation is replaced by plugging in the mode of the conditional distributions. However, in our experience, and in other studies (e.g., Salakhutdinov and Mnih, 2008), sampling usually provides better performance in terms of predictive accuracy, while still being scalable, and is also resistant to overfitting even with an increasing number of factors. More important, it provides a method to automatically obtain estimates of hyperparameters. Thus, we focus on the MCEM algorithm.

Monte Carlo E-Step

Because $E_{\boldsymbol{\Delta}}[\log L(\boldsymbol{\Theta}; \boldsymbol{\Delta}, \boldsymbol{y}) \mid \hat{\boldsymbol{\Theta}}^{(t)}]$ is not available in closed form, we compute the Monte Carlo expectation based on L samples generated by a Gibbs sampler (Gelfand, 1995). We use $(\delta \mid \text{Rest})$, where δ can be one of α_i, β_j, $\boldsymbol{u}_i$, and $\boldsymbol{v}_j$, to denote the conditional distribution of δ given all the other parameters. Let $\mathcal{I}_j$ denote the set of users who responded to item j and $\mathcal{J}_i$ denote the set of items to which user i responded. The Gibbs sampler repeats the following procedure L times:

1. For each user i, sample α_i from $(\alpha_i \mid \text{Rest})$, which is Gaussian:

$$\text{Let } o_{ij} = y_{ij} - b(x_{ij}) - \beta_j - \boldsymbol{u}_i'\boldsymbol{v}_j.$$

$$\text{Var}[\alpha_i|\text{Rest}] = \left(\frac{1}{\sigma_\alpha^2} + \sum_{j \in \mathcal{J}_i} \frac{1}{\sigma^2}\right)^{-1} \tag{8.11}$$

$$E[\alpha_i|\text{Rest}] = \text{Var}[\alpha_i|\text{Rest}] \left(\frac{g(x_i)}{\sigma_\alpha^2} + \sum_{j \in \mathcal{J}_i} \frac{o_{ij}}{\sigma^2}\right).$$

2. For each item j, sample β_j from $(\beta_j \mid \text{Rest})$, which is Gaussian:

$$\text{Let } o_{ij} = y_{ij} - b(x_{ij}) - \alpha_i - \boldsymbol{u}_i'\boldsymbol{v}_j.$$

$$\text{Var}[\beta_j|\text{Rest}] = \left(\frac{1}{\sigma_\beta^2} + \sum_{i \in \mathcal{I}_j} \frac{1}{\sigma^2}\right)^{-1} \tag{8.12}$$

$$E[\beta_j|\text{Rest}] = \text{Var}[\beta_j|\text{Rest}] \left(\frac{h(x_j)}{\sigma_\beta^2} + \sum_{i \in \mathcal{I}_j} \frac{o_{ij}}{\sigma^2}\right).$$

3. For each user i, sample $\boldsymbol{u}_i$ from $(\boldsymbol{u}_i \mid \text{Rest})$, which is Gaussian:

$$\text{Let } o_{ij} = y_{ij} - b(x_{ij}) - \alpha_i - \beta_j.$$

$$\text{Var}[\boldsymbol{u}_i|\text{Rest}] = \left(\frac{1}{\sigma_u^2}I + \sum_{j\in\mathcal{J}_i}\frac{\boldsymbol{v}_j\boldsymbol{v}_j'}{\sigma^2}\right)^{-1} \tag{8.13}$$

$$E[\boldsymbol{u}_i|\text{Rest}] = \text{Var}[\boldsymbol{u}_i|\text{Rest}]\left(\frac{1}{\sigma_u^2}G(x_i) + \sum_{j\in\mathcal{J}_i}\frac{o_{ij}\boldsymbol{v}_j}{\sigma^2}\right).$$

4. For each item j, sample $\boldsymbol{v}_j$ from $(\boldsymbol{v}_j \mid \text{Rest})$, which is Gaussian:

$$\text{Let } o_{ij} = y_{ij} - b(x_{ij}) - \alpha_i - \beta_j.$$

$$\text{Var}[\boldsymbol{v}_j|\text{Rest}] = \left(\frac{1}{\sigma_v^2}I + \sum_{i\in\mathcal{I}_j}\frac{\boldsymbol{u}_i\boldsymbol{u}_i'}{\sigma^2}\right)^{-1} \tag{8.14}$$

$$E[\boldsymbol{v}_j|\text{Rest}] = \text{Var}[\boldsymbol{v}_j|\text{Rest}]\left(\frac{1}{\sigma_v^2}H(x_j) + \sum_{i\in\mathcal{I}_j}\frac{o_{ij}\boldsymbol{u}_i}{\sigma^2}\right).$$

Let $\tilde{E}[\cdot]$ and $\tilde{\text{Var}}[\cdot]$ denote the Monte Carlo mean and variance computed using the L Gibbs samples. The output of the E-step consists of the following:

- $\hat{\alpha}_i = \tilde{E}[\alpha_i]$, $\hat{\beta}_j = \tilde{E}[\beta_j]$, $\hat{\boldsymbol{u}}_i = \tilde{E}[\boldsymbol{u}_i]$, $\hat{\boldsymbol{v}}_j = \tilde{E}[\boldsymbol{v}_j]$, for all i and j.
- $\tilde{E}[\boldsymbol{u}_i'\boldsymbol{v}_j]$, for all observed (i, j) pairs.
- $\sum_{ij}\tilde{\text{Var}}[s_{ij}]$, $\sum_{ik}\tilde{\text{Var}}[u_{ik}]$, where u_{ik} is the kth element in $\boldsymbol{u}_i$.
- $\sum_{jk}\tilde{\text{Var}}[v_{jk}]$, where v_{jk} is the kth element in $\boldsymbol{v}_j$.

These are the sufficient statistics that will be used in the M-step of our fitting procedure.

M-Step

In the M-step, we find the parameter setting $\boldsymbol{\Theta}$ that maximizes the expectation computed in the E-step:

$$\begin{aligned} q_t(\boldsymbol{\Theta}) &= E_{\boldsymbol{\Delta}}[\log L(\boldsymbol{\Theta}; \boldsymbol{\Delta}, \boldsymbol{y}) \mid \hat{\boldsymbol{\Theta}}^{(t)}] \\ &= \text{constant} \\ &\quad - \frac{1}{2\sigma^2}\sum_{ij}\tilde{E}[(y_{ij} - b(x_{ij}) - \alpha_i - \beta_j - \boldsymbol{u}_i'\boldsymbol{v}_j)^2] - \frac{D}{2}\log(\sigma^2) \\ &\quad - \frac{1}{2\sigma_\alpha^2}\sum_i\left((\hat{\alpha}_i - g(x_i))^2 + \tilde{\text{Var}}[\alpha_i]\right) - \frac{M}{2}\log\sigma_\alpha^2 \end{aligned}$$

$$-\frac{1}{2\sigma_\beta^2}\sum_j\left((\hat{\beta}_j - h(x_j))^2 + \tilde{\text{Var}}[\beta_j]\right) - \frac{N}{2}\log\sigma_\beta^2$$
$$-\frac{1}{2\sigma_u^2}\sum_i\left(\|\hat{\boldsymbol{u}}_i - G(x_i)\|^2 + \text{tr}(\tilde{\text{Var}}[\boldsymbol{u}_i])\right) - \frac{Mr}{2}\log\sigma_u^2$$
$$-\frac{1}{2\sigma_v^2}\sum_j\left(\|\hat{\boldsymbol{v}}_j - H(x_j)\|^2 + \text{tr}(\tilde{\text{Var}}[\boldsymbol{v}_j])\right) - \frac{Nr}{2}\log\sigma_v^2. \quad (8.15)$$

It can be easily seen that (b, σ^2), (g, σ_α^2), (h, σ_β^2), (G, σ_u^2), and (H, σ_v^2) can be optimized by separate regressions.

Regression for (b, σ^2). Here we want to minimize

$$\frac{1}{\sigma^2}\sum_{ij}\tilde{E}[(y_{ij} - b(x_{ij}) - \alpha_i - \beta_j - \boldsymbol{u}_i'\boldsymbol{v}_j)^2] + D\log(\sigma^2), \quad (8.16)$$

where D is the number of observed responses. It is easy to see that the optimal solution to b can be found by solving a regression problem with the following settings:

- *Feature vector*: $\boldsymbol{x}_{ij}$
- *Response to predict*: $(y_{ij} - \hat{\alpha}_i - \hat{\beta}_j - \tilde{E}[\boldsymbol{u}_i'\boldsymbol{v}_j])$

Let RSS denote the residual sum of squares from this regression. Then, the optimal σ^2 is $(\sum_{ij}\tilde{\text{Var}}[s_{ij}] + \text{RSS})/D$, where RSS is the residual sum of squares of the regression. Note that b can be any regression model.

Regression for (g, σ_α^2). Similar to the regression for (b, σ^2), the optimal g can be found by solving a regression problem with the following settings:

- *Feature vector*: $\boldsymbol{x}_i$
- *Response to predict*: $\hat{\alpha}_i$

The optimal σ_α^2 is $(\sum_i \tilde{\text{Var}}[\alpha_i] + \text{RSS})/M$, where M is the number of users.

Regression for (h, σ_β^2). The optimal h can be found by solving a regression problem with the following settings:

- *Feature vector*: $\boldsymbol{x}_j$
- *Response to predict*: $\hat{\beta}_j$

The optimal $\sigma_\beta^2 = (\sum_j \tilde{\text{Var}}[\beta_j] + \text{RSS})/N$, where N is the number of items.

Regression for (G, σ_u^2). For multivariate regression models, we find G by solving a regression problem using $\boldsymbol{x}_i$ as features to predict multivariate response $\hat{\boldsymbol{u}}_i$. For univariate regression models, we consider $G(\boldsymbol{x}_i) = (G_1(\boldsymbol{x}_i), \ldots, G_r(\boldsymbol{x}_i))$, where each $G_k(x_i)$ returns a scalar. In this case, for each k, we find G_k by solving a regression problem with the following settings:

- *Feature vector*: $\boldsymbol{x}_i$
- *Response to predict*: $\hat{u}_{ik}$ (the kth element of vector $\hat{\boldsymbol{u}}_i$)

Let RSS denote the total residual sum of squares. Then, $\sigma_u^2 = (\sum_{ik} \tilde{\text{Var}}[u_{ik}] + \text{RSS})/(rM)$.

Regression for (H, σ_v^2). For multivariate regression models, we find H by solving a regression problem using $\boldsymbol{x}_j$ as features to predict multivariate response $\tilde{E}[\boldsymbol{v}_j]$. For univariate regression models, we consider $H(\boldsymbol{x}_j) = (H_1(\boldsymbol{x}_j), \ldots, H_r(\boldsymbol{x}_j))$, where each $H_k(\boldsymbol{x}_j)$ returns a scalar. In this case, for each k, we find H_k by solving a regression problem with the following settings:

- *Feature vector*: $\boldsymbol{x}_j$
- *Response to predict*: $\hat{v}_{jk}$ (the kth element of vector $\hat{\boldsymbol{v}}_j$)

Let RSS denote the total residual sum of squares. Then, $\sigma_v^2 = (\sum_{jk} \tilde{\text{Var}}[v_{jk}] + \text{RSS})/(rN)$.

Remarks

Regularization in the M-step. Any regularization and fitting methods can be applied to the regression problems in the M-step. In practice, regularization is important when the number of features is large or the correlation among features is high.

Number of Gibbs Samples. Replacing the precise E-step with a Monte Carlo average no longer guarantees an increase in the marginal likelihood at each step due to Monte Carlo sampling error. If the Monte Carlo sampling error associated with $\hat{\Theta}^{(t)}$ (an estimate of $\hat{\Theta}_\infty^{(t)}$ that is obtained from an exact E-step, e.g., by using infinite number of samples) is large relative to $\|\hat{\Theta}^{(t-1)} - \hat{\Theta}_\infty^{(t)}\|$, then the Monte Carlo E-step is wasteful Because it is swamped by the Monte Carlo error. A precise solution to this problem does not exist in the literature, except for some practical guidelines (Booth and Hobert, 1999). For instance, it is better to use fewer Monte Carlo simulations during early iterations. We performed extensive experiments with various schemes and found twenty EM iterations with one hundred samples (drawn after ten burn-in samples) at each iteration performed adequately in our experiments. In fact, the performance was not too sensitive to the choice of number of samples; even a small number of samples like fifty did not hurt performance by much. The Gibbs sampler was chosen because of its simplicity; better sampling methods to make the sampler *mix* faster could be investigated.

Scalability. Fixing the factor dimensionality, the number of EM iterations, and the number of Gibbs samples per iteration, the MCEM algorithm is essentially *linear* in the number of observations. In our experience, the MCEM algorithm converges quickly after a fairly small number of EM iterations (usually around ten). The algorithm can also be parallelized. In the E-step, when drawing the ℓth Gibbs sample, the factors for each user can be drawn independently of other users. Thus, this sampling step can be done in parallel. The same holds for items. The M-step requires solving several regression problems. Any scalable software package can be used here.

Shrinkage Estimator for Factors. RLFM estimates the factors as a linear combination of regression function and collaborative filtering. Consider the factor estimate $\boldsymbol{u}_i$ (the same also applies to $\boldsymbol{v}_j$). For simplicity, assume $r = 1$, and let o_{ij} be the response of user i on item j after adjusting for the features $\boldsymbol{x}_{ij}$ and for user and item bias. Then, letting $\lambda = \sigma^2/\sigma_u^2$, we see

$$E[u_i|\text{Rest}] = \frac{\lambda}{\lambda + \sum_{j \in \mathcal{J}_i} v_j^2} G(\boldsymbol{x}_i) + \frac{\sum_{j \in \mathcal{J}_i} v_j o_{ij}}{\lambda + \sum_{j \in \mathcal{J}_i} v_j^2}, \tag{8.17}$$

which for fixed $\boldsymbol{v}$ is a linear combination of regression G and responses o_{ij} of user i. The weights attached to different components in the linear combination depend on both the global shrinkage parameter λ and the item factors for those items that are responded to by the user. The contribution from regression is negligible when $\sum_{j \in \mathcal{J}_i} v_j^2$ is significantly larger than λ; in this scenario, the user factor estimate is obtained by performing a linear regression for each user by treating the user's responses on different items and the factor vectors of those items as the feature vectors in the regression problem. This clearly shows that when a user responds to a large number of items for which we have enough data to obtain reliable item factor estimates, response information takes over and regression is no longer important.

Assuming the hyperparameters are known, remarkably, the marginal expectation of u_i conditional on the data is still a linear combination of regression and responses by user i with the weights being given by

$$E\left[\frac{\lambda}{\lambda+\sum_{j\in\mathcal{J}_i} v_j^2}\right] \text{ and } E\left[\frac{v_j}{\lambda+\sum_{j\in\mathcal{J}_i} v_j^2}\right], \text{ for } j \in \mathcal{J}_i, \tag{8.18}$$

where the expectations are w.r.t. the marginal posterior of item factors v_js. This provides insights on how RLFM is estimating the factors by achieving a compromise between regression and responses. Interestingly, we note that although the shrinkage estimator is a linear combination of responses and regression, the weights are highly nonlinear functions and depend on both global shrinkage parameters and local response information.

8.2.2 ARS-Based EM for Logistic Response

The fitting algorithm for RLFM with binary (or logistic) response $y_{ij} \in \{0, 1\}$ is similar to the EM algorithm for Gaussian response. In this case, the complete data log-likelihood is given by

$$\begin{aligned}
\log L(\boldsymbol{\Theta}; \boldsymbol{\Delta}, \boldsymbol{y}) = \log \Pr[\boldsymbol{y}, \boldsymbol{\Delta}|\boldsymbol{\Theta}] = {} & \text{constant} \\
& - \sum_{ij} \log(1+\exp\{-(2y_{ij}-1)(b(\boldsymbol{x}_{ij})+\alpha_i+\beta_j+\boldsymbol{u}_i'\boldsymbol{v}_j)\}) \\
& - \frac{1}{2\sigma_\alpha^2}\sum_i(\alpha_i - g(\boldsymbol{x}_i))^2 - \frac{M}{2}\log\sigma_\alpha^2 \\
& - \frac{1}{2\sigma_\beta^2}\sum_j(\beta_j - h(\boldsymbol{x}_j))^2 - \frac{N}{2}\log\sigma_\beta^2 \\
& - \frac{1}{2\sigma_u^2}\sum_i\|\boldsymbol{u}_i - G(\boldsymbol{x}_i)\|^2 - \frac{Mr}{2}\log\sigma_u^2 \\
& - \frac{1}{2\sigma_v^2}\sum_j\|\boldsymbol{v}_j - H(\boldsymbol{x}_j)\|^2 - \frac{Nr}{2}\log\sigma_v^2.
\end{aligned} \tag{8.19}$$

The EM algorithm iterates between an E-step and an M-step. We describe a method based on adaptive rejection sampling (ARS) in this subsection and a method based on variational approximation in Section 8.2.3.

ARS-Based E-Step

For binary data and logistic link function, the conditional posterior $p(\alpha_i|\text{Rest})$, $p(\beta_j|\text{Rest})$, $p(\boldsymbol{u}_i|\text{Rest})$, and $p(\boldsymbol{v}_j|\text{Rest})$ are not in closed form. However, precise and efficient sampling from the posterior can still be achieved through ARS

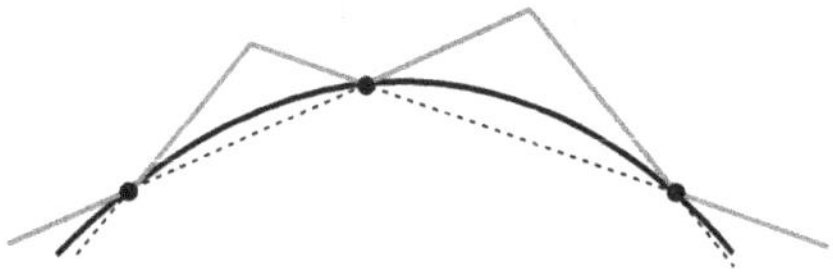

Figure 8.2. Illustration of upper and lower bounds of an arbitrary (log) density function.

(Gilks, 1992). ARS is an efficient method to draw samples from an arbitrary univariate density, provided it is log-concave.

In general, rejection sampling (RS) is a popular method used to sample from a univariate distribution. Suppose we want to draw a sample from a nonstandard distribution with density $p(x)$. If we can find another density $e(x)$ that is easier to sample from and approximates $p(x)$ well and has tails heavier than $p(x)$, then $e(x)$ can be used to do rejection sampling. The key is to find a constant M such that $p(x) \leq Me(x)$ for all points x such that $p(x) > 0$. For example, the gray curve in Figure 8.2 is $Me(x)$, and the black solid curve is $p(x)$. The algorithm then is simple: we repeat the following steps until we obtain a valid sample. First, we draw a number x^* from $e(x)$. Then, with probability $p(x^*)/(Me(x^*))$, we accept x^* as a valid sample; otherwise, we reject it.

Notice that $p(x^*)/(Me(x^*))$ is always between 0 and 1. This algorithm can be shown to provide a sample from $p(x)$, and the acceptance probability is $1/M$. Finding an M that is small often involves knowing the mode of $p(x)$; it is also important to find a good matching density $e(x)$ in practice. ARS addresses both the issues. It finds a good matching density $e(x)$ that is composed of piecewise exponentials; that is, $\log e(x)$ is piecewise linear, like the gray curve in Figure 8.2. ARS does not need to know the mode of $p(x)$, and the only requirement is the log-concavity of $p(x)$, which is true for our problem. The piecewise exponentials are constructed by creating an upper envelope of the target log density. Furthermore, the procedure is adaptive and uses the rejected points to further refine the envelope, which reduces the rejection probability for future samples.

We use the derivative-free ARS process from Gilks (1992), which can be briefly described as follows: suppose we want to obtain a sample x^* from a log-concave target density function $p(x)$. We start from at least three initial points such that at least one point lies on each side of the mode of $p(x)$ (this is ensured by looking at the derivative of the density, which does not require actual mode computation). A lower bound *lower*(x) of $\log p(x)$ is constructed from the chords joining the evaluated points of $p(x)$ with the vertical lines at the extreme points; for example, the dotted piecewise linear curve in Figure 8.2 is *lower*(x), whereas the solid black curve is $\log p(x)$. An upper bound *upper*(x) is also constructed by extending the chords to their intersection points. For example, the gray piecewise linear curve in Figure 8.2 is *upper*(x). The envelope function $e(x)$ (upper bound) and the squeezing function $s(x)$ (lower bound) are created by exponentiating the piece-wise linear upper and lower bounds of $\log p(x)$; that is, $e(x) = \exp(\mathit{upper}(x))$ and $s(x) = \exp(\mathit{lower}(x))$. Let $e_1(x)$ be the corresponding density function derived from $e(x)$; that is,

$$e_1(x) = \frac{e(x)}{\int e(x)dx}. \tag{8.20}$$

The sampling produce works as follows; repeat the following steps until we obtain a valid sample:

1. Draw a number x^* from $e_1(x)$ and another number $z \sim \text{Uniform}(0, 1)$, independently.
2. If $z \leq s(x^*)/e(x^*)$, accept x^* as a valid sample.
3. If $z \leq p(x^*)/e(x^*)$, accept x^* as a valid sample; otherwise, reject x^*.
4. If x^* is rejected, update $e(x)$ and $s(x)$ by constructing new chords using x^*.

This goes on iteratively until one sample is accepted. Note that using the squeezing function as the acceptance criteria implies partial information from the original density $p(x)$; testing x^* based on the squeezing function first is to save computation because the squeezing function is readily available from the constructed envelope, and evaluation of $p(x^*)$ is usually costly.

The ARS-based E-step works as follows; repeat the following steps L times to draw L samples of $\boldsymbol{\Delta}$:

1. Sample α_i from $p(\alpha_i|\text{Rest})$ for each user i using ARS. The log of the target density is given by

$$\begin{aligned}\log p(\alpha_i|\text{Rest}) = {} & \text{constant} \\ & - \sum_{j \in \mathcal{J}_i} \log(1 + \exp\{-(2y_{ij} - 1)(f(x_{ij}) + \alpha_i + \beta_j + \boldsymbol{u}_i'\boldsymbol{v}_j)\}) \\ & - \frac{1}{2\sigma_\alpha^2}(\alpha_i - g(x_i))^2.\end{aligned} \tag{8.21}$$

2. Sample β_j for each item j in a way similar to the sampling of α_i.
3. Sample $\boldsymbol{u}_i$ from $p(\boldsymbol{u}_i|\text{Rest})$ for each user i. Because $\boldsymbol{u}_i$ is an r-dimensional vector, for each $k = 1, \ldots, r$, we sample u_{ik} from $p(u_{ik}|\text{Rest})$ using ARS.

The log of the target density is given by

$$\begin{aligned}\log p(u_{ik}|\text{Rest}) = &\ \text{constant}\\ &-\sum_{j\in\mathcal{J}_i}\log(1+\exp\{-(2y_{ij}-1)(f(x_{ij})+\alpha_i+\beta_j+u_{ik}v_{jk}+\sum_{l\neq k}u_{il}v_{jl})\})\\ &-\frac{1}{2\sigma_u^2}(u_{ik}-G_k(x_i))^2.\end{aligned} \tag{8.22}$$

4. Sample $\boldsymbol{v}_j$ for each item j in a way similar to the sampling of $\boldsymbol{u}_i$.

Initial Points for ARS. The rejection rate of ARS depends on the initial points and the target density function. To reduce the rejection rate, Gilks et al. (1995) suggest using the envelope function from the previous iteration of the Gibbs sampler to construct fifth, fiftieth, and ninety-fifth percentiles as the three starting points. We have adopted this approach in practice and observed roughly 60 percent reduction in rejection rates.

Centering. RLFM is not identifiable. For example, if we let $\tilde{f}(x_{ij}) = f(x_{ij}) - \delta$ and $\tilde{g}(x_i) = g(x_i) + \delta$, the model using $\tilde{f}$ and $\tilde{g}$ is essentially the same as the one using f and g. To help identify the model parameters, we put constraints on the factor values. Specifically, we require $\sum_i \alpha_i = 0$, $\sum_j \beta_j = 0$, $\sum_i \boldsymbol{u}_i = \boldsymbol{0}$, and $\sum_j \boldsymbol{v}_j = \boldsymbol{0}$. These constraints induce dependencies among user factors and item factors. Instead of dealing with these dependencies in sampling, we simply enforce these constraints after sampling by subtracting the sample mean; that is, after sampling all factors, we compute $\bar{\alpha} = \sum_i \hat{\alpha}_i / M$ and set $\hat{\alpha}_i = \hat{\alpha}_i - \bar{\alpha}$ for all i, and so on. Here M is the number of users and $\hat{\alpha}_i$ is the posterior sample mean of α_i.

M-Step

The M-step is the same as that for Gaussian response, except for the regression for $b(\boldsymbol{x}_{ij})$, because only b is involved in the logistic likelihood. In particular, here we need to find b that maximizes the following expectation over $o_{ij} = \alpha_i + \beta_j + \boldsymbol{u}_i'\boldsymbol{v}_j$:

$$\textstyle\sum_{ij} E_{o_{ij}}[\log(1+\exp\{-(2y_{ij}-1)(b(\boldsymbol{x}_{ij})+o_{ij})\})]. \tag{8.23}$$

Because this expectation (8.23) is not available in closed form, we approximate it using a plug-in estimator:

$$\begin{aligned}&\textstyle\sum_{ij} E_{o_{ij}}[\log(1+\exp\{-(2y_{ij}-1)(b(\boldsymbol{x}_{ij})+o_{ij})\})]\\ &\approx \textstyle\sum_{ij}\log(1+\exp\{-(2y_{ij}-1)(b(\boldsymbol{x}_{ij})+\hat{o}_{ij})\}),\end{aligned} \tag{8.24}$$

where $\hat{o}_{ij} = \hat{\alpha}_i + \hat{\beta}_j + \hat{\boldsymbol{u}}_i'\hat{\boldsymbol{v}}_j$ now can be treated as a constant offset. We now have a standard logistic regression problem with binary response y_{ij}, feature vector $\boldsymbol{x}_{ij}$, and offset o_{ij} for each training observation (i, j).

8.2.3 Variational EM for Logistic Response

The variational approximation is based on Jaakkola and Jordan (2000). The basic idea is to transform binary response values into Gaussian response values before each EM iteration based on a variational lower bound of complete data log-likelihood. Then, we just use the E-step and M-step of the Gaussian model.

Let $f(z) = (1 + e^{-z})^{-1}$ denote the sigmoid function. Jaakkola and Jordan (2000) provided the following approximation for $\log f(z)$:

$$\begin{aligned} \log f(z) &= -\log(1 + e^{-z}) = \frac{z}{2} + q(z) \\ q(z) &= -\log(e^{z/2} + e^{-z/2}). \end{aligned} \tag{8.25}$$

By Taylor series expansion, they obtained

$$\begin{aligned} q(z) &\geq q(\xi) + \frac{d\, q(\xi)}{d\,(\xi^2)}(z^2 - \xi^2) \\ &= \log g(\xi) - \frac{\xi}{2} - \lambda(\xi)(z^2 - \xi^2), \end{aligned} \tag{8.26}$$

for any value of ξ, where

$$\lambda(\xi) = \frac{d\, q(\xi)}{d\,(\xi^2)} = \frac{1}{4\xi} \cdot \frac{e^{\xi/2} - e^{-\xi/2}}{e^{\xi/2} + e^{-\xi/2}} = \frac{1}{4\xi} \tanh\left(\frac{\xi}{2}\right). \tag{8.27}$$

This lower bound holds for any value of ξ and is exact when $\xi^2 = z^2$. Let ξ_{ij} denote such a variational parameter associated with each observed y_{ij}. Let $s_{ij} = b(\boldsymbol{x}_{ij}) + \alpha_i + \beta_j + \boldsymbol{u}_i'\boldsymbol{v}_j$. By using the lower bound (8.26), we obtain a lower bound of the complete data log-likelihood defined in Equation (8.19):

$$\begin{aligned} &\log L(\boldsymbol{\Theta}; \boldsymbol{\Delta}, \boldsymbol{y}) \geq \ell(\boldsymbol{\Theta}; \boldsymbol{\Delta}, \boldsymbol{y}, \boldsymbol{\xi}) \\ &= \sum_{ij} \left(\log f(\xi_{ij}) + \frac{(2y_{ij} - 1)s_{ij} - \xi_{ij}}{2} - \lambda(\xi_{ij})(s_{ij}^2 - \xi_{ij}^2) \right) \\ &\quad + \log \Pr(\boldsymbol{\Delta} \mid \boldsymbol{\Theta}), \end{aligned} \tag{8.28}$$

where $\log \Pr(\boldsymbol{\Delta} \mid \boldsymbol{\Theta})$ consists of the last four lines of Equation (8.19). Notice that $\ell(\boldsymbol{\Theta}; \boldsymbol{\Delta}, \boldsymbol{y}, \xi)$ can be written in a form similar to the Gaussian model:

$$\begin{aligned} \ell(\boldsymbol{\Theta}; \boldsymbol{\Delta}, \boldsymbol{y}, \boldsymbol{\xi}) &= \sum_{ij} -\frac{(r_{ij} - s_{ij})^2}{2\sigma_{ij}^2} + \log \Pr(\boldsymbol{\Delta} \mid \boldsymbol{\Theta}) + c(\boldsymbol{\xi}) \\ r_{ij} &= \frac{2y_{ij} - 1}{4\lambda(\xi_{ij})}, \; \sigma_{ij}^2 = \frac{1}{2\lambda(\xi_{ij})}, \end{aligned} \tag{8.29}$$

where $c(\boldsymbol{\xi})$ is a function that only depends on the ξ_{ij}s. Here r_{ij} can be treated as Gaussian response with variance σ_{ij}^2.

Now, the variational EM algorithm works by replacing $\log L(\boldsymbol{\Theta}; \boldsymbol{\Delta}, \boldsymbol{y})$ in the EM algorithm by $\ell(\boldsymbol{\Theta}; \boldsymbol{\Delta}, \boldsymbol{y}, \xi)$. Let $\hat{\boldsymbol{\Theta}}^{(t)}$ and $\hat{\boldsymbol{\xi}}^{(t)}$ denote the estimates of $\boldsymbol{\Theta}$ and $\boldsymbol{\xi}$ at the beginning of the tth iteration. We can set all $\xi_{ij} = 1$ initially. In the tth iteration, do the following:

1. *E-step*: Compute $E_{(\boldsymbol{\Delta} \mid \boldsymbol{y}, \hat{\boldsymbol{\Theta}}^{(t)}, \hat{\boldsymbol{\xi}}^{(t)})}[\ell(\boldsymbol{\Theta}; \boldsymbol{\Delta}, \boldsymbol{y}, \boldsymbol{\xi})]$ based on Equation (8.29). The is the same as the E-step of the Gaussian model with r_{ij} as the response and σ_{ij}^2 as the observation variance.
2. *M-step*: Find $\hat{\boldsymbol{\Theta}}^{(t+1)}$ and $\hat{\boldsymbol{\xi}}^{(t+1)}$ by

$$(\hat{\boldsymbol{\Theta}}^{(t+1)}, \hat{\boldsymbol{\xi}}^{(t+1)}) = \arg\max_{(\boldsymbol{\Theta}, \boldsymbol{\xi})} E_{(\boldsymbol{\Delta} \mid \boldsymbol{y}, \hat{\boldsymbol{\Theta}}^{(t)}, \hat{\boldsymbol{\xi}}^{(t)})}[\ell(\boldsymbol{\Theta}; \boldsymbol{\Delta}, \boldsymbol{y}, \boldsymbol{\xi})]. \tag{8.30}$$

Variational E-Step

The E-step works as follows. Given the pseudo-Gaussian observations (r_{ij}, σ_{ij}^2), which are computed using $\hat{\xi}_{ij}^{(t)}$, repeat the following steps L times to draw L samples of $\boldsymbol{\Delta}$:

1. Draw α_i from the Gaussian posterior of $(\alpha_i|\text{Rest})$ for each user i:

$$\text{Let } o_{ij} = r_{ij} - b(x_{ij}) - \beta_j - \boldsymbol{u}_i'\boldsymbol{v}_j.$$

$$\begin{aligned} \text{Var}[\alpha_i|\text{Rest}] &= \left(\frac{1}{\sigma_\alpha^2} + \sum_{j \in \mathcal{J}_i} \frac{1}{\sigma_{ij}^2} \right)^{-1} \\ E[\alpha_i|\text{Rest}] &= \text{Var}[\alpha_i|\text{Rest}] \left(\frac{g(x_i)}{\sigma_\alpha^2} + \sum_{j \in \mathcal{J}_i} \frac{o_{ij}}{\sigma_{ij}^2} \right). \end{aligned} \tag{8.31}$$

2. Draw β_j for each item j in a way similar to the sampling of α_i.

3. Draw $\boldsymbol{u}_i$ from the Gaussian posterior of $(\boldsymbol{u}_i \mid \text{Rest})$ for each user i:

$$\text{Let } o_{ij} = r_{ij} - b(x_{ij}) - \alpha_i - \beta_j.$$

$$\begin{aligned} \text{Var}[\boldsymbol{u}_i|\text{Rest}] &= \left(\frac{1}{\sigma_u^2} I + \sum_{j \in \mathcal{J}_i} \frac{\boldsymbol{v}_j \boldsymbol{v}_j'}{\sigma_{ij}^2} \right)^{-1} \\ E[\boldsymbol{u}_i|\text{Rest}] &= \text{Var}[\boldsymbol{u}_i|\text{Rest}] \left(\frac{1}{\sigma_u^2} G(x_i) + \sum_{j \in \mathcal{J}_i} \frac{o_{ij} \boldsymbol{v}_j}{\sigma_{ij}^2} \right). \end{aligned} \tag{8.32}$$

4. Draw $\boldsymbol{v}_j$ for each item j in a way similar to the sampling of $\boldsymbol{u}_i$.

Variational M-Step

The M-step is the same as that for Gaussian response, except for the regression for $b(\boldsymbol{x}_{ij})$, because only b is involved in the logistic likelihood. In addition to b, we also need to update the variational parameter $\boldsymbol{\xi}$. In fact, the estimation of b cannot be cleanly separated from estimation of $\boldsymbol{\xi}$. Thus, we repeat the following two steps until convergence.

Regression for b. We use Equation (8.29) to find a new estimate of b, which is included in s_{ij}. It is easy to see that the optimal solution to b can be found by solving a regression problem with the following settings:

- *Feature vector:* $\boldsymbol{x}_{ij}$
- *Response to predict:* $(r_{ij} - \hat{\alpha}_i - \hat{\beta}_j - \tilde{E}[\boldsymbol{u}_i' \boldsymbol{v}_j])$, where r_{ij} is computed based on the last estimate of ξ_{ij}
- *Weight:* $1/\sigma_{ij}^2$, which is computed based on the last estimate of ξ_{ij}

Estimation of $\boldsymbol{\xi}$. We use Equation (8.28) to find the new estimate of ξ_{ij}:

$$\begin{aligned} &\frac{d}{d\xi_{ij}} \tilde{E}[\ell(\boldsymbol{\Theta}; \boldsymbol{\Delta}, \boldsymbol{y}, \boldsymbol{\xi})] \\ &= \frac{d}{d\xi_{ij}} \log f(\xi_{ij}) - \frac{1}{2} - (\tilde{E}[s_{ij}^2] - \xi_{ij}^2) \frac{d\lambda(\xi_{ij})}{d\xi_{ij}} + 2\lambda(\xi_{ij})\xi_{ij} \\ &= \frac{1}{2} + \frac{d}{d\xi_{ij}} q(\xi_{ij}) - \frac{1}{2} - (\tilde{E}[s_{ij}^2] - \xi_{ij}^2) \frac{d\lambda(\xi_{ij})}{d\xi_{ij}} + 2\lambda(\xi_{ij})\xi_{ij} \\ &= -(\tilde{E}[s_{ij}^2] - \xi_{ij}^2) \frac{d\lambda(\xi_{ij})}{d\xi_{ij}}. \end{aligned} \tag{8.33}$$

The maximum is obtained at $\xi_{ij}^2 = \tilde{E}[s_{ij}^2]$. Thus, we set

$$\begin{aligned}\hat{\xi}_{ij}^{(t+1)} &= \sqrt{\tilde{E}[s_{ij}^2]} \\ &= \sqrt{(b(\boldsymbol{x}_{ij}) + \hat{\alpha}_i + \hat{\beta}_j + \tilde{E}[\boldsymbol{u}_i'\boldsymbol{v}_j])^2 + \tilde{\text{Var}}[s_{ij}]},\end{aligned} \tag{8.34}$$

where b is the solution to the regression problem for b.

8.3 Illustration of Cold Start

We illustrate the performance of RLFM with linear-regression priors on two benchmark movie data sets (MovieLens and EachMovie) and on a Yahoo! front page data set. For movie data sets, we use the popular root mean square error (RMSE) as the performance metric. For Yahoo! data, we use ROC curves.

Methods. We evaluate RLFM by comparing it with the following methods:

- *FactorOnly* and *FeatureOnly* are special cases of RLFM.
- *MostPopular* is a baseline method that recommends the most popular items in the training set to users in the test set.
- *FilterBot* (Park et al., 2006) is a hybrid method designed to handle cold-start collaborative filtering. We used thirteen bots based on global popularity, movie genre, and the popularity in each of the eleven user groups defined based on age and gender coupled with an item-based algorithm (Herlocker et al., 1999).

Several other collaborative filtering algorithms (including pure item-item similarity, user-user similarity, regression-based) were also tried. Because *FilterBot* was uniformly better among these, we only report results relative to this baseline.

MovieLens Data. We conducted experiments on two MovieLens data sets: MovieLens-100K, which consists of $100K$ ratings with 943 users and 1,682 movies, and MovieLens-1M, which consists of $1M$ ratings with 6,040 users and 3,706 movies (although the readme file mentions 3,900 movies). User features include age, gender, Zipcode (we used the first digit only), and occupation. Item features include movie genre. MovieLens-100K comes with five pre-specified training-testing splits for five-fold cross-validation. We report the RMSEs of RLFM, FactorOnly, and FeatureOnly on this data set with $r = 5$. For these data, there are no new users and items in the test set; the gain obtained through

Table 8.1. *Test-set RMSE on MovieLens and EachMovie*

Model	MovieLens-1M			EachMovie		
	30%	60%	75%	30%	60%	75%
RLFM	0.9742	0.9528	0.9363	1.281	1.214	1.193
FactorOnly	0.9862	0.9614	0.9422	1.260	1.217	1.197
FeatureOnly	1.0923	1.0914	1.0906	1.277	1.272	1.266
FilterBot	0.9821	0.9648	0.9517	1.300	1.225	1.199
MostPopular	0.9831	0.9744	0.9726	1.300	1.227	1.205
Constant Model	1.118	1.123	1.119	1.306	1.302	1.298
Dyn-RLFM			0.9258			1.182

RLFM relative to FactorOnly is entirely due to better regularization achieved through feature-based priors (see Figure 8.1 for an example).

	RLFM	FactorOnly	FeatureOnly
MovieLens-100K	0.8956	0.9064	1.0968

However, testing methods based on random splits may end up using the *future* to predict the *past*. This does not correspond to the real-world scenario where the goal is to predict ratings for user and item pairs that occur in the future. A more realistic training-test split should be based on time. For MovieLens-1M, we report results on more realistic time-based splits. We set aside the last 25 percent of ratings as the test data and train each model on three training sets, which consist of the first 30 percent, 60 percent and 75 percent of the ratings, respectively. The test-set RMSEs are reported in Table 8.1.

The pure feature based model FeatureOnly has poor performance (although it is better than a constant model). In fact the item popularity model is significantly better than FeatureOnly. The FactorOnly model outperforms all the existing collaborative filtering methods we experimented with. RLFM based on factors regularized through features and item popularity significantly outperforms all other static methods. A large fraction of pairs in the test set (almost 56 percent) involve new users, but most of the items are old. By adaptively estimating factors for new users starting out from a feature based prior through our dynamic RLFM, we obtain a significant boost in predictive accuracy over the static RLFM model.

EachMovie Data. The EachMovie data set is similar to MovieLens but is far more noisy (RMSE for the constant model is close to the best models), with a large fraction of users missing one or more features. It contains 2,811,983 ratings with 72,916 users and 1,628 movies. We cleaned up this data set by only including 2,559,107 "real" ratings (those with weights equal to 1) and then linearly scaled the ratings so that the ratings are from 0 to 5. We created training-test splits in the same way as the MovieLens case. The test-set RMSEs are reported in Table 8.1. The results are qualitatively similar to that of MovieLens. RLFM provides the best offline trained model. The dynamic version of RLFM significantly outperforms all other methods.

Yahoo! Front Page Data. As described in earlier chapters, the Today Module on Yahoo! front page has several tabs and recommends four stories in the Featured tab for each user visit. The goal is to develop algorithms that maximize the number of clicks by recommending relevant stories for each user visit. Stories in this application have short lifetimes (usually less than one day), and for reasons of scalability, models can only be retrained periodically in an offline fashion. Hence, when a model trained offline is deployed, almost all stories (and a large fraction of users) are new. Classical collaborative filtering algorithms that assume stories have some user ratings in the training set do not apply in this scenario. Models that can use both features and users' past ratings are attractive. We only have a few *live* items in the system at any given time, hence online updating of latent item factors is an attractive method to obtain good performance. A data set, which we call Y!FP, was created to evaluate performance of our recommendation algorithms. This data set consists of 1,909,525 "binary ratings" (clicks or views without any subsequent click) given by 30,635 frequent Yahoo! users (each has at least thirty ratings in five months) to 4,316 stories. User features include age, gender, geolocation, and browsing behavior that are inferred based on a user's network wide activity (search, ad clicks, pageviews, subscriptions, etc.) on the Yahoo! portal. A user is assigned an intensity score in a few thousand content categories based on his activity pattern in the recent past; we reduced these to a few hundred features by conducting a principal components analysis on the training data. Item features consist of hand-labeled categories that are assigned to a story by editors.

Results on Y!FP. As shown in Figure 8.3, every model is significantly better than a model that predicts a constant score for all examples (the ROC curve for this model is a straight line). Almost all items that occur in the test set are new in this application. Hence for FactorOnly, the item factors (β_j, v_j) are zero; the only contribution is from the user popularity term α_i. Thus, prediction based on user's click propensity alone performs better than a pure feature-based model. The static RLFM model, which exploits granular user profiles

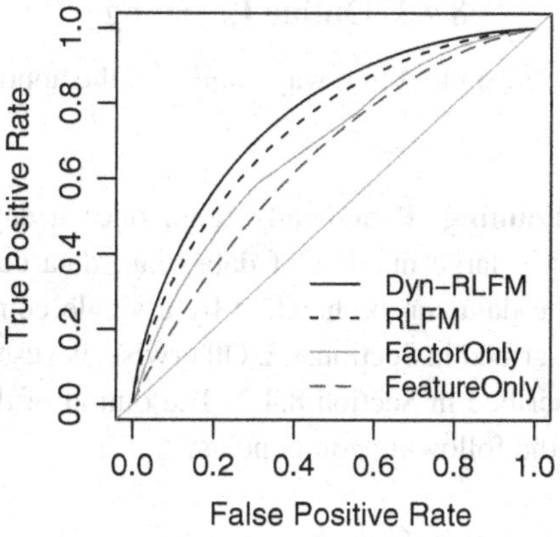

Figure 8.3. ROC curves of different methods on Y!FP data.

along with item features, significantly outperforms FactorOnly, indicating the presence of strong user-item interactions in the data. As for other data sets, the dynamic version of RLFM that estimates item profiles (β_j, v_j) of new items in an online fashion is the most granular model and has the best performance (Figure 8.3).

Discussion of Experimental Results. We observe that models purely based on features are inferior to those based on user-item specific statistics. That said, when features are predictive and combined with past interaction data through our model, they provide significant improvement in accuracy. Online updating of factors is also important because most applications in practice are dynamic. We believe future work in this area should evaluate algorithms using time-based splits to get a realistic estimate of an algorithm's performance. Commonly used evaluation methods that do not use time-based splits at best provide only performance indicators for persistent user-item pairs.

8.4 Large-Scale Recommendation of Time-Sensitive Items

RLFM can be used to solve large-scale time-sensitive recommendation problems. In Section 8.4.1, we begin by discussing the application of online learning to settings where new items (or users) are frequently added or the behavior of items (or users) changes over time. Then, in Section 8.4.2, we provide an algorithm to fit RLFM when the data are too large to fit into the memory of a single computer.

8.4.1 Online Learning

Online learning can be applied in a way similar to the approach introduced in Chapter 7.

Periodic Offline Training. Periodically (e.g., once a day), we retrain the RLFM model using a large number of data (e.g., data collected in the last three months). If the data can be handled by a single computer, we use the fitting algorithm described in Section 8.2. Otherwise, we use the parallel fitting algorithm to be described in Section 8.4.2. The output of this offline training process consists of the following components:

- *Regression functions*: b, g, G, h, H
- *Prior variances*: $\sigma_\alpha^2, \sigma_\beta^2, \sigma_u^2, \sigma_v^2$
- *Posterior means of the factors*: $\hat{\alpha}_i, \hat{\beta}_j, \hat{\boldsymbol{u}}_i, \hat{\boldsymbol{v}}_j$
- *Posterior variances of the factors*: $\tilde{\text{Var}}[\alpha_i]$, $\tilde{\text{Var}}[\boldsymbol{u}_i]$, $\tilde{\text{Cov}}[\alpha_i, \boldsymbol{u}_i]$ if we need online models for users, and $\tilde{\text{Var}}[\beta_j]$, $\tilde{\text{Var}}[\boldsymbol{v}_j]$, $\tilde{\text{Cov}}[\beta_j, \boldsymbol{v}_j]$ if we need online models for items; these variances and covariances can be obtained from the Gibbs samples in the Monte-Carlo E-step in Sections 8.2.1 and 8.2.2

Online Models for Items. It is useful to build an online model for each item j if new items are frequently added into the content pool, or if items have short lifetimes, or if their behavior (e.g., novelty, popularity) changes over time. Let $o_{ijt} = b(\boldsymbol{x}_{ijt}) + \alpha_i$, where we also add a time index t to the feature vector $\boldsymbol{x}_{ijt}$, indicating that it may depend on time. If item j appears in the training data, the prior mean and variance for its online model are its posterior mean and variance from the offline training; that is,

$$\mu_{j0} = (\beta_j, \boldsymbol{v}_j) \text{ (concatenating a scalar and a vector)}$$
$$\Sigma_{j0} = \begin{pmatrix} \tilde{\text{Var}}[\beta_j] & \tilde{\text{Cov}}[\beta_j, \boldsymbol{v}_j] \\ \tilde{\text{Cov}}[\beta_j, \boldsymbol{v}_j] & \tilde{\text{Var}}[\boldsymbol{v}_j] \end{pmatrix}. \tag{8.35}$$

If item j is a new item that does not appear in the training data, the prior mean and variance for its online model are given by feature-based regression; that is,

$$\mu_{j0} = (h(\boldsymbol{x}_j), H(\boldsymbol{x}_j))$$
$$\Sigma_{j0} = \begin{pmatrix} \sigma_\beta^2 & 0 \\ 0 & \sigma_u^2 \boldsymbol{I} \end{pmatrix}. \tag{8.36}$$

The Gaussian online model can be written as

$$\begin{aligned} y_{ijt} &\sim N(o_{ijt} + \boldsymbol{u}_i'\boldsymbol{v}_{jt},\ \sigma^2), \quad \text{for all } i \in \mathcal{I}_{jt} \\ \boldsymbol{v}_{jt} &\sim N(\boldsymbol{\mu}_{j,t-1},\ \rho\boldsymbol{\Sigma}_{j,t-1}), \end{aligned} \tag{8.37}$$

where y_{ijt} is the response that user i gives item j at time t and $\mathcal{I}_{jt}$ denotes the set of users who respond to item j at time t. The logistic online model can be written in a similar way:

$$\begin{aligned} y_{ijt} &\sim \text{Bernoulli}(p_{ijt}), \quad \text{for all } i \in \mathcal{I}_{jt}, \\ \log \frac{p_{ijt}}{1 - p_{ijt}} &= o_{ijt} + \boldsymbol{u}_i'\boldsymbol{v}_{jt}, \\ \boldsymbol{v}_{jt} &\sim N(\boldsymbol{\mu}_{j,t-1},\ \rho\boldsymbol{\Sigma}_{j,t-1}). \end{aligned} \tag{8.38}$$

These two classes of models can be fitted using methods described in Section 7.3

Online Models for Users. If user interests change slowly over time and offline training happens frequently (e.g., daily), then we may not need online models for users because users usually do not respond to many items in a short time span. In this case, the factors for users who appear in the training data are the posterior means (i.e., $\hat{\alpha}_i, \hat{\boldsymbol{u}}_i$) of those factors from offline training; the factors for new users who do not appear in the training data are predicted using feature-based regression (i.e., $g(\boldsymbol{x}_i)$, $G(\boldsymbol{x}_i)$). If online models for users are indeed needed, they can be learned in the same way as the online models for items.

8.4.2 Parallel Fitting Algorithm

For large data sets that reside in distributed clusters and cannot fit into the memory of a single machine, the fitting algorithms described in Section 8.2 do not scale. In this section, we provide a fitting strategy in a the MapReduce framework. We first apply the divide-and-conquer approach to partition the data into small partitions and then run MCEM on each partition to obtain estimates of $\boldsymbol{\Theta}$. The final estimate of $\boldsymbol{\Theta}$ is obtained by averaging over the estimates of $\boldsymbol{\Theta}$ from all the partitions. Finally, given fixed $\boldsymbol{\Theta}$, we do n *ensemble runs* (i.e., repartitioning the data n times using different random seeds), and for each repartitioning, we only run the E-step on the partitions and then average the results to obtain the final estimate of $\boldsymbol{\Delta}$. This is described in Algorithm 8.1.

Algorithm 8.1 Parallel Matrix Factorization

Initialize $\boldsymbol{\Theta}$ and $\boldsymbol{\Delta}$.
Partition data into m partitions using random seed s_0.
for each partition $\ell \in \{1, \ldots, m\}$ running in parallel **do**
  Run MCEM algorithm for K number of iterations using VAR or ARS to obtain $\hat{\boldsymbol{\Theta}}_\ell$, the estimates of $\boldsymbol{\Theta}$ for each partition ℓ.
end for
Let $\hat{\boldsymbol{\Theta}} = \frac{1}{m} \sum_{\ell=1}^{m} \hat{\boldsymbol{\Theta}}_\ell$.
for $k = 1$ to n running in parallel **do**
  Partition data into m partitions using random seed s_k.
  for each partition $\ell \in \{1, \ldots, m\}$ running in parallel **do**
    Run E-Step-Only job given $\hat{\boldsymbol{\Theta}}$ and obtain the posterior sample mean $\hat{\boldsymbol{\Delta}}_{k\ell}$ for all users and items in partition ℓ.
  end for
end for
For each user i, average over all $\hat{\boldsymbol{\Delta}}_{k\ell}$ that contain user i to obtain $\hat{\alpha}_i$ and $\hat{\boldsymbol{u}}_i$.
For each item j, average over all $\hat{\boldsymbol{\Delta}}_{k\ell}$ that contain item j to obtain $\hat{\beta}_i$ and $\hat{\boldsymbol{v}}_i$.

Partitioning the Data. Extensive empirical experiments conducted during our study showed that model performance depends crucially on the data partitioning strategy used in the MapReduce phase, especially when data are sparse. A naive strategy of randomly partitioning observations may not provide good predictive accuracy. On popular websites, the number of users is often much larger than the number of items. Also, the number of observations available per user is small for a large fraction of users; a typical item tends to have a relatively larger sample size than a typical user. In such cases, we recommend partitioning the data by users because it guarantees that all data from a user belong to the same partition and helps in obtaining more reliable user factor estimates. Similarly, when the number of items is larger than the number of users, we recommend partitioning the data by items. An intuitive explanation of this can be obtained by looking at the conditional variance of user factor $\boldsymbol{u}_i$ using variational approximation: $\text{Var}[\boldsymbol{u}_i|\text{Rest}] = (\frac{1}{\sigma_u^2} I + \sum_{j \in \mathcal{J}_i} \frac{\boldsymbol{v}_j \boldsymbol{v}_j'}{\sigma_{ij}^2})^{-1}$. Assuming for the moment that item factors are known (or estimated with high precision), if the user data are split into several partitions, the average information gain (inverse variance) from the partitioned data is the harmonic mean of the information gain from individual partitions. The information gain from the nonpartitioned data can be written as the arithmetic mean of the individual information gains. Because the harmonic mean is less than the arithmetic mean, the information loss in estimating user factor by partitioning is the difference in arithmetic and harmonic means. When the information in partitions becomes weak, this gap increases. Hence, with sparse user(item) data, it is prudent to partition by users (items).

Estimates of $\mathbf{\Theta}$. The $\mathbf{\Theta}$ estimate obtained from each random partition is unbiased. Fitting a model on each partition and then averaging the M-step parameters $\hat{\mathbf{\Theta}}_\ell$ for $\ell = 1, \ldots, m$ provides an estimate that is still unbiased and has low variance due to lack of positive correlations among estimates because of the random partitioning. Before the MCEM algorithm is run, the initial values of $\mathbf{\Theta}$ for all partitions are the same. In particular, we start with zero mean priors; that is, $g(x_i) = h(x_j) = 0$ and $G(x_i) = H(x_j) = \mathbf{0}$. To improve parameter estimation, one may synchronize the parameters among partitions and run another round of MCEM iterations, that is, repartition the data and use the obtained $\hat{\mathbf{\Theta}}$ as the initial values of $\mathbf{\Theta}$ to run another round of MCEM iterations for each partition to obtain a new estimate of $\mathbf{\Theta}$. However, we have observed in practice that iteratively running this process does not give significantly better predictive accuracy but instead adds complexity and training time.

Estimates of $\mathbf{\Delta}$. For each run in the ensemble, it is essential to use a different random seed for partitioning the data, so that the mixes of users and items in partitions across different runs are different. Given $\hat{\mathbf{\Theta}}$, for each run in the ensemble, we only run the E-step once for each partition and obtain the final user and item factors by taking the average. Again, the random partitioning ensures uncorrelated estimates from members of the ensemble and leads to variance reduction through averaging.

Identifiability Issues

After centering, the model is in fact still unidentifiable for two reasons:

1. Because $\boldsymbol{u}_i'\boldsymbol{v}_j = (-\boldsymbol{u}_i)'(-\boldsymbol{v}_j)$, switching the signs of $\boldsymbol{u}$ and $\boldsymbol{v}$ (and the corresponding cold-start parameters) does not change the log-likelihood.
2. For two factors u_{ik}, v_{jk} and u_{il}, v_{jl}, switching u_{ik} with u_{il} and v_{jk} with v_{jl} simultaneously also would not change the log-likelihood, given that the corresponding cold-start parameters are also switched.

We have found empirically that these identifiability issues do not matter for small data sets, especially single-machine runs. However, for large data sets, such as the Yahoo! front page data, with G and H defined as linear regression functions, we observe that for each partition after the MCEM step, we obtain significantly different fitted values of G and H, so that after averaging over all the partitions, the resulting coefficient matrices for G and H become almost zero. Hence the identifiability issue can become severe while fitting parallelized matrix factorization for large data sets.

Solution. For issue 1, we put constraints on the item factor $\boldsymbol{v}$ so that it is always positive. This can be done through simply putting a sampling lower bound (i.e., always sample positive numbers) in the adaptive rejection sampling. After using this approach, we no longer need to do centering on $\boldsymbol{v}$. For issue 2, we first let $\sigma_v^2 = 1$ and change the prior of $\boldsymbol{u}_i$ from $N(G(x_i), \sigma_u^2 I)$ to $N(G(x_i), \Sigma_u)$, where Σ_u is a diagonal variance matrix with diagonal values $\sigma_{u1} \geq \sigma_{u2} \geq \cdots \geq \sigma_{ur}$. The model fitting is very similar; but after each M-step, we re-sort all the factors by the fitted σ_{uk}s for $k = 1, \ldots, r$ to satisfy the constraint.

8.5 Illustration of Large-Scale Problems

We evaluate the proposed methods to address two main questions: (1) How do different techniques for handling binary response compare? (2) How do different methods perform in a real, large-scale web recommender system? For the first question, we compare variational approximation, adaptive rejection sampling, and stochastic gradient descent on balanced and imbalanced binary data sets created from the public MovieLens-1M data set. For the second question, we first evaluate the predictive performance using a small sample of heavy users of the Today module on the Yahoo! front page to allow comparison in the single-machine fitting scenario and then provide complete end-to-end evaluation on massive imbalanced binary response data collected from the Today module through a recently proposed unbiased offline evaluation method (Li et al., 2011), which has been shown to be able to approximate the online click-lift performance. See Section 4.4 for details.

Methods. We consider the following different models and fitting methods, all used with ten factors per user or item throughout the experiments:

- *FEAT-ONLY*: The feature-only factorization model serves as our baseline. Specifically, the model is

$$s_{ij} = b(x_{ij}) + g(x_i) + h(x_j) + G(x_i)' H(x_j),$$

  where g, h, G, and H are unknown regression functions, fitted by the standard conjugate gradient descent method on each partition and averaging over estimates from all partitions to obtain estimates of g, h, G, and H; no ensemble run is needed.

- *MCEM-VAR*: Our matrix factorization model fitted by variational approximation in the MCEM algorithm.
- *MCEM-ARS*: Our matrix factorization model fitted by centered adaptive rejection sampling algorithm in each E-step of the MCEM algorithm.
- *MCEM-ARSID*: Our matrix factorization model fitted by centered adaptive rejection sampling algorithm in each E-step of the MCEM algorithm, incorporating positive constraints on the item factor $\boldsymbol{v}$ and ordered diagonal prior covariance matrix of $\boldsymbol{u}$ (see Section 8.4.2 for more details).
- *SGD*: A popular method that fits a similar factorization model using stochastic gradient descent. We obtained the code for SGD from Charkrabarty et al. (n.d.). The model is

$$s_{ij} = (\alpha_i + \boldsymbol{u}_i + \boldsymbol{U}\boldsymbol{x}_i)'(\beta_j + \boldsymbol{v}_j + \boldsymbol{V}\boldsymbol{x}_j),$$

where $\boldsymbol{U}$ and $\boldsymbol{V}$ are unknown coefficient matrices for cold start to map the feature vectors $\boldsymbol{x}_i$ and $\boldsymbol{x}_j$ into the r-dimensional latent space. For binary response with a logistic link function, it minimizes the following loss function:

$$\sum_{ij} y_{ij} \log(1 + \exp(-s_{ij})) + \sum_{ij}(1 - y_{ij}) \log(1 + \exp(s_{ij}))$$

$$+ \lambda_u \sum_i \|\boldsymbol{u}_i\|^2 + \lambda_v \sum_j \|\boldsymbol{v}_j\|^2 + \lambda_U \|\boldsymbol{U}\|^2 + \lambda_V \|\boldsymbol{V}\|^2,$$

where λ_u, λ_v, λ_U, and λ_V are tuning parameters and $\|\boldsymbol{U}\|$ and $\|\boldsymbol{V}\|$ are Frobenius norms. Because this code has not been parallelized, we only use it in experiments on small data sets. In the experiments, we set $\lambda_u = \lambda_v = \lambda_U = \lambda_V = \lambda$ with λ varying from 0, 10^{-6}, 10^{-5}, 10^{-4}, and 10^{-3}. We also tuned the learning rate by trying 10^{-5}, 10^{-4}, 10^{-3}, 10^{-2}, and 10^{-1}.

In FEAT-ONLY, MCEM-VAR, MCEM-ARS, and MCEM-ARSID, we use linear regression functions for g, h, G, and H.

8.5.1 MovieLens-1M Data

We first compare three techniques for fitting binary response (MCEM-VAR, MCEM-ARS, and SGD) on the benchmark MovieLens-1M data set.

Data. We create training-test splits based on the time stamps of the ratings; the first 75 percent of ratings serve as training data and the remaining 25 percent as

Table 8.2. *AUC of different methods on the imbalanced and balanced MovieLens data sets*

Method	# Partitions[a]	AUC Imbalanced	AUC Balanced
SGD	1	0.8090	0.7413
MCEM-VAR	1	0.8138	0.7576
MCEM-ARS	1	0.8195	0.7563
MCEM-VAR	2	0.7614	0.7599
	5	0.7191	0.7538
	15	0.6584	0.7421
MCEM-ARS	2	0.8194	0.7622
	5	0.7971	0.7597
	15	0.7775	0.7493

[a] Value of 1 indicates a single-machine run.

test data. This split introduces many new users (i.e., cold start) into the test data. To study how different techniques handle binary response with different degree of sparsity of the positive response, we consider two different ways of creating binary response: (1) an imbalanced data set is created by setting the response value to 1 if and only if the original 5-point rating value is 1; otherwise, it is set to 0. The percentage of positive response in this data set is around 5 percent. (2) A balanced data set is created by setting the response to 1 if the original rating is 1, 2, or 3; otherwise, it is set to 0. The percentage of positive response in this data set is approximately 44 percent. We report the predictive performance of SGD, MCEM-VAR, and MCEM-ARS in terms of the area under the ROC curve (AUC) for both data sets in Table 8.2.

Comparison between MCEM-ARS and MCEM-VAR. As can be seen from the Table 8.2, MCEM-ARS and MCEM-VAR have similar performance, and both slightly outperform SGD when running on a single machine (i.e., # partitions = 1). When running on multiple machines with two to fifteen partitions, MCEM-ARS and MCEM-VAR have similar performance on the balanced data set, but on the imbalanced data set, MCEM-VAR becomes much worse when the number of partitions increases (causing more severe data sparsity). The degradation of performance when the number of partitions increases is expected because, with more partitions, each partition has fewer data, which leads to a less accurate model for the partition.

Comparison with SGD. To obtain good performance for SGD, one has to try a large number of different values of the tuning parameters and learning rates, while our method does not need such tuning because all the hyperparameters are obtained through the EM algorithm. Trying different tuning parameter values can be computationally expensive, and it is less efficient in exploring the parameter space than an EM algorithm. After our best-effort tuning using the test data, for imbalanced data, SGD achieves best performance 0.8090 with $\lambda = 10^{-3}$ and learning rate $= 10^{-2}$. For balanced data, SGD achieves best performance 0.7413 with $\lambda = 10^{-6}$ and learning rate $= 10^{-3}$. Even tuning SGD on test data, the best AUC numbers of SGD on both balanced and imbalanced data sets are still slightly worse than the those of MCEM-VAR and MCEM-ARS (which did not use the test data for tuning any parameters in the training phase).

8.5.2 Small Yahoo! Front Page Data

We now evaluate different methods on the Yahoo! front page data set (Y!FP) discussed in Section 8.3. The observations were sorted by their time stamps, and the first 75 percent of them were used as training data and the remaining 25 percent as test data. Because the original set of user features was large, dimension reduction was done through principal component analysis, and finally, we obtained approximately one hundred numerical user features. In this data set, the percentage of positive response is close to 50 percent – it is a balanced data set.

Single-Machine Results. The AUC performance for FEAT-ONLY, MCEM-VAR, MCEM-ARS, and MCEM-ARSID running on a single machine (i.e., one partition) is shown in Table 8.3. MCEM-VAR, MCEM-ARS, MCEM-ARSID, and SGD all outperform FEAT-ONLY significantly because these models allow warm-start user factors (those users having data in the training period) to deviate from purely feature-based predictions, to better fit the data. Conversely, because the test data consist of many new users and new items, handling cold-start scenarios is still important. For this data set, MCEM-VAR significantly improves on matrix factorization models that use zero mean priors for factors, which are commonly applied in many recommender system problems, for example, Netflix. The performances of MCEM-VAR, MCEM-ARS, and MCEM-ARSID are all close. This suggests that for balanced data sets, different fitting methods for logistic models are similar. MCEM-ARSID performs slightly worse than MCEM-ARS, because adding constraints on the item factors $\boldsymbol{v}$ reduces the flexibility of MCEM-ARSID. We defer the discussion on when MCEM-ARSID can provide significant benefit to Section 8.5.3.

Table 8.3. *AUC of different methods on the small Yahoo! front page data set*

Method	# Partitions[a]	Partition method	AUC
FEAT-ONLY	1	–	0.6781
SGD	1	–	0.7252
MCEM-VAR	1	–	0.7374
MCEM-ARS	1	–	0.7364
MCEM-ARSID	1	–	0.7283
MCEM-ARS	2	User	0.7280
	5	User	0.7227
	15	User	0.7178
MCEM-ARSID	2	User	0.7294
	5	User	0.7172
	15	User	0.7133
	15	Event	0.6924
	15	Item	0.6917

[a] Value of 1 indicates a single-machine run.

Comparison with SGD. Similar to what we see in Section 8.5.1, even with SGD tuned on test data, the best AUC is 0.7252 (achieved by using $\lambda = 10^{-6}$ and learning rate $= 10^{-3}$), still slightly worse than the AUC of MCEM-VAR, MCEM-ARS, and MCEM-ARSID for single-machine runs.

Number of Partitions. As the number of partitions grows for MCEM-ARS and MCEM-ARSID (ten ensemble runs for both), we observe the expected degradation of performance because, with more partitions, each partition would have fewer data, which usually leads to a less accurate model for the partition. However, even with fifteen partitions on such a small data set, MCEM-ARS and MCEM-ARSID (user-based partitioning) still significantly outperform FEAT-ONLY. In general, increasing the number of partitions would increase computational efficiency but usually leads to worse performance. We have observed in our experiments that for large data sets, the computation time of $2N$ partitions is roughly half of using N partitions. Therefore we use as few partitions as possible given our computational budget.

Different Partition Methods. In Table 8.3, we also show the performance of our parallel algorithm MCEM-ARSID (ten ensemble runs) with different numbers of partitions and various partition methods. As mentioned in Section 8.4.2, partitioning the data by users is better than event-based or item-based partitioning in our application because, in our application, there are generally more users than items in the data; hence user partitions are less sparse.

8.5.3 Large Yahoo! Front Page Data

We show the performance of our parallel algorithms on a large Yahoo! front page data set using an unbiased evaluation method to estimate the expected click-lifts.

Data. The training data were collected from the Today module on Yahoo! front page during June 2011, whereas the test events were collected during July 2011. The training data include all pageviews by users with at least ten clicks in the Today module and consist of 8 million users, approximately 4,300 items, and 1 billion binary observations. To remove selection bias in evaluating our algorithms, the test data are collected from a randomly chosen user population where, for each user visit, an article is selected at random from the content pool and displayed at the F1 position. This *random bucket* of old users who were seen in the training period as well as new ones consists of around 2.4 million clicks.

Each user is associated with 124 behavior features that reflect various kinds of user activities on the entire Yahoo! network. Each item is associated with forty-three editorial hand-labeled categories. A click on an F1 article link is a positive observation, while a view of an F1 article link without a subsequent click is a negative observation. The percentage of positive response here is much lower than that of the small data set – the increased sparsity and imbalance introduce additional challenges.

Experimental Setup. Because article lifetimes in the Today module are short (six to twenty-four hours), almost all items in the test period are new. Thus, we apply online models for items.

Unbiased Evaluation. The goal of this set of experiments is to maximize total clicks. We provide a brief description of the evaluation metric in what follows.

For each five-minute interval t, we do the following:

1. Compute the predicted CTR of all articles in the pool for each event in t under the model. The estimates can use all data before t.
2. For each event in t, we select the an article j^* from the current pool with the highest predicted probability. If the article that was actually served in the logged data matches j^*, we record this matched event; otherwise, we ignore it.

At the end, we compute CTR metrics based on the recorded events, and these estimates are unbiased (Li et al., 2011). Because each article in the random bucket has an equal probability of being displayed to users, the number of matched view events for any model is expected to be the same. A better model to optimize CTR can match more click events. We can compute the overall CTR from these matched events and use these metrics to compare different models. For large numbers of data, as in our case, the overall CTR metrics for matched events have little variance; all differences reported in our experiments have small p-values and are statistically significant.

Two Baseline Methods. To show that factor-based user features provide state-of-the-art performance to personalize content on Yahoo! front page, we implement two baseline methods for generating user features based on users' past interaction on the front page:

- *ITEM-PROFILE*: Using training data, we pick the one thousand items that have highest number of views. We construct 1,000-dimensional binary user profiles to indicate whether, in the training period, a user has clicked on these item (1 is clicked and 0 is nonclicked). For cold-start users who did not show up in the training data, the binary profile vectors are all 0s.
- *CATEGORY-PROFILE*: Because in this data set each item has forty-three binary features indicating content categories to which the item belongs, we build user-category preference profiles through the following approach: for each user i and category k, denote the number of observed views as v_{ik} and number of clicks as c_{ik}. From the training data, we can obtain the global per-category CTR, denoted γ_k. We then model c_{ik} as $c_{ik} \sim Poisson(v_{ik}\gamma_k\lambda_{ik})$, where λ_{ik} is the unknown user-category preference parameter. We assume λ_{ik} has a Gamma prior $Gamma(a, a)$, hence the posterior of λ_{ik} becomes $(\lambda_{ik}|v_{ik}, c_{ik}) \sim Gamma(c_{ik} + a, v_{ik}\gamma_k + a)$. We use the log of the posterior mean, that is, $\log(\frac{c_{ik}+a}{v_{ik}\gamma_k+a})$, as the profile feature value for user i on category k. Note that if we do not observe any data for user i and category k, the feature value becomes 0. Variable a is a tuning prior sample size parameter and can be obtained through cross-validation. By trying a =1, 5, 10, 15, and 20, we have found that for this data set, $a = 10$ is the optimal value.

Experimental Results. We evaluate all methods by reporting the click-lift obtained through unbiased evaluation relative to an online logistic model that only uses behavioral (BT) features $\boldsymbol{x}_{it}$. Such a model does not incorporate users' past interaction with items – its performance on heavy users has large room for improvement. In Table 8.4, we summarize the overall lift, warm start

Table 8.4. *The overall click-lift over the user behavior feature (BT) – only model*

Method	# Ensembled runs	Overall(%)	Warm start(%)	Cold start(%)
ITEM-PROFILE	–	3.0	14.1	−1.6
CATEGORY-PROFILE	–	6.0	20.0	0.3
MCEM-VAR	10	5.6	18.7	0.2
MCEM-ARS	10	7.4	26.8	−0.5
MCEM-ARSID	1	9.1	24.6	2.8
MCEM-ARSID	10	9.7	26.3	2.9

lifts (users seen in the training set), and cold start lifts (new users). All models produce lifts, but the performance of MCEM-ARSID is the best overall and for cold starts, and MCEM-ARS is the best for warm starts. The reason that we see no lift for cold-start users on MCEM-ARS is the identifiability issues addressed in Section 8.4.2. Although imposing positive constraints on the item factors causes MCEM-ARSID to have slightly inferior performance than MCEM-ARS, it solves the identifiability issues quite well and hence gives the best performance for the cold-start users. MCEM-VAR is worse than CATEGORY-PROFILE, especially for warm starts. We also observe that using the ensemble trick improves results, as is evident from comparing MCEM-ARSID with one- and ten-ensemble runs.

To further investigate the performance of algorithms in different kinds of warm starts based on user activity on the Today module in the training period, we look at click-lifts by Today module activity levels in Figure 8.4. We split the users in the test data into several segments by their number of clicks in the training data. As expected, we see a monotone trend: users with more activity are personalized better by using their prior Today module activity data. From Figure 8.4, we observe that MCEM-ARSID is uniformly better than CATEGORY-PROFILE and ITEM-PROFILE over all the user segments. Comparing the performance of MCEM-ARSID, MCEM-ARS, and MCEM-VAR, we find the MCEM-VAR to be quite inferior to MCEM-ARS and MCEM-ARSID.

Potential Issue with Variational Approximation. To investigate issues with MCEM-VAR with data sparsity, we examine the factor estimates in Figure 8.5, which shows the histograms of the fitted $\boldsymbol{u}_i$ and $\boldsymbol{v}_j$ after thirty EM iterations for MCEM-VAR and MCEM-ARS, both with ten factors and one hundred partitions. While the fitted user factors for both MCEM-VAR and MCEM-ARS are

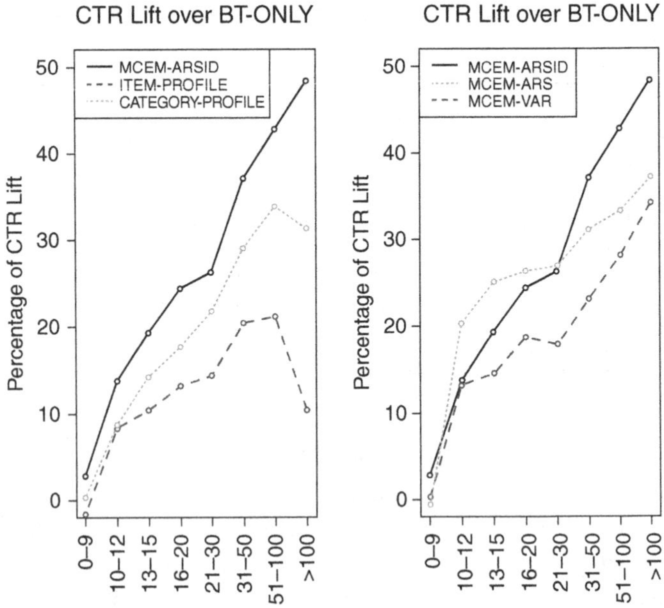

Figure 8.4. The click-lift over the user behavior feature (BT)-only model for different user segments. The segments are created from the number of clicks in the training data.

on a similar scale, the item factors produced by variational approximation are approximately one order of magnitude smaller than those produced by MCEM-ARS. This phenomenon is in fact surprising and shows that MCEM-VAR tends to overshrink the factor estimates when fitting rare response. This explains why the performance of MCEM-VAR deteriorates as the binary response gets rare. It seems that variational approximation leads to too much shrinkage when working with rare response.

8.5.4 Discussion of Results

The experiments clearly show that factorization for binary response and using a divide-and-conquer strategy to scale the method in a Hadoop framework involve several subtle issues. For scenarios where we can fit the model using a single machine, all methods work equally well on balanced binary response, the case widely studied in prior work.

For highly imbalanced data, MCEM-VAR tends to deteriorate; we do not recommend its use in such scenarios. SGD works well provided learning rates and regularization parameters are tuned carefully, but we do not recommend

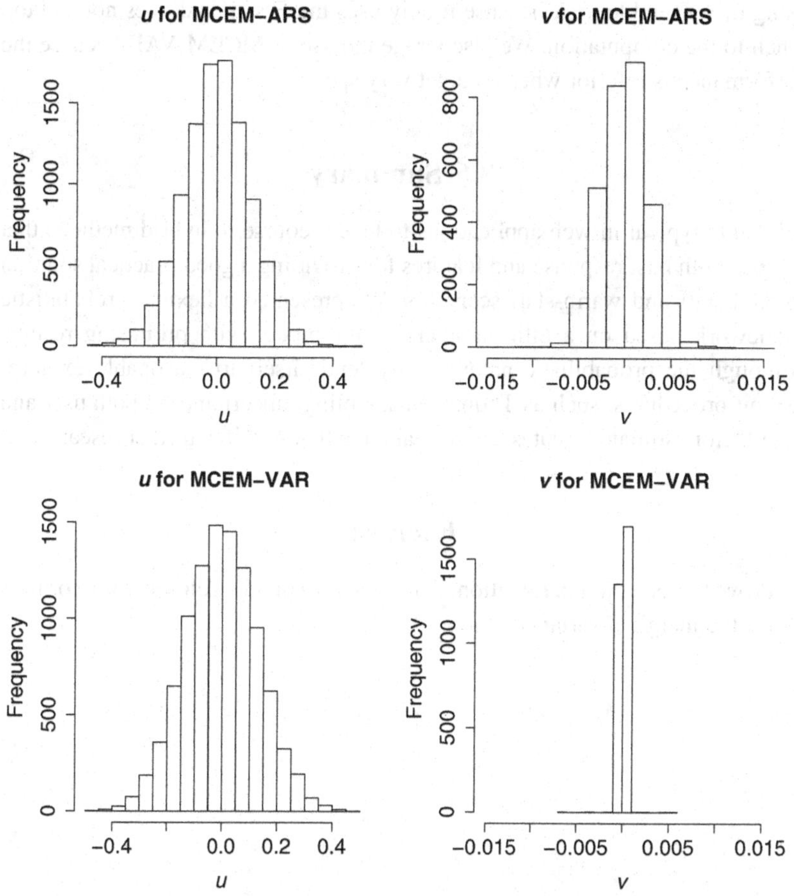

Figure 8.5. The histogram of the fitted $\boldsymbol{u}_i$ and $\boldsymbol{v}_j$ after thirty iterations of the MCEM step for MCEM-VAR and MCEM-ARS, both with ten factors and four hundred partitions.

its use unless such tuning is undertaken seriously. Even after tuning, it is inferior to MCEM methods, and hence we recommend using MCEM if possible. For single-machine MCEM, imposing positivity constraints in MCEM-ARSID hurts performance because it adds additional constraints. We do not recommend it; instead, we recommend fitting MCEM-ARS.

The story is different when fitting MapReduce with divide and conquer. Because the factor models are multimodal, each partition may converge to a very different regression estimate and may lead to poor performance. Here we highly recommend making all possible efforts to impose identifiability through MCEM-ARSID and synchronizing the initializations. We also recommend using the ensemble trick because it only uses the E-step and does not add too much to the computation. We discourage the use of MCEM-VAR because the performance is inferior when data get very sparse.

8.6 Summary

It is quite typical in web applications to take recourse to hybrid methods that can use both past response and features for providing a good practical solution to cold-start and warm-start scenarios. We presented a flexible probabilistic framework based on a bilinear latent factor model with promising results. Although the probabilistic nature easily lends itself to reasonable explore-exploit procedures, such as Thompson sampling, uncertainty in both user and item factor estimates creates a new challenge that requires further research.

Exercise

1. Prove the assertion in Equation (8.18). Can we obtain a closed-form formula for the marginal variance of u_i?

PART III

Advanced Topics

9
Factorization through Latent Dirichlet Allocation

9.1 Introduction

In Chapter 8, we described a bilinear latent factor model RLFM that captured user-item interactions through a multiplicative function $u_i'v_j$; u_i and v_j are unknown vectors associated with user i and item j, respectively (often referred to as latent factors). The latent factors live in a Euclidean space and are regularized with a Gaussian prior with mean determined by a regression function that is based on user and item features. This incorporates both cold-start and warm-start aspects into a single modeling framework. In this chapter, we describe a new factor model called factorized latent Dirichlet allocation (fLDA), which is suited to the task of incorporating both rich bag-of-words-type features on items and user response simultaneously to enhance predictions. Such scenarios are commonplace in web applications like content recommendation, advertising, and web search. We note that "word" in our context is a general term used to denote elements like *phrases*, *entities*, and others. We empirically show that this model provides better accuracy compared to state-of-the-art factor models for items with textual metadata that is amenable to topic modeling. As a by-product, interpretable item topics help in explaining recommendations. We also show that when rich item metadata is not available or noisy, this method is still comparable in accuracy to state-of-the-art factorization models. However, the model fitting is computationally more intensive than in RLFM.

The key idea in fLDA is to let the user factors (or profiles) take values in a Euclidean space, as in RLFM, but to assign item factors through a richer prior based on LDA (Blei et al., 2003). Specifically, we model the affinity between user i and item j as $u_i'\bar{z}_j$, where $\bar{z}_j$ is a multinomial probability vector representing the soft cluster membership score of item j for K different latent topics; u_i represents user i's affinity to those topics. The main idea in LDA is to attach a *discrete* latent factor to each word of an item that can take K different values (K topics) and produce item topics by averaging the per-word topics in the item. Thus, a news article where 80 percent of the words are assigned to politics and the rest to education can be thought of as being an article about politics but perhaps related to an issue in education. Because the number of latent factors in fLDA is large, regularization is key. In LDA, this is done by modeling the word-topic association and the item-topic association, and finally averaging the word topics for each item. In fLDA, we also include user responses on items as an additional source of information when determining the item topics. In fact, responses on items influence the estimation of the *global* word-topic association matrix, which in turn influences the *local* assignment of topics to words in each item. For instance, if many users respond positively to political articles with mention of the word "Obama," they may form a separate topic in fLDA; this may not happen with unsupervised LDA, because it is only influenced by word occurrences. The overwhelming number of positive responses for articles with mention of "Obama" forces them to cluster together to increase the likelihood of observing the response. In fact, one can think of response as providing additional information to attach importance scores to different words in an item. The key is the ability of fLDA to learn these scores automatically from the data. We also note that the latent profiles of users who respond to items play a crucial role in determining item topics, and vice versa. This simultaneous estimation of both user profiles and topic attribution distinguishes fLDA from other supervised LDA, such as sLDA (Blei and McAuliffe, 2008), which also incorporates a response variable in deciding LDA topics, but through a *global* regression. fLDA, conversely, performs per-user local regression.

The topical representation of items in fLDA provides interpretability and may help to explain recommendations for users. For well-understood topics, user factors can be thought of as providing an interest profile for the LDA topics. In Section 9.2, we define the fLDA model. Then, we describe the model training algorithm in Section 9.3 and present experimental results in Section 9.4. Finally, we provide a brief literature review in Section 9.5 and conclude the chapter in Section 9.6.

9.2 Model

In this section, we define the fLDA model. We begin with a high level overview and draw distinction from other existing work in this area. This is followed by a detailed mathematical specification. We then describe the fitting procedure based on a Monte-Carlo EM (MCEM) algorithm.

9.2.1 Overview

As in previous chapters, we use (i, j) to denote a user-item pair and y_{ij} to denote the response. We are interested in scenarios where each item has a natural bag-of-words representation that is amenable to unsupervised topic modeling. Needless to say, this is pervasive in recommender problems for web applications.

Our prediction method is based on fitting a two-stage hierarchical mixed-effects model to training data. In particular, we attach latent factors $(\alpha_i, \boldsymbol{u}_i^{r\times 1})$ to user i and $(\beta_j, \bar{z}_j^{r\times 1})$ to item j. Item factors $\bar{z}_j$ are obtained by averaging $\{z_{jn}\}$,

$$\bar{z}_j = \sum_{n=1}^{W_j} \frac{z_{jn}}{W_j},$$

where z_{jn} is a discrete latent factor (with r possible topics) that is attached to the nth word in item j and W_j denotes the number of words in item j. This is one of the key differences between fLDA and factor models, like RLFM, that attach r continuous latent factors $\boldsymbol{v}_j^{r\times 1}$ to each item. Note that we abuse the notation a bit by using z_{jn} to denote both a discrete variable with r possible values and a vector of length r, where there is exactly one element equal to 1 and all the others are 0.

The fLDA model specifies a generative process for responses and words in two stages. The first stage specifies the relationship between response y_{ij} conditional on the latent factors. In fact, the mean of y_{ij} (or some monotone function of the mean) and the latent factors are connected through an easily interpretable bilinear function of factors

$$\alpha_i + \beta_j + \boldsymbol{u}_i'\bar{z}_j,$$

where α_i is the bias for user i, β_j is the item bias representing the global popularity of item j, vector $\bar{z}_j$ is the (empirical) probability distribution for item j over the r topics, and vector $\boldsymbol{u}_i$ quantifies user i's affinity to each of the r topics.

The estimation of the multiplicative term $\boldsymbol{u}_i'\bar{z}_j$ that captures user interaction with items is the main modeling challenge. In fact, given the data incompleteness in applications (typically, we have response available for 1 percent to 5 percent of all possible pairs), it is clear that latent factors cannot be estimated reliably even for small number of topics r. A second stage that constrains the factors through priors reduces the effective degrees of freedom and results in good performance.

The crux of the problem is in specifying such a prior; the first-stage model alone is too flexible and overfits the data. Factor models that assume both user and item factors take values in an r-dimensional Euclidean space moderate the factor values through an L_2 norm constraint or equivalently a zero-mean Gaussian prior. The regression-based latent factor model (RLFM) in Chapter 8 relaxes the prior to have a flexible mean that is obtained by regressing factor values on user(item) features. Yu et al. (2009) go further and regularize the factors through a nonlinear kernel function of features. Other than providing better regularization, such strategies help in providing better prediction in cold-start scenarios.

The fLDA model is similar in spirit, but although it assumes the user factors still take values in a Euclidean space, item factors are discrete with r possible values (topics). Moreover, we attach a latent topic to each word in an item and assume the average of per-word topics to provide the item topics that capture user-item interactions. The granular topics at the word level are regularized through user response and the LDA prior on items.

9.2.2 Model Specification

We provide a detailed description of fLDA in this section. We begin by setting up notations.

Notation. As before, i indexes a user and j indexes an item. We use index k to denote item topics and index n to denote a word in an item. Let M, N, r, and W denote the numbers of users, items, topics, and distinct words in the item corpus, respectively. We use W_j to denote item length, that is, the number of words in item j. As in earlier chapters, $\boldsymbol{x}_i$, $\boldsymbol{x}_j$, and $\boldsymbol{x}_{ij}$ denote the feature vectors for user i, item j, and the user-item pair (i, j), respectively. In addition to $\boldsymbol{x}_j$, items have a bag-of-words vector $\boldsymbol{w}_j$, where w_{jn} denotes the nth word in item j $(n = 1, \ldots, W_j)$.

First-Stage Observation Model. Our first-stage observation model specifies the distribution of response conditional on the latent factors and topics, as follows:

- for the Gaussian model, the continuous response $y_{ij} \sim \mathcal{N}(\mu_{ij}, \sigma^2)$, where

$$\mu_{ij} = \boldsymbol{x}'_{ij}\boldsymbol{b} + \alpha_i + \beta_j + \boldsymbol{u}'_i \bar{\boldsymbol{z}}_j$$

- for the logistic model, the binary response $y_{ij} \sim \text{Bernoulli}(\mu_{ij})$, where

$$\log\left(\frac{\mu_{ij}}{1 - \mu_{ij}}\right) = \boldsymbol{x}'_{ij}\boldsymbol{b} + \alpha_i + \beta_j + \boldsymbol{u}'_i \bar{\boldsymbol{z}}_j$$

Note that b is the regression weight vector for features $\boldsymbol{x}_{ij}$ and α_i, β_j, $\boldsymbol{u}_i$, and z_{jn} are unknown latent factors. Each word w_{jn} in item j has an underlying latent topic z_{jn}, and $\bar{z}_j = \sum_{n=1}^{W_j} \frac{z_{jn}}{W_j}$ denotes the empirical distribution of topics for item j averaged over the topic distribution of words in item j (z_{jn} is a vector of zeros with length K, except the kth position equals 1 if z_{jn} represents topic k). In typical applications, $\boldsymbol{b}$ is a global parameter whose dimension is small and hence does not require further regularization.

Second-Stage State Model. We specify the prior distribution on latent factors $[\{\alpha_i\}, \{\beta_j\}, \{\boldsymbol{u}_i\}, \{z_{jn}\}]$ conditional on the features $[\{\boldsymbol{x}_i\}, \{\boldsymbol{x}_j\}, \{w_{jn}\}]$. We assume that the factor distributions are statistically independent, that is,

$$[\{\alpha_i\}, \{\beta_j\}, \boldsymbol{u}_i\}, \{z_{jn}\}] = \left(\prod_i [\alpha_i] \prod_j [\beta_j] \prod_i [\boldsymbol{u}_i] \right) \cdot [\{z_{jn}\}],$$

with priors given as follows:

1. User bias $\alpha_i = \boldsymbol{g}_0' \boldsymbol{x}_i + \epsilon_i^\alpha$, where $\epsilon_i^\alpha \sim \mathcal{N}(0, a_\alpha)$, and $\boldsymbol{g}_0$ is the regression weight vector on user features $\boldsymbol{x}_i$.
2. User factor $\boldsymbol{u}_i = \boldsymbol{H}\boldsymbol{x}_i + \epsilon_i^u$ is a $r \times 1$ vector of topic affinity scores, where $\epsilon_i^u \sim \mathcal{N}(\boldsymbol{0}, \boldsymbol{A}_u)$, and $\boldsymbol{H}$ is the regression weight matrix on user features $\boldsymbol{x}_i$.
3. Item popularity $\beta_j = \boldsymbol{d}_0' \boldsymbol{x}_j + \epsilon_j^\beta$, where $\epsilon_j^\beta \sim \mathcal{N}(0, a_\beta)$ and $\boldsymbol{d}_0$ is the regression weight vector on item features $\boldsymbol{x}_j$.

The prior for $\{z_{jn}\}$ is given by the LDA model (Griffiths and Steyvers, 2004; Blei et al., 2003).

LDA Prior. The LDA model is an unsupervised clustering method that works well when each element to be clustered has a bag-of-words representation. Thus, it clusters data that are categorical and high-dimensional, but sparse. It has found widespread use in text mining applications, where it provides a soft clustering of each document into topics that are typically easy to interpret.

The LDA model works by assuming that the occurrence probabilities in the three-way (word, item, topic) contingency table can be modeled in terms of (word, topic) and (item, topic) interactions. It assumes that word vectors for items are generated in the following way. Associate with each topic k a multinomial distribution $\boldsymbol{\Phi}_k^{1\times W}$ over the words in the entire corpus; that is, $\Phi_{k\ell}$ = Pr[observe word ℓ | topic k]. Also assume a multinomial distribution $\boldsymbol{\theta}_j^{r\times 1}$ for item j over the r topics; that is, θ_{jk} = Pr[the latent topic of a

Table 9.1. *LDA-based factorization model*

Rating	$y_{ij} \sim \mathcal{N}(\mu_{ij}, \sigma^2)$, or (Gaussian) $y_{ij} \sim \text{Bernoulli}(\mu_{ij})$ (Logistic) $l(\mu_{ij}) = \boldsymbol{x}'_{ij}\boldsymbol{b} + \alpha_i + \beta_j + \boldsymbol{u}'_i\bar{\boldsymbol{z}}_j$	
User factors	$\alpha_i = \boldsymbol{g}'_0\boldsymbol{x}_i + \epsilon^\alpha_i$, $\boldsymbol{u}_i = \boldsymbol{H}\boldsymbol{x}_i + \epsilon^u_i$,	$\epsilon^\alpha_i \sim \mathcal{N}(0, a_\alpha)$ $\epsilon^u_i \sim \mathcal{N}(\boldsymbol{0}, \boldsymbol{A}_u)$
Item factors	$\beta_j = \boldsymbol{d}'_0\boldsymbol{x}_j + \epsilon^\beta_j$, $\bar{\boldsymbol{z}}_j = \sum_n \boldsymbol{z}_{jn} / W_j$	$\epsilon^\beta_j \sim \mathcal{N}(0, a_\beta)$
Topic model	$\boldsymbol{\theta}_j \sim \text{Dirichlet}(\lambda)$ $\boldsymbol{\Phi}_k \sim \text{Dirichlet}(\eta)$ $z_{jn} \sim \text{Multinom}(\boldsymbol{\theta}_j)$ $w_{jn} \sim \text{Multinom}(\boldsymbol{\Phi}_{z_{jn}})$	

Note: $l(\mu_{ij}) = \mu_{ij}$ for Gaussian; $l(\mu_{ij}) = \log \frac{\mu_{ij}}{1-\mu_{ij}}$ for logistic.

word is k | item j]. Now, the generative model for the corpus is modeled as $[\{w_{jn}\}, \{z_{jn}\}|\{\boldsymbol{\Phi}_k\}, \{\boldsymbol{\theta}_j\}] \propto [\{w_{jn}\}|\{z_{jn}\}, \{\boldsymbol{\Phi}_k\}] \cdot [\{z_{jn}\}|\{\boldsymbol{\theta}_j\}]$, where

1. $z_{jn} \mid \boldsymbol{\theta}_j \sim \text{Multinom}(\boldsymbol{\theta}_j)$, that is, we draw a latent topic for each word in item j from the document specific multinomial
2. $w_{jn} \mid z_{jn} \sim \text{Multinom}(\boldsymbol{\Phi}_{z_{jn}})$, that is, after drawing the latent topics for each word in the item, the words are drawn from the topic-specific (document-independent) multinomial distributions with topic = z_{jn}

To regularize the multinomial probabilities associated with high-dimensional simplex, we assume $\theta_j \sim \text{Dirichlet}(\lambda)$ and $\boldsymbol{\Phi}_k \sim \text{Dirichlet}(\eta)$. Here λ and η are hyperparameters of symmetric Dirichlet priors that indirectly control the entropy induced in the posterior distribution $[\bar{z}_j|\{w_{jn}\}]$. Large values of hyperparameters would lead to less concentration and higher entropy. The Dirichlet-multinomial conjugacy enables us to marginalize over $\{\boldsymbol{\Phi}_k\}$ and $\{\boldsymbol{\theta}_j\}$ and work directly with $[\{w_{jn}\}, \{z_{jn}\}|\eta, \lambda]$ to draw samples from the posterior of latent topics efficiently through a collapsed Gibbs sampler, as proposed in Griffiths and Steyvers (2004). In fLDA, we shall also work with the marginalized prior because the item factors are functions of latent topic variables $\{z_{jn}\}$ that do not depend on the multinomial probabilities $\{\boldsymbol{\Phi}_k\}$ or $\{\boldsymbol{\theta}_j\}$. However, the functional form of the collapsed Gibbs sampler for fLDA gets modified multiplicatively through the contribution from the log-likelihood part of the first-stage model that depends on the response (see Section 9.3). For easy reference, we summarize our two-stage model succinctly in Table 9.1 and show the graphical representation in Figure 9.1.

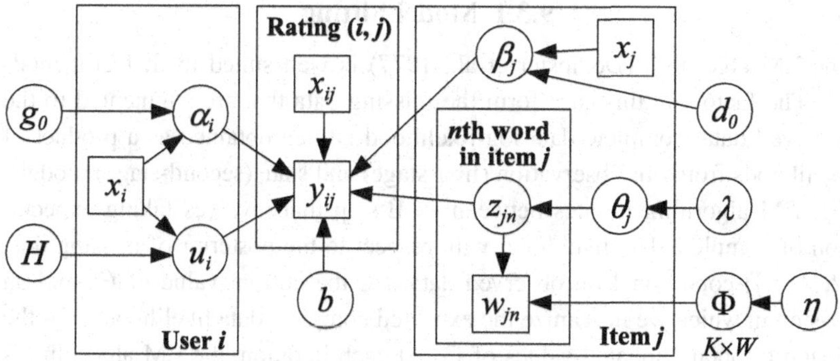

Figure 9.1. Graphical representation of fLDA. Variance components (σ^2, a_α, a_β, A_s) are omitted for succinctness.

We end this section with a brief discussion of why we chose $\bar{z}_j$ to capture interactions in the first-stage model, instead of $\boldsymbol{\theta}_j$, the item multinomial topic probability vector. The main intuition is that $\bar{z}_j$, the empirical distribution of word latent factors in an item, has more variability than $\boldsymbol{\theta}_j$, which helps in better behaved user-level regressions and leads to faster convergence.

9.3 Training and Prediction

In this section, we first provide a detailed description of model training based on a Monte Carlo expectation maximization (MCEM) algorithm and then discuss the prediction procedure. We begin with a precise formulation of the optimization problem in the model training phase, followed by a description of the EM algorithm. For ease of exposition, we focus on the Gaussian first-stage model and discuss the logistic model in Section 9.3.1.

Let $\boldsymbol{X}_{ij} = [\boldsymbol{x}_i, \boldsymbol{x}_j, \boldsymbol{x}_{ij}]$ denote the features, $\boldsymbol{\Delta}_{ij} = [\alpha_i, \beta_j, \boldsymbol{u}_i]$ denote the continuous latent factors, and $\boldsymbol{\Theta} = [\boldsymbol{b}, \boldsymbol{g}_0, \boldsymbol{d}_0, \boldsymbol{H}, \sigma^2, a_\alpha, a_\beta, \boldsymbol{A}_u, \lambda, \eta]$ denote the model parameters. We use the convention that $\boldsymbol{y} = \{y_{ij}\}$, $\boldsymbol{X} = \{\boldsymbol{X}_{ij}\}$, $\boldsymbol{\Delta} = \{\boldsymbol{\Delta}_{ij}\}$, $\boldsymbol{z} = \{z_{jn}\}$, and $\boldsymbol{w} = \{w_{jn}\}$.

Following the empirical Bayes approach, given observed response y and words w, the goal of training is to find the parameter setting $\hat{\boldsymbol{\Theta}}$ that maximizes the incomplete data likelihood (marginalizing over latent factors $\boldsymbol{\Delta}$ and $\{z_{jn}\}$):

$$\hat{\boldsymbol{\Theta}} = \arg\max_{\boldsymbol{\Theta}} \Pr[\boldsymbol{y}, \boldsymbol{w} \mid \boldsymbol{\Theta}, \boldsymbol{X}].$$

Having obtained the optimal value of $\boldsymbol{\Theta}$ after optimizing the incomplete data likelihood, inference and predictions can be done through the posterior $[\boldsymbol{\Delta}, \{z_{jn}\} \mid \boldsymbol{y}, \boldsymbol{w}, \hat{\boldsymbol{\Theta}}, \boldsymbol{X}]$.

9.3.1 Model Fitting

The EM algorithm (Dempster et al., 1977) is well suited to fit factor models. The factors in this case form the missing data that are augmented to the observed data; complete data log-likelihood is then obtained as a product of likelihoods from our observation (first-stage) and state (second-stage) models. The EM algorithm iterates between an E-step that involves taking expectation of complete data likelihood with respect to the posterior of missing data $(\boldsymbol{\Delta}, \{z_{jn}\})$ conditional on observed data and the current value of $\boldsymbol{\Theta}$, and an M-step in which we maximize the expected complete data likelihood from the E-step to obtain updated values of $\boldsymbol{\Theta}$. At each iteration, the EM algorithm is guaranteed not to deteriorate the value of incomplete data log-likelihood. The major computational bottleneck is in the E-step because the posterior of factors are not available in closed form. Hence, we take recourse to Monte Carlo methods. We draw samples from this posterior and approximate the expectation in E-step by taking the Monte Carlo mean. This is known as the Monte Carlo EM (MCEM) algorithm (Booth and Hobert, 1999). Alternatively, one can apply variational approximation to derive a closed-form formula for the expectation or apply the iterative conditional mode (ICM) algorithm, in which the expectation computation is replaced by plugging in the mode of the conditional distributions. However,in our experience and that of other studies (Salakhutdinov and Mnih, 2008), sampling usually provides better performance in terms of predictive accuracy, while still being scalable. One reason for this behavior is the highly multimodal nature of the posterior; sampling in our experience ensures we do not get stuck in shallow minima. In fact, we have found sampling to be resistant to overfitting even with an increasing number of factors; this is not the case with mode-finding approaches that may overfit (see, e.g., Agarwal and Chen, 2009). Thus, in this section, we focus on the MCEM algorithm.

Let $LL(\boldsymbol{\Theta}; \boldsymbol{\Delta}, z, \boldsymbol{y}, \boldsymbol{w}, X) = \log(\Pr[\boldsymbol{\Delta}, z, \boldsymbol{y}, \boldsymbol{w} \mid \boldsymbol{\Theta}, X])$ denote the complete data log-likelihood. Let $\hat{\boldsymbol{\Theta}}^{(t)}$ denote our current estimate of $\boldsymbol{\Theta}$ at the tth iteration. The EM algorithm iterates through the following two steps until convergence:

1. *E-step*: Compute $E_{\boldsymbol{\Delta},z}[LL(\boldsymbol{\Theta}; \boldsymbol{\Delta}, z, \boldsymbol{y}, \boldsymbol{w}, X) \mid \hat{\boldsymbol{\Theta}}^{(t)}]$ as a function of $\boldsymbol{\Theta}$, where the expectation is taken over the posterior distribution of $(\boldsymbol{\Delta}, z \mid \hat{\boldsymbol{\Theta}}^{(t)}, \boldsymbol{y}, \boldsymbol{w}, X)$.
2. *M-step*: Find the Θ that maximizes the expectation computed in the E-step:

$$\hat{\boldsymbol{\Theta}}^{(t+1)} = \arg\max_{\boldsymbol{\Theta}} E_{\boldsymbol{\Delta},z}[LL(\boldsymbol{\Theta}; \boldsymbol{\Delta}, z, \boldsymbol{y}, \boldsymbol{w}, X) \mid \hat{\boldsymbol{\Theta}}^{(t)}].$$

Monte Carlo E-Step

Because $E_{\Delta,z}[LL(\Theta; \Delta, z, y, w, X) \mid \hat{\Theta}^{(t)}]$ is not available in closed form, we compute the Monte Carlo expectation based on L samples generated by a Gibbs sampler (Gelfand, 1995). The Gibbs sampler repeats the following procedure L times. In the following, we use $(\delta \mid \text{Rest})$, where δ can be one of α_i, β_j, $\boldsymbol{u}_i$, and z_{jn}, to denote the conditional distribution of δ given all the others. Let $\mathcal{I}_j$ denote the set of users who responded to item j, and $\mathcal{J}_i$ denote the set of items to which user i responded.

1. For each user i, sample α_i from $(\alpha_i \mid \text{Rest})$, which is Gaussian:

$$\text{Let } o_{ij} = y_{ij} - \boldsymbol{x}_{ij}'\boldsymbol{b} - \beta_j - \boldsymbol{u}_i'\bar{\boldsymbol{z}}_j.$$

$$\text{Var}[\alpha_i|\text{Rest}] = \left(\frac{1}{a_\alpha} + \sum_{j\in\mathcal{J}_i} \frac{1}{\sigma^2}\right)^{-1}$$

$$E[\alpha_i|\text{Rest}] = \text{Var}[\alpha_i|\text{Rest}] \left(\frac{\boldsymbol{g}_0'\boldsymbol{x}_i}{a_\alpha} + \sum_{j\in\mathcal{J}_i} \frac{o_{ij}}{\sigma^2}\right).$$

2. For each item j, sample β_j from $(\beta_j \mid \text{Rest})$, which is Gaussian:

$$\text{Let } o_{ij} = y_{ij} - \boldsymbol{x}_{ij}'\boldsymbol{b} - \alpha_i - \boldsymbol{u}_i'\bar{\boldsymbol{z}}_j.$$

$$\text{Var}[\beta_j|\text{Rest}] = \left(\frac{1}{a_\beta} + \sum_{i\in\mathcal{I}_j} \frac{1}{\sigma^2}\right)^{-1}$$

$$E[\beta_j|\text{Rest}] = \text{Var}[\beta_j|\text{Rest}] \left(\frac{\boldsymbol{d}_0'\boldsymbol{x}_j}{a_\beta} + \sum_{i\in\mathcal{I}_j} \frac{o_{ij}}{\sigma^2}\right).$$

3. For each user i, sample $\boldsymbol{u}_i$ from $(\boldsymbol{u}_i \mid \text{Rest})$, which is Gaussian, for all i:

$$\text{Let } o_{ij} = y_{ij} - \boldsymbol{x}_{ij}'\boldsymbol{b} - \alpha_i - \beta_j.$$

$$\text{Var}[\boldsymbol{u}_i|\text{Rest}] = \left(\boldsymbol{A}_u^{-1} + \sum_{j\in\mathcal{J}_i} \frac{\bar{\boldsymbol{z}}_j\bar{\boldsymbol{z}}_j'}{\sigma^2}\right)^{-1}$$

$$E[\boldsymbol{u}_i|\text{Rest}] = \text{Var}[\boldsymbol{u}_i|\text{Rest}] \left(\boldsymbol{A}_u^{-1}\boldsymbol{H}\boldsymbol{x}_i + \sum_{j\in\mathcal{J}_i} \frac{o_{ij}\bar{\boldsymbol{z}}_j}{\sigma^2}\right).$$

4. For each item j and each word n in item j, sample z_{jn} from $(z_{jn} \mid \text{Rest})$, which is multinomial. Assume the word corresponding to z_{jn} is $w_{jn} = \ell$. Let $Z_{j'k\ell}^{\neg jn}$ denote the number of times word ℓ belongs to topic k in item j'

with z_{jn} removed; that is,

$$Z_{jk\ell}^{\neg jn} = \sum_{n' \neq n} \mathbf{1}\{z_{jn'} = k \text{ and } w_{jn'} = \ell\} \text{ and}$$

$$Z_{j'k\ell}^{\neg jn} = \sum_{n'} \mathbf{1}\{z_{j'n'} = k \text{ and } w_{j'n'} = \ell\}, \text{ for } j' \neq j.$$

Then, the multinomial probabilities are given by

$$\Pr[z_{jn} = k \mid \text{Rest}] \propto \frac{Z_{k\ell}^{\neg jn} + \eta}{Z_k^{\neg jn} + W\eta} (Z_{jk}^{\neg jn} + \lambda_k)\, g(y),$$

where $Z_{k\ell}^{\neg jn} = \sum_{j'} Z_{j'k\ell}^{\neg jn}$, $Z_k^{\neg jn} = \sum_\ell Z_{k\ell}^{\neg jn}$, $Z_{jk}^{\neg jn} = \sum_\ell Z_{jk\ell}^{\neg jn}$ and, letting $o_{ij} = y_{ij} - \boldsymbol{x}_{ij}' \boldsymbol{b} - \alpha_i - \beta_j$,

$$g(y) = \exp\left\{\bar{z}_j' \boldsymbol{B}_j - \frac{1}{2}\bar{z}_j' \boldsymbol{C}_j \bar{z}_j\right\}$$

$$\boldsymbol{B}_j = \sum_{i \in \mathcal{I}_j} \frac{o_{ij}\boldsymbol{u}_i}{\sigma^2} \text{ and } \boldsymbol{C}_j = \sum_{i \in \mathcal{I}_j} \frac{\boldsymbol{u}_i \boldsymbol{u}_i'}{\sigma^2}.$$

Note that here $\bar{z}_j = \sum_{n'} z_{jn'} \,/\, W_j$ is the empirical topic distribution of item j with z_{jn} set to topic k.

In the following, we derive the formula for $\Pr[z_{jn} = k \mid \text{Rest}]$. Let $z_{\neg jn}$ denote z with z_{jn} removed, and $w_{jn} = \ell$. We have

$$\Pr[z_{jn} = k \mid \text{Rest}] \propto \Pr[z_{jn} = k, \boldsymbol{y} \mid z_{\neg jn}, \boldsymbol{\Delta}, \hat{\boldsymbol{\Theta}}^{(t)}, \boldsymbol{w}, \boldsymbol{X}]$$

$$\propto \Pr[z_{jn} = k \mid \boldsymbol{w}, z_{\neg jn}, \hat{\boldsymbol{\Theta}}^{(t)}] \prod_{i \in I_j} \Pr[y_{ij} \mid z_{jn} = k, z_{\neg jn}, \boldsymbol{\Delta}, \hat{\boldsymbol{\Theta}}^{(t)}, \boldsymbol{X}]$$

$$\begin{aligned}
&\Pr[z_{jn} = k \mid \boldsymbol{w}, z_{\neg jn}, \hat{\boldsymbol{\Theta}}^{(t)}] \\
&\propto \Pr[z_{jn} = k, w_{jn} = \ell \mid \boldsymbol{w}_{\neg jn}, z_{\neg jn}, \hat{\boldsymbol{\Theta}}^{(t)}] \\
&= \Pr[w_{jn} = \ell \mid \boldsymbol{w}_{\neg jn}, z_{jn} = k, z_{\neg jn}, \eta]\; \Pr[z_{jn} = k \mid z_{\neg jn}, \lambda] \\
&= E[\Phi_{k\ell} \mid \boldsymbol{w}_{\neg jn}, z_{\neg jn}, \eta]\; E[\theta_{jk} \mid z_{\neg jn}, \lambda] \\
&= \frac{Z_{k\ell}^{\neg jn} + \eta}{Z_k^{\neg jn} + W\eta} \, \frac{Z_{jk}^{\neg jn} + \lambda_k}{Z_j^{\neg jn} + \sum_k \lambda_k}.
\end{aligned}$$

Note that the denominator of the second term $(Z_j^{\neg jn} + \sum_k \lambda_k)$ is independent of k. Thus, we obtain

$$\Pr[z_{jn} = k \mid \text{Rest}] \propto \frac{Z_{k\ell}^{\neg jn} + \eta}{Z_k^{\neg jn} + W\eta} (Z_{jk}^{\neg jn} + \lambda_k) \prod_{i \in \mathcal{I}_j} f_{ij}(y_{ij}),$$

where $f_{ij}(y_{ij})$ is the probability density at y_{ij}, which is Gaussian with mean $\boldsymbol{x}'_{ij}\boldsymbol{b} + \alpha_i + \beta_j + \boldsymbol{u}'_i\bar{\boldsymbol{z}}_j$ and variance σ^2, and $\bar{\boldsymbol{z}}_j$ is computed by setting $z_{jn} = k$. Let $o_{ij} = y_{ij} - \boldsymbol{x}'_{ij}\boldsymbol{b} - \alpha_i - \beta_j$:

$$\prod_{i \in \mathcal{I}_j} f_{ij}(y_{ij}) \propto \exp\left\{-\frac{1}{2}\sum_{i \in \mathcal{I}_j}\frac{(o_{ij} - \boldsymbol{u}'_i\bar{\boldsymbol{z}}_j)^2}{\sigma^2}\right\}$$

$$\propto \exp\left\{\bar{\boldsymbol{z}}'_j\boldsymbol{B}_j - \frac{1}{2}\bar{\boldsymbol{z}}'_j\boldsymbol{C}_j\bar{\boldsymbol{z}}_j\right\}$$

$$\text{where } \boldsymbol{B}_j = \sum_{i \in \mathcal{I}_j}\frac{o_{ij}\boldsymbol{u}_i}{\sigma^2} \text{ and } \boldsymbol{C}_j = \sum_{i \in \mathcal{I}_j}\frac{\boldsymbol{u}_i\boldsymbol{u}'_i}{\sigma^2}.$$

M-Step

In the M-step, we want to find the parameter setting $\Theta = [\boldsymbol{b}, \boldsymbol{g}_0, \boldsymbol{d}_0, \boldsymbol{H}, \sigma^2, a_\alpha, a_\beta, \boldsymbol{A}_u, \lambda, \eta]$ that maximizes the expected complete data likelihood computed in the E-step:

$$\hat{\boldsymbol{\Theta}}^{(t+1)} = \arg\max_{\boldsymbol{\Theta}} E_{\boldsymbol{\Delta},z}[LL(\boldsymbol{\Theta}; \boldsymbol{\Delta}, z, \boldsymbol{y}, \boldsymbol{w}, \boldsymbol{X}) \mid \hat{\boldsymbol{\Theta}}^{(t)}],$$

where

$$\begin{aligned}
-LL(\boldsymbol{\Theta}; \boldsymbol{\Delta}, z, \boldsymbol{y}, \boldsymbol{w}, \boldsymbol{X}) &= \text{constant} \\
&+ \frac{1}{2}\sum_{ij}\left(\frac{1}{\sigma^2}(y_{ij} - \alpha_i - \beta_j - \boldsymbol{x}'_{ij}\boldsymbol{b} - \boldsymbol{u}'_i\bar{\boldsymbol{z}}_j)^2 + \log\sigma^2\right) \\
&+ \frac{1}{2a_\alpha}\sum_i(\alpha_i - \boldsymbol{g}'_0\boldsymbol{x}_i)^2 + \frac{M}{2}\log a_\alpha \\
&+ \frac{1}{2}\sum_i(\boldsymbol{u}_i - \boldsymbol{H}\boldsymbol{x}_i)'\boldsymbol{A}_u^{-1}(\boldsymbol{u}_i - \boldsymbol{H}\boldsymbol{x}_i) + \frac{M}{2}\log(\det\boldsymbol{A}_u) \\
&+ \frac{1}{2a_\beta}\sum_j(\beta_j - \boldsymbol{d}'_0\boldsymbol{x}_j)^2 + \frac{N}{2}\log a_\beta \\
&+ N\,(r\log\Gamma(\lambda) - \log\Gamma(r\lambda)) \\
&+ \sum_j\left(\log\Gamma\left(Z_j + r\lambda\right) - \sum_k\log\Gamma(Z_{jk} + \lambda)\right) \\
&+ r\,(W\log\Gamma(\eta) - \log\Gamma(W\eta)) \\
&+ \sum_k\left(\log\Gamma(Z_k + W\eta) - \sum_\ell\log\Gamma(Z_{k\ell} + \eta)\right).
\end{aligned}$$

In the preceding equation, $(\boldsymbol{b}, \sigma^2)$, $(\boldsymbol{g}_0, a_\alpha)$, $(\boldsymbol{d}_0, a_\beta)$, $(\boldsymbol{H}, \boldsymbol{A}_u)$, λ, and η can be optimized separately. In particular, the first four can be optimized by solving four regression problems. The last two are single-dimensional and can be solved easily by a grid search. In the rest of this section, we provide the details. We use $\tilde{E}[\cdot]$ and $\tilde{\mathrm{Var}}[\cdot]$ to denote the Monte Carlo mean and variance.

Regression for $(\boldsymbol{b}, \boldsymbol{\sigma^2})$. Let $o_{ij} = \alpha_i + \beta_j + \boldsymbol{u}_i' \bar{z}_j$. Here we want to minimize

$$\frac{1}{\sigma^2} \sum_{ij} \tilde{E}[(y_{ij} - \boldsymbol{x}_{ij}'\boldsymbol{b} - o_{ij})^2] + D \log(\sigma^2),$$

where D is the number of observed ratings. It can be seen that the optimal solution to b can be found by least squares regression using $\boldsymbol{x}_{ij}$ as features to predict $(y_{ij} - \tilde{E}[o_{ij}])$. Let RSS denote the residual sum of squares from this regression. Then, the optimal σ^2 is $(\sum_{ij} \tilde{\mathrm{Var}}[o_{ij}] + \mathrm{RSS})/D$, where RSS is the residual sum of squares of the regression.

Regression for $(\boldsymbol{g}_0, \boldsymbol{a}_\alpha)$. Similar to the previous case, the optimal $\boldsymbol{g}_0$ can be found by solving a regression problem using $\boldsymbol{x}_i$ as features to predict $\tilde{E}[\alpha_i]$, and the optimal a_α is $(\sum_i \tilde{\mathrm{Var}}[\alpha_i] + \mathrm{RSS})/M$.

Regression for $(\boldsymbol{d}_0, \boldsymbol{a}_\beta)$. The optimal $\boldsymbol{d}_0$ can be found by solving a regression problem using $\boldsymbol{x}_j$ as features to predict $\tilde{E}[\beta_j]$, and the optimal $a_\beta = (\sum_j \tilde{\mathrm{Var}}[\beta_j] + \mathrm{RSS})/N$.

Regression for $(\boldsymbol{H}, \boldsymbol{A}_u)$. For simplicity, we assume the variance-covariance matrix to be diagonal; that is, $\boldsymbol{A}_u = a_u \boldsymbol{I}$. Let $\boldsymbol{H}_k$ denote the kth row of $\boldsymbol{H}$ and u_{ik} be the kth component in $\boldsymbol{u}_i$. We find $\boldsymbol{H}_k$ by solving a regression problem using $\boldsymbol{x}_i$ as features to predict $\tilde{E}[u_{ik}]$, for each topic k. Let RSS_k denote the residual sum of squares of the kth regression. Then, $a_u = (\sum_{ik} \tilde{\mathrm{Var}}[u_{ik}] + \sum_k \mathrm{RSS}_k)/rM$.

Optimization Over $\boldsymbol{\eta}$. We find η that minimizes

$$\begin{aligned} & r\,(W \log \Gamma(\eta) - \log \Gamma(W\eta)) \\ & + \textstyle\sum_k \left(\tilde{E}[\log \Gamma(Z_k + W\eta)] - \sum_\ell \tilde{E}[\log \Gamma(Z_{k\ell} + \eta)]\right). \end{aligned}$$

Because this optimization is just one-dimensional and η is a nuisance parameter, we can simply try a number of fixed possible η values.

Optimization Over $\boldsymbol{\lambda}$. We find λ that minimizes

$$\begin{aligned} & N\,(r \log \Gamma(\lambda) - \log \Gamma(r\lambda)) \\ & + \textstyle\sum_j \left(\tilde{E}[\log \Gamma\left(Z_j + r\lambda\right)] - \sum_k \tilde{E}[\log \Gamma(Z_{jk} + \lambda)]\right). \end{aligned}$$

Again, this optimization is single-dimensional. We search through a number of fixed points to find the best λ value.

Discussion

Regularizing Regressions. In the M-step, each regression is performed by using a t-prior on the coefficients to avoid overfitting.

Number of Topics. Based on several experiments in the past and simulation studies, we have found the MCEM algorithm to be resistant to overfitting even when the number of factors is misspecified to be large; we did not try several r values on the test data because that may inadvertently lead to overfitting and undermine the validity of our experiments. Hence, in our experiments, we run fLDA using a large number of factors (twenty to twenty-five). In practice, one can also perform cross-validation within the training data to find the best number of factors.

Scalability. Fixing the number of topics, the number of EM iterations, and the number of Gibbs samples per iteration, the MCEM algorithm is essentially *linear* in the number of (response + word) observations. In our experience, the MCEM algorithm converges quickly after a fairly small number of EM iterations (usually around ten). The algorithm is also highly parallelizable. In particular, when drawing a sample for user (or item) factors, one can partition the users (or items) and draw a sample for each partition independently. For parallel algorithms to draw LDA samples, see, for example, Wang et al. (2009) and Smola and Narayanamurthy (2010).

Fitting Logistic Regression. This is done through a variational approximation that involves a weighted Gaussian regression after each EM iteration (for details, see Agarwal and Chen, 2009).

9.3.2 Prediction

Given the observed ratings y and words w in the training data, our goal is to predict the response y_{ij}^{new} of user i on item j. We can predict the response by the posterior mean $E[y_{ij}^{\text{new}} | \boldsymbol{y}, \boldsymbol{w}, \hat{\boldsymbol{\Theta}}, X]$. For computational efficiency, we approximate the posterior mean by

$$\begin{aligned} E[y_{ij}^{\text{new}} \mid \boldsymbol{y}, \boldsymbol{w}, \hat{\boldsymbol{\Theta}}, X] &= \boldsymbol{x}_{ij}' \hat{\boldsymbol{b}} + \hat{\alpha}_i + \hat{\beta}_j + E[\boldsymbol{u}_i' \bar{\boldsymbol{z}}_j] \\ &\approx \boldsymbol{x}_{ij}' \hat{\boldsymbol{b}} + \hat{\alpha}_i + \hat{\beta}_j + \hat{\boldsymbol{u}}_i' \hat{\bar{\boldsymbol{z}}}_j, \end{aligned}$$

where $\hat{\delta} = E[\delta \mid \boldsymbol{y}, \boldsymbol{w}, \hat{\boldsymbol{\Theta}}, X]$ (δ take values in $\{\alpha_i\}, \{\beta_j\}, \{\boldsymbol{u}_i\}$) is estimated in the training phase. For estimating $\hat{\bar{\boldsymbol{z}}}_j$ for a new item j in cold-start scenarios, we use Gibbs sampling to obtain topic distribution of words w_j in item j through unsupervised LDA sampling formula. However, the topic$\times$word matrix $\mathbf{\Phi}$ used during the sampling is the one obtained from fLDA; hence, the predictions are influenced by response even for new items.

9.4 Experiments

We show the effectiveness of fLDA using three real-life data sets. We use the widely studied MovieLens (movie rating) data set to show that the predictive accuracy of fLDA is among the best compared to six popular collaborative filtering methods. Here, because each movie in the test set has enough ratings in the training set to estimate the movie factors, fLDA does not provide improved accuracy. Next, we report a case study of how fLDA can be used to provide interpretable, personalized recommendations on a social news service site using the Yahoo! Buzz data set. We show that fLDA significantly outperforms the state-of-the-art method when there are many new items that do not appear in the training data set, and it can also identify high-quality topics from news stories. Finally, we present another case study using a book rating data set. Again, we show that fLDA can provide better predictive performance than state-of-the-art methods.

9.4.1 MovieLens Data

In this section, we illustrate the effectiveness of the flDA method on the widely studied movie recommender problem. Because both user and item features are central to our method, we did not consider the Netflix data for experimentation (no user features are available for Netflix). Instead, we analyzed the MovieLens data that consist of 1 million ratings for 6,040 users and 3,706 movies. User features include age, gender, ZIPcode (we used the first digit only), and occupation; item features include movie genre (this was only used with RLFM). To construct bag-of-word features, we supplemented the movie features with actor, actress, and director names, and we extracted words from movie titles and plots. We further split the data into a training set and a test set based on time; the first 75 percent of ratings in chronological order are used for training, whereas the rest are used for testing. These data were analyzed in Agarwal and Chen (2009) and compared to several benchmark methods; we report RMSE along with results from fLDA in Table 9.2.

Methods. The Constant model predicts the rating as training data average for all test cases; Feature-Only is a regression model trained on user and item

Table 9.2. *Test-set RMSE on MovieLens*

Model	Test RMSE
fLDA	0.9381
RLFM	0.9363
unsup-LDA	0.9520
Factor-Only	0.9422
Feature-Only	1.0906
FilterBot	0.9517
MostPopular	0.9726
Constant	1.1190

features (genre) only; Factor-Only is the usual matrix factorization model with zero-mean priors; Most-Popular is a model based only on user and item bias, which are regularized using features; and Filter-Bot is a collaborative filtering method that is used to deal with warm-start and cold-start problems simultaneously, as discussed in Chapter 8 (we do not report on other collaborative filtering methods, such as item-item similarity, because they were all worse than Filter-Bot). RLFM is the regression-based latent factor model discussed in Chapter 8. unsup-LDA is a variant of fLDA obtained by using unsupervised LDA; that is, it first applies unsupervised LDA to identify topics of each word in each item and then fits fLDA by fixing $\bar{z}_j$ as the unsupervised topics.

For this data set, a large fraction of ratings in the test set (almost 56 percent) involved new users, but most of them involved old items for which ratings are available in the training data. The key to having good accuracy is whether a model can handle cold start for users, which is not the target application scenario for fLDA. Thus, we did not expect substantial improvements from fLDA relative to RLFM, which is the best among the methods we tried on this data set. The main purpose of this analysis was to demonstrate that fLDA performs equally well in warm-start scenarios where we have ratings on most items that are scored in the test set.

9.4.2 Yahoo! Buzz Application

Yahoo! Buzz (at http://buzz.yahoo.com/) was a social news service site that recommended "buzzing" news stories to users; votes on articles ("buzz up" or "buzz down") were an important source of information used in deciding recommendations. The site has been shut down by Yahoo! In this section, we describe results from an offline analysis that was conducted on data collected when the site was live.

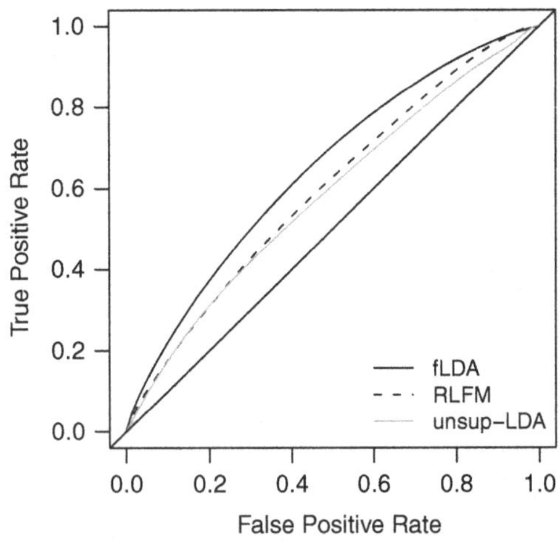

(a) Yahoo! Buzz data

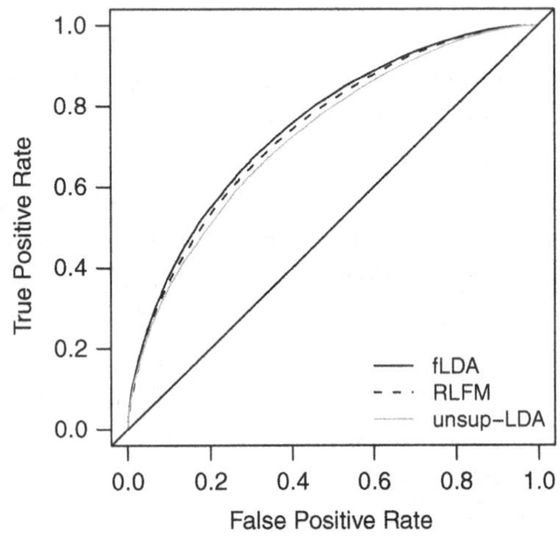

(b) BookCrossing data

Figure 9.2. ROC curves of different methods.

We collected 620,883 votes that were generated by 4,026 users rating 10,468 articles over a three-month period. To minimize the effect of spamming votes, we only selected articles from trusted sources and users with reasonable numbers of votes (no more than one thousand votes). We treat "buzz up" votes as ratings with value 1 and "buzz down" votes as ratings with value -1. In this application, the majority of votes are "buzz up" because users usually "buzz down" an article only when they dislike it; it is difficult to obtain explicit feedback on articles that are not of interest to them. Thus, for each user who had N votes, we randomly selected N articles not voted by the user and gave them a user rating of 0. Because users usually like a small number of articles, it is reasonable to assume that random articles would not interest them. Each user is associated with her age and gender. We converted age values into ten age groups (each of which has an equal number of users). Each article is associated with its title, description, and a set of categories determined by Yahoo! Buzz. We removed the stop words, ran an entity recognizer to identify named entities, and stemmed the terms by the Porter stemmer. Then, we created a training data set by using the first two months and a test data set using the last one month of data. Because the articles are related to news, most articles in the test data set are new and do not appear in the training data set.

We compare three models: fLDA with twenty-five supervised topics, RLFM (the state-of-the-art method) with twenty-five factors, and unsup-LDA with twenty-five unsupervised topics. The ROC curves (reviewed in Section 4.1.3) are shown in Figure 9.2(a). We treat ratings with value 1 as positives and ratings with value 0 or -1 as negatives. It can be clearly seen that fLDA significantly outperforms RLFM and unsup-LDA, and RLFM is slightly better than unsup-LDA.

In Table 9.3, we list interesting topics identified by fLDA. As can be seen, fLDA was able to identify important news topics in Yahoo! Buzz, for example, the CIA's harsh interrogation techniques in the Bush administration (topic 1), swine flu (topic 2), the gay marriage issue (topic 4), the economy downturn (topic 13), the North Korean issue (topic 14), and the American International Group and General Motor issue (topic 25). Most of the topics are quite easy to interpret, but six out of twenty-five topics are too general to be useful. Unsupervised LDA also identified interpretable topics. Roughly half of the topics look similar to those identified by fLDA. However, the predictive performance of unsup-LDA is much worse than that of fLDA.

9.4.3 BookCrossing Data Set

BookCrossing (at http://www.bookcrossing.com) is an online book club. Users can rate books on a scale of 1–10. In prior work, Ziegler et al. (2005) collected book ratings from the site.[1] The data are quite noisy; there are invalid ISBNs, and some of the ISBNs in the rating file cannot be found in the book description file. We cleaned up the data set by only taking the books that have at least three ratings and have reviews from the product description pages of Amazon.com. We then took the book reviews from Amazon.com as the text description about the books. For each book, we took the top seventy terms in the review with

Table 9.3. *Some topics identified by fLDA from the Yahoo! Buzz data*

Topic	Terms (after stemming)
1	bush, tortur, interrog, terror, administr, cia, offici, suspect, releas, investig, georg, memo, al, prison, george_w._bush, guantanamo, us, secret, harsh, depart, attornei, detaine, justic, iraq, alleg, probe, case, said, secur, waterboard
3	mexico, flu, pirat, swine, drug, ship, somali, border, mexican, hostag, offici, somalia, captain, navi, health, us, attack, cartel, outbreak, coast, case, piraci, violenc, u.s., held, spread, pandem, kill
4	nfl, player, team, suleman, game, nadya, star, high, octuplet, nadya_suleman, michael, week, school, sport, fan, get, vick, leagu, coach, season, mother, run, footbal, end, dai, bowl, draft, basebal
6	court, gai, marriag, suprem, right, judg, rule, sex, pope, supreme_court, appeal, ban, legal, allow, state, stem, case, church, california, immigr, law, fridai, cell, decis, feder, hear, cathol, justic
8	palin, republican, parti, obama, limbaugh, sarah, rush, gop, presid, sarah_palin, sai, gov, alaska, steel, right, conserv, host, fox, democrat, rush_limbaugh, new, bristol, tea, senat, levi, stewart, polit, said
9	brown, chri, rihanna, chris_brown, onlin, star, richardson, natasha, actor, actress, natasha_richardson, sai, madonna, milei, singer, divorc, hospit, cyru, angel, wife, charg, adopt, lo, assault, di, ski, accid, year, famili, music
10	idol, american, night, star, look, michel, win, dress, susan, danc, judg, boyl, michelle_obama, susan_boyl, perform, ladi, fashion, hot, miss, leno, got, contest, photo, tv, talent, sing, wear, week, bachelor
11	nation, scienc, christian, monitor, new, obama, christian_science_monitor, com, time, american, us, world, america, climat, peopl, week, dai, michel, just, warm, ann, coulter, chang, state, public, hous, global
12	obama, presid, hous, budget, republican, tax, barack, democrat, barack_obama, parti, sai, senat, congress, tea, administr, palin, group, spend, white, lawmak, politico, offic, gop, right, american, stimulu, feder, anti, health
13	economi, recess, job, percent, econom, bank, expect, rate, jobless, year, unemploy, month, record, market, stock, financi, week, wall, street, new, number, sale, rise, fall, march, billion, februari, crisi, reserv, quarter
14	north, korea, china, north_korea, launch, nuclear, rocket, missil, south, said, russia, chines, iran, militari, weapon, countri, chavez, korean, defens, journalist, japan, secur, nkorea, us, council, u.n., leader, talk, summit, warn
20	com, studi, space, livesci, research, earth, scientist, new, like, year, ic, station, nasa, water, univers, diseas, planet, human, discov, ancient, rare, intern, risk, live, find, expert, red, size, centuri, million
22	israel, iran, said, isra, pakistan, kill, palestinian, presid, iraq, war, gaza, taliban, soldier, leader, attack, troop, milit, govern, afghanistan, countri, offici, peac, group, us, minist, mondai, bomb, militari, polic, iraqi
23	plane, citi, air, high, resid, volcano, mondai, peopl, crash, jet, flight, erupt, south, itali, forc, flood, mile, alaska, small, hit, near, pilot, dai, mount, island, storm, river, travel, crew, earthquak
25	bonus, american_international_group, bank, billion, gener, compani, million, madoff, motor, financi, insur, treasuri, govern, bailout, bankruptci, execut, chrysler, gm, corp, general_motor, monei, pai, auto, ceo, giant, group, automak

Table 9.4. *Test-set RMSE for BookCrossing*

Model	RMSE	MAE
fLDA	1.3088	1.0317
RLFM	1.3278	1.0553
unsup-LDA	1.3539	1.0835

high TF/IDF scores. We selected users with at least six ratings. Each user in the data set is associated with his age and location. We converted age values into ten age groups and only took countries with at least fifty users as the location feature. We removed all the "implicit" ratings because they are not real ratings and their meaning is unclear. To prevent test-set errors from being dominated by a small number of outliers, we removed ratings with values from 1 to 4 (which accounts for less than 5 percent of explicit ratings) and rescaled rating values from the range between 5 and 10 to the range between −2.5 and 2.5. At the end, we have 149,879 ratings for 25,137 books from 6,981 users. We then create a training-test split by threefold cross-validation. For each user, we randomly put the books that she rated into three buckets. In the nth fold, ratings in the nth bucket are used as test data, and the rest are used as training data.

The test-set RMSEs, MAEs of fLDA with twenty-five supervised topics, RLFM with twenty-five factors, and unsup-LDA with twenty-five unsupervised topics are listed in Table 9.4. The ROC curves (by treating ratings above zero as positives and ratings below zero as negatives) are shown in Figure 9.2(b). For this data set, fLDA outperforms RLFM, which outperforms unsup-LDA. However, the differences are small.

9.5 Related Work

Recommender systems have a rich literature by now and have seen rapid progress in the past few years primarily triggered by the Netflix competition. Although several new methods have been proposed, those based on matrix factorization (Mnih and Salakhutdinov, 2007; Salakhutdinov and Mnih, 2008; Bell et al., 2007; Koren et al., 2009) and neighborhood-based methods (Koren, 2008; Bell and Koren, 2007) have become popular and are widely used. Neighborhood-based methods are popular because of their easy interpretation; a user gets an item recommendation if other users with similar tastes have liked the item. Factorization-based methods are in general more accurate, but the factors are hard to interpret. Recently, several papers have explored models to better regularize the latent factors, primarily inspired by the task of improving RMSE for Netflix data (Lawrence and Urtasun, 2009). Using unsupervised LDA topics as features in recommender systems was explored in Jin et al. (2005). In Section 9.4, we showed that fLDA can significantly outperform unsupervised LDA.

Models to address both cold start and warm start that have been studied in collaborative filtering are also related to fLDA. Although it has been studied extensively (Balabanović and Shoham, 1997; Claypool et al., 1999; Good et al., 1999; Park et al., 2006; Schein et al., 2002), only recently has this topic started getting attention in a factorization model framework (Yu et al., 2009; Agarwal and Chen, 2009; Stern et al., 2009). Our fLDA model is an addition to this literature and works with discrete factors for items regularized through an LDA prior. In addition to providing good predictive performance, it provides interpretations that are useful in some applications.

Our work is related to supervised LDA (Blei and McAuliffe, 2008), a variation of LDA that incorporates regression in estimating the topics. However, sLDA only fits a single global regression to item factors; we fit one per user. This work was also inspired by conjoint analysis, which is often conducted in marketing (Rossi et al., 2005). The goal is to estimate individual partworths (user factors) to items. However, item characteristics in this analysis are known features, and fLDA obtains item factors by converting item metadata that are in bag-of-words form into concise topic vectors.

Relational learning (Getoor and Taskar, 2007) is also related. In a very general sense, fLDA is a relational model. However, joint modeling of ratings given by users to items and words in items has not been studied in the literature. In related work, Porteous et al. (2008) apply LDA to cluster users and items into groups and model ratings using the group membership; Singh and Gordon (2008) propose to jointly model user-to-item rating relation, user-to-feature relation, and item-to-feature relation via joint factorization of multiple matrices.

9.6 Summary

We presented a new factorization model fLDA that provides significantly better performance in applications where items have a bag-of-words representation, commonplace in many web applications. The key idea that differentiates fLDA from previous work in the area is the use of an LDA prior to regularize item factors. As an additional benefit, fLDA may provide interpretable user factors as affinities to latent item topics. In fact, we illustrate both prediction accuracy and interpretability on a real-world example related to content recommendation on Yahoo! Buzz.

Our work has opened up several avenues for future research. In Section 9.1, we discussed the potential benefit of using output from fLDA for applications like content programming to help in *media-scheduling* problems and user targeting in display advertising. This requires more follow-up work. On the algorithmic front, updating the posterior of $\boldsymbol{u}_i$ requires inverting a $K \times K$ matrix, which can be computationally expensive for large K. One solution to this problem could be to express $\boldsymbol{u}_i'\bar{\boldsymbol{z}}_j$ as $\boldsymbol{U}_i' \boldsymbol{Q}\bar{\boldsymbol{z}}_j$ where $\boldsymbol{Q}_{K_s \times K}$ is a global matrix estimated from data and $K_s < K$. Finally, although we have illustrated fLDA on a real world application and on benchmark data sets, we are currently scaling up computations in a MapReduce framework to work with massive data sets on several other applications in advertising and content recommendation.

10

Context-Dependent Recommendation

The availability of additional contextual information can have a significant impact on recommendations. In this chapters, we discuss algorithms to provide context-dependent recommendations to users. We describe some example scenarios in the following.

- *Related-item recommendation*: Recommending items (such as news articles) that are related to the one that the user is interacting with is useful in many applications. In this case, the item being interacted with provides the context. For instance, when a user is reading a news article or viewing a product on an e-commerce site, it is useful to recommend other news articles or products related to the one that the user is currently reading or viewing.
- *Multicategory recommendation*: Many websites organize their items using human-understandable categories and recommend top items for each category. Here the categories provide context. An item may be classified into multiple categories, and it is desirable for recommendations within a category to be both semantically relevant and personalized.
- *Location-dependent recommendation*: In several applications, geographical location is an important context, and it is desirable to provide recommendations that are germane to a user's current location.
- *Multiapplication recommendation*: A recommendation system may serve multiple applications, for example, modules on a website and apps for different devices. Because different applications have varying screen sizes, layouts, and different ways to present items, it is important to tailor recommendations to incorporate application specific user behavior. Here each application provides context.

If personalized recommendation is not required in a given context, the models presented in Chapters 7 and 8 can be easily modified to provide context-dependent recommendation. For example, the RLFM model described in Chapter 8 can be modified for related-item recommendation, as follows. Let y_{jk} denote the response that a user would give to item j in context k (e.g., reading context article k in related-news recommendation). Then, we predict y_{jk} by

$$b(\boldsymbol{x}_{jk}) + \alpha_k + \beta_j + \boldsymbol{u}_k' \boldsymbol{v}_j, \tag{10.1}$$

where

- b is a regression function based on feature vector $\boldsymbol{x}_{jk}$ that characterizes (item j, context k) pair (e.g., the similarity between the two bags of words for articles j and k in related-news recommendation)
- α_k is the bias of context k
- β_j is the popularity of item j
- $\boldsymbol{u}_k$ and $\boldsymbol{v}_j$ are the two latent factor vectors for context k and item j

Note that, in Chapter 8, we use index i to denote a user and α_i and $\boldsymbol{u}_i$ to denote the user bias and factor vector, respectively. Changing user index i to context index k does not change the model-fitting algorithms.

When personalization is desired for each context, models that can capture the three-way interaction among user i, item j, and context k are required. In the rest of this chapter, we first introduce tensor factorization models in Section 10.1, where a tensor is an n-dimensional array for $n > 2$, and we seek to approximate a three-dimensional tensor (with size = number users $\times$ number of items $\times$ number of contexts, representing users' responses in different contexts) by several low-rank matrices. We then discuss how to extend tensor factorization through hierarchical shrinkage in Section 10.2. Then, we illustrate the proposed models using a multifaceted news article recommendation problem in Section 10.3. Finally, we discuss special considerations in related-item recommendation in Section 10.4.

10.1 Tensor Factorization Models

When we personalize context-dependent recommendation, we seek to model the three-way interaction among user i, item j, and context k. Tensor models capture this three-way interaction using tensor factorization. We use the following notations:

- $\langle \boldsymbol{u}_i, \boldsymbol{v}_j \rangle = \boldsymbol{u}_i' \boldsymbol{v}_j$ denotes the inner product of two vectors $\boldsymbol{u}_i$ and $\boldsymbol{v}_j$.
- $\langle \boldsymbol{u}_i, \boldsymbol{v}_j, \boldsymbol{w}_k \rangle = \sum_\ell u_{i\ell} v_{j\ell} w_{k\ell}$ denotes a simple form of tensor product, where $u_{i\ell}$, $v_{j\ell}$, and $w_{k\ell}$ are the ℓth elements of vectors $\boldsymbol{u}_i$, $\boldsymbol{v}_j$, and $\boldsymbol{w}_k$ respectively.

10.1.1 Modeling

We model the response y_{ijk} that user i gives item j in context k as follows:

$$\begin{aligned} y_{ijk} \sim\ & b(\boldsymbol{x}_{ijk}) + \alpha_i + \beta_j + \gamma_k \\ & + \langle \boldsymbol{u}_i^{(1)}, \boldsymbol{v}_j^{(1)} \rangle + \langle \boldsymbol{u}_i^{(2)}, \boldsymbol{w}_k^{(1)} \rangle + \langle \boldsymbol{v}_j^{(2)}, \boldsymbol{w}_k^{(2)} \rangle \\ & + \langle \boldsymbol{u}_i^{(3)}, \boldsymbol{v}_j^{(3)}, \boldsymbol{w}_k^{(3)} \rangle, \end{aligned} \tag{10.2}$$

where "$y_{ijk} \sim \ldots$" represents any response model, including Gaussian and logistic. Intuitively, y_{ijk} is predicted based on some distribution and link function that are not explicitly specified here for the sake of succinctness.

Feature-based Regression. Response y_{ijk} is first predicted by a regression function b based on feature vector $\boldsymbol{x}_{ijk}$; this can include user features $\boldsymbol{x}_i$, item features $\boldsymbol{x}_j$, context features $\boldsymbol{x}_k$, and any interaction among them. One choice of the regression function that works well for web applications is

$$b(\boldsymbol{x}_{ijk}) = \boldsymbol{x}_i' \boldsymbol{A} \boldsymbol{x}_j + \boldsymbol{x}_i' \boldsymbol{B} \boldsymbol{x}_k + \boldsymbol{x}_j' \boldsymbol{C} \boldsymbol{x}_k, \tag{10.3}$$

where $\boldsymbol{A}$, $\boldsymbol{B}$, and $\boldsymbol{C}$ are the matrices of regression coefficients for the two-way interaction between user features and item features, two-way interaction between user features and context features, and two-way interaction between item features and context features, respectively. In this case, estimating regression function b entails estimating $\boldsymbol{A}$, $\boldsymbol{B}$, and $\boldsymbol{C}$, which are usually high-dimensional. Another choice is to use a set of predefined "similarity" functions to reduce dimensionality. Let $s_1(\boldsymbol{x}_i, \boldsymbol{x}_j)$, $s_2(\boldsymbol{x}_i, \boldsymbol{x}_k)$, and $s_3(\boldsymbol{x}_j, \boldsymbol{x}_k)$ denote similarity functions, each of which returns a vector of similarity (or affinity) measures between two entities. For example, $s_1(\boldsymbol{x}_i, \boldsymbol{x}_j)$ may return a vector of similarity measures, each of which measures the similarity between user i and item j from a different perspective. A possible similarity measure between a user and an item is the cosine similarity between the user-profile bag of words and the item bag of words. The regression function for similarity measures is

$$b(\boldsymbol{x}_{ijk}) = \boldsymbol{c}_1' s_1(\boldsymbol{x}_i, \boldsymbol{x}_j) + \boldsymbol{c}_2' s_2(\boldsymbol{x}_i, \boldsymbol{x}_k) + \boldsymbol{c}_3' s_3(\boldsymbol{x}_j, \boldsymbol{x}_k), \tag{10.4}$$

where $\boldsymbol{c}_1$, $\boldsymbol{c}_2$, and $\boldsymbol{c}_3$ are vectors of regression coefficients.

Bias and Popularity. In addition to feature-based regression, we include a bias term for each entity (user, item, or context). Intuitively, the user bias α_i represents the average response of user i to a random item in a random context, β_j represents the global (instead of context-specific) popularity of item j, and the context bias γ_k represents the average response of a random user to a random item in context k.

Two-way Interactions of Factors. Similar to RLFM, $\langle \boldsymbol{u}_i^{(1)}, \boldsymbol{v}_j^{(1)} \rangle$ represents the affinity between user i and item j, where $\boldsymbol{u}_i^{(1)}$ and $\boldsymbol{v}_j^{(1)}$ are unknown vectors representing latent factors. Similarly, $\langle \boldsymbol{u}_i^{(2)}, \boldsymbol{w}_k^{(1)} \rangle$ and $\langle \boldsymbol{v}_j^{(2)}, \boldsymbol{w}_k^{(2)} \rangle$ represent the affinity between user i and context k and the affinity between item j and context k, respectively. Unlike RLFM, here each user has two factors ($\boldsymbol{u}_i^{(1)}$ and $\boldsymbol{u}_i^{(2)}$), one for user-item interaction and the other for user-context interaction. Each item or each context also has two factors. One can choose to constrain $\boldsymbol{u}_i^{(1)} = \boldsymbol{u}_i^{(2)} = \boldsymbol{u}_i$, $\boldsymbol{v}_j^{(1)} = \boldsymbol{v}_j^{(2)} = \boldsymbol{v}_j$, and/or $\boldsymbol{w}_k^{(1)} = \boldsymbol{w}_k^{(2)} = \boldsymbol{w}_k$. For example, if we choose to enforce these three constraints, then the two-way interaction of factors becomes

$$\langle \boldsymbol{u}_i, \boldsymbol{v}_j \rangle + \langle \boldsymbol{u}_i, \boldsymbol{w}_k \rangle + \langle \boldsymbol{v}_j, \boldsymbol{w}_k \rangle. \tag{10.5}$$

Three-way Interaction of Factors. For behavior that cannot be captured by only using two-way interactions, we can use three-way interaction $\langle \boldsymbol{u}_i^{(3)}, \boldsymbol{v}_j^{(3)}, \boldsymbol{w}_k^{(3)} \rangle$, where $\boldsymbol{u}_i^{(3)}$, $\boldsymbol{v}_j^{(3)}$, and $\boldsymbol{w}_k^{(3)}$ are to be learned from data. One interpretation of this tensor product $\langle \boldsymbol{u}_i, \boldsymbol{v}_j, \boldsymbol{w}_k \rangle = \sum_\ell u_{i\ell} v_{j\ell} w_{k\ell}$ is that the affinity between user i and item j in context k is a "weighted" inner product between user factor $\boldsymbol{u}_i$ and item factor $\boldsymbol{v}_j$, where the weight $w_{k\ell}$ on each dimension ℓ depends on the context k. Similar to the discussion in two-way interactions, one can choose to constrain $\boldsymbol{u}_i^{(1)} = \boldsymbol{u}_i^{(2)} = \boldsymbol{u}_i^{(3)} = \boldsymbol{u}_i$, $\boldsymbol{v}_j^{(1)} = \boldsymbol{v}_j^{(2)} = \boldsymbol{v}_j^{(3)} = \boldsymbol{v}_j$, and/or $\boldsymbol{w}_k^{(1)} = \boldsymbol{w}_k^{(2)} = \boldsymbol{w}_k^{(3)} = \boldsymbol{w}_k$.

Regression Priors. Similar to RLFM, we can put a regression prior on each factor to handle cold-start situations. For example, we can specify

$$\boldsymbol{w}_k^{(3)} \sim N(F^{(3)}(\boldsymbol{x}_k), \sigma_w^2 I), \tag{10.6}$$

where $F^{(3)}(\boldsymbol{x}_k)$ is a regression function that captures the characteristics of context k. It returns a vector that has the same number of dimensions as $\boldsymbol{w}_k^{(3)}$. The features help us predict the factors even in the absence of training data for the corresponding entities. For details, see Section 8.1.

10.1.2 Model Fitting

The Monte Carlo EM (MCEM) algorithm introduced in Section 8.2 can also be extended for fitting tensor factorization models. The computations in the E-step for the bias and popularity factors (α_i, β_j, and γ_k), and two-way interaction factors ($\boldsymbol{u}_i^{(1)}$, $\boldsymbol{u}_i^{(2)}$, $\boldsymbol{v}_j^{(1)}$, $\boldsymbol{v}_j^{(2)}$, $\boldsymbol{w}_k^{(1)}$, and $\boldsymbol{w}_k^{(2)}$) are similar. The M-step computation method also remains the same. The only new kind of computation is for the three-way interaction factors ($\boldsymbol{u}_i^{(3)}$, $\boldsymbol{v}_j^{(3)}$, and $\boldsymbol{w}_k^{(3)}$) factors. We describe the steps for sampling $\boldsymbol{w}_k^{(3)}$ as an example; other three-way interaction factors can be handled similarly.

In the E-step of MCEM, we use the Gibbs sampler to draw posterior samples of the factors. When drawing a sample of $\boldsymbol{w}_k^{(3)}$, we fix the rest of the factors at their current sampled values. For the Gaussian model, it is easy to see that $(\boldsymbol{w}_k \mid \text{Rest})$ is Gaussian. Let

$$\begin{aligned} o_{ijk} &= y_{ijk} - b(x_{ijk}) - \alpha_i - \beta_j - \gamma_k \\ &\quad - \langle \boldsymbol{u}_i^{(1)}, \boldsymbol{v}_j^{(1)} \rangle - \langle \boldsymbol{u}_i^{(2)}, \boldsymbol{w}_k^{(1)} \rangle - \langle \boldsymbol{v}_j^{(2)}, \boldsymbol{w}_k^{(2)} \rangle \qquad (10.7) \\ z_{ij} &= (u_{i1}v_{j1}, \ldots, u_{id}v_{jd}), \end{aligned}$$

where z_{ij} is the element-wise product between $\boldsymbol{u}_i$ and $\boldsymbol{v}_j$. Then,

$$\begin{aligned} \text{Var}[\boldsymbol{w}_k^{(3)}|\text{Rest}] &= \left(\frac{1}{\sigma_w^2} I + \sum_{ij \in \mathcal{IJ}_k} \frac{z_{ij} z'_{ij}}{\sigma^2} \right)^{-1} \qquad (10.8) \\ E[\boldsymbol{w}_k^{(3)}|\text{Rest}] &= \text{Var}[\boldsymbol{w}_k|\text{Rest}] \left(\frac{1}{\sigma_w^2} F^{(3)}(x_k) + \sum_{ij \in \mathcal{IJ}_k} \frac{o_{ijk} z_{ij}}{\sigma^2} \right). \end{aligned}$$

10.1.3 Discussion

The tensor factorization in Equation (10.2) specifies a flexible class of models. Depending on the application, one can choose to drop different terms from the model formula and/or enforce constraints like $\boldsymbol{u}_i^{(1)} = \boldsymbol{u}_i^{(2)}$. For example, Agarwal et al. (2011b) consider the problem of recommending comments in a comment rating environment. The rating y_{ijk} that user i would give to comment j posted by user k (called poster) is modeled as

$$y_{ijk} \sim \alpha_i + \beta_j + \gamma_k + \langle \boldsymbol{u}_i^{(1)}, \boldsymbol{v}_j^{(1)} \rangle + \langle \boldsymbol{u}_i^{(2)}, \boldsymbol{u}_k^{(2)} \rangle, \qquad (10.9)$$

where $\langle \boldsymbol{u}_i^{(1)}, \boldsymbol{v}_j^{(1)} \rangle$ represents the affinity between user i and comment j and $\langle \boldsymbol{u}_i^{(2)}, \boldsymbol{u}_k^{(2)} \rangle$ represents the agreement in opinions between user i and user k. Here each user i has two factors: $\boldsymbol{u}_i^{(1)}$ for item preferences and $\boldsymbol{u}_i^{(2)}$ for opinions. Compared to Equation (10.2), they drop the tensor product and the comment-poster interaction and enforce constraint $\boldsymbol{w}_k^{(1)} = \boldsymbol{u}_k^{(2)}$.

We can also employ a more general form of tensor product,

$$\langle \boldsymbol{u}_i, \boldsymbol{v}_j, \boldsymbol{w}_k, \boldsymbol{T} \rangle = \sum_{\ell} \sum_{m} \sum_{n} u_{i\ell} v_{jm} w_{kn} T_{\ell mn}, \tag{10.10}$$

where $\boldsymbol{T}$ is a tensor (or three-dimensional array) also to be learned from data and $T_{\ell mn}$ is the (ℓ, m, n)th entry of the tensor. Unlike the basic tensor product $\langle \boldsymbol{u}_i, \boldsymbol{v}_j, \boldsymbol{w}_k \rangle$, which only considers the three-way interaction terms of factors on the diagonal (i.e., $\langle \boldsymbol{u}_i, \boldsymbol{v}_j, \boldsymbol{w}_k \rangle = \langle \boldsymbol{u}_i, \boldsymbol{v}_j, \boldsymbol{w}_k, \boldsymbol{I} \rangle$, where $\boldsymbol{I}$ is the identify matrix), this more general form of tensor product includes all three-way interaction terms among user factors, item factors, and context factors. For an empirical study comparing these two kinds of tensor products, see Rendle and Schmidt-Thieme (2010).

10.2 Hierarchical Shrinkage

Response data in the three-dimensional tensor of users×items×contexts are sparse – we only observe a very small fraction of entries in the tensor. Tensor factorization models deal with this sparsity issue through low rank approximation. Another way to address the sparsity issue is through hierarchical shrinkage. A simple example is to predict the response y_{ijk} that user i would give to item j in context k as

$$y_{ijk} \sim \alpha_{ik} + \beta_{jk}, \tag{10.11}$$

where α_{ik} represents the bias of user i in context k and β_{jk} represents the popularity of item j in context k; both factors α_{ik} and β_{jk} are context specific and to be learned from data. If we have a sufficient number of data for each context to accurately estimate all the factors, then we can easily estimate the parameters. However, this is rarely the case in practice. We often need to leverage the data in one context to estimate the factors in another. Hierarchical models achieve this by adding a set of context-independent global factors and assuming context-specific factors are "generated" from a distribution centered around those global factors. For example, we can add a global user bias factor α_i for each user i and assume that the context-specific user bias factor α_{ik} is generated from α_i,

$$\alpha_{ik} \sim N(\alpha_i, \sigma^2), \tag{10.12}$$

which specifies the prior distribution of α_{ik}. The global factor α_i is estimated using data from all contexts, whereas the context-specific factor α_{ik} is estimated using the data in context k. Because α_i is the prior mean of α_{ik}, if we lack data in context k, the estimated α_{ik} would be close to its prior mean α_i; in other words, we "shrink" α_{ik} toward α_i, where α_i and α_{ik} form a two-level hierarchy. If we have a large number of data in context k for user i, the estimated α_{ik} can deviate from α_i significantly to fit the behavior of user i specific to context k.

10.2.1 Modeling

In this section, we extend the simple hierarchical model in Equations (10.11) and (10.12) to include tensor factorization and feature-based regression priors. As discussed in Section 10.1.3, we can pick and choose different terms in Equation (10.2) to produce different tensor models for different application scenarios. For ease of exposition, we choose to only include the three-way interaction term $\langle \boldsymbol{u}_i^{(3)}, \boldsymbol{v}_j^{(3)}, \boldsymbol{w}_k^{(3)} \rangle$ and drop the superscript $*^{(3)}$. It is straightforward to include other terms.

Bias Smoothed Tensor (BST) Model. We model the response y_{ijk} that user i gives item j in context k as

$$y_{ijk} \sim b(\boldsymbol{x}_{ijk}) + \alpha_{ik} + \beta_{jk} + \langle \boldsymbol{u}_i, \boldsymbol{v}_j, \boldsymbol{w}_k \rangle, \tag{10.13}$$

$$\alpha_{ik} \sim N(\boldsymbol{g}_k' \boldsymbol{x}_{ik} + q_k \alpha_i,\ \sigma_{\alpha,k}^2), \qquad \alpha_i \sim N(0, 1), \tag{10.14}$$

$$\beta_{jk} \sim N(\boldsymbol{d}_k' \boldsymbol{x}_{jk} + r_k \beta_j,\ \sigma_{\beta,k}^2), \qquad \beta_j \sim N(0, 1), \tag{10.15}$$

$$\boldsymbol{u}_i \sim N(\boldsymbol{G}(\boldsymbol{x}_i),\ \sigma_u^2 I), \tag{10.16}$$

$$\boldsymbol{v}_j \sim N(\boldsymbol{D}(\boldsymbol{x}_j),\ \sigma_v^2 I), \tag{10.17}$$

$$\boldsymbol{w}_k \sim N(\boldsymbol{F}(\boldsymbol{x}_k),\ \sigma_w^2 I). \tag{10.18}$$

The main components of the model are as follows.

Feature Vectors. Vector $\boldsymbol{x}_{ijk}$ is the feature vector associated with the instance that user i sees item j in context k. Vector $\boldsymbol{x}_i$ is the feature vector of user i. Vector $\boldsymbol{x}_j$ is the feature vector of item j, and $\boldsymbol{x}_k$ is the feature vector of context k.

User Bias. Term α_i is the *global* user bias term that captures the context-independent general behavior of user i. Term α_{ik} is the *context-specific* user bias that captures the behavior of user i specific for context k. If we have a large number of past observations for user i in context k, we should be able to estimate α_{ik} accurately without the hierarchical prior – a simple zero-mean prior (i.e., $\alpha_{ik} \sim N(0, \sigma_{\alpha,k}^2)$) should be sufficient. However, in many application settings, we do not have many past observations for several users, and it is useful to use user features $\boldsymbol{x}_i$ to predict the user bias. If a user has many past observations in some contexts but not in other contexts, it is also useful to use the user's global bias (α_i, which can be learned using the user's data across all contexts to predict the context-specific user bias terms for the contexts that lack past observations.

Hierarchical Regression Prior. Vectors $\boldsymbol{g}_k$ and scalar q_k are the context-specific regression coefficient vector on user features $\boldsymbol{x}_{ik}$ and the regression coefficient on the global user bias α_i, respectively. When we do not have data to estimate the the context-specific user bias α_{ik}, we can still predict it based on the user features and the global user bias through a linear regression as α_{ik}'s prior mean $\boldsymbol{g}_k'\boldsymbol{x}_{ik} + q_k\alpha_i$. When we have some data, the model also allows the posterior of α_{ik} to deviate from its prior mean to capture the user's unique behavior in context k that the linear regression does not capture.

Item Bias. Term β_{jk} is the context-specific bias (i.e., popularity) of item j in context k. It has a hierarchical regression prior based on the global item bias β_j and the regression coefficients $\boldsymbol{d}_k$ and r_k.

Tensor Factorization. The tensor factorization term $\langle \boldsymbol{u}_i, \boldsymbol{v}_j, \boldsymbol{w}_k \rangle$ and the priors of $\boldsymbol{u}_i$, $\boldsymbol{v}_j$, and $\boldsymbol{w}_k$ are the same as those in Section 10.1.

10.2.2 Model Fitting

The MCEM algorithm introduced in Section 8.2 can be used here.

Let η denote the set of latent factors $(\alpha_i, \alpha_{ik}, \beta_j, \beta_{jk}, \boldsymbol{u}_i, \boldsymbol{v}_j, \boldsymbol{w}_k)$ and $\boldsymbol{\Theta}$ denote the set of prior parameters $(\boldsymbol{g}_k, q_k, \boldsymbol{d}_k, r_k, \boldsymbol{G}, \boldsymbol{D}, \boldsymbol{F})$. Let R = the number observations, N_k = the number of users, M_k = the number of items in context k, and H = the number of latent dimensions (i.e., the length of vector $\boldsymbol{u}_i$, which has the same length as $\boldsymbol{v}_j$ and $\boldsymbol{w}_k$). Let $\hat{a}$ and $\hat{V}[a]$ denote the posterior mean and variance of factor a, and $\hat{V}[a, b]$ denote the covariance between factor a and b, which are computed as the sample mean, variance, covariance based on the Monte Carlo samples obtained in the E-step. Let $\mu_{ijk} = b(\boldsymbol{x}_{ijk}) + \alpha_{ik} + \beta_{jk} + \langle \boldsymbol{u}_i, \boldsymbol{v}_j, \boldsymbol{w}_k \rangle$. The complete data log-likelihood of the Gaussian bias-smoothed tensor model is

$$
\begin{aligned}
2 \log \Pr(\mathbf{y}, \eta \mid \boldsymbol{\Theta}) = {} & \text{some constant} \\
& - R \log \sigma_y^2 - \sum_{ijk} (y_{ijk} - \mu_{ijk})^2 / \sigma_y^2 \\
& - \sum_i \alpha_i^2 - \sum_k N_k \log \sigma_{\alpha,k}^2 - \sum_k \sum_i (\alpha_{ik} - \boldsymbol{g}_k' \boldsymbol{x}_{ik} - q_k \alpha_i)^2 / \sigma_{\alpha,k}^2
\end{aligned}
$$

$$
\begin{aligned}
&-\sum_j \beta_j^2 - \sum_k M_k \log\sigma_{\beta,k}^2 - \sum_k\sum_j(\beta_{jk} - \boldsymbol{d}_k'\boldsymbol{x}_{jk} - r_k\beta_j)^2/\sigma_{\beta,k}^2 \\
&-\sum_i \left(H \log\sigma_u^2 + \|\boldsymbol{u}_i - \boldsymbol{G}(\boldsymbol{x}_i)\|^2/\sigma_u^2\right) \\
&-\sum_j \left(H \log\sigma_v^2 + \|\boldsymbol{v}_j - \boldsymbol{D}(\boldsymbol{x}_j)\|^2/\sigma_v^2\right) \\
&-\sum_k \left(H \log\sigma_w^2 + \|\boldsymbol{w}_k - \boldsymbol{F}(\boldsymbol{x}_k)\|^2/\sigma_w^2\right). \qquad (10.19)
\end{aligned}
$$

The expected log-likelihood (over $\boldsymbol{\eta}$) is

$$
\begin{aligned}
&2\,E_{\eta}[\log \Pr(\mathbf{y}, \boldsymbol{\eta} \mid \boldsymbol{\Theta})] = \text{ some constant} \\
&- R \log\sigma_y^2 - \sum_{ijk}\left((y_{ijk} - \hat{\mu}_{ijk})^2 + \hat{V}[\mu_{ijk}]\right)/\sigma_y^2 \\
&-\sum_i E[\alpha_i^2] - \sum_k N_k \log\sigma_{\alpha,k}^2 \\
&-\sum_k\sum_i \frac{(\hat{\alpha}_{ik} - g_k'x_{ik} - q_k\hat{\alpha}_i)^2 + \hat{V}[\alpha_{ik}] - 2q_k\hat{V}[\alpha_{ik},\alpha_i] + q_k^2\hat{V}[\alpha_i]}{\sigma_{\alpha,k}^2} \\
&-\sum_j E[\beta_j^2] - \sum_k M_k \log\sigma_{\beta,k}^2 \\
&-\sum_k\sum_j \frac{(\hat{\beta}_{jk} - d_k'x_{jk} - r_k\hat{\beta}_j)^2 + \hat{V}[\beta_{jk}] - 2r_k\hat{V}[\beta_{jk},\beta_j] + r_k^2\hat{V}[\beta_j]}{\sigma_{\beta,k}^2} \\
&-\sum_i \left(H \log\sigma_u^2 + \left(\|\hat{\boldsymbol{u}}_i - \boldsymbol{G}(\boldsymbol{x}_i)\|^2 + \text{trace}(\hat{V}[\boldsymbol{u}_i])\right)/\sigma_u^2\right) \\
&-\sum_j \left(H \log\sigma_v^2 + \left(\|\hat{\boldsymbol{v}}_j - \boldsymbol{D}(\boldsymbol{x}_j)\|^2 + \text{trace}(\hat{V}[\boldsymbol{v}_j])\right)/\sigma_v^2\right) \\
&-\sum_k \left(H \log\sigma_w^2 + \left(\|\hat{\boldsymbol{w}}_k - \boldsymbol{F}(\boldsymbol{x}_k)\|^2 + \text{trace}(\hat{V}[\boldsymbol{w}_k])\right)/\sigma_w^2\right).
\end{aligned}
$$

(10.20)

E-Step

In the E-step, we would like to draw L Gibbs samples for all of the latent factors in $\boldsymbol{\eta}$ and then use these samples to compute the means and variances in Equation (10.20). Each sample can be drawn in the following way.

Draw $\boldsymbol{\alpha_i}$ and $\boldsymbol{\alpha_{ik}}$. Assume that all the other factors are given. Let $o_{ijk} = y_{ijk} - \beta_{jk} - \langle \boldsymbol{u}_i, \boldsymbol{v}_j, \boldsymbol{w}_k \rangle - \boldsymbol{g}_k' \boldsymbol{x}_{ik}$ and $\alpha_{ik}^* = \alpha_{ik} - \boldsymbol{g}_k' \boldsymbol{x}_{ik}$. Then, we have

$$\begin{aligned} o_{ijk} &\sim N(\alpha_{ik}^*,\ \sigma_y^2), \\ \alpha_{ik}^* &\sim N(q_k \alpha_i,\ \sigma_{\alpha,k}^2), \\ \alpha_i &\sim N(0, 1). \end{aligned} \tag{10.21}$$

Let $\mathcal{J}_{ik}$ denote the set of items that user i has responded to in context k. Let $\boldsymbol{o}_{ik} = \{o_{ijk}\}_{\forall j \in \mathcal{J}_{ik}}$. Because all the distributions are normal, the distribution of $(\alpha_i | \boldsymbol{o}_{ik})$ is also normal and can be obtained by $\int p(\alpha_i, \alpha_{ik}^* \mid \boldsymbol{o}_{ik})\, d\,\alpha_{ik}^*$. Let $\rho_{ik} = (1 + |\mathcal{J}_{ik}|\, \sigma_{\alpha,k}^2 / \sigma_y^2)^{-1}$. We have

$$\begin{aligned} E[\alpha_i \mid \boldsymbol{o}_{ik}] &= \mathrm{Var}[\alpha_i \mid \boldsymbol{o}_{ik}] \Big(\rho_{ik}\, q_k \sum_{j \in \mathcal{J}_{ik}} \frac{o_{ijk}}{\sigma_y^2} \Big) \\ \mathrm{Var}[\alpha_i \mid \boldsymbol{o}_{ik}] &= \left(1 + \frac{q_k^2}{\sigma_{\alpha,k}^2} (1 - \rho_{ik}) \right)^{-1}. \end{aligned} \tag{10.22}$$

Then, letting $\boldsymbol{o}_i = \{\boldsymbol{o}_{ik}\}_{\forall k}$, we obtain the distribution of $(\alpha_i \mid \boldsymbol{o}_i)$, which is normal with

$$\begin{aligned} E[\alpha_i \mid \boldsymbol{o}_i] &= \mathrm{Var}[\alpha_i \mid \boldsymbol{o}_i] \left(\sum_k \frac{E[\alpha_i \mid \boldsymbol{o}_{ik}]}{\mathrm{Var}[\alpha_i \mid \boldsymbol{o}_{ik}]} \right) \\ \mathrm{Var}[\alpha_i \mid \boldsymbol{o}_i] &= \left(1 + \sum_k \left(\frac{1}{\mathrm{Var}[\alpha_i \mid \boldsymbol{o}_{ik}]} - 1 \right) \right)^{-1}. \end{aligned} \tag{10.23}$$

Now, we draw α_i from this distribution. Then, for each k, we draw α_{ik} from the distribution of $(\alpha_{ik} \mid \alpha_i, \boldsymbol{o}_i)$, which is normal with

$$\begin{aligned} E[\alpha_{ik} \mid \alpha_i, \boldsymbol{o}_i] &= V_{ik}^{(\alpha)} \left(\frac{q_k \alpha_i}{\sigma_{\alpha,k}^2} + \sum_{j \in \mathcal{J}_{ik}} \frac{o_{ijk}}{\sigma_y^2} \right) + \boldsymbol{g}_k' x_{ik} \\ \mathrm{Var}[\alpha_{ik} \mid \alpha_i, \boldsymbol{o}_i] &= V_{ik}^{(\alpha)} = \left(\frac{1}{\sigma_{\alpha,k}^2} + \frac{1}{\sigma_y^2} |\mathcal{J}_{ik}| \right)^{-1}. \end{aligned} \tag{10.24}$$

Draw $\boldsymbol{\beta_j}$ and $\boldsymbol{\beta_{jk}}$. This is similar to the procedure for drawing α_i and α_{ik}.

Draw $\boldsymbol{u_i}$, $\boldsymbol{v_j}$, and $\boldsymbol{w_k}$. This is can be done in the same way as the Gibbs sampling process discussed in Section 10.1.2.

M-Step

In the M-step, we would like to find the prior parameters in $\mathbf{\Theta}$ that maximize Equation (10.20).

Estimating $(g_k, q_k, \sigma^2_{\alpha,k})$. Let $\boldsymbol{\theta}_k = (q_k, g_k)$, $z_{ik} = (\hat{\alpha}_i, \boldsymbol{x}_{ik})$, $\Delta_i = \text{diag}(\hat{V}[\alpha_i], \mathbf{0})$, and $\boldsymbol{c}_{ik} = (\hat{V}[\alpha_{ik}, \alpha_i], \mathbf{0})$. We want to find $\boldsymbol{\theta}_k$ and $\sigma_{\alpha,k}$ that minimize

$$\frac{1}{\sigma^2_{\alpha,k}} \sum_i \left((\hat{\alpha}_{ik} - \boldsymbol{\theta}'_k z_{ik})^2 + \boldsymbol{\theta}'_k \Delta_i \boldsymbol{\theta}_k - 2\boldsymbol{\theta}'_k \boldsymbol{c}_{ik} + \hat{V}[\alpha_{ik}] \right) + N_k \log \sigma^2_{\alpha,k}. \tag{10.25}$$

By setting the derivative to zero, we obtain

$$\begin{aligned} \hat{\boldsymbol{\theta}}_k &= \left(\sum_i (\Delta_i + z_{ik} z'_{ik}) \right)^{-1} \left(\sum_i (z_{ik} \hat{\alpha}_{ik} + \boldsymbol{c}_{ik}) \right) \\ \hat{\sigma}^2_{\alpha,k} &= \left((\hat{\alpha}_{ik} - \hat{\boldsymbol{\theta}}'_k z_{ik})^2 + \hat{\boldsymbol{\theta}}'_k \Delta_i \hat{\boldsymbol{\theta}}_k - 2\hat{\boldsymbol{\theta}}'_k \boldsymbol{c}_{ik} + \hat{V}[\alpha_{ik}] \right) / N_k. \end{aligned} \tag{10.26}$$

Estimating $(d_k, r_k, \sigma^2_{\beta,k})$. This is similar to the procedure for estimating $(g_k, q_k, \sigma^2_{\alpha,k})$.

Estimating (G, σ^2_u), (D, σ^2_v), and (F, σ^2_w). This can be done in the same way as the M-step in Section 8.2.

10.2.3 Locally Augmented Tensor Model

In this section, we introduce an extension to the BST model defined in Section 10.2.1. We start by discussing two simple baseline matrix factorization models for context-dependent recommendation.

- *Separate matrix factorization* (SMF) treats observations in K different contexts as K separate matrices and applies factorization to each of them independently; that is,

$$y_{ijk} \sim \alpha_{ik} + \beta_{jk} + \boldsymbol{u}'_{ik} \boldsymbol{v}_{jk}.$$

- *Collapsed matrix factorization* (CMF) collapses observations in all contexts into a single matrix and applies factorization to it; that is,

$$y_{ijk} \sim \alpha_i + \beta_j + \boldsymbol{u}'_i \boldsymbol{v}_j,$$

  where the right-hand side does not depend on type k.

SMF is a strong baseline because the context-specific factors for users and items with large numbers of training samples in different contexts can be estimated accurately. For users and items without much training data, their factors can still be predicted by features. Compared to CMF, SMF has K times more factors to be estimated from data and is more sensitive to data sparsity. Although CMF is less sensitive to data sparsity, it ignores the behavioral differences across different contexts, which may lead to bias and poor performance. BST addresses the bias issue of CMF by tensor factorization and hierarchical priors. However, compared to SMF, BST may still lack the capacity to capture the behavioral differences across different contexts, especially when we have a large number of data for each context.

Modeling. The locally augmented tensor (LAT) model bridges the gap between BST and SMF by factorizing the residuals of BST locally for each context. The response y_{ijk} that user i gives item j in context k is modeled as

$$y_{ijk} \sim \alpha_{ik} + \beta_{jk} + \langle \boldsymbol{u}_i, \boldsymbol{v}_j, \boldsymbol{w}_k \rangle + \boldsymbol{u}'_{ik}\boldsymbol{v}_{jk}. \tag{10.27}$$

The intuitive meanings of the factors are as follows:

- α_{ik} is the context-specific bias of user i.
- β_{jk} is the context-specific popularity of item j.
- $\langle \boldsymbol{u}_i, \boldsymbol{v}_j, \boldsymbol{w}_k \rangle$ measures the similarity between user i's global profile $\boldsymbol{u}_i$ and item j's global profile $\boldsymbol{v}_j$ weighted by a context-specific weight vector $\boldsymbol{w}_k$. These profiles are called global because they are not context specific. This weighted inner product (i.e., tensor product) imposes a constraint when we try to use it to approximate the observations y_{ijk}. Specifically, it may not be flexible enough to accurately model users' response when there is diverse behavior across contexts. However, this constraint in the parametrization helps to avoid overfitting when data are sparse.
- $\boldsymbol{u}'_{ik}\boldsymbol{v}_{jk}$ also measures the similarity between user i and item j in context k and is more flexible than the tensor product. Thus, the residuals that the tensor product does not capture can be captured by this inner product of context-specific user factor $\boldsymbol{u}'_{ik}$ and item factor $\boldsymbol{v}_{jk}$.

We call the context-specific factors $\boldsymbol{u}_{ik}, \boldsymbol{v}_{jk}$ *local factors*, in contrast to the global factors $\boldsymbol{u}_i, \boldsymbol{v}_j$. Because we augment the tensor product with the inner product of local factors, the resulting model is called the locally augmented tensor model. The priors of the factors are specified as follows:

$$\alpha_{ik} \sim N(\boldsymbol{g}'_k\boldsymbol{x}_{ik} + q_k\alpha_i,\, \sigma^2_{\alpha,k}), \quad \alpha_i \sim N(0, 1), \tag{10.28}$$

$$\beta_{jk} \sim N(\boldsymbol{d}'_k\boldsymbol{x}_{jk} + r_k\beta_j,\, \sigma^2_{\beta,k}), \quad \beta_j \sim N(0, 1), \tag{10.29}$$

$$\boldsymbol{u}_{ik} \sim N(\boldsymbol{G}_k(\boldsymbol{x}_i),\, \sigma^2_{uk}\boldsymbol{I}), \quad \boldsymbol{v}_{jk} \sim N(\boldsymbol{D}_k(\boldsymbol{x}_j),\, \sigma^2_{vk}\boldsymbol{I}), \tag{10.30}$$

$$\boldsymbol{u}_i \sim N(\boldsymbol{0},\, \sigma^2_{u0}\boldsymbol{I}),\ \boldsymbol{v}_j \sim N(\boldsymbol{0},\, \sigma^2_{v0}\boldsymbol{I}),\ \boldsymbol{w}_k \sim N(\boldsymbol{0}, \boldsymbol{I}), \tag{10.31}$$

where $\boldsymbol{g}_k$, q_k, $\boldsymbol{d}_k$, r_k, $\boldsymbol{G}_k$, and $\boldsymbol{D}_k$ are regression coefficient vectors and regression functions. These regression coefficients and functions are to be learned from data and provide the ability to make predictions for users or items that do not appear in training data. The factors of these new users or items will be predicted based on their features through regression.

Model Fitting. The MCEM algorithm can be easily applied to fit the LAT model. All of the needed formulas are discussed in Sections 8.2, 10.1.2, and 10.2.2.

10.3 Multifaceted News Article Recommendation

Recommending links to news articles has become important to facilitating information discovery on the web. One of the most widely used indicators of user engagement with such recommender systems is the observed click-through rate or CTR, that is, the probability that the user will click a recommended article. It is customary to rank articles to optimize CTR (Das et al., 2007; Agarwal et al., 2008; Li et al., 2010). However, merely using CTR to rank news articles may not be sufficient because user interaction with online news is multifaceted. Users do not merely click on news links and read articles – as shown in Figure 10.1, they can share articles with friends, tweet about them, write and read comments, rate other users' comments, e-mail links to friends and themselves, print articles to read more meticulously offline, and so on. These different types of "post-read" actions are indicators of deeper user engagement and provide additional signals for tailoring recommendations. We will use *facet* and *post-read action type* interchangeably. For example, news articles can be ranked for individual facets based on the predicted action rates. We can also

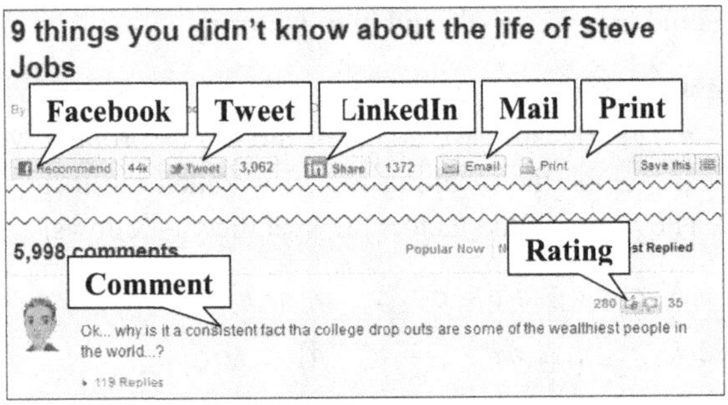

Figure 10.1. Illustration of post-read actions.

consider using combinations of CTR and post-read action rates to blend news articles to ensure the ranking can be potentially useful for users not only clicking on the articles but also sharing or commenting about them after reading.

In this section, we treat each facet (i.e., post-read action type) as a context and apply context-dependent models to this problem. We start with an exploratory analysis of this problem and then report an empirical comparison of different models.

10.3.1 Exploratory Data Analysis

We study post-read behavior based on data collected from U.S. Yahoo! News in early 2012 with several million user visits per month. Although this does not represent the entire news-reading population, it has a large enough market share to study online news consumption behavior in the United States. The site provides various functionalities for users to act on after reading an article. Figure 10.1 shows a portion of a typical news article page. On top are links or buttons that allow a user to share articles on various social media websites such as Facebook, Twitter, and LinkedIn. The user can also share the article with others or herself via e-mail or by printing a hard copy. At the bottom portion of the page, the user can leave comments on the article or rate other users, comments with a thumb-up or thumb-down.

In addition to links or buttons that facilitate post-read actions, most article pages on this site publish a module that recommends interesting article links to users. This module is an important way to generate pageviews on the site and hence tries to recommend article links that maximize overall click-through rates. A small portion of the user visits are shown a random list of articles, and the CTR estimated from this small portion of traffic is used for our analysis.

Source of Data. We collect two kinds of data: (1) all pageviews on the news site to study post-read actions (these page views are generated via clicks on links to news articles published by the site on the web) and (2) click logs from the module. To distinguish link views on the module from page views of news article pages after article links are clicked, we shall refer to the former as *linkview* and to the latter as *pageview*. The pre-read article click-through rate (CTR) is computed as the number of clicks divided by the number of linkviews on the module, and post-read Facebook share rate (FSR) is computed as the number of sharing actions divided by the number of pageviews. Post-read action rates of other types can be computed similarly; we focus on the following post-read actions: Facebook share, e-mail, print, comment, and rating.

Data Diversity. The data used in our analysis were collected over a period of several months in 2011. We selected articles that were shown on the module and were clicked at least once and that received at least one comment and one post-read action type out of Facebook share, e-mail, and print. This gives us approximately eight thousand articles, which were already classified into a hierarchical directory by the publishers. We use the top three levels of the hierarchy for our analysis. The first level of the hierarchy has seventeen categories; the distribution of article frequency in these categories is shown in Figure 10.2. As evident from this figure, news articles published on the site are diverse and provide a good source to study user interaction with online news. We also obtain user demographic information, which includes age, gender, and geolocation (identified through IP address). All user IDs are anonymized. We have hundreds of millions of pageview events in our data, which is sufficient for us to estimate the post-read action rates.

Pre-read versus Post-read. We investigate the relationship between pre-read (click) and post-read actions. For example, is a highly clicked article also highly shared or commented on by users? For each article, we compute the article's overall CTR on the module and post-read action rates of different types. In Figure 10.3, we show the correlation between clicks and other action types using Pearson's correlation (the first column or the last row). We observe very low correlation between click rates and other post-read action rates. We also computed the correlations after stratifying articles by categories and found that the correlations are still very low. This lack of correlation is perhaps not surprising: clicks are driven by a user's topical interest in certain articles versus others, whereas post-click behaviors are inherently conditioned on clicks and hence on topical interest. Ranking articles using CTR and other post-click indicators would perhaps lead to different rankings. For instance, if the goal of a news website is to maximize CTR but also ensure a certain minimum amount of tweeting and it is possible to predict articles that are more likely to be tweeted, the rankings could be altered based on CTR and tweeting rates to achieve such an objective.

Correlations among Post-read Actions. In Figure 10.3, we also show all pairwise Pearson's correlations among post-read action types, computed using article-level action rates. We observe positive correlations among various post-read action types; mail has high correlation with Facebook and print, but not with comment and rating. There are high correlations among Facebook, mail, and print. Not surprisingly, comment and rating are also highly correlated.

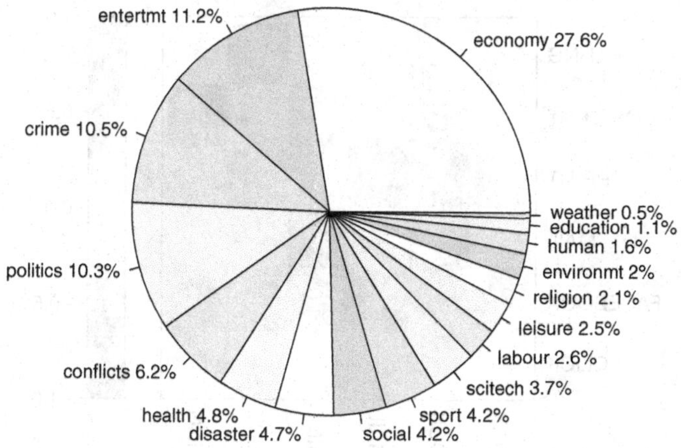

Abbreviation	Full name
economy	economy, business and finance
entertmt	arts, culture and entertainment
crime	crime, law and justice
conflicts	unrest, conflicts and war
disaster	disaster and accident
social	social issue
scitech	science and technology
leisure	lifestyle and leisure
religion	religion and belief
environmt	environmental issue
human	human interest

Figure 10.2. Distribution of news articles over categories.

These provide evidence of being able to leverage correlations among post-read action types to improve estimation.

A word of caution – correlations do not necessarily hold when the data are disaggregated at the (user, item) level because our data are observational and subject to various sources of bias. It is not possible to study correlations at the (user, item) level through exploratory analysis because of the lack of replicates.

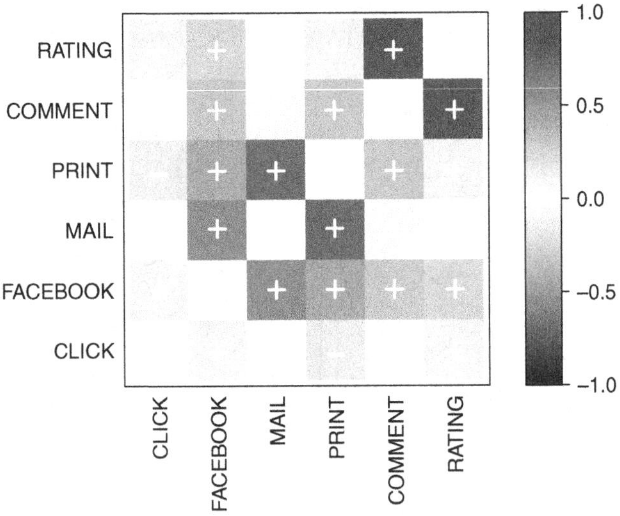

Figure 10.3. Correlation between different action types (diagonal cells are not of interest).

The exploratory analysis is shown to provide a flavor to our data and to gain some insights at an aggregate level.

Read versus Post-read: Private versus Public. We now compare users' reading behavior with their post-read behavior. Specifically, is post-read behavior uniform across different article types or user types? Does a typical young male from California comment and share most of the articles he reads?

To understand this, we use a vector of the fractions of pageviews in different article categories to represent the reading behavior. One can think of this vector as a multinomial probability distribution over categories, that is, the probability that a random pageview is in a given category. Similarly, marginal post-read behavior of an action type in a category is represented as a vector of fractions of post-read actions of that type in that category. To compare a post-read behavior vector with the reading behavior vector, we compute the element-wise ratio between the two vectors. Figure 10.4(a) shows these ratios on the log-scale using the top ten most viewed categories, where the categories are ordered according to the numbers of pageviews they received (highest on the left). All the sample sizes are sufficiently large (with at least tens of thousands of post-read actions) to ensure statistical significance. To help understand this plot, let us consider the negative value in the (mail, conflicts) cell. It indicates that a typical user is more likely to read an article about conflicts than e-mail it. In general, if post-read action behavior of users were the same as reading

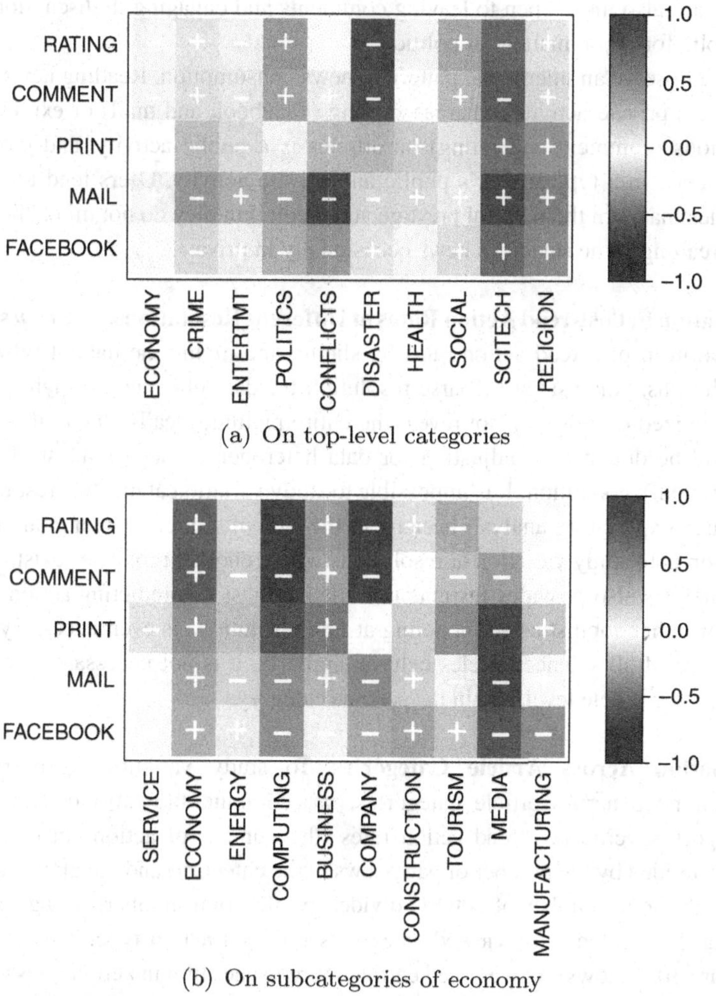

Figure 10.4. Difference between pageview and post-read actions. This also shows variations in post-read action rates of different types by article category.

behavior or uniform across news types, the ratios (on log-scale) should be clustered around zero. Obviously this is not the case for all action types, as we see both positive and negative cells in the plot.

Users are more likely to read articles about crime, politics, and conflicts than to share them with friends via e-mail or on Facebook; they are more likely to read about disaster and science and technology but are reluctant to comment on them. When it comes to science and religion, they are eager to share more.

They are also more open to leaving comments and engaging in discussions in a public forum on matters of politics.

We observe an interesting pattern in news consumption. Reading news articles is a private activity, whereas sharing (Facebook and mail) or expressing opinions (comment and rating) on articles is a public activity, and there is difference in a typical user's public and private activity. Users tend to share articles that earn them social prestige and credit, but they do not mind clicking and reading some salacious news occasionally in private.

Variation in Post-read Action Rates at Different Resolutions. We now study variation in post-read action rates by slicing and dicing the data at different resolutions. Analysis at a coarse resolution for data obtained through a non-randomized design may not reveal the entire picture; ideally, such inferences should be drawn after adjusting for data heterogeneity at the finest, that is, (user, item), resolution. It is impossible to study variation at this fine resolution through exploratory analysis because of the lack of replicates. Our goal in this section is to study variation at resolutions where enough replicates exist. Such an analysis also provides insights into the hardness of predicting action rates and whether sophisticated modeling at fine resolutions is even necessary. For instance, if all science articles behave similarly, it is not necessary to model data at the article level within the science category.

Variation Across Article Categories. To study variation in post-read action rates across article categories, we compute the ratio between the category-specific post-read action rates (the number of actions in the category divided by the number of pageviews in the category) and the global action rate (the total number of actions divided by the total number of pageviews) using the top ten most viewed categories for each action type. This is what Figure 10.4 shows. As we noted earlier, there is variation in action rates at this resolution, as is evident from the positive and negative cells.

Variation Across User Segments. We segment users by age and gender and show post-read action rates for the two genders across different age groups in Figure 10.5. Once again, we see variation. Facebook share rates are highest among young and middle-aged users. Users in older age groups tend to mail more, but young users tend to share more on Facebook and also print more. We see that women have surprisingly high share rates and that male users tend to comment more on articles. We also include pre-read click actions in this figure and observe that users in older age groups tend to click more; men across all age groups are more active clickers than women.

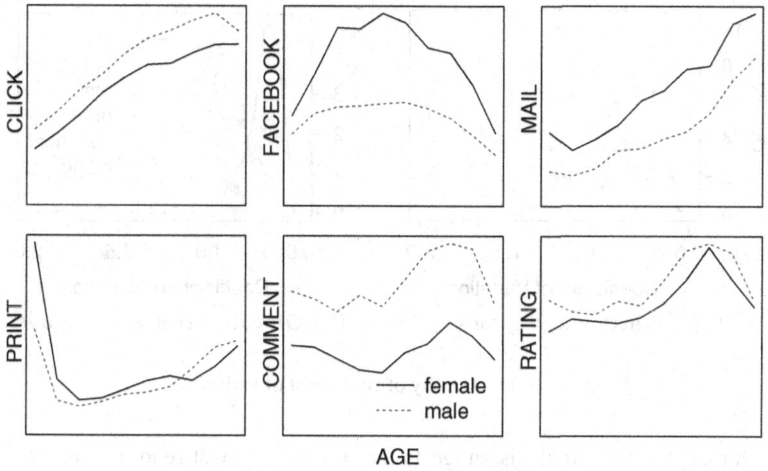

Figure 10.5. Post-read action rate variation over age-gender segments.

Variation within Categories and Segments. We now dig deeper and analyze variation at the article resolution after stratifying our data by article categories and user segments. High within-category or within-segment variations at the article level indicate excessive heterogeneity with categories and segments and suggest the need to model the rates at finer resolutions. To study such variation, we leverage the coefficient of variation σ/μ, where σ is the standard deviation of article action rates within a given category (or category $\times$ user segment); and μ is the average article action rate in the category (or category $\times$ user segment). σ/μ is a positive number, and smaller values indicate less variation. In general, values higher than 0.2 are indicative of high variation.

In Figure 10.6, we show the distribution of coefficient of variation with respect to article categories and the cross-product of categories with user age-gender. From these two figures, we can see that all post-read actions have much larger coefficients of variation than click. This means that although there is variation in average post-read behavior across categories and user segments, the variation at the article resolution within each such stratum is high, making it more difficult to predict article post-read action rates than to predict article click rates based on the category information. Comparing the two figures, we can see that adding user features helps little in terms of reducing coefficients of variation, indicating that stratification by user segments does not help in explaining article-level variation within each category. Perhaps users in a given (age, gender) segment have different news consumption behaviors at the article level.

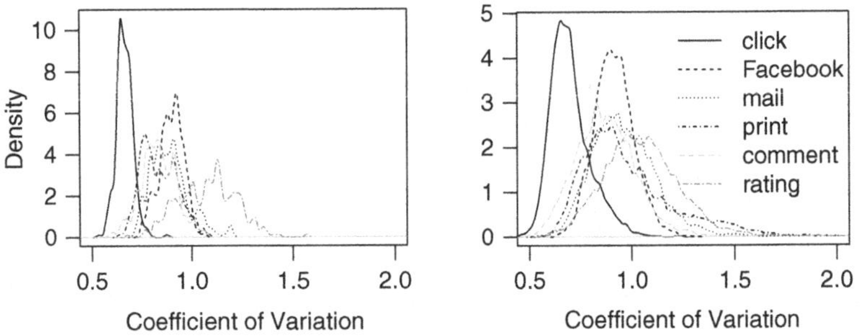

(a) On article categories (b) On categories × age-gender

Figure 10.6. Density of coefficient of variation.

Our exploratory analysis suggests that predicting post-read actions of any type is harder than estimating CTR. We see that although using features like article category and user demographics is useful, there is heterogeneity at the article and user resolution that has to be modeled. We also see evidence of positive correlations among post-read action types. The LAT model defined in Section 10.2.3 can use such correlations to improve prediction performance.

10.3.2 Empirical Evaluation

We evaluate the following models presented in Sections 10.2.1 and 10.2.3 using post-read data collected from U.S. Yahoo! News.

- *LAT:* Locally augmented tensor model (defined in Section 10.2.3), where context k corresponds to facet (i.e., post-read action type) k
- *BST:* Bias-smoothed tensor model (defined in Section 10.2.1), which is a special case of LAT
- *SMF:* Separate matrix factorization (defined in Section 10.2.3)
- *CMF:* Collapsed matrix factorization (defined in Section 10.2.3)
- *Bilinear:* This model uses the user features $\boldsymbol{x}_i$ and item features $\boldsymbol{x}_j$ to predict whether a user would take an action on an item. Specifically,

$$y_{ijk} \sim \boldsymbol{x}_i' W_k \boldsymbol{x}_j,$$

  where W_k is the regression coefficient matrix for facet k. This model has a regression coefficient for every pair of an individual user feature and an individual item feature, which is fitted using Liblinear (Fan et al., 2008) with L_2 regularization, where the regularization weight is selected using five-fold cross-validation.

We also compare these models to a set of baseline IR models. In all of the following IR models, we build a user profile based on the training data by aggregating all the text information of the items on which the user took positive actions. We treat such user profiles as queries and then use different retrieval functions to rank the items. The IR models include

- *COS:* Vector space model with cosine similarity
- *LM:* The Dirichlet smoothed language model (Zhai and Lafferty, 2001)
- *BM25:* The best variant of Okapi retrieval methods (Robertson et al., 1995)

For the factor models, the Gaussian version gives better performance on the tuning set than the logistic version, so we report the performance of the Gaussian version.

Data. We collected post-read actions from 13,739 users, each of whom has at least five actions for at least one facet, on 8,069 items, each of which received at least one action for each type of post-read action. As a result, we obtain 2,548,111 post-read action events, where each *event* is identified by (user, facet, item). If the user took an action on the item in the facet, the event is positive or *relevant* (meaning that the item is relevant to the user in the facet); if the user saw the item but did not take an action in the facet, the event is negative or *irrelevant*. In this setting, it is natural to treat each (user, facet) pair as a *query*; the set of events associated with that pair defines the set of items to be ranked with relevance judgments coming from user actions. It is difficult to use editorial judgments in our setting because different users have different preferences for their news consumption.

Evaluation Metrics. We use mean precision at k (P@k) and mean average precision (MAP) as our evaluation metrics, where mean is taken over the test (user, facet) pairs. P@k of a model is computed as follows: for each test (user, facet) pair, we use the model predictions to rank the items seen by the user in that facet and compute the precision at rank k, and then we average the precision numbers over all the test pairs. MAP is computed in a similar way. To help comparison among different models, we define *P@k Lift* and *MAP Lift* over SMF of a model as the lift in P@k and MAP of the model over the SMF model, which is a strong baseline. For example, if P@k of a model is A and P@k of SMF is B, then the lift is $\frac{A-B}{B}$.

Experimental Setup. We create a training set, a tuning set, and a test set as follows. For each user, we randomly select one facet in which the user took some action and put the events associated with this (user, facet) pair into set $\mathcal{A}$.

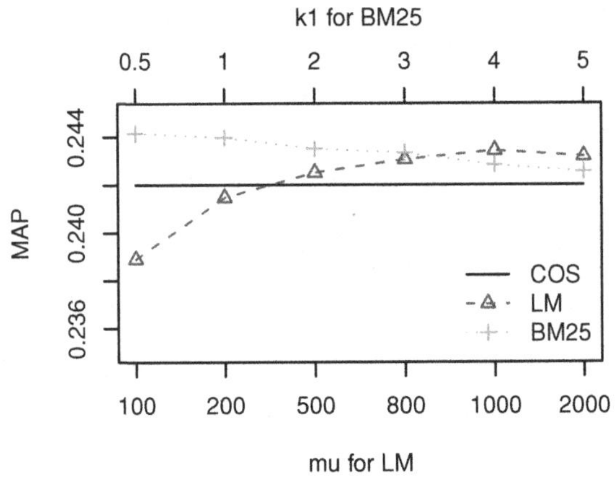

Figure 10.7. Performance of different IR models.

The rest of the (user, facet) pairs form the *training set*. We put one-third of set $\mathcal{A}$ into the *tuning set* and the remaining two-thirds into the *test set*. The tuning set is used to select the number of latent dimensions of the factor models (i.e., the numbers of dimensions of $\boldsymbol{u}_i$, $\boldsymbol{v}_j$, $\boldsymbol{w}_k$, $\boldsymbol{u}_{ik}$, $\boldsymbol{v}_{jk}$). The EM algorithm automatically determines all the model parameters, except for the number of latent dimensions. For each model, we only report the test-set performance of the best number of dimensions selected using the tuning set.

The user features used in our experiments are age, gender, and geolocation identified based on users' IP addresses. We only consider logged-in users; their user IDs are anonymized and not used in any way. The item features consist of article categories tagged by the publishers and the bag of words in the article titles and abstracts.

Performance of IR Models. We first compare the baseline IR models in Figure 10.7. In this figure, the parameter μ for LM and the parameter k_1 for BM25 vary. The other two parameters are set at the recommended default values $k_3 = 1000$ and $b = 0.75$ in all the experiments. We can see that both LM and BM25 can outperform COS, but the difference is not large. In the rest of this section, we use the BM25 with $k_1 = 1$ as the IR model to compare with other learning-based methods.

Overall Performance. The precision-recall curves averaged over all (user,facet) pairs in the test data of different models are shown in Figure 10.8(a), and P@1, P@3, P@5, and MAP are reported in Table 10.1. As k increases, the precision drops, because post-read actions are rare events; many users do not

Table 10.1. *Overall performance of different models*

	Precision			
Model	P@1	P@3	P@5	MAP
LAT	**0.3180**	**0.2853**	**0.2648**	**0.3048**
BST	0.2962	0.2654	0.2486	0.2873
SMF	0.2827	0.2639	0.2469	0.2910
Bilinear	0.2609	0.2472	0.2350	0.2755
CMF	0.2301	0.2101	0.2005	0.2439
BM25	0.2256	0.2247	0.2207	0.2440

have 3 or 5 post-read actions in the test set. For example, if a user only had one action and saw at least five items in the test set, his P@5 is at most 1/5. To test the significance of the performance difference between two models, we look at P@k and MAP for each individual (user, facet) pair and conduct a paired t-test for the two models over all test (user, facet) pairs. The test result is shown in Table 10.2. In particular, LAT significantly outperforms all other models. We find that the difference between BST and SMF and the difference between CMF and BM25 are insignificant.

Bilinear outperforms CMF because CMF completely ignores the behavioral differences among action types. The fact that Bilinear outperforms CMF shows that user and item features have some predictive power, but compared to SMF, these features are not sufficient to capture the behavior of individual users or

Table 10.2. *Paired* t-*test result*

Comparison	Significance level
LAT $>$ BST	0.05 (P@1), 10^{-4} (P@3, P@5, MAP)
LAT $>$ BST	10^{-4} (all metrics)
BST $\approx$ SMF	insignificant
BST $>$ Bilinear	10^{-3} (all metrics)
SMF $>$ Bilinear	0.05 (P@1), 10^{-3} (P@3, P@5, MAP)
BST $>$ CMF	10^{-4} (all metrics)
SMF $>$ BM25	10^{-4} (all metrics)
Bilinear $>$ CMF	10^{-3} (all metrics)
Bilinear $>$ BM25	10^{-3} (all metrics)
CMF $\approx$ BM25	insignificant

Note: Smaller level values represent stronger significance.

Table 10.3. *P@1 broken down by facet*

Model	Facet				
	Comment	Thumb	Facebook	Mail	Print
LAT	**0.3477**	**0.3966**	**0.2565**	0.2069	**0.2722**
BST	0.3310	0.3743	0.2457	0.1936	0.1772
SMF	0.2949	0.3408	0.2306	**0.2255**	0.2532
Bilinear	0.2837	0.2947	0.2328	**0.2255**	0.1709
CMF	0.2990	0.2905	0.1638	0.1114	0.1203
BM25	0.2726	0.3198	0.1509	0.1061	0.0886

Note: Boldface signifies the best performance among all models for each facet.

items. BM25 is one of the worst performing models probably because it is the only model without supervised learning.

Breakdown by Facets. In Table 10.3, we break the test data down by facets and report P@1 for different models; the results for other metrics are similar. Here we focus on the comparison between LAT, BST, and SMF. We see that BST outperforms SMF for the first three facets but underperforms for the last two facets. The first three facets have more events in our data set than the last two. The advantage of BST over SMF is that it has global factors; thus, the training actions in one facet are utilized to predict the test actions in other facets through the correlation among facets. However, BST is less flexible than SMF. In particular, it is not flexible enough to capture the differences among facets; thus, it is forced to fit some facets better than others. As expected, it fits the actions in facets with more data better than those with fewer data. LAT addresses this problem by adding facet-specific factors ($\boldsymbol{u}_{ik}$ and $\boldsymbol{v}_{jk}$) to model the residuals of BST. As can be seen, LAT uniformly outperforms BST. It also outperforms SMF, except for mail. The fact that SMF and Bilinear have the same performance for mail suggests the difficulty of using latent factors to improve accuracy. Because LAT has more factors than SMF, it has a higher chance of overfitting.

Breakdown by User Activity Level. In Figure 10.8, we break test users down by their activity levels in terms of the numbers of post-read actions that they took in the training data. Here our focus is also on comparing LAT and BST to SMF. Each curve represents the P@1 lift or MAP lift of each model over the SMF model as a function of the user activity level specified on the x-axis. LAT almost uniformly outperforms all other models. For users with low activity levels

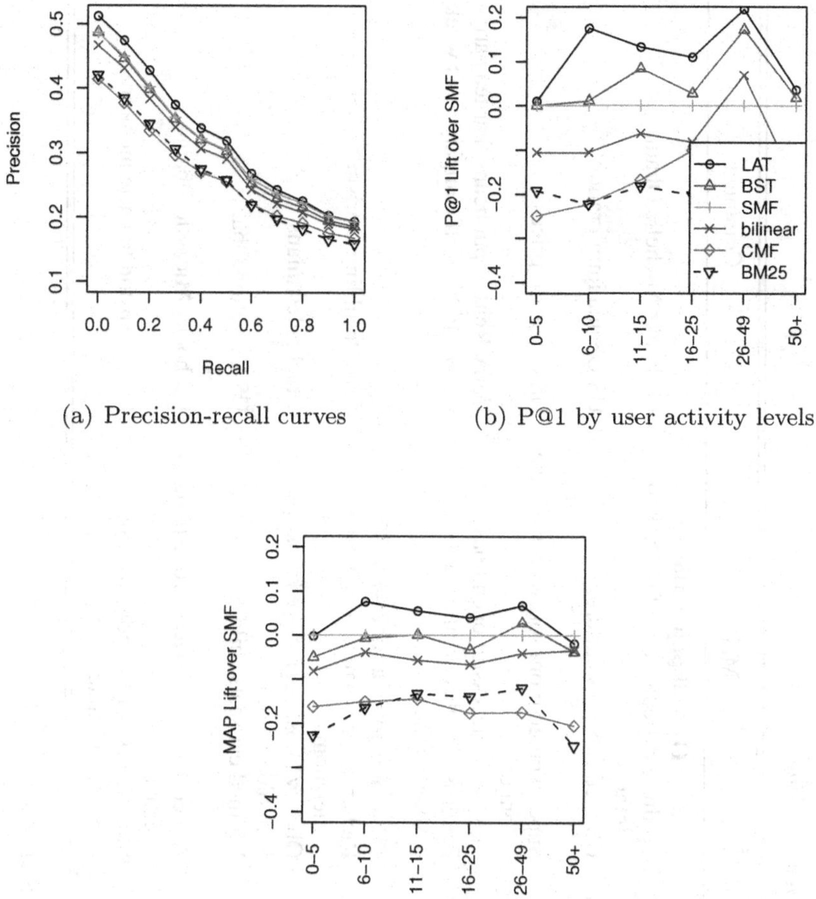

(a) Precision-recall curves (b) P@1 by user activity levels

(c) MAP by user activity levels

Figure 10.8. Performance of different models.

(0–5), there is almost no difference between LAT, BST, and SMF because they all lack data and the predictions are mostly based on features. We see the largest advantage of using LAT for users who took five to fifty post-read actions.

Perceived Differences Among Facets. In Table 10.4, we show some examples of the result of multifaceted news ranking. In the top half of the table, we show top-ranked articles for an average user. In the bottom half, we show top-ranked articles for men with ages between forty-one and forty-five years. We see that different facets have very different ranking results. For example, in the

Table 10.4. *Examples of multifaceted news ranking*

Facebook	Mail	Comment
	Overall population	
US weather tornado Japan disaster aid	Teething remedies pose fatal risk to infants	US books Michelle Obama
Eight ways monsanto is destroying our health	US med car seats children	US Obama immigration
Teething remedies pose fatal risk to infants	Super women mom soft wins may live longer	US exxon oil prices
New zombie ant fungi found	Tips for a successful open house	Harry Reid: republicans fear tea party
Indy voters would rather have Charlie Sheen . . .	Painless diabetes monitor talks to smartphone	Obama to kick off campaign this week
	For male at age 41 to 45	
Oxford English dictionary added new words	Richer white women more prone to melanoma	Israel troubling tourism
US exxon oil prices	Obesity boost aggressive breast cancer in older women	Israel palestinians
Children make parents happy eventually	US med car seats children	USA election Obama
Qatar Saudi politics Internet	Are coffee drinkers less prone to breast cancer	US books Michelle Obama
Lawmakers seek to outlaw prank calls	Short course of hormone therapy boosts prostate cancer	Levi Johnston to write memoir

Note: Only the titles of the news articles are shown.

Facebook and mail facets, many health-related articles are highly ranked. But for the comment facet, political articles are usually preferred. Furthermore, if we compare the men in their early forties with the overall population, we also see notable differences. For example, although both populations have health-related articles in the mail facet, men in their early forties tend to mail more cancer-related articles. These differences confirm the need for personalized multifacet ranking.

10.4 Related-Item Recommendation

One common type of recommendation with item k on the prime region of a web page is to recommend other items related to item k. For example, on a news site, when a user is reading an article k, it is useful to recommend other articles related (or similar) to article k. On an e-commerce site, when a user is viewing a product k, it is useful to recommend other products related to product k. We call article k and product k in these examples *context items* because they are the context on which the recommendations are dependent.

In related-item recommendation, given a user i and a context item k, we seek to recommend other items j that satisfy both of the following criteria:

- *Semantic relatedness*: The recommended items need to be related to the context item according to some application-dependent definition of relatedness.
- *High response rates*: We also want to make sure that the user is likely to respond to the recommended items positively (e.g., click on the recommended items).

In this section, we first introduce how to measure relatedness between items, then we describe how to predict response rates, and, we discuss how to combine the two criteria to produce the final recommendations.

10.4.1 Semantic Relatedness

The definition of relatedness usually depends on the application. For example, related articles or products can be "similar" articles or products, where similarity could be measured using the cosine similarity (see Section 2.3.1) between the bag-of-words representation (see Section 2.1.2) of two articles or products. In some cases, we do not want to recommend related items that are too similar to the context item; very similar items provide very little additional information. Related articles can be defined as articles that are on the same topic but that are not too similar to the context article. There are various ways to classify articles into topics and to define similarity. Topics can be discovered using the LDA model (see Section 2.1.3), and similarity can be measured using cosine between the bags of words of two articles.

In general, it is difficult to define a relatedness function without having examples of related items, which may depend on the application. Given examples of related items and unrelated items for an application, we can apply any supervised learning method to learn the relatedness function. Let $\boldsymbol{x}_j$ and $\boldsymbol{x}_k$ denote the feature vectors of item j and item k and $\boldsymbol{x}_{jk}$ denote a vector of different measures of the relationship (e.g., similarity) between item j and item k. One model is to predict the probability that item j is related to item k using $\boldsymbol{x}_j' \boldsymbol{A} \boldsymbol{x}_k + \boldsymbol{x}_{jk}' \boldsymbol{b}$ based on logistic regression, where $\boldsymbol{A}$ is a matrix of regression coefficients and $\boldsymbol{b}$ is a vector of regression coefficients (see Section 2.3.2 on how to fit such a model). We call the output from a model that quantifies the propensity that item j is related to item k the *relatedness score* from j to k, which may or may not be symmetric, depending on the application requirements.

10.4.2 Response Prediction

When we recommend related items, it is important to make sure that users would like to respond to them positively by clicking, sharing, liking, giving high ratings and so on. In some applications, related items are recommended solely based on predicted response without using semantic relatedness scores. One example commonly seen on online shopping websites has the following form: people who bought item k also buy item j. This kind of recommendation is usually based on the probability that a user would buy j given that she just bought k; that is, Pr(a user buys j | the user bought k), where item k is the context item. This probability can be estimated by the number of users who bought both items j and k divided by the number of users who bought item k. If the denominator is large, this conditional probability can be estimated accurately. However, for items that have not been bought many times, accurate probability estimation is difficult. Furthermore, if we want to personalize related-item recommendation, we need to add the user i into the conditioning and estimate Pr(buying item j | bought item k, user i). The data become sparser and the counting-based estimation usually does not work.

To predict the response y_{ijk} that user i would give item j given the context item k, we can use the tensor factorization models introduced in Section 10.1 and hierarchical shrinkage models introduced in Section 10.2. Because the total number of context items is large, tensor factorization models are usually better suited for related-item recommendation. Hierarchical shrinkage models (e.g., the BST model) are usually better suited for recommender problems with a relatively small number of contexts because the memory required to store α_{ik} and β_{jk} is $MK + NK$, where M is the number of users, N is the number of items, and K is the number of contexts. $MK + NK$ is usually too large for related-item recommendation because the number of contexts is the number of items; that is, $K = N$.

10.4.3 Combining Predicted Response and Relatedness

After building a model to predict how user i will respond to item j given the context item k and a model to predict the relatedness score from item j to item k, we can generate the final recommendations using one of the following strategies.

1. Rank items based on a weighted sum of the predicted response and the relatedness score.
2. Rank items based on relatedness scores for items with predicted response higher than a threshold.
3. Rank items based on predicted response for items with relatedness scores higher than a threshold.

We usually prefer strategy 3 because, in many related-item recommendation applications, it is usually unacceptable to recommend items that are not semantically related to the context item; that is, the relatedness scores for recommended items must be higher than some threshold. Then, it is natural to rank related items according to predicted response to maximize users' positive response.

10.5 Summary

In this chapter, we discussed how to make recommendations to a user in a given context. We introduced two classes of models to predict the user's response, tensor factorization models and hierarchical models, which can also be mixed together to further improve predictive power. Tensor factorization addresses data sparsity in the three-dimensional space of users, items, and contexts through a low-rank decomposition, which approximates this three-dimensional tensor by the products of low-rank matrices of user latent factors, item latent factors, and context latent factors. Hierarchical shrinkage addresses data sparsity through hierarchical priors that shrink context-specific user and item factors (e.g., α_{ik} and β_{jk} in Equation (10.11)) toward global user and item factors (e.g., α_i and β_j that do not depend on context k). Context-specific factors (e.g., α_{ik}) give a model more capacity to accurately model context-specific behavior than low-rank factorization (e.g., $\langle \boldsymbol{u}_i, \boldsymbol{w}_k \rangle$, where the number of dimensions of $\boldsymbol{u}_i$ and $\boldsymbol{w}_k$ is much small than the number of contexts). However, this capacity comes with a much larger number of parameters to be fitted than does factorization (e.g., the total number of α_{ik}s is the number of users times the number of contexts) when the number of contexts is large. Thus, for applications with a large number of contexts (e.g., related-item recommendation), tensor factorization is usually used.

Related-item recommendation usually has two criteria: the recommended items need to be semantically related to the context item and also must have high response rates. If the two criteria are highly correlated, then we can choose to focus on any single criterion and the other will automatically be satisfied. Otherwise, we need to make a trade-off because we cannot achieve both maximal relatedness and maximal response at the same time. This relatedness-response trade-off is an example of multiobjective trade-off. How to optimize multiple objectives is a topic we discuss in Chapter 11.

11
Multiobjective Optimization

The approaches that we discussed in previous chapters typically recommend items to optimize for a single objective, usually clicks on recommended items. However, a click is only the starting point of a user's journey, and subsequent downstream utilities, such as time spent on the website after the click and revenue generated through displaying advertisements on web pages, are also important. Here clicks, time spent, and revenue are three different objectives for which a website may want to optimize. When different objectives have strong positive correlation, maximizing one would automatically maximize others. In reality, this is not a typical scenario. For example, the advertisements on real estate articles tend to generate higher revenue than those on entertainment articles, but users usually click more and spend more time on entertainment articles. In situations like this, it is not feasible to reach optimality for all objectives. The goal, instead, is to find a good trade-off among competing objectives. For example, we maximize revenue such that clicks and time spent are still within 95 percent of the achievable number of clicks and 90 percent of the achievable time spent relative to some normative serving scheme (e.g., CTR maximization). How to set the constraints (the 95 percent and 90 percent thresholds) depends on the business goals and strategies of the website and is application specific. This chapter provides a methodology based on multiobjective programming to optimize a recommender system for a given set of predetermined constraints. Such a formulation can easily incorporate various application-driven requirements.

We present two approaches to multiobjective optimization. Section 11.2 describes a *segmented approach* (originally published in Agarwal et al., 2011a), where users are classified into user segments in a way similar to segmented postpopular recommendation (discussed in Sections 3.3.2 and 6.5.3) and the optimization is at the segment level. Although useful, this segmented approach assumes that users are partitioned into a few coarse, nonoverlapping segments.

In many applications, a user is characterized by a high-dimensional feature vector (thousands of dimensions with large number of all possible combinations) – the segmented approach fails to provide recommendations at such granular resolutions because decisions are made at coarse user-segment resolutions. Section 11.3 describes a *personalized approach* (originally published in Agarwal et al., 2012) that improves the segmented approach by optimizing the objectives at the individual-user level. The challenges of the personalized approach are solved through Lagrangian duality in Section 11.3 and approximation methods in Section 11.4. Then, in Section 11.5, we demonstrate multiobjective optimization using the Yahoo! front page data. The experimental results show interesting characteristics of different formulations, and the findings may provide valuable guidance in designing of recommender systems for web portals.

11.1 Application Setting

We consider a content recommendation module on the front page of a portal, such as Yahoo!, that has several *properties* (e.g., Yahoo! News, Finance, Sports). The goal is to simultaneously optimize for user engagement with the module and the objectives of each property (e.g., advertising revenue and time spent in the property). Extension to other problem settings is straightforward, as long as the objectives can be formulated as weighted sums of the decision variables, that is, the problem can be still be represented as a linear program.

We bucketize time into epochs. In each epoch t, there is a set of candidate items available for recommendation, denoted by $\mathcal{A}_t$. Each item $j \in \mathcal{A}_t$ belongs to one of K different properties of the portal. Let $\mathcal{P} = \{P_1, \ldots, P_K\}$ denote the set of properties and $j \in P_k$ means the landing page of item j belongs to property P_k; that is, a click on item j leads the user to a web page in property P_k. Let $\mathcal{U}_t$ denote the set of all users in epoch t. A user $u \in \mathcal{U}_t$ visits the front page and is recommended an item from $\mathcal{A}_t$. For simplicity, we only consider the problem of recommending a single item for each user visit. When the user clicks the recommended item, the system routes him to a web page in the property to which the clicked item belongs. User visits to different properties are usually significantly influenced by the clicks on the front page. For the sake of illustration, consider that the portal wants to optimize for two different objectives: (1) total number of clicks on the front page and (2) total time spent in landing properties by users who click recommended items on the front page. As discussed in Section 11.2.2, other objectives, such as revenue, can be easily incorporated into this framework, and the properties $(P_1, \ldots, P_K)$ can be replaced by arbitrary categories of items on which one may want to define constraints.

Content recommendation is an explore-exploit problem. To optimize for any metric (that measures an objective), we need to estimate the performance of each candidate item in terms of that metric. Without displaying an item to any user, it is difficult to know the performance of that item. The explore-exploit problem for a single objective is well studied (see Chapter 6 and Section 7.3.3). Developing explore-exploit methods for multiple objectives that ensure a certain notion of optimality is an open problem. Here we assume that some explore-exploit scheme is running in the system. We use a simple ϵ-greedy scheme, which has been empirically shown to achieve good performance (Vermorel and Mohri, 2005). This scheme works as follows: we serve a small fraction of randomly selected user visits (called the exploration population) with items selected uniformly at random from the current content pool to collect data for every item. For the remaining visits (called the exploitation population), we serve the item with the highest estimated click-through rate (CTR) if the goal is to maximize clicks. With multiple objectives, the serving scheme for the exploitation population is different from that of displaying the highest CTR item.

11.2 Segmented Approach

In this section, we describe the problem setting of segmented multiobjective optimization. At any point in time, the system makes a serving plan for the next serving epoch (e.g., five-minute intervals): for each user segment i and each candidate item j, allocate a certain fraction x_{ij} of user visits in that segment to that item in a way that maximizes one particular objective under the constraint that the drops in other objectives are bounded. When the objectives can be computed as a weighted sum of the *decision variables* x_{ij}, the multiobjective problem can be represented as a linear program (LP) in a straightforward manner and solved by using a standard LP solver.

11.2.1 Problem Setup

Segmented Models. In the segmented approach, users are partitioned into m segments. Let $\mathcal{S}$ denote the set of segments and $i \in \mathcal{S}$ denote a segment in the rest of the chapter. To measure the utility of an item j, statistical models are used to estimate (1) the probability p_{ijt} that a user in segment i would click item j when it is displayed in epoch t and (2) the time d_{ijt} that a user in segment i would spend postclick in the landing property of item j. We call p_{ijt} CTR and d_{ijt} *time spent*, which can be estimated using Gamma-Poisson models as described in Section 6.3. If the goal is to maximize clicks (or time spent, but not both), the optimal solution is to recommend the item j with the highest p_{ijt} (or $p_{ijt} \cdot d_{ijt}$) to users in segment i.

Segmented Serving Scheme. We call an algorithm that recommends items to users a *serving scheme*. For each epoch t, a segmented serving scheme uses information obtained before the epoch to produce a *segmented serving plan* $\mathbf{x}_t = \{x_{ijt} : i \in \mathcal{S}, j \in \mathcal{A}_t\}$, where x_{ijt} is the probability that the serving scheme will recommend item j to users in segment i in epoch t. When a user visits the front page in epoch t, she is first assigned to an appropriate segment, and then an item is served through a multinomial draw according to $\{x_{ijt} : j \in \mathcal{A}_t\}$. It should be clear that $x_{ijt} \geq 0$ and $\sum_j x_{ijt} = 1$. Different optimization methods generate different serving plans according to different criteria. For example, the click maximization method would set x_{ij^*t} to 1 if j^* has the highest CTR item, and to 0 for the remaining items. Note that the serving plan for epoch t is made before epoch t, that is, in epoch $t-1$.

11.2.2 Objective Optimization

Objectives. For simplicity, we consider two objectives, number of clicks and time spent. Let N_t denote the total number of visits during epoch t, and let $\boldsymbol{\pi}_t = (\pi_{1t}, \ldots, \pi_{mt})$ denote the fraction of visits in different user segments. Obviously, $\sum_{i \in \mathcal{S}} \pi_{it} = 1$, and $N_t \pi_{it}$ is the total number of visits of segment i. Usually, $\boldsymbol{\pi}_t$ can be estimated based on past user visits (Agarwal et al., 2011a). For succinctness, we drop subscript t because we always consider the current epoch t. Given serving plan $\mathbf{x} = \{x_{ij}\}$ for the current epoch, the two objectives are as follows:

- the expected total number of clicks on the front page:

$$TotalClicks(\mathbf{x}) = N \sum_{i \in \mathcal{S}} \sum_{j \in \mathcal{A}} \pi_i x_{ij} p_{ij} \tag{11.1}$$

- the expected total time spent on property P_k:

$$TotalTime(\mathbf{x}, P_k) = N \sum_{i \in \mathcal{S}} \sum_{j \in P_k} \pi_i x_{ij} p_{ij} d_{ij} \tag{11.2}$$

We use $TotalTime(\mathbf{x}) = TotalTime(\mathbf{x}, \mathcal{A})$ to denote the total time spent on all properties.

Other Objectives. Although only time spent is used to illustrate multiobjective optimization, we show that a few other common objectives can be easily defined (and thus added into the linear program) in a way similar to time spent:

- The expected total revenue on property P_k is defined as

$$\mathit{TotalRevenue}(\mathbf{x}, P_k) = N \sum_{i \in \mathcal{S}} \sum_{j \in P_k} \pi_i x_{ij} p_{ij} r_{ij}, \tag{11.3}$$

  where r_{ij} is the expected (predicted) revenue of a click on item j for a user in segment i. If item j is a sponsored item or an advertisement, it generates direct revenue. Otherwise, revenue may be generated by the ads displayed on the destination page of item j.
- The expected total pageviews on property P_k is defined as

$$\mathit{TotalPageView}(\mathbf{x}, P_k) = N \sum_{i \in \mathcal{S}} \sum_{j \in P_k} \pi_i x_{ij} p_{ij} v_{ij}, \tag{11.4}$$

  where v_{ij} is the expected (predicted) number of pageviews in the property to which item j belongs after a user in segment i clicks item j. Notice that $v_{ij} \geq 1$ because the click on item j already generates one pageview.

Click Maximization Scheme. One baseline method is to solely optimize the total number of clicks, which we call the *status-quo algorithm*, because, before considering multiple objectives, we usually seek to maximize clicks. We obtain the serving plan $\mathbf{z} = \{z_{ij}\}$ as follows:

$$z_{ij} = \begin{cases} 1 \text{ when } j = \arg\max_{j'} p_{ij'} \\ 0 \text{ otherwise.} \end{cases} \tag{11.5}$$

We use $\mathit{TotalClicks}^* = \mathit{TotalClicks}(\mathbf{z})$ and $\mathit{TotalTime}^*(P_k) = \mathit{TotalTime}(\mathbf{z}, P_k)$ to denote the values of the two objectives for the click maximization scheme; by the definition of $\mathbf{z}$, they are constants.

Scalarization. One simple method for combining the two objectives is to define a weighted sum of the two as the new objective to be optimized. To construct the serving plan, we find the $\mathbf{x}$ that maximizes

$$\lambda \cdot \mathit{TotalClicks}(\mathbf{x}) + (1 - \lambda) \cdot \mathit{TotalTime}(\mathbf{x}),$$

where $\lambda \in [0, 1]$ represents the trade-off between total clicks and total time spent; with a smaller λ, we allow more loss in clicks to obtain higher total time spent. The solution is given by

$$x_{ij} = \begin{cases} 1, \text{ if } j = \arg\max_J \lambda \cdot p_{iJ} + (1 - \lambda) \cdot p_{iJ} d_{iJ} \\ 0, \text{ otherwise.} \end{cases} \tag{11.6}$$

The trade-off between objectives for a constant λ may vary significantly across epochs. In fact, in some epochs, the loss in clicks could be significant, and this may be a problem for some applications. However, the ability to lose a significant number of clicks in some epochs to obtain substantial gains in engagement may lead to better results over a long time horizon. This approach is attractive when the website owner is interested in a weighted combination of multiple objectives and it does not hurt if any one of them deteriorates significantly. Because the objectives are both linear, one drawback of this approach is the inability to explore all possible points on the Pareto optimal curve (see Chapter 7 of Boyd and Vandenberghe, 2004); it may miss out on some interesting solutions. Another drawback of this method is that it is not easy to introduce application-driven business constraints.

Linear Program. A variety of multiobjective programs (MOP) are introduced in Agarwal et al. (2011a). Here we only discuss the most flexible formulation, the *localized multiobjective program* (ℓ-MOP). Formally, the optimization problem is

$$\begin{aligned} &\max_{\mathbf{x}} \; \mathit{TotalTime}(\mathbf{x}) \\ &\quad \text{s.t. } \mathit{TotalClicks}(\mathbf{x}) \geq \alpha \cdot \mathit{TotalClicks}^* \\ &\quad\quad \mathit{TotalTime}(\mathbf{x}, P_k) \geq \beta \cdot \mathit{TotalTime}^*(P_k), \; \forall P_k \in \mathcal{P}^*, \end{aligned} \tag{11.7}$$

where $\mathcal{P}^*$ is a subset of $\mathcal{P}$, for which we want to ensure a certain level of time spent. This linear program seeks to maximize the total time spent on all properties such that the potential loss in the total number of clicks is bounded by α ($0 \leq \alpha \leq 1$) compared to the status quo click maximization scheme. For each of the key properties $P_k \in \mathcal{P}^*$, the total time spent on P_k is guaranteed to be at least β ($0 \leq \beta \leq 1$) times that of the click maximization scheme. This linear program can be easily solved by standard LP solvers.

Any linear constraint can be added to the linear program. Linear Program (11.7) is useful in our application setting and serves as a running example for illustration purposes. In every epoch, we use statistical models to predict p_{ij}, d_{ij}, and π_i and then solve the linear program to obtain the serving plan $\mathbf{x}$ for the next epoch. Thus, user visits in the next epoch will be served according to the plan made before we actually see the users.

It is straightforward to add other objectives. For example, we can replace *TotalTime*($\mathbf{x}$) by *TotalRevenue*($\mathbf{x}$) or *TotalPageView*($\mathbf{x}$). We can also add more constraints into Linear Program (11.7), such as

$$\begin{aligned} &\mathit{TotalRevenue}(\mathbf{x}, P_k) \geq \gamma \cdot \mathit{TotalRevenue}^*(P_k), \; \forall P_k \in \mathcal{P}^* \\ &\mathit{TotalPageView}(\mathbf{x}, P_k) \geq \delta \cdot \mathit{TotalPageView}^*(P_k), \; \forall P_k \in \mathcal{P}^*. \end{aligned} \tag{11.8}$$

11.3 Personalized Approach

Linear programs can be effectively used to perform segmented multiobjective optimization. However, such a segmented serving scheme treats all the users in a segment in the same way – it lacks the ability of serving each individual user differently to satisfy his unique personal information need. In this section, we extend the segmented approach to provide personalized serving plans for individual users.

Optimization at the individual-user level is challenging. A naive extension of the segmented approach by using one variable x_{uj} for each (user u, item j) pair in the LP is infeasible because (1) this makes the LP ill-defined in the online setting because there are *unseen* users that are observed for the first time in the *next* epoch, and so the "personalized LP" has to predict the set of unseen users and include corresponding user variables to serve them in the next epoch, and (2) even if we can accurately predict which users will be seen in the next epoch, such an extension increases the size of the LP dramatically because there can be hundreds of thousands of users per epoch.

11.3.1 Primal Formulation

We define the *primal* formulation of personalized multiobjective optimization by extending the segment-based Linear Program (11.7) through redefining the form of serving plan **x**.

Personalized Serving Plan. In personalized multiobjective optimization, we have a user-specific serving plan for each user u, instead of segment-specific ones. The personalized serving plan is defined as $\mathbf{x} = \{x_{uj} : u \in \mathcal{U}, j \in \mathcal{A}\}$, where x_{uj} is the probability that user u will be served with item j in the next epoch. Because the x_{uj}s are probabilities, we have $x_{uj} \geq 0$ and $\sum_j x_{uj} = 1$. A personalized serving scheme serves items to each individual user according to these probabilities.

Objectives. Because the form of serving plan **x** changed, the definitions of *TotalClicks*(**x**) and *TotalTime*(**x**, P_k) also need to be updated:

$$\begin{aligned} \mathit{TotalClicks}(\mathbf{x}) &= \sum_{u \in \mathcal{U}} \sum_{j \in \mathcal{A}} x_{uj} p_{uj} \\ \mathit{TotalTime}(\mathbf{x}, P_k) &= \sum_{u \in \mathcal{U}} \sum_{j \in P_k} x_{uj} p_{uj} d_{uj}, \end{aligned} \tag{11.9}$$

where p_{uj} is the predicted probability that user u would click item j and d_{uj} is the predicted length of time that user u would spend on pages in the landing property of item j after he clicks the item. Both the prediction of p_{uj} and the prediction of d_{uj} are orthogonal to our problem formulation, and any personalized statistical model, such as the online regression proposed in previous work (see Section 7.3 or Agarwal et al., 2008, 2009), can be plugged in. Given predicted CTR p_{uj}, we can compute the click optimization serving scheme similarly to Equation (11.5) and define the status quo constants $TotalClicks^*$ and $TotalTime^*$ for personalized serving accordingly.

Personalized serving plans are more flexible than segmented ones and include segmented ones as special cases. If we instantiate p_{uj} and d_{uj} using a segment-based model (i.e., $p_{uj} = p_{ij}$ and $d_{uj} = d_{ij}$ for all u in segment i), Equation (11.9) will reduce to Equation (11.1) and Equation (11.2).

Challenges. With these new definitions of $\mathbf{x}$, *TotalClicks* and *TotalTime*, it seems that Linear Program (11.7) can be trivially applied to personalized multiobjective optimization: We could solve this linear program in each epoch and use the solution to serve users in the next epoch. However, solving such a formulation is challenging for the following reasons:

- *Unseen users*: In the linear program, the variables x_{uj} are defined for every user u who will visit the web portal in the *next* epoch. For those users who have not visited the portal before, computing x_{uj} is challenging. Although it is usually easy to estimate the number of users (which determines the number of variables), the linear program input parameters p_{uj} and d_{uj} are difficult to predict for unseen users but must be determined for all users before solving the linear program.
- *Scalability*: The linear program requires a set of variables $\{x_{uj}\}_{\forall j \in \mathcal{A}}$ for each user u. Even if we know p_{uj} and d_{uj} for all the users in the next epoch, when the number of users is large (e.g., millions), the large number of variables results in a very large linear program and thus causes scalability issues.

Key Idea. To tackle these challenges, we exploit the Lagrangian duality formulation of our constrained optimization problem. In the primal program of Linear Program (11.7), x_{uj}s are the primal variables. Although we have a large number of *user-specific* primal variables, there are only a small number of nontrivial constraints in the primal formulation. Our key idea is to explore Lagrangian duality to capture the primal variables by using a small number of *user-independent* dual variables, one per constraint in the primal program. Now, suppose that we can efficiently compute the optimal dual solution for the next epoch (which is discussed in Section 11.4). Also, suppose that in the next epoch, we can efficiently convert the dual solution on the fly to the primal solution (i.e., serving plan) for each individual user at serving time. Then, the challenges are solved.

Unfortunately, linear programs do not allow easy conversion from dual solutions to primal solutions, and vice versa, because the derivatives of the Lagrangian vanish (Boyd and Vandenberghe, 2004). To ensure convertibility, we slightly modify the originally linear objective function so that it becomes strongly convex. Let $\mathbf{q} = \{q_{uj} : u \in \mathcal{U}, j \in \mathcal{A}\}$ denote some baseline serving plan. We add terms to the objective function to penalize serving plans $\mathbf{x}$ that are far away from $\mathbf{q}$. There are a few choices for the baseline $\mathbf{q}$. One is the click maximization plan $\mathbf{z}$. Another is the uniform serving plan $q_{uj} = 1/|\mathcal{A}|$, which will encourage some notion of "fairness" among items. These penalty terms can be the L2 norm or KL divergence. Here we choose the L2 norm penalty term and the uniform serving plan $\mathbf{q}$:

$$||\mathbf{x} - \mathbf{q}||^2 = \sum_{u \in \mathcal{U}} \sum_{j \in \mathcal{A}} (x_{uj} - q_{uj})^2.$$

Revised Primal Program. After adding the penalty term, we obtain the revised primal program:

$$\begin{aligned} &\min\nolimits_{\mathbf{x}} \ \frac{1}{2}\gamma||\mathbf{x} - \mathbf{q}||^2 - \mathit{TotalTime}(\mathbf{x}) \\ &\quad \text{s.t. } \mathit{TotalClicks}(\mathbf{x}) \geq \alpha \cdot \mathit{TotalClicks}^* \\ &\quad \mathit{TotalTime}(\mathbf{x}, P_k) \geq \beta \cdot \mathit{TotalTime}^*(P_k), \ \forall P_k \in \mathcal{P}^*, \end{aligned} \tag{11.10}$$

where γ specifies the importance of the penalty. Such a modification is generic because it can be applied to any linear-program-based multiobjective optimization. Notice that we also change from maximization to its equivalent minimization to put the primal program in the standard form of quadratic programming problem. In some sense, the added penalty term serves as regularization and can potentially reduce the variance of the solution.

11.3.2 Lagrangian Duality

We now introduce the dual variables and an algorithm to efficiently convert a dual solution to its corresponding primal solution. Let

$$g_0 = \alpha \cdot \mathit{TotalClicks}^* \ \text{ and } \ g_k = \beta \cdot \mathit{TotalTime}^*(P_k).$$

The Lagrangian function of the primal program is

$$\begin{aligned}\Lambda(\mathbf{x}, \boldsymbol{\mu}, \boldsymbol{\nu}, \boldsymbol{\delta}) = &\tfrac{1}{2}\gamma \textstyle\sum_u \sum_j (x_{uj} - q_{uj})^2 - \sum_u \sum_j p_{uj} d_{uj} x_{uj} \\ &- \mu_0 (\textstyle\sum_u \sum_j p_{uj} x_{uj} - g_0) \\ &- \textstyle\sum_{k \in \mathcal{I}} \mu_k (\sum_u \sum_{j \in P_k} p_{uj} d_{uj} x_{uj} - g_k) \\ &- \textstyle\sum_u \nu_u (\sum_j x_{uj} - 1) - \sum_u \sum_j \delta_{uj} x_{uj},\end{aligned}$$

where $\mu_0 \geq 0$, $\mu_k \geq 0$, for all $k \in \mathcal{I}$ and $\delta_{uj} \geq 0$, for all u and j. This is obtained by expanding *TotalTime* and *TotalClick* according to Equation (11.9) and applying the Lagrange multipliers μ_0 to ensure the total click constraint, μ_k to ensure the per-property total time constraint, ν_u to ensure $\sum_j x_{uj} = 1$, and δ_{uj} to ensure $x_{uj} \geq 0$. Note that μ_0, μ_k, ν_u, and δ_{uj} are also called the *dual variables*.

By setting $\frac{\partial}{\partial x_{uj}} \Lambda(\mathbf{x}, \boldsymbol{\mu}, \boldsymbol{\nu}, \boldsymbol{\delta}) = 0$, we obtain

$$x_{uj} = \frac{c_{uj} + \nu_u + \delta_{uj}}{\gamma}, \tag{11.11}$$

where

$$c_{uj} = p_{uj} d_{uj} + \mu_0 p_{uj} + \mathbf{1}\{j \in P_k \wedge k \in \mathcal{I}\}\, \mu_k p_{uj} d_{uj} + \gamma q_{uj}. \tag{11.12}$$

Note that $\mathbf{1}\{\text{True}\} = 1$ and $\mathbf{1}\{\text{False}\} = 0$. Thus, if we have the dual solution for μ_0, μ_k, ν_u, and δ_{uj}, we can reconstruct the primal solution x_{uj}. However, this does not help to solve the challenges, because ν_u and δ_{uj} still depend on the user's u in the next epoch. In the following, we provide an efficient algorithm that reconstructs x_{uj} from $\boldsymbol{\mu} = \{\mu_0, \mu_k\}_{\forall P_k \in \mathcal{P}^*}$ alone, without the need for ν_u and δ_{uj}.

Dual Serving Plan. We call $\boldsymbol{\mu}$ the *dual serving plan*, which does not include any user-specific variables. The algorithm that converts a dual plan to its corresponding primal serving plan is based on the following proposition.

Proposition 11.1. *In the optimal solution, given user u and two items j_1 and j_2, if $c_{uj_1} \geq c_{uj_2}$ and $x_{uj_2} > 0$, then $x_{uj_1} > 0$.*

Proof sketch: According to the Karush-Kuhn-Tucker (KKT) conditions (for details, see Boyd and Vandenberghe, 2004), at the optimum point, $\delta_{uj_2} = 0$ because $x_{uj_2} > 0$. Then, because $c_{uj_1} \geq c_{uj_2}$ and $\delta_{uj_1} \geq 0$, we have

$$x_{uj_1} = \frac{c_{uj_1} + \nu_u + \delta_{uj_1}}{\gamma} \geq \frac{c_{uj_2} + \nu_u}{\gamma} = x_{uj_2} > 0. \qquad \square$$

Without loss of generality, for each user u, we reindex items such that $c_{u1} \geq c_{u2} \cdots \geq c_{un}$, where n is the number of items. Notice that this ordering is user-specific. Based on Proposition 11.1, there exists a number $1 \leq t \leq n$ such that, in the optimal solution, $x_{uj} > 0$ for $j \leq t$ and $x_{uj} = 0$ for $j > t$. To find the value of t, we check from $t = 1$ to n whether the following linear system has a feasible solution:

$$x_{uj} = \frac{c_{uj} + \nu_u}{\gamma} \quad \text{and} \quad x_{uj} > 0, \text{ for } 1 \leq j \leq t$$

$$\textstyle\sum_{j=1}^{t} x_{uj} = 1.$$

Notice that $\delta_{uj} = 0$ if $x_{uj} > 0$. The largest t value that still gives a feasible solution is what we are looking for. By some algebra, given t, we have $\nu_u = (\gamma - \sum_{j=1}^{t} c_{uj})/t$. The preceding system is feasible if the smallest $x_{ut} > 0$, that is, if

$$x_{ut} \propto c_{ut} + \frac{\gamma - \sum_{j=1}^{t} c_{uj}}{t} > 0. \tag{11.13}$$

Conversion Algorithm. Given dual plan $\boldsymbol{\mu}$ and an incoming user u, the primal serving plan $\{x_{uj}\}$ for u is obtained by the conversion algorithm, which is summarized in Algorithm 11.2.

Proposition 11.2. *If the input dual plan $\boldsymbol{\mu}$ is optimal for a set of users, then the output serving plan from the conversion algorithm is also optimal for the same set of users.*

Proof sketch: Based on dual variable $\boldsymbol{\mu}$, the conversion algorithm gives us $\boldsymbol{\nu}$ and $\mathbf{x}$. We can further compute δ_{uj} for all $x_{uj} = 0$ based on Equation (11.11). It can be verified that all these values satisfy all the KKT conditions. □

The complexity of the conversion algorithm is dominated by the prediction of p_{uj} and d_{uj} and the sorting of c_{uj}s. Because the number of candidate items is usually small or can be made small (from hundreds to thousands), the conversion algorithm is very efficient. Furthermore, the computation can be easily paralleled by users because each user can be computed independently from others.

The preceding formulation is similar to a simple scalarization that linearly combines different objectives in that the weights μ_k in Equation (11.12) can be thought of as the importance for different objectives or constraints. However, scalarization is limited in its ability to obtain all the meaningful Pareto optimal points because it does not allow for fractional serving (Agarwal et al., 2011a; Boyd and Vandenberghe, 2004). The existence of ν_u in our formulation can

---

Algorithm 11.2 Conversion algorithm

Input: dual plan $\boldsymbol{\mu}$ and an incoming user u

Output: primal plan $\{x_{uj}\}$

 1: Predict p_{uj} and d_{uj} for each item j
 2: Compute c_{uj} based on $\boldsymbol{\mu}$, p_{uj} and d_{uj}
 3: Order items by c_{uj} so that $c_{u1} \geq c_{u2} \geq \cdots$
 4: Set $a = \gamma$ and $t = 1$
 5: **repeat**
 6:   **if** $c_{ut} + (a - c_{ut})/t \leq 0$ **then**
 7:     $t = t - 1$ and break
 8:   **else**
 9:     $a = a - c_{ut}$ and continue
10:   **end if**
11:   $t = t + 1$
12: **until** $t \geq |\mathcal{A}|$
13: $v_u = a/t$
14: **for** $j = 1$ to t **do**
15:   $x_{uj} = (c_{uj} + v_u)/\gamma$
16: **end for**
17: **return** $\{x_{uj}\}$

---

achieve fractional serving and thus can move the Pareto optimal solutions in a more controlled way than scalarization.

11.4 Approximation Methods

Because we do not observe all the users who will visit the web portal in the next epoch, we can only solve the QP approximately. The main idea is to exploit the observation that the distribution of users in the next epoch is similar to that in the current one. This is a mild requirement because each epoch is usually of short duration (ten minutes in the experiments) and user population usually does not change significantly. If we use the primal solution directly for serving, we can only serve the set of seen users because we do not have primal variables for unseen users. However, if we use the dual plan for serving, we can convert it to the per-user serving plan on the fly for all users. The dual plan only requires that the sets of user features in the two adjacent epochs be statistically similar (we do not require users themselves to be similar). For this reason, the dual formulation can even work with a sample of users. In this section, because of the potentially large number of users in an epoch, we explore two techniques to reduce computational cost: clustering and sampling.

11.4.1 Clustering

Our goal is to obtain the dual solution for the QP defined in Equation (11.10). To reduce the QP problem size, one choice is to cluster users, and then we have a small number of primal variables. Specifically, we define a set of primal variables $\{x_{ij}\}_{\forall j \in \mathcal{A}}$ for each cluster i, instead of each user u. An off-the-shelf QP solver is then used to find the dual solution $\boldsymbol{\mu}$ of the small QP problem. Finally, at serving time, $\boldsymbol{\mu}$ is used to compute the personalized serving plan $\{x_{uj}\}_{\forall j \in \mathcal{A}}$ for each individual user u using Algorithm 11.2. We consider two clustering methods:

- *k-means*: The standard k-means algorithm is applied to the set of users in the current epoch to create m clusters based on the similarity between users.
- *Top1Item*: This method puts all the users having the same highest CTR item into the same cluster. Specifically, we name clusters by item ID. The set of users in cluster j is

$$S_j = \{u \in \mathcal{U} : j = \arg\max_{j' \in \mathcal{A}} \; p_{uj'}\}.$$

For consistency, we still use index i to refer to such a cluster in general. The number of clusters in this method does not need to be specified.

After we get the user clusters, we approximate the QP as follows: for each cluster i, we estimate p_{ij} and d_{ij} by averaging the per-user p_{uj} and d_{uj} over users u in the cluster. Also, to ensure feasibility, the baseline performance *TotalClicks** and *TotalTime** are defined based on the click maximization scheme in Equation (11.5). We then solve the QP to get the dual optimal values $\boldsymbol{\mu}$.

11.4.2 Sampling

Another way to reduce computational cost is to down-sample users. We consider two types of sampling methods:

- *Random sampling*: Given a sample rate r, we randomly select r percent users uniformly in the current epoch.
- *Stratified sampling*: Given a set of user clusters, we randomly sample r percent users for each individual user cluster. The clusters can be created by k-means or Top1Item.

After sampling, we obtain a subset of users in the current epoch. When we solve the QP, we define a set of primal variables $\{x_{uj}\}_{\forall j \in \mathcal{A}}$ only for sampled users

Table 11.1. *Summary of the methods*

Name	Method description
Segment-LP	Segment-based linear program, same as Agarwal et al. (2011a).
	Clustering-based (Section 11.4.1)
kMeans-QP-Dual	k-means clustering and personalized serving using the dual solution
Top1Item-QP-Dual	Top1Item clustering and personalized serving using the dual solution
	Sampling-based (Section 11.4.2)
Random-Sampling	Random sampling and personalized serving using the dual solution
Stratified-kMeans	Stratified sampling using k-means, and personalized serving using dual
Stratified-Top1Item	Stratified sampling using Top1Item, and personalized serving using dual

u. Again, we update the baseline performance *TotalClicks** and *TotalTime** by only considering the sampled users. Then, the small QP is solved to obtain the dual solution $\boldsymbol{\mu}$, which is used by the conversion algorithm for online personalized serving.

11.5 Experiments

In this section, we compare different methods for multiobjective optimization as summarized in Table 11.1. Segement-LP relies on the primal solution directly for *segmented* serving, whereas kMeans-QP-Dual and Top1Item-QP-Dual rely on dual solution for *personalized* serving. We report empirical results using the unbiased offline replay evaluation method (see Section 4.4 or Li et al., 2011) based on Yahoo! front page log data. We mainly compare the personalized multiobjective optimization with the most effective segmented ones in Agarwal et al. (2011a). We also compare the proposed methods in terms of their abilities to enforce constraints and achieve the desired trade-off between clicks and time spent.

11.5.1 Experimental Setup

Data. Our data are derived from Yahoo! front page web server logs, which record users' clicks and views of items displayed in the Today module on the

Yahoo! front page. The data were collected from a "random bucket" of users in August 2010 for the purpose of evaluating different serving schemes. A random sample of users was assigned to the random bucket, in which each user visit was served with an item uniformly randomly picked from an editor-selected item pool. Based on the replay evaluation method (Section 4.4 and Li et al., 2011), these random bucket data allow us to perform *provably unbiased* comparisons among different serving schemes. Approximately 2 million click and view events were collected per day. To compute downstream time spent, we also collected postclick information on all the pages that a user visited within Yahoo! after clicking on a Today module item. Each user is identified by an anonymized browser cookie and has a profile consisting of demographics (age and gender) and affinities to different categories (such as sports, finance, and entertainment) based on the user's activities in the Yahoo! network. No personally identifiable information is used in the experiments. To create user segments or clusters, we use the best method proposed in Agarwal et al. (2011a). Specifically, we collected ten days of data in April 2010 and created an activity vector for each user. Each entry in the vector corresponds to an item in the data set and the value is the predicted CTR of the item based on the user profile. Users were then clustered using the k-means algorithm based on the activity vectors, and new users were assigned to a cluster based on cosine similarity. This applies to all k-means-related methods.

Metrics. We define the time spent d_{uj} of a user u after clicking article $j \in P_k$ as the length (in seconds) of the *session* of the user's events, which starts from the click and ends at the last pageview inside property P_k, before the user either leaves the property or has no activity for more than thirty minutes. For confidentiality reasons, we cannot reveal the total number of clicks or total time spent. Thus, we only report the relative CTR and relative time spent as defined subsequently. After running a replay experiment using serving scheme A, we compute the average number of clicks per view p_{A} (i.e., CTR) and the average time spent per view q_{A}. Fixing one baseline algorithm B, we report the performance of algorithm A by two ratios: CTR ratio $\rho_{\text{CTR}} = p_{\mathsf{A}}/p_{\mathsf{B}}$ and TS ratio $\rho_{\text{TS}} = q_{\mathsf{A}}/q_{\mathsf{B}}$.

Estimation of p_{uj} and d_{uj}. Predicted CTR p_{uj} and time spent d_{uj} are necessary input to our quadratic program. The choice of statistical models for such prediction is orthogonal to the methods presented in this chapter, and any model can be used here. In our experiments, we use the online logistic regression (OLR) model described in Section 7.3 to predict CTR p_{ujt} based on the feature vector (i.e., the profile consisting of demographics and category affinities) of user u. One OLR model is trained for each item and updated per

Table 11.2. *Comparison of time spent prediction*

Age-gender model		Linear regression	
MAE	RMSE	MAE	RMSE
86.11	**119.44**	87.75	122.02

epoch, to quickly capture the unique behavior of each item that does not generalize well through item features. Time spent d_{uj} is predicted by an age-gender model. We discretize ages into ten groups and have three gender groups (male, female, and unknown); this gives thirty groups in total. For each group, we use a dynamic Gamma-Poisson model to track the mean of time spent d_{uj} on item j by a random user u in the group. Because time spent is very noisy, this simple age-gender model cuts down the variance and provides good prediction performance. More fine-grained models, such as building a linear regression model on user features for each item, were tested but did not provide improvement: Table 11.2 compares the mean absolute error (MAE) and root mean square error (RMSE) of the two methods using two-fold cross-validation. The age-gender model performs just slightly better. A better time-spent model needs further research and is not the focus here.

11.5.2 Experimental Results

Advantage of the Personalized Approach. We first show that the personalized multiobjective optimization significantly outperforms the segmented version in Figure 11.1. We start with a simplified special case that only considers the trade-off between total clicks and total time spent and does not have any property-specific constraint. We show the results of Random-Sampling method with sampling rate $r = 20$ percent and $\beta = 0$. The trade-off curve is generated by varying α from 1 to 0 (where each point is produced by averaging over five sampling runs). In this simplified setting without property-specific constraints, *scalarization* is also applicable: serving each user u with the item j that has the highest weighted sum of the two objectives, $\lambda \cdot p_{uj} + (1 - \lambda) \cdot p_{uj} d_{uj}$. By varying λ from 1 to 0, we obtain a trade-off curve for scalarization in Figure 11.1. Each specific value of λ or α gives us a serving scheme that, after running through the data set, generates a pair of CTR ratio and TS ratio. To compare with the segmented approach in this setting, we also plot the trade-off curve using the scalarization method with different number of segments. All the implementation details are the same as in Agarwal et al. (2011a). These

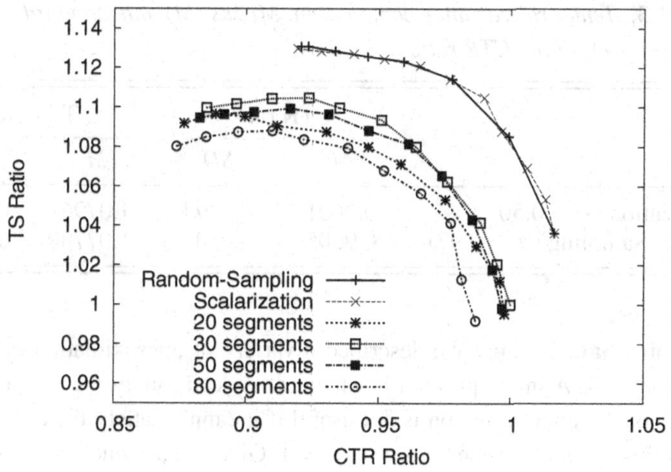

Figure 11.1. Personalized versus segmented method.

methods are labeled as *k segments* in the figure. We can see that both versions of personalized multiobjective optimizations outperform all the segmented ones for all points on the trade-off curves. For example, when $\lambda = 1$ and $\alpha = 1$, the personalized models achieve 2 percent CTR lift (statistically significant at level 0.1) and 4 percent TS lift (statistically significant at level 0.05). Segmented multiobjective optimization achieves the best performance when the number of segments is thirty. When the number of segments becomes large, the performance drops mainly because we have few users in each cluster and the prediction of p_{ij} and d_{ij} (based on Gamma-Poisson) has high variances because of smaller sample sizes.

Figure 11.1 also shows that both Random-Sampling and scalarization achieve similar trade-offs. This means that our dual formulation combined with sampling-based approximation is very effective to trade off competing objectives. In Table 11.3, we show the temporal variances of both methods on the TS ratio and CTR ratio over all the epochs. As can be seen, the variances of scalarization are much larger than those of Random-Sampling, meaning that Random-Sampling is a more stable method. This observation is similar to that of Agarwal et al. (2011a), where primal plans are used. This shows that the dual formulation enjoys the same desirable property of constrained optimization, which makes sure there is no significant deviation from the status quo performance in most epochs. Scalarization cannot provide detailed control over per-property performance constraints (as shown in Agarwal et al., 2011a). Thus, we do not further discuss scalarization.

Table 11.3. *Temporal variance comparison. Means (M) and standard deviations (SD) of the CTR ratio and TS ratio*

	CTR ratio		TS ratio	
Method	*M*	*SD*	*M*	*SD*
Scalarization ($\lambda = 0.50$)	0.9601	0.0394	1.0796	0.0403
Random-Sampling ($\alpha = 0.97$)	0.9605	0.0306	1.0778	0.0322

Constraint Satisfaction. We described a variety of approximation methods in Section 11.4. A main question is whether they can satisfy the per-property constraints. An approximation is not useful if it cannot satisfy the constraints well. In this set of experiments, we set $\beta = 1$. Given an α value and a property P_k, we look at the relative difference in time spent on that property between an approximation method and the baseline click maximization scheme:

$$\phi_\alpha(P_k) = \frac{TotalTime_\alpha(P_k) - TotalTime^*(P_k)}{TotalTime^*(P_k)}.$$

Here $\phi_\alpha(P_k) < 0$ means that the constraint on property P_k is violated and $|\phi_\alpha(P_k)|$ represents the degree of violation. We then define a satisfaction measure over all the per-property constraints as

$$\Phi_\alpha = 1 + \frac{1}{|\mathcal{V}|} \sum_{k \in \mathcal{V}} \phi_\alpha(P_k),$$

where $\mathcal{V} = \{k \mid \phi_\alpha(P_k) < 0, k \in \mathcal{I}\}$ is the set of properties for which constraints are violated.

In Figure 11.2, we set $\alpha = 0.95$ and plot the satisfaction measure for each method. We set the sampling rate $r = 20$ percent for all sampling-based methods. As can be seen, all the methods except for clustering-based dual methods have $\Phi_\alpha \approx 1$ and thus satisfy the per-property constraints very well. In particular, all sampling-based dual methods satisfy the constraints well. However, clustering-based dual methods (kMeans-QP-Dual and Top1Item-QP-Dual) significantly violate the constraints. To further understand this behavior, we plot kMeans-QP-Dual and Top1Item-QP-Dual in Figure 11.3 for each individual property using $\phi_\alpha(P_k)$ with $\alpha = 0.95$. It can be seen that neither respects the constraints and both give some properties more traffic than sufficient and others less than necessary. This means that the clustering we tried is not a good approximation for personalized multiobjective optimization.

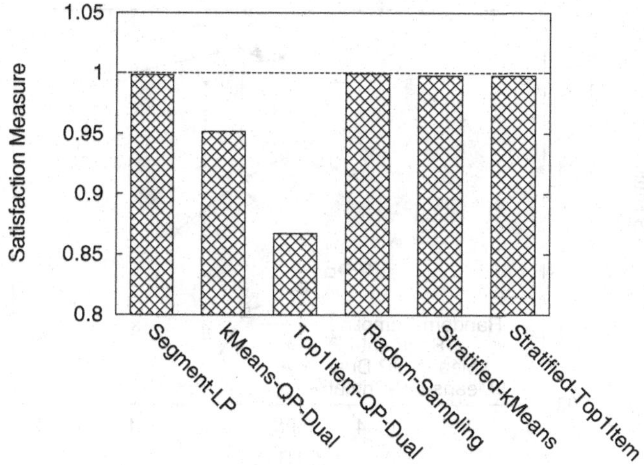

Figure 11.2. Satisfaction of constraints.

Tradeoff Comparison. In Figure 11.4, we compare the trade-off curves of different methods with per-property constraints by setting $\beta = 1$. Each curve is generated by varying α from 1 to 0. As shown later when we discuss Figure 11.10, stratified sampling methods have very similar performance to Random-Sampling. Thus, for plot clarity, we only show the trade-off curve for Random-Sampling (for which we ran the experiments five times and show the average curve).

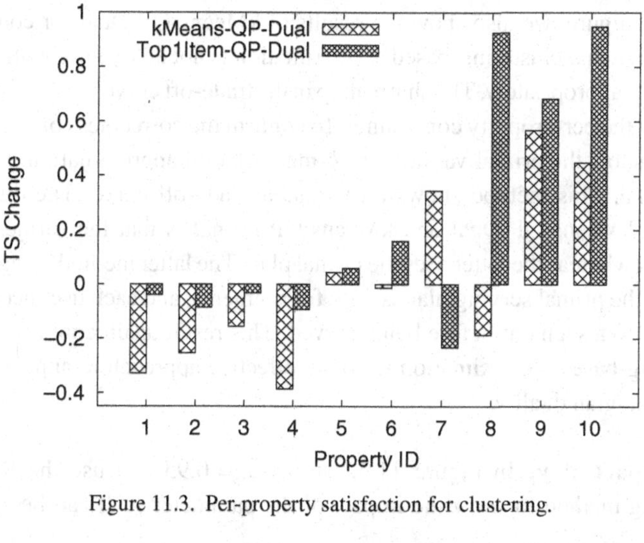

Figure 11.3. Per-property satisfaction for clustering.

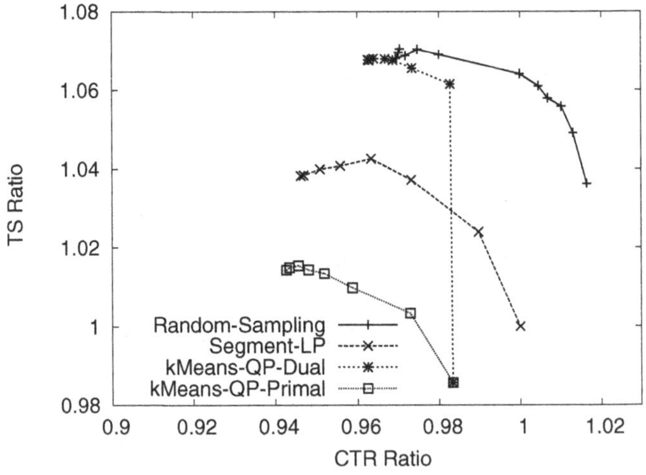

Figure 11.4. Trade-off curves of different methods.

From Figure 11.4, we can see that the Random-Sampling method performs much better than the Segmented-LP method, under the per-property constraints. We can also see that Random-Sampling has the same ability to trade off the two competing objectives as Segmented-LP. Random-Sampling is personalized multiobjective optimization based on a dual plan, whereas Segmented-LP is based on a primal plan. This result confirms that the Lagrangian duality formulation is not only mathematically sound but practically effective to incorporate personalization into multiobjective optimization.

In this figure, we also show the results of kMeans-QP-Dual for contrast. It can be seen that clustering-based approximation is not able to trade off the two objectives appropriately. The sharp jump in the trade-off curve is a by-product of violating the per-property constraints. To confirm the correctness of our results, we also show the primal variation of k-means-based approximation: kMeans-QP-Primal. This method shows a reasonable trade-off curve. The difference between kMeans-QP-Dual and kMeans-QP-Primal is that the former uses a dual plan whereas the latter uses the primal plan. The latter method is segmented because the primal serving plan is only for segments, and each user needs to be assigned to a segment before being served. This result again confirms that the clustering-based approximation is not an effective approach to approximating the Lagrangian duality.

The Impact of γ. In Figure 11.5, we set $\alpha = 0.95$ and use the Random-Sampling method to show the impact of the parameter γ. It can be seen that

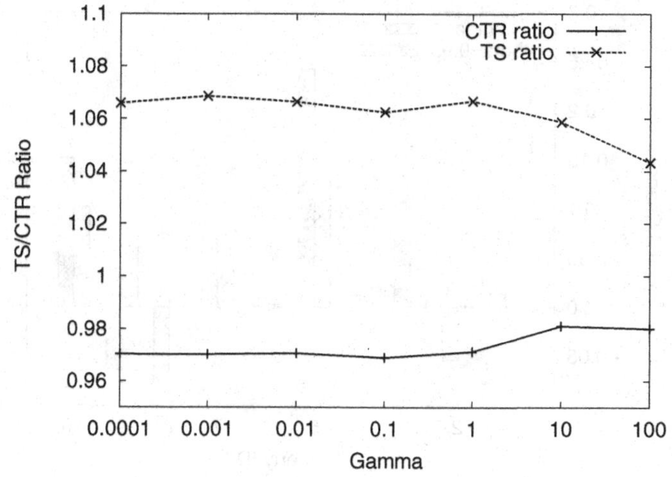

Figure 11.5. The impact of γ.

when γ is less than 1, the results are not sensitive to the choice of γ. When γ is too large, the penalty term has high weight and thus the TS lift gets smaller. In all the experiments, we set $\gamma = 0.001$.

Relaxation of the Per-property Constraints. In Figure 11.6, we show the trade-off curves for $\beta = 1$ and $\beta = 0.95$. For each parameter setting, we have five runs of experiments and we show the mean of these five runs. We also plot

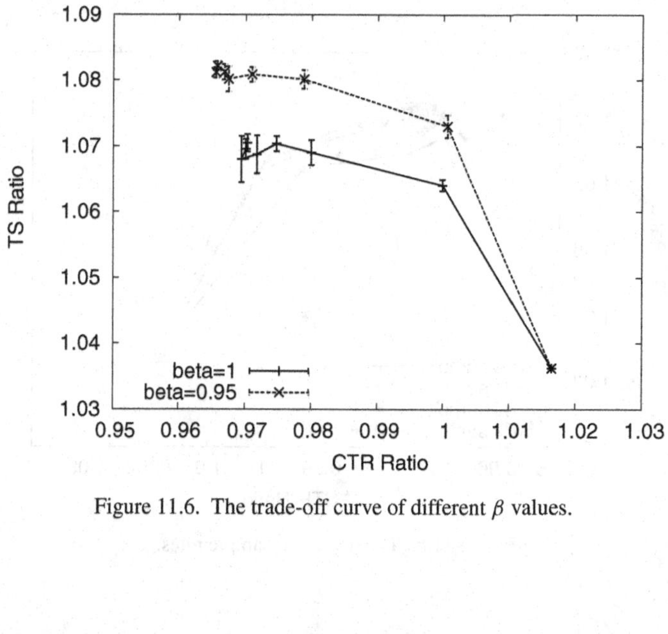

Figure 11.6. The trade-off curve of different β values.

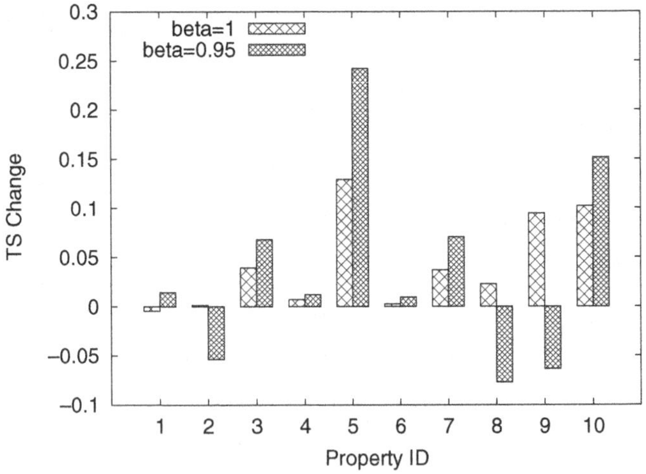

Figure 11.7. The impact of β on time-spent difference.

the error bars of TS ratio. It can be seen that we can achieve a better trade-off when β is smaller because the constraints are less restrictive. We also show the $\phi_{\alpha=0.95}$ for both methods in Figure 11.7. The Random-Sampling method can roughly guarantee the per-property constraints. For $\beta = 1$, ϕ_α are almost all nonnegative. For $\beta = 0.95$, ϕ_α are almost all ≥ -0.05.

Comparing Different Sampling Methods. In Figure 11.8, we study the sampling rate for Random-Sampling. As expected, when we have a larger sample, our approximation becomes better, thus achieving a better trade-off curve. In

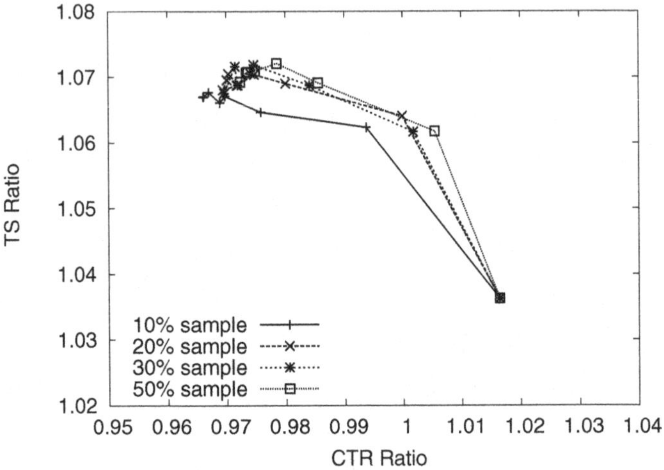

Figure 11.8. The impact of sample rates.

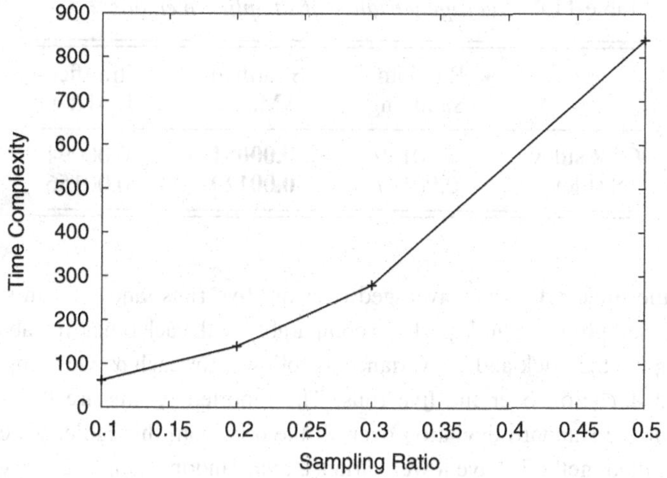

Figure 11.9. Time complexity versus sampling rate.

Figure 11.9, we show the (relative) running time needed for one run of our replay, and we compare different sampling rates. The running time is super-linear, and this shows that sampling is necessary to handle a large number of users. As shown in Figure 11.8, a 20 percent sampling rate can achieve similar results to a 50 percent sampling rate, and thus sampling is an effective way of reducing the time complexity while retaining the effectiveness of our methods.

In Figure 11.10 and Table 11.4, we compare different sampling methods based on five sampling runs with a 20 percent sampling rate. Figure 11.10

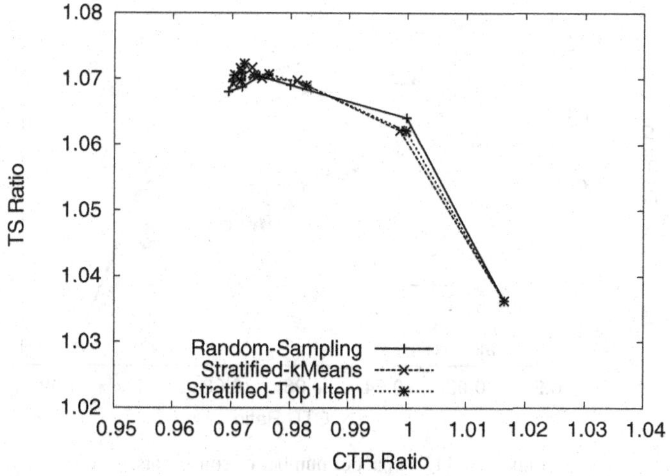

Figure 11.10. Comparison of different sampling methods (sampling ratio = 0.2).

Table 11.4. *Average variance of sampling methods*

	Random-Sampling	Stratified-kMeans	Stratified-Top1Item
CTR stdev	0.00139	**0.00081**	0.00094
TS stdev	0.00187	**0.00129**	0.00156

shows the trade-off curves averaged over the five runs, and we can see that different sampling methods perform comparably with each other. In Table 11.4, we compute the click and TS variance as follows: for each α, we compute the standard deviation over the five runs. The reported results are the average values of the standard deviation over all the αs. From this table, we can see that stratified methods have lower variance than random sampling. Among the two stratified methods, Stratified-kMeans has lower variance than Stratified-Top1Item. This means that k-means creates more homogeneous clusters than the Top1Item method.

Top N Properties. In Figure 11.11, we relax the number of per-property constraints in the Random-Sampling method and show the results when we only have the per-property constraints for the top three, five, and seven properties. When the number of per-property constraints is reduced, we have a better

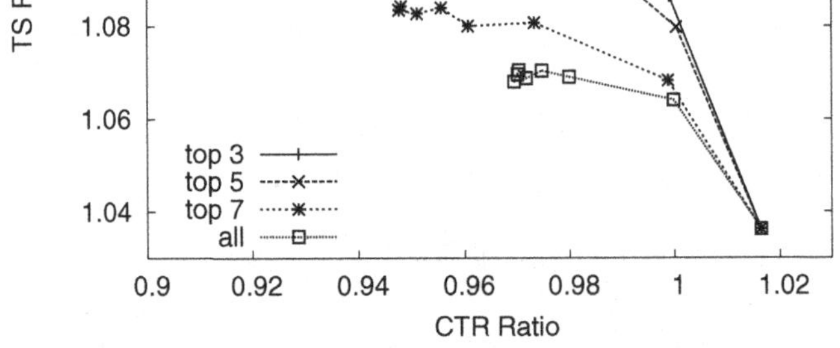

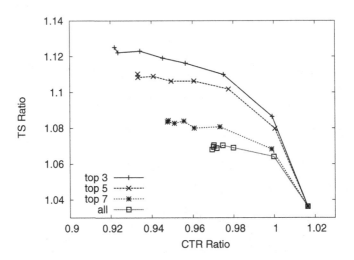

Figure 11.11. Impact of number of constraints.

trade-off curve. This again shows the effectiveness of the dual formulation for personalized multiobjective optimization.

11.6 Related Work

The content of this chapter is based on Agarwal et al. (2011a, 2012). The former introduced the segmented approach, whereas the latter proposed the personalized approach. Research on how to make a good trade-off among multiple objectives for web recommender systems is still in its early stage. Adomavicius et al. (2011) provided a survey of multicriteria recommender systems, where the focus was on multicriteria rating systems and the aspect of multi-objective optimization did not receive much attention. Rodriguez et al. (2012) described an example of multiobjective optimization for job recommendation, and Ribeiro et al. (2013) provided an example that combines objectives like prediction accuracy, novelty, and diversity.

The constrained optimization formulation described in this chapter is similar to the guaranteed delivery problem in display advertising (Vee et al., 2010; Chen et al., 2011), where incoming users are allocated to see different ads to optimize ad-related utilities. For example, Vee et al. (2010) consider multiobjective programming and provide techniques to simultaneously optimize for revenue of remnant inventory and overall ad quality delivered to advertisers with theoretical properties. The use of duality in this chapter is similar to the use of Vee et al. (2010), but the content recommendation setting is very different from the advertising setting.

Multiobjective optimization is also discussed in a number of other problem settings. For instance, auctions in sponsored search incorporate both revenue (measured by bids) and ad quality (measured by CTR) for ads ranking (Fain and Pedersen, 2006). A common approach is simply to rank ads by the product of bid value and CTR. Sculley et al. (2009) also study ad CTR and quality in sponsored search and define a new measure called *bounce rate* to capture ad quality by inferring abandonment rate on the ad landing page. However, this study is exploratory and focuses on bounce rate prediction instead of multiobjective optimization. Besides online advertising, Jambor and Wang (2010) consider constraints like limited supply of the items in a collaborative filtering setting; Svore et al. (2011) consider several objectives in learning to rank. These two studies are in a static setting, different from the online recommendation setting.

Finally, there is a rich literature in multiobjective programming (e.g., Steuer, 1986), convex optimization (e.g., Boyd and Vandenberghe, 2004), and stochastic optimization (e.g., Hentenryck and Bent, 2006). This chapter shows an effective application of optimization techniques to online personalized content recommendation.

11.7 Summary

In this chapter, we study the problem of personalized multiobjective optimization, which combines personalization with multiobjective optimization. We formulate multiobjective problems as linear programs and show that Lagrangian duality can be effectively used to solve the two challenges in applying constrained optimization to personalized serving – unseen users and scalability. By slightly modifying the objective function to achieve strong convexity, we are able to efficiently convert a *dual plan*, which consists of a small number of *user-independent* dual variables, to its corresponding primal serving plan at the time when a new user comes. Based on extensive experiments on a large, real data set, we show that the set of Pareto optimal points of the personalized version significantly outperforms and uniformly dominates the set of the segmented version.

Interesting problems for future research include how to extend the multiobjective programming method to the scenario where multiple items can be simultaneously recommended at multiple positions on a portal page and how to extend the current per-epoch constraints (e.g., requiring click loss to be bounded for every epoch) to long-term constraints (e.g., only requiring the total click loss in any n-epoch period to be bounded).

Endnotes

Chapter 1

1. We call each time the recommender displays an item to a user a *view* of the item by the user, which is also sometimes called an *impression*.

Chapter 2

1. Recommendation is also called *information filtering*.

Chapter 5

1. Because of the private nature of NMs, we do not show screenshots of NMs.
2. http://www.project-voldemort.com/.
3. http://hadoop.apache.org/.

Chapter 6

1. It is straightforward to replace the Poisson distribution with the binomial distribution if there is a concern that some of the predicted CTRs might be greater than 1. For applications in which CTRs are small, we do not have such a concern.

Chapter 9

1. The BookCrossing data set can be downloaded from http://www.informatik.uni-freiburg.de/~cziegler/BX/.

References

Adomavicius, G., and Tuzhilin, A. 2005. Toward the next generation of recommender systems: A survey of the state-of-the-art and possible extensions. *IEEE Transactions on Knowledge and Data Engineering*, **17**, 734–49.

Adomavicius, Gediminas, Manouselis, Nikos, and Kwon, YoungOk. 2011. Multi-criteria recommender systems. Pages 769–803 of *Recommender Systems Handbook*. Springer.

Agarwal, D., and Chen, B.-C. 2009. Regression-based latent factor models. Pages 19–28 of *Proceedings of the 15th ACM SIGKDD International Conference on Knowledge Discovery and Data Mining (KDD'09)*.

Agarwal, D., Chen, B.-C., Elango, P., Motgi, N., Park, S.-T., Ramakrishnan, R., Roy, S., and Zachariah, J. 2008. Online models for content optimization. Pages 17–24 of *Proceedings of the Twenty-Second Annual Conference on Neural Information Processing Systems (NIPS'08)*.

Agarwal, D., Chen, B.-C., and Elango, P. 2009. Spatio-temporal models for estimating click-through rate. Pages 21–30 of *Proceedings of the 18th International Conference on World Wide Web (WWW'09)*.

Agarwal, D., Chen, B.-C., Elango, P., and Wang, X. 2011a. Click shaping to optimize multiple objectives. Pages 132–40 of *Proceedings of the 17th ACM SIGKDD International Conference on Knowledge Discovery and Data Mining (KDD'11)*.

Agarwal, Deepak, Chen, Bee-Chung, and Pang, Bo. 2011b. Personalized recommendation of user comments via factor models. Pages 571–82 of *Proceedings of the Conference on Empirical Methods in Natural Language Processing*. Association for Computational Linguistics.

Agarwal, Deepak, Chen, Bee-Chung, Elango, Pradheep, and Wang, Xuanhui. 2012. Personalized click shaping through Lagrangian duality for online recommendation. Pages 485–94 of *Proceedings of the 35th International ACM SIGIR Conference on Research and Development in Information Retrieval*.

Agarwal, D., Chen, B.-C., Elango, P., and Ramakrishnan, R. 2013. Content recommendation on web portals. *Communications of the ACM*, **56**, 92–101.

Anderson, Theodore Wilbur. 1951. Estimating linear restrictions on regression coefficients for multivariate normal distributions. *Annals of Mathematical Statistics*, **22**(3), 327–51.

Auer, P. 2002. Using confidence bounds for exploitation-exploration trade-offs. *Journal of Machine Learning Research*, **3**, 397–422.

Auer, P., Cesa-Bianchi, N., Freund, Y., and Schapire, R. E. 1995. Gambling in a rigged casino: The adversarial multi-armed bandit problem. Pages 322–31 of *Proceedings of the 36th Annual Symposium on Foundations of Computer Science (FOCS'95)*.

Auer, P., Cesa-Bianchi, N., and Fischer, P. 2002. Finite-time analysis of the multiarmed bandit problem. *Machine Learning*, **47**, 235–56.

Balabanović, Marko, and Shoham, Yoav. 1997. Fab: content-based, collaborative recommendation. *Communications of the ACM*, **40**(3), 66–72.

Bell, Robert M., and Koren, Yehuda. 2007. Scalable collaborative filtering with jointly derived neighborhood interpolation weights. Pages 43–52 *Data Mining of Proceedings of the 7th IEEE International Conference on Data Mining (ICDM'07)*.

Bell, R., Koren, Y., and Volinsky, C. 2007. Modeling relationships at multiple scales to improve accuracy of large recommender systems. Pages 95–104 of *Proceedings of the 13th ACM SIGKDD International Conference on Knowledge Discovery and Data Mining (KDD'07)*.

Bengio, Yoshua, Ducharme, Réjean, Vincent, Pascal, and Janvin, Christian. 2003. A neural probabilistic language model. *Journal of Machine Learning Research*, **3**(Mar.), 1137–55.

Besag, Julian. 1986. On the statistical analysis of dirty pictures. *Journal of the Royal Statistical Society, Series B (Methodological)*, **48**(3), 259–302.

Bingham, Ella, and Mannila, Heikki. 2001. Random projection in dimensionality reduction: applications to image and text data. Pages 245–50 of *Proceedings of the seventh ACM SIGKDD International Conference on Knowledge Discovery and Mining (KDD'01)*.

Blei, David, and McAuliffe, Jon. 2008. Supervised topic models. Pages 121–28 of Platt, J. C., Koller, D., Singer, Y., and Roweis, S. (eds), *Advances in Neural Information Processing Systems 20*. Cambridge, MA: MIT Press.

Blei, David M., Ng, Andrew Y., and Jordan, Michael I. 2003. Latent Dirichlet allocation. *Journal of Machine Learning Research*, **3**(Mar.), 993–1022.

Booth, James G., and Hobert, James P. 1999. Maximizing generalized linear mixed model likelihoods with an automated Monte Carlo EM algorithm. *Journal of the Royal Statistical Society: Series B (Statistical Methodology)*, **61**(1), 265–85.

Bottou, Léon. 2010. Large-scale machine learning with stochastic gradient descent. Pages 177–87 of *Proceedings of the 19th International Conference on Computational Statistics (COMPSTAT'2010)*. Springer.

Boyd, Stephen Poythress, and Vandenberghe, Lieven. 2004. *Convex Optimization*. Cambridge University Press.

Celeux, G., and Govaert, G. 1992. A classification EM algorithm for clustering and two stochastic versions. *Computational Statistics and Data Analysis*, **14**, 315–32.

Charkrabarty, Deepay, Chu, Wei, Smola, Alex, and Weimer, Markus. *From Collaborative Filtering to Multitask Learning*. Tech. rept.

Chen, Ye, Pavlov, Dmitry, and Canny, John F. 2009. Large-scale behavioral targeting. Pages 209–18 of *Proceedings of the 15th ACM SIGKDD International Conference on Knowledge Discovery and Data Mining (KDD'09)*.

Chen, Ye, Berkhin, Pavel, Anderson, Bo, and Devanur, Nikhil R. 2011. Real-time bidding algorithms for performance-based display ad allocation. Pages 1307–15 of

Proceedings of the 17th ACM SIGKDD International Conference on Knowledge Discovery and Data Mining (KDD'09).

Claypool, Mark, Gokhale, Anuja, Miranda, Tim, Murnikov, Pavel, Netes, Dmitry, and Sartin, Matthew. 1999. Combining content-based and collaborative filters in an online newspaper. In *Proceedings of ACM SIGIR workshop on recommender systems*, vol. 60. ACM.

Das, A. S., Datar, M., Garg, A., and Rajaram, S. 2007. Google news personalization: scalable online collaborative filtering. Pages 271–80 of *Proceedings of the 16th International Conference on World Wide Web (WWW'07).*

Datta, Ritendra, Joshi, Dhiraj, Li, Jia, and Wang, James Z. 2008. Image retrieval: Ideas, influences, and trends of the new age. *ACM Computing Surveys (CSUR)*, **40**(2), 5.

DeGroot, M. H. 2004. *Optimal Statistical Decisions*. John Wiley.

Dempster, Arthur P., Laird, Nan M., and Rubin, Donald B. 1977. Maximum likelihood from incomplete data via the EM algorithm. *Journal of the Royal Statistical Society, Series B (Methodological)*, **39**(1), 1–38.

Deselaers, Thomas, Keysers, Daniel, and Ney, Hermann. 2008. Features for image retrieval: an experimental comparison. *Information Retrieval*, **11**(2), 77–107.

Desrosiers, C., and Karypis, G. 2011. A comprehensive survey of neighborhood-based recommendation methods. In *Recommender Systems Handbook*, 107–44.

Duchi, John, Hazan, Elad, and Singer, Yoram. 2011. Adaptive subgradient methods for online learning and stochastic optimization. *Journal of Machine Learning Research*, **12**, 2121–59.

Efron, Brad, and Tibshirani, Rob. 1993. *An Introduction to the Bootstrap*. Chapman and Hall/CRC.

Fain, Daniel C., and Pedersen, Jan O. 2006. Sponsored search: A brief history. *Bulletin of the American Society for Information Science and Technology*, **32**(2), 12–13.

Fan, Rong-En, Chang, Kai-Wei, Hsieh, Cho-Jui, Wang, Xiang-Rui, and Lin, Chih-Jen. 2008. LIBLINEAR: A library for large linear classification. *Journal of Machine Learning Research*, **9**, 1871–74.

Fontoura, Marcus, Josifovski, Vanja, Liu, Jinhui, Venkatesan, Srihari, Zhu, Xiangfei, and Zien, Jason. 2011. Evaluation strategies for top-k queries over memory-resident inverted indexes. *Proceedings of the VLDB Endowment*, **4**(12), 1213–1224.

Fu, Zhouyu, Lu, Guojun, Ting, Kai Ming, and Zhang, Dengsheng. 2011. A survey of audio-based music classification and annotation. *IEEE Transactions on Multimedia*, **13**(2), 303–19.

Fürnkranz, Johannes, and Hüllermeier, Eyke. 2003. Pairwise preference learning and ranking. Pages 145–56 of *Proceedings of the 14th European Conference on Machine Learning (ECML'03).*

Gelfand, Alan E. 1995. Gibbs sampling. *Journal of the American Statistical Association*, **452**, 1300–1304.

Getoor, Lise, and Taskar, Ben. 2007. *Introduction to Statistical Relational Learning*. MIT Press.

Gilks, W. R. 1992. Derivative-free adaptive rejection sampling for Gibbs sampling. *Bayesian Statistics*, **4**, 641–49.

Gilks, Walter R., Best, N. G., and Tan, K. K. C. 1995. Adaptive rejection metropolis sampling within Gibbs sampling. *Journal of the Royal Statistical Society. Series C (Applied Statistics)*, **44**(4), 455–72.

Gittins, J. C. 1979. Bandit processes and dynamic allocation indices. *Journal of the Royal Statistical Society. Series B (Methodological)*, **41**(2), 148–77.

Glazebrook, K. D., Ansell, P. S., Dunn, R. T., and Lumley, R. R. 2004. On the optimal allocation of service to impatient tasks. *Journal of Applied Probability*, **41**, 51–72.

Golub, Gene H., and Van Loan, Charles F. 2013. *Matrix Computations*. Vol. 4. Johns Hopkins University Press.

Good, Nathaniel, Schafer, J. Ben, Konstan, Joseph A., Borchers, Al, Sarwar, Badrul, Herlocker, Jon, and Riedl, John. 1999. Combining collaborative filtering with personal agents for better recommendations. Pages 439–46 of *Proceedings of the Sixteenth National Conference on Artificial Intelligence and the Eleventh Innovative Applications of Artificial Intelligence Conference Innovative Applications of Artificial Intelligence (AAAI/IAAI)*.

Griffiths, Thomas L., and Steyvers, Mark. 2004. Finding scientific topics. *Proceedings of the National Academy of Sciences of the United States of America*, **101**(Suppl 1), 5228–35.

Guyon, Isabelle, and Elisseeff, André. 2003. An introduction to variable and feature selection. *Journal of Machine Learning Research*, **3**(Mar.), 1157–82.

Hastie, T., Tibshirani, R., and Friedman, J. 2009. *The Elements of Statistical Learning*. Springer.

Hentenryck, Pascal Van, and Bent, Russell. 2006. *Online Stochastic Combinatorial Optimization*. MIT Press.

Herlocker, Jonathan L., Konstan, Joseph A., Borchers, Al, and Riedl, John. 1999. An algorithmic framework for performing collaborative filtering. Pages 230–37 of *Proceedings of the 22nd annual International ACM SIGIR Conference on Research and Development in Information Retrieval (SIGIR'99)*.

Jaakkola, Tommi S., and Jordan, Michael I. 2000. Bayesian parameter estimation via variational methods. *Statistics and Computing*, **10**(1), 25–37.

Jaccard, Paul. 1901. Étude comparative de la distribution florale dans une portion des Alpes et des Jura. *Bulletin del la Société Vaudoise des Sciences Naturelles*, **37**, 547–79.

Jambor, Tamas, and Wang, Jun. 2010. Optimizing multiple objectives in collaborative filtering. Pages 55–62 of *Proceedings of the fourth ACM Conference on Recommender Systems (RecSys'10)*.

Jannach, D., Zanker, M., Felfernig, A., and Friedrich, G. 2010. *Recommender Systems: An Introduction*. Cambridge University Press.

Jin, Xin, Zhou, Yanzan, and Mobasher, Bamshad. 2005. A maximum entropy web recommendation system: Combining collaborative and content features. Pages 612–17 of *Proceedings of the eleventh ACM SIGKDD International Conference on Knowledge Discovery and Data Mining (KDD'05)*.

Jones, David Morian, and Gittins, John C. 1972. *A dynamic allocation index for the sequential design of experiments*. University of Cambridge, Department of Engineering.

Kakade, S. M., Shalev-Shwartz, S., and Tewari, A. 2008. Efficient bandit algorithms for online multiclass prediction. Pages 440–47 of *Proceedings of the Twenty-Fifth International Conference on Machine Learning (ICML'08)*.

Katehakis, Michael N., and Veinott, Arthur F. 1987. The multi-armed bandit problem: Decomposition and computation. *Mathematics of Operations Research*, **12**(2), 262–68.

Kocsis, L., and Szepesvari, C. 2006. Bandit based Monte-Carlo planning. Pages 282–93 of *Machine Learning: ECML*. Lecture Notes in Computer Science. Springer.

Konstan, J. A., Riedl, J., Borchers, A., and Herlocker, J. L. 1998. Recommender systems: A grouplens perspective. In *Proc. Recommender Systems, Papers from 1998 Workshop, Technical Report WS-98-08*.

Koren, Yehuda. 2008. Factorization meets the neighborhood: A multifaceted collaborative filtering model. Pages 426–34 of *Proceedings of the 14th ACM SIGKDD International Conference on Knowledge Discovery and Data Mining (KDD'08)*.

Koren, Y., Bell, R., and Volinsky, C. 2009. Matrix factorization techniques for recommender systems. *Computer*, **42**(8), 30–37.

Lai, Tze Leung, and Robbins, Herbert. 1985. Asymptotically efficient adaptive allocation rules. *Advances in Applied Mathematics*, **6**(1), 4–22.

Langford, J., and Zhang, T. 2007. The Epoch-Greedy algorithm for contextual multi-armed bandits. Pages 817–24 of *Proceedings of the Twenty-First Annual Conference on Neural Information Processing Systems (NIPS'07)*.

Lawrence, Neil D., and Urtasun, Raquel. 2009. Non-linear matrix factorization with Gaussian processes. Pages 601–8 of *Proceedings of the 26th annual International Conference on Machine Learning (ICML'09)*.

Li, L., Chu, W., Langford, J., and Schapire, R. E. 2010. A contextual-bandit approach to personalized news article recommendation. Pages 661–70 of *Proceedings of the 19th International Conference on World Wide Web (WWW'10)*.

Li, Lihong, Chu, Wei, Langford, John, and Wang, Xuanhui. 2011. Unbiased offline evaluation of contextual-bandit-based news article recommendation algorithms. Pages 297–306 of *Proceedings of the fourth ACM International Conference on Web Search and Data Mining (WSDM'11)*.

Lin, Chih-Jen, Weng, Ruby C., and Keerthi, S. Sathiya. 2008. Trust region Newton method for logistic regression. *Journal of Machine Learning Research*, **9**, 627–50.

McCullagh, P. 1980. Regression models for ordinal data. *Journal of the Royal Statistical Society, Series B (Methodological)*, **42**(2), 109–42.

Mitchell, Thomas M. 1997. *Machine Learning*. 1st ed. McGraw-Hill.

Mitrović, Dalibor, Zeppelzauer, Matthias, and Breiteneder, Christian. 2010. Features for content-based audio retrieval. *Advances in Computers*, **78**, 71–150.

Mnih, Andriy, and Salakhutdinov, Ruslan. 2007. Probabilistic matrix factorization. Pages 1257–64 of *Proceedings of the Twenty-First Annual Conference on Neural Information Processing Systems (NIPS'07)*.

Montgomery, Douglas. 2012. *Design and Analysis of Experiments*. 8th ed. John Wiley.

Nadeau, David, and Sekine, Satoshi. 2007. A survey of named entity recognition and classification. *Lingvisticae Investigationes*, **30**(1), 3–26.

Nelder, J. A., and Wedderburn, R. W. M. 1972. Generalized linear models. *Journal of the Royal Statistical Society, Series A (General)*, **135**, 370–84.

Niño-Mora, José. 2007. A $(2/3)n^3$ fast-pivoting algorithm for the Gittins index and optimal stopping of a Markov chain. *INFORMS Journal on Computing*, **19**(4), 596–606.

Pandey, S., Agarwal, D., Chakrabarti, D., and Josifovski, V. 2007. Bandits for taxonomies: A model-based approach. Pages 216–27 of *Proceedings of the Seventh SIAM International Conference on Data Mining (SDM'07).*

Park, Seung-Taek, Pennock, David, Madani, Omid, Good, Nathan, and DeCoste, Dennis. 2006. Naïve filterbots for robust cold-start recommendations. Pages 699–705 of *Proceedings of the 12th ACM SIGKDD International Conference on Knowledge Discovery and Data Mining (KDD'06).*

Pilászy, István, and Tikk, Domonkos. 2009. Recommending new movies: Even a few ratings are more valuable than metadata. Pages 93–100 of *Proceedings of the third ACM Conference on Recommender Systems (RecSys'09).*

Pole, A., West, M., and Harrison, P. J. 1994. *Applied Bayesian Forecasting and Time Series Analysis.* Chapman-Hall.

Porteous, Ian, Bart, Evgeniy, and Welling, Max. 2008. Multi-HDP: A non parametric Bayesian model for tensor factorization. Pages 1487–90 of *Proceedings of the Twenty-Third AAAI Conference on Artificial Intelligence (AAAI'08).*

Princeton University. 2010. *WordNet.* http://wordnet.princeton.edu.

Puterman, Martin L. 2009. *Markov Decision Processes: Discrete Stochastic Dynamic Programming.* Vol. 414. John Wiley.

Rendle, Steffen, and Schmidt-Thieme, Lars. 2010. Pairwise interaction tensor factorization for personalized tag recommendation. Pages 81–90 of *Proceedings of the third ACM International Conference on Web Search and Data Mining (WSDM'10).*

Resnick, Paul, Iacovou, Neophytos, Suchak, Mitesh, Bergstrom, Peter, and Riedl, John. 1994. GroupLens: An open architecture for collaborative filtering of netnews. Pages 175–186 of *Proceedings of the 1994 ACM Conference on Computer Supported Cooperative Work (CSCW'94).*

Ribeiro, Marco Tulio, Lacerda, Anisio, de Moura, Edleno Silva, Veloso, A., and Ziviani, N. 2013. Multi-objective Pareto-efficient approaches for recommender systems. *ACM Transactions on Intelligent Systems and Technology*, **9**(1), 1–20.

Ricci, Francesco, Rokach, Lior, Shapira, Bracha, and Kantor, Paul B. (eds). 2011. *Recommender Systems Handbook.* Springer.

Robbins, H. 1952. Some aspects of the sequential design of experiments. *Bulletin of the American Mathematical Society*, **58**, 527–35.

Robertson, S. E., Walker, S., Jones, S., Hancock-Beaulieu, M., and Gatford, M. 1995. Okapi at TREC-3. In Harman, D. K. (ed), *The Third Text REtrieval Conference (TREC-3).*

Rodriguez, Mario, Posse, Christian, and Zhang, Ethan. 2012. Multiple objective optimization in recommender systems. Pages 11–18 of *Proceedings of the sixth ACM Conference on Recommender Systems (RecSys'12).*

Rossi, Peter E., Allenby, Greg, and McCulloch, Rob P. 2005. *Bayesian Statistics and Marketing.* John Wiley.

Salakhutdinov, Ruslan, and Mnih, Andriy. 2008. Bayesian probabilistic matrix factorization using Markov chain Monte Carlo. Pages 880–87 of *Proceedings of the 25th International Conference on Machine Learning (ICML'08).*

Salton, G., Wong, A., and Yang, C. S. 1975. A vector space model for automatic indexing. *Communications of the ACM*, **18**(11), 613–20.

Sarkar, Jyotirmoy. 1991. One-armed bandit problems with covariates. *Annals of Statistics*, **19**(4), 1978–2002.

Schein, Andrew I., Popescul, Alexandrin, Ungar, Lyle H., and Pennock, David M. 2002. Methods and metrics for cold-start recommendations. Pages 253–60 of *Proceedings of the 25th annual International ACM SIGIR Conference on Research and Development in Information Retrieval (SIGIR'02)*.

Sculley, D., Malkin, Robert G., Basu, Sugato, and Bayardo, Roberto J. 2009. Predicting bounce rates in sponsored search advertisements. Pages 1325–34 of *Proceedings of the 15th ACM SIGKDD International Conference on Knowledge Discovery and Data Mining (KDD'09)*.

Sebastiani, Fabrizio. 2002. Machine learning in automated text categorization. *ACM Computing Surveys*, **34**(1), 1–47.

Singh, Ajit P., and Gordon, Geoffrey J. 2008. Relational learning via collective matrix factorization. Pages 650–58 of *Proceedings of the 14th ACM SIGKDD International Conference on Knowledge Discovery and Data Mining (KDD'08)*.

Smola, Alexander J., and Narayanamurthy, Shravan M. 2010. An architecture for parallel topic models. *PVLDB*, **3**(1), 703–10.

Stern, D. H., Herbrich, R., and Graepel, T. 2009. Matchbox: Large scale online bayesian recommendations. Pages 111–20 of *Proceedings of the 18th International Conference on World Wide Web (WWW'09)*.

Steuer, R. 1986. *Multi-criteria Optimization: Theory, Computation and Application*. John Wiley.

Svore, Krysta M., Volkovs, Maksims N., and Burges, Christopher J. C. 2011. Learning to rank with multiple objective functions. Pages 367–76 of *Proceedings of the 20th International Conference on World Wide Web (WWW'11)*.

Thompson, William R. 1933. On the likelihood that one unknown probability exceeps another in view of the evidence of two samples. *Biometrika*, **25**, 285–94.

Varaiya, Pravin, Walrand, Jean, and Buyukkoc, Cagatay. 1985. Extensions of the multiarmed bandit problem: the discounted case. *IEEE Transactions on Automatic Control*, **30**(5), 426–39.

Vee, Erik, Vassilvitskii, Sergei, and Shanmugasundaram, Jayavel. 2010. Optimal online assignment with forecasts. Pages 109–18 of *Proceedings of the 11th ACM Conference on Electronic Commerce (EC'10)*.

Vermorel, J., and Mohri, M. 2005. Multi-armed bandit algorithms and empirical evaluation. Pages 437–48 of *Machine Learning: ECML*. Lecture Notes in Computer Science. Springer.

Wang, Yi, Bai, Hongjie, Stanton, Matt, Chen, Wen-Yen, and Chang, Edward Y. 2009. pLDA: Parallel latent Dirichlet allocation for large-scale applications. Pages 301–14 of *Algorithmic Aspects in Information and Management*. Springer.

West, M., and Harrison, J. 1997. *Bayesian Forecasting and Dynamic Models*. Springer.

Whittle, P. 1988. Restless bandits: Activity allocation in a changing world. *Journal of Applied Probability*, **25**, 287–98.

Yu, Kai, Lafferty, John, Zhu, Shenghuo, and Gong, Yihong. 2009. Large-scale collaborative prediction using a nonparametric random effects model. Pages 1185–92 of *Proceedings of the 26th annual International Conference on Machine Learning (ICML'09)*.

Zhai, Chengxiang, and Lafferty, John. 2001. A study of smoothing methods for language models applied to ad hoc information retrieval. Pages 334–42 of *Proceedings of the 24th annual International ACM SIGIR Conference on Research and Development in Information Retrieval (SIGIR'01)*.

Zhang, Liang, Agarwal, Deepak, and Chen, Bee-Chung. 2011. Generalizing matrix factorization through flexible regression priors. Pages 13–20 of *Proceedings of the fifth ACM Conference on Recommender Systems (RecSys'11)*.

Zhu, Ciyou, Byrd, Richard H., Lu, Peihuang, and Nocedal, Jorge. 1997. Algorithm 778: L-BFGS-B: Fortran subroutines for large-scale bound-constrained optimization. *ACM Transactions on Mathematical Software*, **23**(4), 550–560.

Ziegler, Cai-Nicolas, McNee, Sean M., Konstan, Joseph A., and Lausen, Georg. 2005. Improving recommendation lists through topic diversification. Pages 22–32 of *Proceedings of the 14th International Conference on World Wide Web (WWW'05)*.

Index

Note to index: An *f* following a page number indicates a figure; a *t* following a page number indicates a table.

Printed in the United States
By Bookmasters